World Histories of Crime, Culture and Violence

Palgrave's World Histories of Crime, Culture and Violence seeks to publish research monographs, collections of scholarly essays, multi-authored books, and Palgrave Pivots addressing themes and issues of interdisciplinary histories of crime, criminal justice, criminal policy, culture and violence globally and on a wide chronological scale (from the ancient to the modern period). It focuses on interdisciplinary studies, historically contextualized, across various cultures and spaces employing a wide range of methodologies and conceptual frameworks.

More information about this series at
http://www.palgrave.com/gp/series/14383

Lisa Featherstone

Sexual Violence in Australia, 1970s–1980s

Rape and Child Sexual Abuse

palgrave
macmillan

Lisa Featherstone
University of Queensland
Brisbane, QLD, Australia

ISSN 2730-9630 ISSN 2730-9649 (electronic)
World Histories of Crime, Culture and Violence
ISBN 978-3-030-73309-4 ISBN 978-3-030-73310-0 (eBook)
https://doi.org/10.1007/978-3-030-73310-0

Cover illustration: AztecBlue / Alamy Stock Photo

This Palgrave Macmillan imprint is published by the registered company Springer Nature Switzerland AG.
The registered company address is: Gewerbestrasse 11, 6330 Cham, Switzerland

For friends and strangers who are survivors.

Acknowledgements

It was never my intention to write a second book on sexual violence. Yet, once I began, it was a topic so compelling that I did not stop. Along the way, I have gathered many people to thank.

This work was funded by an ARC Discovery Project, DP150101798 (2015–2018), held with Andy Kaladelfos, Carolyn Strange and Nina Westera. During the term of the grant, Nina Westera passed away: both personally and professionally, this was an intense, encompassing loss. Nina remains an inspiration, as a friend and colleague. She is an enduring example of how to write compassionate, victim-centred scholarship on sexual assault. She is gone, but her memory remains.

The University of Queensland (UQ) has provided significant institutional support, including travel funding and study leave. The Institute of Advanced Humanities (IASH) provided a very much appreciated Fellowship, which allowed me time and space to write. My colleagues in the School of Historical and Philosophical Inquiry have provided friendship and companionship, and the chance to talk about histories that were not only about violence. I have been influenced, too, by the work and friendship of other scholars at UQ including Jon Willis and Uncle Shane Coghill: our meetings are often the highlight of my working week.

From near and afar, I have benefited from mentoring from some pretty amazing scholars. Professor Philip Dwyer started me thinking about violence, and has been a continuing support. Professor Joanna Bourke was an intellectual inspiration well before I met her and has continued to be so after. Professor Peter Cryle has encouraged and supported my work on sexuality at UQ, as well as being an excellent lunchtime companion.

Professor Joy Damousi has long provided sage advice and mentoring. Professor Mary Spongberg began it all, stimulting my early interest in gender history—and has provided much support ever since. Thank you all.

Professor Mark Finnane has encouraged my work on crime, and included me in various aspects of the Prosecution Project. I am grateful for the time I spent at Griffith University under his mentorship. Other links made or strengthened through the Prosecution Project—including Alana Piper, Sarah Wilson, Karen Terry and Rachel Zajac—have stimulated my thinking about criminology and sociolegal studies.

When I arrived at UQ, I established a Gender History Writing Group, which has now graduated numerous honours and PhD candidates. At UQ, I have been blessed to have met some amazing postgraduate students (some now doctors themselves!) who have both inspired me and cheered me on. Thank you, my smart and sassy coven, especially Gemmia Burden, Cassandra Byrnes and Anna Temby, who have all read chapters of this work. You made a difference.

I have benefited from 'historical' friendships with Adam Bowles, Shirleene Robinson, Alison Holland, Rebecca Jennings, Frank Bongiorno, Beth Spacey, Nancy Cushing, Victoria Haskins and James Bennett, as well as many others, on Facebook and in real life. Other friends, especially Byron Golby, have kept me company across the ups and downs of writing on this topic. Thank you.

Over the years, I have been fortunate to have a raft of Research Assistants work on various aspects of this book, including Altin Gavranovic, Cassandra Byrnes, Anna Temby, Naomi Parry, Kyle Harvey, Hayley Stokes and especially Paige Doherty. Your contributions have made this a better book.

This book would not have been written without the love and support of my dearest friends, Andy Kaladelfos and Yorick Smaal. They've shared—and contributed to—this journey. Andy and Yorick, I couldn't do it without you.

Finally, a deep and heartfelt thank you to my family, Craig and Lachlan Macdemid. Your love keeps me going, every day.

Contents

CHAPTER 1

Introduction: Sexual Violence

In 2013, an eighteen-year-old woman and her friend from the Central Coast of New South Wales (NSW) travelled two hours on the train to Sydney, for a night on the town. She had planned to hit the clubs: it was the first time she had been to Kings Cross, one of city's main nightclub precincts.[1] A little after eleven o'clock that night, the two young women met with other friends at McDonalds at the Cross, where they finished their premixed drinks. For the next five hours, the two friends moved between the World Bar and Soho Nightclub.

It was on the dance floor at the Soho that the young woman met Luke Lazarus. He told her he was a part-owner of the nightclub, and asked if she had met the DJ. In fact, it was his father who was a part-owner of the club, where Lazarus worked part-time. He introduced her very briefly to the DJ: according to CCTV footage, this took only two minutes or so. Lazarus would later give evidence in court that while they talked to the DJ, he had kissed her and touched her, including grabbing her on her bottom. This intimacy, he argued, encouraged him to think she would have sex with him. In contrast, the young woman gave evidence that they had held hands.

[1]Details of this case are taken from *Lazarus v R* [2016] NSWCCA 52; *R v Lazarus* (Unreported, District Court of NSW, Tupman DCJ, 4 May 2017); *R v Lazarus* [2017] NSWCCA 279.

L. Featherstone, *Sexual Violence in Australia, 1970s–1980s*, World Histories of Crime, Culture and Violence,
https://doi.org/10.1007/978-3-030-73310-0_1

Minutes later, Lazarus guided her to what he had told her was the VIP area. He led her from the dance floor down a flight of stairs to a cloakroom, and then outside to a dead-end alley behind the nightclub. They walked approximately 50 metres up the road and began to kiss. The young woman gave testimony that she repeatedly told Lazarus she wanted to return to her friends. She told the court that when she had turned to go, he pulled down her stockings a few inches. Her evidence continued:

> A. I turned back to him and I pulled them back up and I said 'I really have to go'.
>
> Q. And did he reply to that?
>
> A. He—that's when he said 'Put your fucking hands on the wall'.
>
> Q. What was the tone of his voice like when he said that?
>
> A. He—he was getting frustrated and impatient I guess frustrated and impatient would be the tone, more aggressive than [the] previous conversation.
>
> Q. And what did you do then?
>
> A. Put both my hands on the—on the fence.
>
> Q. Are you able to tell the Court why you did that?
>
> A. I was just scared I guess, I didn't know what to do so I just did what he said.

The interpretation of *her* actions in these moments—and the moments that follow—were central to *his* trial.

After some courtroom discussion about the location, the young woman's evidence continued. She recorded that he told her, 'Just get on your hands and knees and arch your back.' When asked about the tone of his voice, she replied, 'Like authoritarian like do, not—not aggressive but not nice I guess, just do that if you know what I mean.' And so she gave testimony that she complied: 'I—I was scared, I can't—I was just doing what he asked.' At this point, the defendant had anal sex with the complainant. The complainant gave testimony that she asked him to stop: 'I asked him to—I said "Stop" at the start like at the beginning after—after he said "Oh shit, really" and then I just kept saying "I need to go back to my friend".'

The complainant gave evidence of immediate complaint of sexual assault to the friend she had gone to the club with, then shortly afterwards to her sister and other friends. This can be important in a trial, as it goes towards her credibility as a witness. There was evidence from multiple people that she had been seen crying and in shock. The complainant went to the Chatswood Police Station the following morning and made a report. She was taken to Royal North Shore Hospital, and the medical examination revealed grazes on her knees, and small tears around her anus. She gave a statement to police at Kings Cross Station on the same day (defence would later suggest that there were some inconsistencies in the various reports provided). Luke Lazarus was charged with one count of sexual intercourse without consent.

At trial, the young woman came under considerable scrutiny, particularly on the issue of her consent. Under cross-examination, the defence attempted to challenge her credibility. By questioning her on highly specific details, defence aimed to show that she was lying about what had happened in the alleyway and to show that the complainant was a willing participant in sex. It was claimed that she had changed her mind only when she saw she was part of a 'trophy' list of girls in the defendant's phone.

Much of the evidence presented at the original trial was around the young woman's drinking. The complainant told the court she had consumed around sixteen standard drinks; her friend recorded they had drunk around ten. Under Section 61HA(6)(a) of the Crimes Act, a person could not be said to have consented to sex if 'the person has sexual intercourse while substantially intoxicated by alcohol or any drug'. At trial, neither side denied that anal sex had taken place: instead, the trial swung on whether or not it was consensual, and on whether or not the complainant was capable of consent. In this trial, the prosecution argued that the complainant was too drunk to consent to sex. The complainant gave evidence that 'I was drunk but yeah, and I was pretty out of it I guess and just very, I don't know, drunk is the only way I can really think to describe it'. There was CCTV evidence of her steadying herself as she left the club. In contrast, the defence argued that the complainant had exaggerated her drinking, and claimed that she had not been steadying herself as they left the building. Witnesses reported that the complainant had been 'moderately' drunk that evening.

Other evidence was given, on the defendant's behaviour on the night and afterwards. It was suggested that Lazarus took the complainant to the laneway, as he knew the CCTV would not cover that area. Revealing text messages between Lazarus and his friends and father had also been obtained by the police, and these suggested a certain unease about the encounter. However, Lazarus strenuously denied force had been used, and claimed that the sex was consensual throughout. Under NSW law, to be found guilty, the defendant had to perform the guilty act (*actus reus*) but also do so with a guilty mind (*mens rea*). The prosecution had to show that the defendant actually knew the complainant did not consent, was reckless over whether the complainant consented, or had no reasonable grounds for believing the complainant consented.[2] Thus, in this trial, the prosecution had to prove that Luke Lazarus knew that the woman had not consented to sex, or that he was reckless in his assumptions, or that there were no reasonable grounds for believing she had consented.

In the District Court in 2015, Luke Lazarus was found guilty by a jury of one count of sexual intercourse without consent. He was sentenced to imprisonment for five years, with a non-parole period of three years. He was to serve ten months of this sentence. The verdict was appealed on three grounds, with two grounds going forward. First, there was a challenge that 'the verdict of the jury was unreasonable and contrary to the evidence'. The second ground for appeal was even more complicated. During the trial, the judge had given directions to the jury, that the defendant had no reasonable grounds for believing the young woman was consenting to sex. This, the appeal argued, imposed an objective test of 'reasonableness of belief in consent where no such test existed', and misstated the onus of proof. The appeal hearing reserved a decision on the first ground of appeal, but on the second ground found that the judge had indeed given erroneous directions regarding consent. A retrial was ordered.

The case was retried before a judge alone, with no jury, in 2017. Judge Robyn Tupman addressed the first part of the appeal, and found that the Crown had proven lack of consent beyond a reasonable doubt. However, Judge Tupman ultimately found Lazarus not guilty, stating that the defendant *believed* the complainant was consenting. Judge Tupman stated that the complainant 'did not take any physical action to move away from the intercourse or attempted intercourse'. The judge stated:

> I accept that this series of circumstances on the early morning of 12 May 2013 amounts to reasonable grounds in the circumstances for the accused to have formed the belief, which I accept was a genuine belief, that in fact the complainant was consenting to what was occurring even though it was quick, unromantic, they had both been drinking and in the case of both of them [it] may not [have] occurred if each had been sober.[3]

* * *

[2] *Crimes Act 1900* (NSW) s 61HA(3) (a)–(c).

[3] Georgina Mitchell, 'Court of Criminal Appeal Upholds Luke Lazarus Rape Acquittal', *Sydney Morning Herald (SMH)*, 27 November 2017, https://www.smh.com.au/national/nsw/court-of-criminal-appeal-upholds-luke-lazarus-rape-acquittal-20171127-gzteon.html.

Tupman J's judgement reverberated through Australian communities. There was an almost visceral reaction to what must have been a physically and emotionally painful sexual experience for the young woman—the speed of the encounter, the ugliness, the lack of basic care by a young man to a young woman. For many reading the news, it highlighted the ruthless way a young woman might be simply a receptacle, a vessel, for a young man's sexual needs. Reading the reports, I myself felt a sinking horror at just how little *her* needs and desires were considered, in this sexual encounter. Further, there were legal questions. Using the standard of 'reasonable grounds', how would someone in Lazarus' position think that a young, sexually and socially inexperienced girl would consent to anal sex in a back alley, with a man she had just met?[4] While legally the Crown had to prove that Lazarus himself had 'no reasonable grounds for believing' that there was consent (as Fullerton J suggested), public opinion was not focused on this. Instead, there was much critique in the media of an affluent and privileged young man who appeared to have been distinctly disinterested in issues of a woman's pleasure or her desire.

The NSW Court of Criminal Appeal upheld the rape acquittal of Luke Lazarus, finding that he should not face another retrial because it would 'give rise to oppression and unfairness'. The narrative during and around the Lazarus trials was often about *him*: about Luke's potential. As he stated at his sentencing hearing, 'I could have been a CEO.'[5] The victim was originally absent and her trauma was silenced, though, as we will see, this would change over time.

The Lazarus case (the trial, the retrial and the two appeals) brought to mind a number of recent trials in other Western nations, including the controversial criminal trial of American student Brock Turner, in 2016.[6] Turner had been apprehended by two international students on Stanford Campus, after they had seen him sexually assaulting 'Emily Doe' while she was unconscious. She would later state clearly that she had not consented to any sexual activity that night. At trial, Turner was found guilty of three

[4] For discussion on 'reasonable' in this case, see Andrew Dyer, 'Sexual Assault Law Reform in New South Wales: Why the Lazarus Litigation Demonstrates No Need for Section 61HE of the Crimes Act to Be Changed (Except in One Minor Respect)', *Criminal Law Journal* 43:2 (2019): 91–3.

[5] Louise Hall, 'Convicted Rapist Luke Lazarus Jailed for at Least Three Years', *SMH*, 27 March 2015.

[6] *People of the State of California v. Brock Allen Turner*. Turner was originally indicted on five counts, but two were withdrawn before the trial began.

counts of felony sexual assault. The charges held a minimum penalty of two years and a maximum of fourteen years. In a conviction that made headlines across the world, Judge Aaron Persky sentenced Turner to just six months in county jail, of which he served only three months.

Feminists and others read the judgement as prioritising the future of a young affluent white man, a 'promising' swimmer, over the trauma he had caused to a young woman.[7] The judge (himself a former athlete at Stanford) had suggested that the imprisonment would have a 'severe impact' on Turner.[8] Turner's father had written to the court to say any prison sentence 'is a steep price to pay for 20 minutes of action out of 20 plus years of his life'.[9] But as Emily Doe herself would state:

> The probation officer weighed the fact that he has surrendered a hard-earned swimming scholarship. How fast Brock swims does not lessen the severity of what happened to me, and should not lessen the severity of his punishment. If a first-time offender from an underprivileged background was accused of three felonies and displayed no accountability for his actions other than drinking, what would his sentence be? The fact that Brock was an athlete at a private university should not be seen as an entitlement to leniency, but as an opportunity to send a message that sexual assault is against the law regardless of social class.
>
> The Probation Officer has stated that this case, when compared to other crimes of similar nature, may be considered less serious due to the defendant's level of intoxication. It felt serious. That's all I'm going to say.[10]

There was a significant political backlash against the sentence, and Judge Persky was recalled from the bench in 2018, the first time this had happened in over eighty years. Nonetheless, the sentence remained. These

[7] On the issue of swimming, see, amongst others, Michael E. Miller, 'All American Swimmer Found Guilty of Sexually Assaulting Unconscious Woman on Stanford Campus', *Washington Post*, 31 March 2016, downloaded 12 September 2019; Alice Phillips, 'Freshman Swimmer Brock Turner Faces Five Felony Counts After Alleged Rape', *The Stanford Daily*, 27 January 2015, downloaded 12 September 2019.

[8] Elle Hunt, '"20 Minutes of Action": Father Defends Stanford Student Son Convicted of Sexual Assault', *The Guardian*, 6 June 2016, downloaded 21 September, 2019.

[9] Elle Hunt, '20 minutes of Action'.

[10] Katie J. M. Baker, 'Here's the Powerful Letter the Stanford Victim Read to Her Attacker', *Buzzfeed News*, 3 June 2016, https://www.buzzfeednews.com/article/katiejm-baker/heres-the-powerful-letter-the-stanford-victim-read-to-her-ra.

cases—and many others like them—begged a serious question. After fifty years of feminism, were young women becoming expendable?

As I read the press around the Lazarus case (and the Brock case, and the Federal Government's Royal Commission into Institutional Reponses into Child Sexual Abuse, and so many other press releases, official reports, social media posts, blogs and public commentaries on sexual violence), one thing became terribly clear. Not so very much had changed. As a historian, I had co-written a book on sexual assault in the 1950s. I was currently working on sexual offences in court cases from the 1970s and 1980s. Here, with Lazarus in 2017, I was reading a story that was all too familiar. How had there been so much change, and yet so little?

This book explores the conundrum at the heart of sexual violence: Why does it continue? This book asks difficult questions of our recent past. Using Australia as an important case study, it asks why we do not act more decisively to eradicate sexual and gender violence? What prevented our culture from looking seriously at abuse? How did we fail to protect victims, both inside institutions and beyond? *Why, after several decades of agitation around sexual violence, does the problem remain?* At the core of this book is the question that resonates deeply right now: Why does sexual violence appear seemingly insurmountable, despite significant change?

To answer these questions, I focus on Australia in the 1970s and 1980s, a period of intense social and legal change. Impelled by the sexual revolutions, second-wave feminism, and ideas of the rights of the child, this was a period of substantial public interest in the sexual assault of women and children. Australia was a world leader in many aspects of rape law reform. The rape of adult women was studied, surveyed and discussed more than ever before in Australian society. Yet, despite this, there remained substantial inaction by government, from community and on the part of individuals, across the final decades of the twentieth century. It was, and is, survivors who have literally demanded change.

Speaking Out

As I wrote this book, the #MeToo movement had garnered strength, becoming a global phenomenon. The #MeToo movement was started by Tarana Burke, a black American civil rights activist in 2006, to raise awareness of sexual assault, in particular amongst women of colour. The hashtag was not popularised until 2017, when the actor Alyssa Milano encouraged women to take to social media, particular Twitter, and voice their own experiences. In the wake of the Harvey Weinstein exposé, the hashtag would be used over twelve million times in twenty-four hours. It was adopted by women in diverse countries the world over, spawning local variations too.[11] Australian women joined in, with journalist Tracey Spicer leading the NOW campaign, while other corresponding campaigns grew in size and prominence.[12]

At its best, #MeToo movement has revealed the commonality, even the banality, of sexual abuse and harassment of women in the workplace, in the home and in the street. It highlighted the shared experiences of many women, and revealed the multiple ways that institutions, including workplaces, covered up gendered abuse. Nonetheless, the #MeToo movement has been rightly controversial.[13] As criminologist Michael Salter has suggested, 'online justice' lacks the specificity of more nuanced discussions about sexual assault.[14] Critics have also highlighted the potential for the commodification of sexual violence, with the hashtag driving media clicks and potentially revenue, while not truly challenging industries that profit from gender violence.[15] In Australia, there have been controversies about

[11] Bianca Fileborn and Rachel Loney-Howes, 'Introduction: Mapping the Emergence of #MeToo', in *#MeToo and the Politics of Social Change*, eds. Biance Fileborn and Rachel Loney-Howes (London: Palgrave Macmillan, 2019), 3–4; Sarah Wildman, '#MeToo Goes Global', *Foreign Policy*, Winter 2019, https://foreignpolicy.com/gt-essay/metoo-goes-global-feminism-activism/; '#MeToo Movement's Second Anniversary', *Human Rights Watch*, 14 October 2019, https://www.hrw.org/news/2019/10/14/metoo-movements-second-anniversary.

[12] www.now.org.au. See also Destroy The Joint's social media on #Counting Dead Women and Sherele Moody's Red Heart Campaign, theredheartcampaign.org. On social media and gender violence, see Ana Stevenson and Bridget Lewis, 'From Page to Meme: The Print and Digital Revolutions Against Gender Violence', in *Gender Violence in Australia: Historical Perspectives*, eds. Alana Piper and Ana Stevenson (Melbourne: Monash University Publishing, 2019), 184–190.

[13] See Bianca Fileborn and Nickie Phillips, 'From "Me Too" to "Too Far"? Contesting the Boundaries of Sexual Violence in Contemporary Activism', in *#MeToo and the Politics of Social Change*, eds. Bianca Fileborn and Rachel Loney-Howes (London: Palgrave Macmillan, 2019), 99–115.

[14] Michael Salter, 'Want #MeToo to Serve Justice? Use it Responsibly', *The Ethics Centre*, 31 January 2019, https://ethics.org.au/want-metoo-to-serve-justice-use-it-responsibly.

[15] Rosalind Gill and Shani Orgad, 'The Shifting Terrains of Sex and Power', *Sexualities* 21:8 (2018): 1320; Michael Salter, 'Online Justice in the Circuit of Capital: #MeToo, Marketization and the Deformation of Sexual Ethics', in *#MeToo and the Politics of Social Change*, eds. Bianca Fileborn and Rachel Loney-Howes (London: Palgrave Macmillan, 2019), 317–334.

the use of women's private information in the media without their consent.[16]

Most damningly, #MeToo has been strongly critiqued for being a movement for white women, especially elite white women.[17] As Bianca Fileborn and Rachel Loney-Howes suggest, we must ask '*who* is able to speak and be heard... *whose* experiences are included and perceived as worthy of redress'.[18] Neha Kagal, Leah Cowan and Huda Jawad and others have argued that the campaign centres the 'experiences of white, affluent and educated women with access to a significant social media following and offline clout'.[19] The movement tends towards the 'erasure of poor, informally educated, low-paid, disabled, LGBT and non-urban women', as well as women of colour, migrant women and sex workers.[20] The exclusiveness of #MeToo is a very real limitation to its effectiveness. Nonetheless, #MeToo has driven an impetus to disclosure of sexual assault which has been powerful, far beyond Twitter.

A Voice

Speaking out—whether inspired by #MeToo or not—has offered (some) survivors a chance to take control of their own narrative, and to potentially navigate and negotiate change. In 2018, Saxon Mullins, the survivor of the Lazarus case, spoke out. It was a formidable moment. The young woman gave a powerful and moving interview with the current affair

[16] Nina Funnell, '"Unprofessional, unethical, unsafe": ABC breaches rape victim's privacy in new Tracey Spicer documentary', news.com.au November 13, 2019.

[17] Angela Onwuachi-Willig, 'What About #UsToo? The Invisibility of Race in the #MeToo Movement', *Yale Law Journal Forum* 128 (2018): 105–120.

[18] Fileborn and Loney-Howes, 'Introduction: Mapping the Emergence of #MeToo', 5 (italics in original).

[19] Neha Kagal, Leah Cowan, and Huda Jawad, 'Beyond the Bright Lights: Are Minoritized Women Outside the Spotlight Able to Say #MeToo?', in *#MeToo and the Politics of Social Change*, eds. Bianca Fileborn and Rachel Loney-Howes (London: Palgrave Macmillan, 2019): 134.

[20] Kagal, Cowan, and Jawad, 'Beyond the Bright Lights: Are Minoritized Women Outside the Spotlight Able to Say #MeToo?', 134; Jess Ison, 'It's Not Just Men and Women': LGBTQIA People and #MeToo', in *#MeToo and the Politics of Social Change*, eds. Bianca Fileborn and Rachel Loney-Howes (London: Palgrave Macmillan, 2019): 151–167; Tess Ryan, 'This Black Body is Not Yours for the Taking', in *#MeToo and the Politics of Social Change*, eds. Bianca Fileborn and Rachel Loney-Howes (London: Palgrave Macmillan, 2019): 117–132.

program *Four Corners*.[21] So, too, in the United States, 'Emily Doe' spoke out about her sexual assault by Brock Turner, sharing an extraordinary statement she read at her sentencing hearing publicly on *Palo Alto Online* and *BuzzFeed*, where it went viral.[22] The statement was so moving, so commanding, that it was even read in the US House of Representatives, to raise awareness of sexual assaults on campus.[23] In 2019, revealing her identity, Chanel Miller released a powerful memoir, *Know My Name*, on her experiences of the assault and its terrible aftermath.[24]

Here, in the bravery of these survivors, perhaps we see a moment of hope, though it cannot be the only answer to the problem of sexual violence. There are significant costs in speaking out: loss of anonymity, the likelihood for personal attacks, threats to mental health and the potential for media misrepresentation. As criminologist Tanya Seisner has shown, even the so-called feminist media has often co-opted or sensationalised survivors' stories.[25] Speaking out has had impact, both personal and political.[26] Survivors who speak out inhabit a peculiar space that crosses the individual and the collective: they are now are understood by the public as both individuals (victims of a specific crime) and yet somehow representative of all survivors (victims of all sexual crime). This leaves survivors both as vulnerable to vicious personal and online attack and as powerful voices for systemic, structural change. On an individual level, survivors have noted the somewhat 'ephemeral' changes in themselves and in their confidence in dealing with harassment and abuse, alongside improvements in local, workplace and community policies.[27]

[21] ABC, 'I Am That Girl', *Four Corners*, 7 May 2018, http://www.abc.net.au/4corners/i-am-that-girl/9736126, downloaded 2 August, 2019.

[22] Baker, 'Here's the Powerful Letter'.

[23] Concepción de León, 'You Know Emily Doe's Story. Now Learn Her Name', *New York Times*, 4 September 2019, https://www.nytimes.com/2019/09/04/books/chanel-miller-brock-turner-assault-stanford.html, downloaded 5 September 2019.

[24] Concepción de León, 'You Know Emily Doe's Story. Now Learn Her Name', *New York Times*, 4 September 2019, https://www.nytimes.com/2019/09/04/books/chanel-miller-brock-turner-assault-stanford.html, downloaded 5 September 2019.

[25] Tanya Serisier, 'Speaking Out, and Beginning to be Heard: Feminism, Survivor Narratives and Representations of Rape in the 1980s', *Continuum* 32:1 (2018): 52–61.

[26] Loney-Howes, 'The Politics of the Personal', 33.

[27] Kaitlynn Mendes and Jessica Ringrose, 'Digital Feminist Activism: #MeToo and the Everyday Experiences of Challenging Rape Culture', in *#MeToo and the Politics of Social Change*, eds. Bianca Fileborn and Rachel Loney-Howes (London: Palgrave Macmillan, 2019), 46.

On a macro level, too, there have been tangible moves towards change. Not long after Saxon Mullins spoke on *Four Corners*, the state of NSW announced that the Law Reform Commission would review the provisions of consent, and in May 2021 the NSW government poposed the adoption of an affirmative consent model, to go through parliament in late 2021.[28] In Queensland, there have been calls to reform the defence of 'mistaken belief', which allows a defendant—often successfully—to argue that he believed his victim had consented to sex, even if she had not.[29] The author and survivor Bri Lee drove a campaign that successfully had consent laws and mistake of fact laws referred to the Law Reform Commission in Queensland for review.[30] In late 2019 in Tasmania, the #LetHerSpeak campaign convinced the Attorney General Elise Archer to amend section 194K of the *Evidence Act 2001* (Tas), which had effectively gagged survivors from talking about their own experiences of, and responses to, sexual assault.[31]

This recent activism was not, of course, the first time women had spoken out about sexual violence.[32] In this book, I chart the previous moment, during second-wave feminism in Australia, when women as a collective began to speak out about both rape and the sexual assault of children. The 1970s and 1980s were a critical turning point in the politics and culture of

[28] Mark Speakman and Pru Goward, 'Sexual Consent Laws to Be Reviewed', NSW Government Media Release, 8 May 2018, https://www.justice.nsw.gov.au/Documents/Media%20Releases/2018/sexual-assault-consent-laws-to-be-reviewed.pdf.

[29] Under the Queensland Criminal Code 1899, section 24(1) states: 'A person who does or omits to do an act under an honest and reasonable, but mistaken, belief in the existence of any state of things is not criminally responsible for the act or omission.' For feminist interpretations of the law, see Kate McKenna, 'Queensland Consent Laws Confuse Juries and Need Reform, Women's Advocate Argues', *ABC News*, 13 August 2019, downloaded 13 August 2019.

[30] See consentlawqld.com. Bri Lee is the author of *Eggshell Skull* (Sydney: Allen and Unwin, 2018).

[31] Nina Funnell, '#LetHerSpeak', conference paper Sex and Consent in the Age of #MeToo Workshop, Macquarie University, 6–7 November 2019; Lisa Martin, 'Tasmania Sex Assault Gag Law to Face Overhaul Early Next Year', *The Guardian*, 19 August 2019; Lauren Roberts, "Gag Laws' Stopping Sexual Assault Survivors in the NT from Speaking Out', *ABC News*, 22 October 2019, https://www.abc.net.au/news/2019-10-22/nt-sexual-assault-victims-stopped-from-speaking-out/11622468. Similar legislation still exists in the Northern Territory at the end of 2019, meaning survivors are denied agency in telling their own stories, and journalists risk jail time in reporting on survivor's experiences.

[32] For studies historicising responses to sexual assault in the United States, see Tanya Serisier, 'Speaking Out Against Rape: Feminist (Her)stories and Anti-Rape Politics', *Lilith* 16 (2007): 84–95; Maria Bevacqua, *Rape on the Public Agenda: Feminism and the Politics of Sexual Assault* (Boston: Northeastern University Press, 2000).

sexual violence, requiring further, detailed investigation. Australia makes an important case study. The Australian situation is read here as one shaped by international networks of knowledge and practice: Australians have engaged with aspects of the law, feminism and violence as a settler colonial state, and the flow of information from other developed nations. In particular, Australia has been informed by the United Kingdom and the United States. Yet, Australia also led the way in many developments, including the involvement of feminists in the government and bureaucracy, and the criminalising of some offences including rape in marriage. Throughout this book, I trace these shifts and transformations—influenced by feminism—in thinking about sexual assault and child sexual abuse in Australia. These changes were social, cultural, political and legal, all intertwined. Social change drove legal reform; at the same time, legal change influenced the wider culture. So how did this coalescence operate in Australia, and what did it mean? How was sexual violence imagined in law and in society? Understanding Australia—in this period of rapid transition—helps us to understand our own contemporary attitudes towards gendered violence and to consider the options for further change.

Sexual Assault in the Law

As historians including Joanna Bourke have shown, rape has been defined in multiple ways, changing over time and place.[33] In some jurisdictions, rape might only include penile-vaginal penetration; at other moments, it might include penetration of a number of orifices by a range of body parts or objects. The twentieth century saw substantial shifts in how rape and other forms of sexual violence were imagined, understood, defined and treated in the criminal justice system. For instance, in Australian jurisdictions during the colonial period and for much of the twentieth century, homosexual sex between consenting men was a crime. From 1975 to 1997, consenting gay sex was decriminalised across Australian states, though there remained provisions for the sexual assault of boys, and for non-consensual sexual assault on men.[34]

[33] Joanna Bourke, *Rape: A History from 1860 to the Present Day* (London: Virago, 2007), 8–10.

[34] Claire Parker and Paul Sendziuk, 'It's Time: The Duncan Case and the Decriminalisation of Homosexual Acts in South Australia, 1972', in *Out Here: Gay and Lesbian Perspectives VI*, eds. Yorick Smaal and Graham Willett (Melbourne: Monash University Publishing, 2011), 17–35.

Australian laws around rape itself originated from seventeenth-century British common law, though the states had no one single definition of rape, either before Federation or after. Rape was commonly understood as 'unlawful sexual intercourse with a woman without her consent, by force, fear or fraud'.[35] Consent here was understood to mean physical resistance: to prove her non-consent, a woman needed to physically resist sexual intercourse.[36] By the late 1960s, the authoritative Jowitt's *Dictionary of English Law* defined rape as 'carnal knowledge of a woman against her will or without her conscious permission, or where her permission has been extorted by force or fear of immediate bodily harm', whereas carnal knowledge was defined as 'the penetration to the slightest degree of the male organ of generation'.[37]

Australian states took up these basic ideas in various ways. Australia is, on the whole, a common law nation: this means that judgements made in courts must be followed by later judges, due to the doctrine of precedent. Some states and territories codified criminal law in the late nineteenth century, including Queensland, Tasmania, Western Australia, the ACT and the Northern Territory. Nonetheless, if there was an ambiguity in the law, or the legislation did not adequately define a problem, judges might still form common law decisions, which then become part of the broader law for the state. In contrast, New South Wales, Victoria and South Australia were common law jurisdictions, guided by the relevant *Crimes Acts*, but where the crimes themselves were defined by common law. Thus, in NSW, for instance, under the *Crimes Act* 1900, rape itself was not defined, but the statute guided that 'the consent of the woman, if obtained by threats or terror, shall be no defence to a charge'.[38] As legal experts would suggest, this ensured 'the onus is upon the prosecution to prove that the woman did not consent'.[39]

[35] NSW Parliament, *Report of the Criminal Law Review Division of the Department of the Attorney-General and of Justice into Rape and Other Sexual Offences* (Sydney: Government Printer, 1977), 11.

[36] See Carol Backhouse, 'A Comparative Study of Canadian and American Rape Law', *Canada-United States Law Journal* 7 (1984): 182–3.

[37] NSW Government, *Report from the Select Committee on Violence Sex Crimes in New South Wales* (Sydney: Government Printer, 1969), viii.

[38] *Crimes Act 1900* (NSW) s 62.

[39] Montgomerie H. Hamilton and G. C. Addison, *Criminal Law and Procedure, New South Wales: Containing the Crimes Act, 1900, the Criminal Appeal Act of 1912 and Other Statues, vol. 2*, 5th edition, ed. C. E. Weigall (Sydney: Law Book Co., 1947), 80.

What all Australian states had in common was that rape was understood as sexual penetration of a woman by a man, without her consent. This definition of the crime of rape led, however, to a number of problems. In 1970, at the start of this study, rape was defined narrowly as penetrative sexual intercourse between a man and woman: it did not include non-consensual anal sex, non-consensual oral penetration or penetration by an object.[40] Further, the definition meant that rape could only be committed on a woman by a man,[41] yet men and boys were clearly suffering from sexual assaults that were similar to rape, but could not be named as such.

Other males could not be held criminally responsible under the law for rape. A boy under the age of fourteen could not be convicted of rape, though he could be convicted of indecent assault, or aiding and abetting rape.[42] Even more notably, a married man could not be charged with raping his wife: he was not liable under law, no matter how vicious or violent the assault. At marriage, his wife was considered to have granted ongoing consent for any penile-vaginal sexual encounter at any time in the marriage.[43] As we will see, this was one of the most controversial of all aspects of rape law reform, and remained an urgent but difficult issue, resistant to both social and legal change.

The problem of sexual violence against adult women was not a simple lack of legal capacity to define sexual assault, which was codified in law, albeit imperfectly. There were manifest, systemic problems in negotiating and utilising the law, in the reporting of crime, in the policing of sexual assaults, in the prosecution of offenders (and the safeguards they were offered) and, of course, with the protection of victims. These problems, along with a series of rape myths that were heightened by gendered and racial denigrations, permeated the social and legal landscape of the late twentieth century.

[40] For example, NSW Parliament, *Report of the Criminal Law Review Division*, 12.

[41] Royal Commission on Human Relationships (hereafter RCHR), *Final Report vol. 5* (Canberra: Government Printer, 1977), 196.

[42] NSW Parliament, *Report of the Criminal Law Review Division*, 21.

[43] Lisa Featherstone, '"That's What Being a Woman is For": Opposition to Marital Rape Law Reform in Late Twentieth-Century Australia', *Gender & History* 29:1 (2017): 87–103.

Child Sexual Assault

If public interventions focused imperfectly on adult women as victims, it slowly became clear that children, too, were vulnerable to sexual abuse. Gradually, across the 1970s and 1980s, sexual abuse emerged as a public problem, alongside increased attention to 'baby battering' and neglect, and a growing awareness about the 'Rights of the Child'. We might now think that the protracted 'discovery' of child sexual abuse is strange: after all, assault on children had long been a core business of the court, as studies in criminal records across the nineteenth and twentieth centuries show.[44] Further, across the twentieth century, crimes were reported in the press, often with surprisingly graphic details.[45] Offenders were routinely policed and prosecuted, with more success if the victim was a child than an adult.[46] And as Shurlee Swain has shown, the nineteenth and twentieth centuries saw numerous national and state inquiries into the physical and sexual abuse of children both inside and outside of institutions.[47]

Yet before feminist interventions, sexual abuse of children was understood as the unusual, grisly crime of pathological men. Child sexual assault continued to be imagined as the work of the deviant, aberrant man, and was thus to be dealt with as individual crimes, rather than as something requiring structural or community change.[48] It took activism from femi-

[44] See, for example, Louise A. Jackson, *Child Sexual Abuse in Victorian England* (London: Routledge, 2000); Stephen Robertson, *Crimes Against Children: Sexual Violence and Legal Culture in New York City, 1880–1960* (Chapel Hill: UNC Press, 2005). In Australia, see Judith Allen, *Sex and Secrets: Crimes Involving Australian Women Since 1880* (Melbourne: OUP, 1990; Jill Bavin-Mizzi, *Ravished: Sexual Violence in Victoria Australia* (Sydney: UNSW Press, 1995); Yorick Smaal, '"Keeping it in the family": Prosecuting Incest in Colonial Queensland', *Journal of Australian Studies* 37:3 (2013): 316–32; Juliet Peers, 'The Tribe of Mary Jane Hicks: Imagining Women Through the Mount Rennie Rape Case 1886', *Australian Cultural History* 12 (1993): 127–144; Lisa Featherstone and Andy Kaladelfos, *Sex Crimes in the Fifties* (Carlton: Melbourne University Press, 2016).

[45] Andy Kaladelfos, 'Crime and Outrage: Sexual Villains and Sexual Violence in New South Wales, 1870–1939', PhD thesis, University of Sydney, 2010.

[46] Featherstone and Kaladelfos, *Sex Crimes in the Fifties*, 76–80.

[47] Johanna Sköld and Shurlee Swain, eds., *Apologies and the Legacy of Abuse of Children in "Care"* (London: Palgrave Macmillan, 2015); Shurlee Swain, *History of Australian Inquiries: Reviewing Institutions Providing Care for Children*, 2014, https://www.childabuseroyalcommission.gov.au/sites/default/files/file-list/Research%20Report%20-%20History%20of%20Australian%20inquiries%20reviewing%20institutions%20providing%20care%20for%20children%20-%20Institutional%20responses.pdf.

[48] See Conclusion for comments on the Northern Territory Intervention, this volume.

nists, especially women working in domestic violence shelters and rape crisis centres, to draw attention to the structural components of child suffering. Still, it took significant time, and some resistance, for child sexual abuse to emerge as a community problem, as this book will trace.

It was not until relatively recently that child sexual assault has come into the spotlight in the mainstream, and major studies in Canada, Ireland, Australia and the United States have proven the proliferation of sexual assaults against children within institutions, with cultures of secrecy that failed to protect victims.[49] When I began this book, the Australian Federal Government's Royal Commission into Institutional Responses to Child Sexual Abuse was already underway, and in 2017 it reported. In total, the Royal Commission held over 8000 private sessions, took over 42,000 phone calls and almost 26,000 emails and letters, and investigated 57 in-depth case studies. The final report ran to seventeen volumes, plus an executive summary. Taking a victim-centred approach, the Royal Commission was a vast yet intricate body of work documenting and critiquing the handling of child sexual assault in institutions in Australia's past. It made far-reaching recommendations for making institutions safer for children, but also recommending ways forward to support survivors, including redress and civil litigation.[50] The Royal Commission, alongside other state-based investigations, garnered widespread media coverage: never before had sexual violence against children received so much public scrutiny.[51]

[49] Karen Terry et al., 'The Causes and Context of Sexual Abuse of Minors by Catholic Priests in the United States, 1950–2010: A Report Presented to the United States Conference of Catholic Bishops by the John Jay College Research Team', United States Conference of Catholic Bishops, Washington, DC, 2011; *The Report of the Archdiocesan Commission of Enquiry into the Sexual Abuse of Children by Members of the Clergy*, 3 volumes (Archdiocese of St John's, Newfoundland, Canada, 1990); Francis D. Murphy, Helen Buckley, and Larain Joyce, *The Ferns Report: Presented to the Minister for Health and Children* (Dublin: Government Publications, 2005).

[50] www.childabuseroyalcommission.gov.au. See also the Special Issue 'The Royal Commission into Institutional Responses to Child Sexual Abuse', *Journal of Australian Studies* 42:2 (2018), especially Katie Wright and Shurlee Swain, 'Introduction: Speaking the Unspeakable, Naming the Unnameable: The Royal Commission into Institutional Responses to Child Sexual Abuse', 139–152.

[51] For other important works, see Human Rights and Equal Opportunity Commission, *Bringing Them Home: Report of the National Inquiry into the Separation of Aboriginal and Torres Strait Islander Children from Their Families* (Canberra: Government Printer, 1997); E. P. Mullighan, *Children on Anangu Pitjantjatjara Yankunytjatjara (APY) Lands Commission of Inquiry: Report into Sexual Abuse* (Adelaide: Office of the Commissioner,

We cannot yet know the full and final impact of the Royal Commission into Institutional Reponses to Child Sexual Abuse. Running parallel to and beyond the Royal Commission, the courts were and are addressing a number of criminal and civil trials for historical child sexual assault. Most notorious is the trial and subsequent appeals of Archbishop George Pell, the highest-ranking Catholic to have been found guilty of child sexual abuse, convictions that have since been quashed. In December 2018, Pell was convicted by a jury of five counts of historic child sexual abuse, including four charges of an indecent act with or in the presence of a child under sixteen and one charge of sexual penetration of a child under sixteen. Pell was sentenced to six years imprisonment, with a non-parole period of three years and eight months.[52] His initial appeal, on the grounds that the jury might have had reasonable doubt, was overturned by two of three judges. The High Court of Australia allowed special leave to appeal, on the grounds that the Court of Appeal had misapplied the legal test, leading to a miscarriage of justice. Finally, the High Court ruled that the two judges at the Court of Appeal should have found that there could have been sufficient doubt by the jury. This does not mean that the High Court ruled him not guilty of the original crimes as charged, but rather that legal process was not correctly followed.[53] Civil action in the courts is ongoing as this book goes to press.

Whatever the outcome, it has truly been a series of trials and appeals that divided the nation. Many Australians have condemned his actions (in respect to both this individual case and his wider involvement with paedophile priests).[54] Other Australians remained convinced of his innocence, and eagerly awaited the overturning of his guilty verdict. Indeed, a string of high-profile community leaders wrote letters of character reference for

2008); Family and Community Development Committee, Victorian Government, *Betrayal of Trust—Inquiry into the Handling of Child Abuse by Religious and Other Non-Government Institutions* (Victoria: Government Printer, 2013); Victorian Government, *Royal Commission into Family Violence Report* (Victoria: Government Printer, 2016).

[52] *DPP v Pell* (sentence) [2019] VCC 260 (13 March 2019), www.austlii.edu.au/cgi-bin/viewdoc/au/cases/vic/VCC/2019/260.html.

[53] At the time of press, full legal analysis of the High Court decision has not yet occurred. A good summary appeared at Ben Mathews and Mark Thomas, 'How George Pell won in the High Court on a legal technicality', *The Conversation* April 7, 2020, https://theconversation.com/how-george-pell-won-in-the-high-court-on-a-legal-technicality-133156.

[54] On Pell's relationships with other priests, see Louise Milligan, *Cardinal: The Rise and Fall of George Pell* (Melbourne: Melbourne University Press, 2017); David Marr, 'The Prince: Faith, Abuse and George Pell', *Quarterly Essay* 51 (2013): 1–98.

the convicted Pell, including the former prime minister John Howard.[55] Yet what was perhaps most remarkable was the courage of the two young men who came forward, to press charges, in what they knew would be a volatile political, social and religious environment.[56]

Vulnerabilities

It is clear that women and children and some men were (and are) routinely subject to sexual violence. The 2016 *Personal Safety Survey of Australians* reports that one in five women and one in twenty men have experienced sexual violence.[57] But it is also clear that some groups are more vulnerable than others. Problems (including cultural attitudes towards consent, the policing of sexual crime, the prosecution of cases, and racial, class and gendered bias within the courtroom) were and are heightened for marginalised groups. Notions of an ideal or worthy victim have profound implications for seeking justice: as Linda Alcoff has suggested, some victims are more 'palatable' than others.[58] And as intersectional feminism has shown, this burden is intensified for survivors who suffer discrimination or marginalisation on multiple fronts.

In Australia, Indigenous women and children were and are a group vulnerable to sexual assault: one recent study suggests Aboriginal and Torres Strait Islander women are 3.1 times more likely to suffer from physical and sexual abuse.[59] This vulnerability is grounded in the racism and sexism of the coloniser, and the systemic oppression and intergenerational trauma experienced by many Indigenous Australians.[60] As Eugenia

[55] Scanned copies cited at theaustralianatnewscorpau.files.wordpress.com/2019/02/statements.pdf, downloaded 7 March 2019.

[56] One of the young men, known as R, died before trial.

[57] ABS, Personal Safety, Australia, 2016, https://www.abs.gov.au/ausstats/abs@.nsf/mf/4906.0.

[58] Linda Alcoff, *Rape and Resistance* (Cambridge: Polity Press, 2018), 52.

[59] Our Watch, *Changing the Picture: A National Resource to Support the Prevention of Violence against Aboriginal and Torres Strait Islander Women and Their Children* (Melbourne: Our Watch, 2018), Executive Summary, np.

[60] Judy Atkinson, 'Violence in Aboriginal Australia: Colonisation and Gender', *Aboriginal and Islander Health Worker Journal* 14:2 (June 1990): 5–21.

Flynn has written, 'there is nowhere on this continent that has been untouched by white patriarchal violence.'[61]

One aspect of this appropriation of Indigenous bodies is that black women have been rendered always available for sex, as part of the colonial spoils.[62] Tess Ryan, a proud Biripi woman, has recently argued in her powerful piece on Indigenous women and gendered violence:

> Since colonization in Australia, Black Women have been viewed as lascivious and manipulative beasts, erotic curios, and domicile victims at the whims of men.[63]

Strong Indigenous women have (over and over) spoken out against multiple forms of violence. However, black women are still at a high risk of physical, verbal and sexual abuse, and as a recent study by Our Watch has suggested, this violence 'is often more severe and complex in its impacts'.[64] Reporting a crime—indeed any interactions with police—makes women further vulnerable in the criminal justice sector.[65] The mainstream media reports continue to report Aboriginal victims as promiscuous, addicts, and poor mothers.[66] Further, white attitudes towards Indigenous survivors have not necessarily improved. As Ryan and Flynn have both suggested, black women have once again been 'forgotten' in the #MeToo movement in Australia.[67]

In many ways, this book cannot overcome these omissions, not due to a lack of interest or a lack of care, but because of a resounding, even embarrassing, lack of sources. To build a picture of sexual violence in the

[61] Eugenia Flynn, 'This Place', in *#MeToo: Stories from the Australian Movement*, eds. Miriam Sved, Christie Nieman, Maggie Scott, Natalie Kon-yu (Sydney: Pan Macmillan, 2019), 17.

[62] Larissa Behrendt, 'Consent in a (Neo)Colonial Society: Aboriginal Women as Sexual and Legal 'Other', *Australian Feminist Studies* 15:33 (2000): 353.

[63] Ryan, 'This Black Body is Not Yours for the Taking', 120.

[64] Our Watch, *Changing the Picture: A National Resource to Support the Prevention of Violence against Aboriginal and Torres Strait Islander Women and Their Children*, Executive Summary, np.

[65] Amy McQuire, 'The More Things Change: Female Black Lives Don't Matter. If They Did, Ms Dhu Would Still Be Alive', *New Matilda*, 24 November 2015, https://newmatilda.com/2015/11/24/the-more-things-change-female-black-lives-dont-matter-if-they-did-ms-dhu-would-still-be-alive/.

[66] Flynn, 'This Place', 20.

[67] Ryan, 'This Black Body is Not Yours for the Taking', 117.

1970s and 1980s, I have drawn on four main forms of sources: feminist writings, government reports, media and court records. All of these groups—without exception—have not prioritised the voices of Indigenous women. White feminism has been widely critiqued by black women, for its exclusionary politics.[68] Indigenous women were rendered largely invisible in late twentieth-century mainstream media, and government reports might sometimes include statistics on Indigenous people, but gave no voice to women (or men). Court records tell us little about Indigenous women's experience of sexual violence, though I have utilised them when applicable. There were a small number of Indigenous women writing in this time period, including activists.[69] As a white woman living on unceded, colonised land, I have not attempted to tell—or take—the story of sexual assault on Indigenous women, but to acknowledge black voices when possible. This is done with a deep and saddening knowledge that sexual violence is at the core of the colonial process, and that so much more needs to be done by white Australia to address all forms of violence against First Nations people, in the past and in the present.

LGBTIQ+ people are also over-represented in sexual violence statistics, and under-represented in 1970s and 1980s material. We do not have good statistics on rates of assault and abuse against LGBTIQ+ communities, and there are significant differences between groups within queer communities, though much of the violence has at its core homophobic, transphobic and heterosexist values.[70] Gay men were notoriously subject to

[68] Pat O'Shane, 'Is There Any Relevance in the Women's Movement for Aboriginal Women?', *Refractory Girl* 12 (1976): 32–34; Melissa Lucashenko, 'No Other Truth?: Aboriginal Women and Australian Feminism', *Social Alternatives* 12:4 (1994): 21–24; Aileen Moreton-Robinson, *Talkin' Up to the White Woman: Aboriginal Women and Feminism* (St Lucia, Qld: University of Queensland Press, 2000); Larissa Behrendt, 'Aborignal Women and the White Lies of the Feminist Movement: Implication for AboriginalWomen in Rights Discourse', *The Australian Feminist Law Journal* 1 (1993): 27–44; A. Maguire, 'All Feminists Are Created Equal, But Some Are More Equal Than Others', *New Matilda*, 5 March 2015, https://newmatilda.com/2015/03/05/all-feminists-are-created-equal-some-aremore-equal-others/, downloaded December 2019.

[69] Edie Carter, *Aboriginal Women Speak Out About Rape and Child Sexual Abuse* (Adelaide: Adelaide Rape Crisis Centre, 1987). See also Vivian Bligh, 'A Study of the Needs of Aboriginal Women Who Have Been Raped or Sexually Assaulted', in *We Are Bosses Ourselves: The Status and Role of Aboriginal Women Today*, ed. Fay Gale (Canberra: Australian Institute of Aboriginal Studies, 1983).

[70] See Bianca Fileborn, 'Sexual Violence and Gay, Lesbian, Bisexual, Trans, Intersex, and Queer Communities', *Australian Institute of Family Studies* (March 2012): 3–7; Gail Mason and Stephen Tomsen, *Homophobic Violence* (Sydney: Hawkins Press, 1997); Alan Berman

physical and sexual assault in this period, including almost ninety deaths in Sydney alone from 1976 to the late 1990s.[71] Even so, homosexual men were more often imagined as offenders, rather than victims, with consistent mainstream messaging about the links between paedophilia and homosexuality.[72] Lesbian women were also subject to sexual and gendered assault across this time period, as Rebecca Jennings' work has shown.[73] Yet they too were not the focus of any sustained interest by either liberal feminism or government stakeholders, and few cases reached the courts. Recent studies show survivors feared reporting, in case they were not believed, or were maligned by police, or because they were afraid of bringing negative attention to their community.[74]

Transpeople, and the violence they endured, were even less visible in the late twentieth century. A recent study into reported rates of sexual violence or coercion in trans and gender diverse communities recorded rates four times higher than found in the broader Australian community.[75] In total, 53.2% of surveyed participants reported experiencing sexual violence or coercion, compared to 13.3% across the Australian community.[76] Though we do not have good statistics or other evidence on sexual violence and trans- or gender-diverse people in Australia's past, historical studies have captured instances of sexual assault, and it is likely rates of assault were high in the past as well as the present. Beyond the important

and Shirleene Robinson, *Speaking Out: Stopping Homophobic and Transphobic Abuse in Queensland* (Brisbane: Australian Academic Press, 2000).

[71] Lucy Cormack, 'Ugly Part of Our History': Sydney's Wave of Gay-Hate Deaths Exposed', *SMH*, 26 June 2018.

[72] Steven Angelides, 'The Homosexualization of Pedophilia: The Case of Alison Thorne and the Australian Pedophile Support Group', in *Homophobias: Lust and Loathing Across Time and Space*, ed. David A. B. Murray (Duke University Press, 2009), 64–81; Steven Angelides, 'The Emergence of the Paedophile in the Late Twentieth Century', *Australian Historical Studies* 36:126 (2005): 272–295.

[73] Rebecca Jennings, "It Was Quite a Scary Time': Lesbians and Violence in Post-War Australia', in *Gender Violence in Australia: Historical Perspectives*, eds. Alana Piper and Ana Stevenson (Melbourne: Monash University Publishing, 2019), 153–8.

[74] See Fileborn, 'Sexual Violence', 8.

[75] D. Callander, J. Wiggins, S. Rosenberg, V. J. Cornelisse, E. Duck-Chong, M. Holt, M. Pony, E. Vlahakis, J. MacGibbon, and T. Cook, *The 2018 Australian Trans and Gender Diverse Sexual Health Survey: Report of Findings* (Sydney: The Kirby Institute, UNSW, 2019), 10.

[76] Callander et al., *The 2018 Australian Trans and Gender Diverse Sexual Health Survey*, 10.

work of activist and academic Roberta Perkins,[77] I uncovered almost no mention of gender diverse people in my investigations in the 1970s and 1980s. Feminist groups in particular focused on straight and lesbian women's experiences of violence, and showed little interest in thinking outside of gender binaries. Court records in my sample did not reveal trans victims or offenders, nor aspects of gender diversity. This absence is replicated in more recent activism, too, with the voices of trans- and gender-diverse people excluded from the #MeToo movement.[78] Yet it is important to acknowledge the vulnerability and strengths of trans communities, even where primary sources do not reveal their stories.

* * *

This book explores the profound problems of dealing with sexual violence, both historically and in the contemporary world. In broader culture, women and children have too often been seen as sexually available, with little regard to their consent (in the case of adults), or ability to make informed decisions about consent (in the case of children). This was compounded by policing, where victims were unheard or disbelieved or their voices silenced. Legislation all too often privileged offenders (the long-lasting immunity of a husband from prosecution of rape of his wife is just one example). Cases were (and are) whittled away before a small number reached trial. In the courtroom, complainants were subject to a raft of invasive questions and demeaning practices, meaning the victim themselves felt on trial. In the community, all too often survivors were seen as complicit in their assaults: she had dressed in a certain way; she had been drunk; she had 'asked for it'.

Many of these ideas are based on a series of rape myths. Ideas about rape myths were developed in the 1970s and 1980s, when theorists including Susan Brownmiller, Susan Estrich and others began to suggest that sexual violence was accompanied by powerful sets of gendered

[77] See amongst others Roberta Perkins, *The Drag Queen Scene: Transsexuals in Kings Cross* (Sydney: George Allen & Unwin, 1983); Roberta Perkins, *Working Girls: Prostitutes, Their Life and Social Control* (Canberra: Australian Institute of Criminology, 1991).

[78] Meredith Talusan, 'Trans Women and Femmes Are Shouting #MeToo—But Are You Listening?', *Them*, 2 March 2018, https://www.them.us/story/trans-women-me-too. One recent exception is Kaya Wilson, 'Among Men', in *#MeToo: Stories from the Australian Movement*, eds. Miriam Sved, Christie Nieman, Maggie Scott, Natalie Kon-yu (Sydney: Pan Macmillan, 2019), 315–322.

assumptions, that operated to undermine the seriousness of sexual violence.[79] The most common rape myths include the following: the idea that the survivor was to blame; that physical assault and physical resistance is necessary for sex to be rape; that men have sexual needs that must be met; and that rape is perpetrated by strangers and monsters, and not by ordinary men.[80] Studies of rape myths highlighted that they continue to be persuasive at trial, not the least because worrying ideas about rape were perpetuated by police, journalists and legal professionals.[81]

Throughout this book, I trace these complex problems in modern Australia, considering how rape myths continued to co-exist (and clash) with alternative views that framed sexual assault as violent, patriarchal and a threat to all women. How, in this period of intense social and legal change, did ideas about sexual violence compete and contest? This work tracks five key themes over two decades: ideas of consent; ways of understanding trauma; ways of understanding victims and offenders; the structural impediments to justice; and changing awareness about sexual violence. I will introduce these themes here, but they are interwoven throughout the chapters. I seek to explain how all five themes are understood and interpreted over two decades of substantial social, cultural, economic and political change.

Culture and Consent

First, this book engages with the problem of consent. How might consent be defined? The idea that a victim had not consented was key to the crime of rape, yet the law (in either legislation or the common law) had not

[79] Susan Brownmiller, *Against Our Will: Men, Women and Rape* (New York: Simon & Schuster, 1975); M. R. Burt, 'Cultural Myths and Support for Rape', *Journal of Personality and Social Psychology* 38 (1980): 217–230; Susan Estrich, *Real Rape* (Cambridge: Harvard University Press, 1987).

[80] For an excellent summary on rape myths and the literature on them, see Olivia Smith, *Rape Trials in England and Wales: Observing Justice and Rethinking Rape Myths* (Springer, 2018), 54–57.

[81] See O. Smith and T. Skinner, 'How Rape Myths Are Used and Challenged in Rape and Sexual Assault Trials', *Social & Legal Studies* 26:4 (2017): 4–6. On the impact of rape myths in journalism, see Jane Gilmore, *Violence and the Representation of Women in the Media* (Melbourne: Penguin, 2019); R. Franiuk, J. L. Seefelt, and J. A. Vandello, 'Prevalence of Rape Myths in Headlines and Their Effects on Attitudes Toward Rape', *Sex Roles* 58 (2008): 790–801.

defined a standard of non-consent.[82] The common law demanded some form of resistance, but it did not dictate precisely how much and what forms it should take. Further, the idea of physical resistance was an unsubtle or clumsy one. As Constance Backhouse has argued, 'Some threats, intimidation and forms of bodily harm might be too minimal to count, for judges and jurors seemed to believe that "normal" heterosexual relations often manifested varying degrees of physical and psychological coercion.'[83]

In Australia in the 1970s and 1980s, the confusion over consent within the courtroom was a reflection of the disorder in broader society, where issues of consent were unclear. In part, this drew on the long Western tradition of gender roles, where men were constructed as 'naturally' sexually active and women as passive. Men were conditioned to think that their own sexual desires were paramount, that women might reject initial advances but not deny men sex, and that if a woman showed any sign of flirtation or sexual contact, she must—deep down—want sexual intercourse.[84] The slippages between flirtation and consent were so profound that the police and others developed terminology to describe a rape where the complainant had shown some degree of familiarity with the accused: 'victim precipitated rapes' was a term used to describe what would later be known as date rape. The very term suggested that the victim had been complicit in her assault.[85]

There is gripping evidence to suggest that at least a proportion of men convicted of sexual crimes did not view their sexual act as an assault, as rape, or even as especially violent. In 1969, four students from the University of Melbourne's Criminology Department researched a group of sixty-nine offenders who had been gaoled for rape, attempted rape or abduction with intent to rape. Information was gathered by interview and through written evidence including prison files, court transcripts and pre-sentence reports. Their report revealed a number of important attitudes towards consent, sexuality and rape, most notably that 'it was considered

[82] Anne Edwards and Melanie Heenan, 'Rape Trials in Victoria: Gender, Socio-cultural Factors and Justice', *Australian and New Zealand Journal of Criminology* 27:3 (December 1994): 215.

[83] Constance Backhouse, "Her Protests Were Unavailing': Australian Legal Understandings of Rape, Consent and Sexuality in the 'Roaring Twenties'', *Journal of Australia Studies* 24:64 (2000): 21.

[84] RCHR, *Final Report vol. 5*, 163, 164.

[85] Paul Ward, and Greg Woods, *Law and Order in Australia* (Sydney: Angus and Robertson, 1972), 93.

"right" that the girl must be coaxed'. The prisoners believed that women required coercion to have sex: 'all girls put up a bit of a fight', as one man revealed, and 'they all say "no" at first', suggested another. The assumption—or perhaps the justification—by men who raped was that all women needed coercion, and that she would have to be convinced to consent. Women, then, did not ever *really* refuse sex. Further, the prisoners believed—as did many in general society—that one man could not rape a woman without using violence. By this logic, it seems that the prisoners believed that unwanted sex with a woman was acceptable as long as she was not 'knocked about'—without extreme violence, she must have been a willing party.[86]

On the whole, the prisoners believed—or claimed to believe—that they had not raped a woman, even if sex had been unwanted. This allowed offenders to understand a woman as a 'partner', not a victim.[87] Many men lacked awareness of the basic concept of consent. For instance, criminologists of the period suggest that many men who were involved in gang rapes did not understand this as sexual assault, but rather made 'no attempt to hide their identities and on apprehension seem surprised by the fuss made about a normal activity'.[88] As one accused man explained, the woman had not specifically rejected him: 'She might have been raped before I came ... I heard her yelling and screaming... but she didn't try to stop me.'[89] Here, shock, trauma, exhaustion or unconsciousness might be read by the perpetrator as 'consent'. Further, it was believed that some women had given up the right to be able to consent to sex. Sex workers, in particular, were rarely successful in charging a man with rape. While feminists and criminologists suggested that any woman had the right to say 'no' to any man, it was notoriously difficult to prosecute cases where

[86] E. J. Hodgens, I. H. McFadyen, R. J. Failla and F. M. Daly, 'The Offence of Rape in Victoria', *Australian and New Zealand Journal of Criminology* 5:4 (December 1972): 227, 234.

[87] RCHR, *Final Report vol. 5*, 161.

[88] Ward and Woods, *Law and Order in Australia*, 93. See also Menachim Amir, 'Victim Precipitated Forcible Rape', *Journal of Criminal Law and Criminology* 58:4 (1967): 493–502.

[89] Beverley Scholz, 'Profile of a Gang Rape', in *Delinquency in Australia: A Critical Appraisal*, ed. Paul R. Wilson (St. Lucia, Qld: University of Queensland Press, 1977), 119.

sex workers were complainants, for their consent was always assumed, and the harm to them remained unacknowledged.[90]

Trauma Narratives

Ideas of trauma and harm are the second major theme of this book. It might seem obvious to us now that concepts of trauma and harm are central to how we understand sexual assault, and the impacts that violence has on victims/survivors. Yet this was not always the case. As recently as the 1950s, there was almost no discussion about trauma and the psychological impact of sexual assault on either adult or child victims. In the mid-twentieth century, concern focused on two key areas: first, physical injuries caused particularly by penetration, and second, social injuries that led to long-term effects including teenage pregnancy, or problems with establishing or maintaining heterosexual relationships.[91] In medical care and in the courtroom, there was almost no discussion of psychological harm. While concepts of trauma existed more broadly in medicine—particularly for the returned soldier—in Australia these were simply not applied to the survivor of a sexual assault or sexual abuse.[92]

This book will trace the new understandings of trauma and sexual assault that would occur only slowly, beginning in the 1970s. Feminists began to notice the common traits of trauma across women who had been victims of sexual assault, child sexual abuse and domestic violence. On the ground, feminists who worked in the newly emerging rape crisis centres and women's refuges saw that adult women remained traumatised not just by recent abuse, but by assaults they had suffered as children. Feminist scholars, journalists and activists developed a narrative of ongoing trauma.[93] These ideas were disseminated widely in the 1970s and 1980s,

[90] Paul Wilson, interview, *Royal Commission on Human Relationships: Official transcript of proceedings* (Sydney: Commonwealth Reporting Service, 1974–1976), 1667; 'All Women Have The Right To Say No', *WEL-Informed*, October 1979, 17. See also Olivia Plunkett, 'Innocent Even When Proven Guilty: Sexual Assault of Female Sex Workers in Australia 1966–1996', BA Honours Thesis, University of Queensland, 2019.

[91] Featherstone and Kaladelfos, *Sex Crimes*, 14.

[92] See Lisa Featherstone, 'Trauma and Sexual Violence: Narratives and Cases in Australia in the Late Twentieth Century', in Paula Michaels and Christina Twomey (eds.) Gender and Trauma since 1900 (London: Bloomsbury Press, 2021).

[93] Cathy Waldby, *Breaking the Silence: A Report Based Upon the Findings of the Women Against Incest Phone-in Survey* (Sydney: Women Against Incest, 1985), 4; 'Sexual Abuse of Children', *WEL-Informed*, August 1978, 6.

through a raft of articles in newspapers, women's magazines and mainstream media. Across the chapters, I acknowledge this remarkable change: over a period of less than two decades, it became impossible to discuss sexual assault without considering the trauma of the victim.

Victims and Offenders

The third theme of this book is a broader consideration of the voices and experiences of victims and survivors, and this work makes a concentrated effort to prioritise and highlight the ways sexual violence impacted on survivors, and also their families and communities. This is a challenge: sexual assault is often shrouded in secrecy. It is a crime that often occurs beyond the public sphere, though it may be brought into the public sphere through policing, medical care and prosecution. Sexual violence sits on the boundary of the public and the private. Because of this tension, it is notoriously difficult to capture the views of the women and children who experienced sexual crime in the past, even in our recent history.

I have not undertaken oral histories for this book, largely because I do not believe I have the skills to engage in interviews that may traumatise or re-traumatise the subjects. Though oral history may be therapeutic for some,[94] it was a risk I was unwilling to take, for myself, and for potential interviewees. I have instead attempted to forensically detail the voices of survivors, wherever possible, and to hear and acknowledge these voices.

I note here that this book focuses on women and children as victims and survivors. This is not, of course, because I believe men are not subject to sexual violence, or that their trauma is not worth reporting. I was led to exclude adult male victims in this study for a simple reason: in 1970s and 1980s Australia, men were very rarely represented, discussed or acknowledged in public discussions about sexual assault. My source base is elusive on men as victims or survivors. The feminist and activist movements of the 1970s and 1980s were often little concerned with violence against men: indeed, rape crisis centres sometimes actively rejected male patients, for they were seen as still part of a patriarchal order. Women's liberation groups quite self-consciously focused on the victimisation of women and children (especially girls). This is not to say that this violence did not

[94] Rebecca Campbell et al., '"What Has It Been Like for You to Talk with Me Today?": The Impact of Participating in Interview Research on Rape Survivors', *Violence Against Women* 16:1 (2010): 60–83.

occur, but that it was almost never scrutinised, leaving fewer sources for the historian to consider. Media debates and panics also did not focus on the adult man as a target of sexual assault: ironically, the seemingly inviolable white man's body meant any victimisation was rendered invisible. Even in terms of the criminal trial, there were far fewer criminal trials involving adult male complainants. To interrogate male sexual victimisation, this study would need to include additional work in vastly different sources, including prison records, military records and writing on gay hate crimes. Due to the disparity in the sources, the potential for male survivors to experience abuse and disclosure differently, the distinctiveness in public discourses about adult male victims and the already-broad scope of this project, I felt that male victims/survivors require a separate study and future research.[95]

Conversely, men appear overwhelmingly as offenders. Again, this is not because I do not believe women cannot commit sexual crimes. Female offenders, however, are statistically less likely.[96] They are also less likely to be discussed in public debates over offending—women are not so readily imagined as a sexual predator (though if she is, the commentary can be particularly brutal). But in many of my sources, female offenders are rarely conceived. Further, there is evidence to suggest that female offenders are less obvious as subjects for policing and prosecution, ensuring that in multiple ways the woman as offender is less visible, and less likely to be recorded in historical sources. There is, however, significant evidence about male offending, across multiple kinds of evidence, including femi-

[95] For historical studies of male victimisation, see Andy Kaladelfos and Yorick Smaal, 'Sexual Violence and Male Prisons: An Australian Queer Genealogy', *Current Issues in Criminal Justice* 31:3 (2019), 349–364; Yorick Smaal and Graham Willett, 'Conduct Unbecoming: Homosex, Discipline and Military Cultures in the Second World War', in *Criminologies of the Military, Militarism, National Security and Justice*, eds. Ben Wadham and Andrew Goldsmith (Oxford: Hart Publishing 2018), 169–188; Shurlee Swain, 'Gender-Based Violence in Out-of-Home Care', in *Gender Violence in Australia: Historical Perspectives*, eds. Alana Piper and Ana Stevenson (Melbourne: Monash University Publishing, 2019), 131–145.

[96] ABS, '4125.0—Gender Indicators, Australia, Sep 2018' https://www.abs.gov.au/ausstats/abs@.nsf/Lookup/by%20Subject/4125.0~Sep%202018~Main%20Features~Safety%20and%20Justice~8. For some of the problems in identifying female offenders, see David Axlyn McLeod, 'Female Offenders in Child Sexual Abuse Cases: A National Picture', *Journal of Child Sexual Abuse* 24:1(2015): 97–114; Sarah Michal Greathouse et al., 'Female Sexual Assault Perpetrators,' in their *A Review of the Literature on Sexual Assault Perpetrator Characteristics and Behaviors* (Santa Monica: Rand Corporation, 2015), 37–42.

nist writing, media reports, criminological studies, memoirs and medical sources, and throughout evidence from the criminal justice sector. Male offenders were omnipresent in all forms of testimony utilised in this work.

One discourse that was unexpectedly pervasive, however, was that of the offender as a 'good bloke', and I trace this idea throughout the chapters. The 'good bloke' defence spoke, paradoxically, to both a rape myth and a truism. It could be a truism in the fact that in many ways these were ordinary men—everyday neighbours, family members, citizens from the community. Nonetheless, that a man might be found guilty of a sexual crime, and still be imagined as a good man, spoke to a patriarchal myth where a man's (private) crimes were mitigated by his otherwise exemplary public life. A sexual offender who was a 'good bloke' was often a man who held a public position, and performed voluntary or paid work in community organisations. He might be a schoolteacher, a scout master, a guardian, a member of the local footy club or a surf lifesaver. He might be a man of the church. At trial, at sentencing and in the media, character witnesses reimagined these offenders as hard-working men, community volunteers, advocates for children or just generally as men of good character, despite their crimes.

Seeking Justice

The fantasy of the 'good bloke' was merely one challenge to the successful prosecution of a sexual offence. There were many and diverse difficulties, and as is widely reported in both the past and the present, problems of attrition during reporting, policing and prosecution are manifest. Unpacking the difficulties of the successful policing and prosecution of sexual crime is a constant theme throughout this work.

Studies of sexual assault are built on a problematic edifice, for we do not know precisely how many people were sexually assaulted in either the past or present. There are layers of inconsistency. We cannot rely on police or court statistics, for these reveal only cases reported or prosecuted. Victim surveys reveal higher rates of sexual violence against both adults and children, but again, we cannot be sure of their accuracy, for we cannot account for who responds to surveys, and why. We do know that there is a significant gap between alleged sexual assaults and reporting. The 2016 *Australian Safety Survey* revealed that almost one in five women (18%)

and one in twenty men (4.7%) had experienced sexual violence.[97] Of the women, the vast majority (87%) did not report the assault to the police.[98]

Women make informed decisions not to report, based on legitimate fears of not being believed, or of being shamed, or through fear of the court processes, which act to re-victimise the already vulnerable. Now, victims' rights groups generally support that it is an adult's choice whether or not to report sexual assault: only the victim can balance out the benefits and costs of reporting. At a structural level, however, this leads to high rates of non-reporting, both in the past and in the present. Non-reporting is highest in cases where the victim was affected by drugs and alcohol, or engaging in risky behaviour. It is also low amongst vulnerable groups, where women are less likely to be believed. Further, reports are lowered in cases of domestic abuse, where a victim might suffer further consequences at the hands of her partner, or ex-partner. Reporting from Indigenous women is low, because Aboriginal and Torres Strait Islander women are vulnerable from all policing and legal interactions, even when they are victims of crime.[99]

Yet attrition did not simply take place due to non-reporting by a victim/survivor. Instead, decisions made by police and later prosecutors meant that the majority of reported cases of sexual assault did not reach court. The attrition rate is staggering. In 2017–2018, ABS Crime Victimisation records suggest that 50,200 Australians over the age of eighteen experienced a sexual assault in the past twelve months.[100] In the same time period across Australia, there were 9,885 defendants who were finalised through the criminal justice system. Of these 9,885 defendants, 4,266 were found guilty, while 880 were found not guilty. Of the rest, 1,516 cases were withdrawn by the prosecution. A further 5,148 were adjudicated and dealt with in other legal systems, while 3,117 were trans-

[97] https://www.abs.gov.au/ausstats/abs@.nsf/mf/4906.0 accessed December 2019.

[98] https://www.abs.gov.au/ausstats/abs@.nsf/mf/4906.0 accessed December 2019.

[99] *Indigenous Deaths in Custody: A Report Prepared by the Office of the Aboriginal and Torres Strait Islander Social Justice Commissioner* (Canberra: Government Printer, 1996), Chap. 6, https://www.humanrights.gov.au/our-work/indigenous-deaths-custody-chapter-6-police-practices; The Senate, Finance and Public Administration References Committee, *Report: Aboriginal and Torres Strait Islander Experience of Law Enforcement and Justice Services* (Canberra: Government Printer, 2016), https://www.aph.gov.au/Parliamentary_Business/Committees/Senate/Finance_and_Public_Administration/Legalassistanceservices/Report.

[100] https://www.abs.gov.au/AUSSTATS/abs@.nsf/DetailsPage/4530.02017-18?OpenDocument.

ferred to other courts.[101] As these statistics show, cases can be dropped at multiple points—by the victim before or after reporting, by police or by prosecutors—and even for cases that end at trial, not all ended in a guilty verdict.

Kathy Daly and Brigitte Bouhours' exhaustive study of the attrition of rape cases across five countries is illustrative of the trends, with cases lost at the stage of policing, then by prosecutors and, finally, during the court process. Using data from multiple studies, Daly and Bouhours suggest that in Australia across the late twentieth century, about 80% of all reports of sexual assault were eroded during the early stages in the criminal justice sector. This means that after a victim's report, only 20% of cases flow into court, with flow highest in child sexual assault cases, and lower when the complainant is an adult woman.[102]

Daly and Bouhours show that there was further attrition at the next stage, too. In South Australia, between 2001 and 2005, for example, of 463 charges of rape, attempted rape and unlawful sexual intercourse, 37% had a guilty plea, 32% went to trial, and 31% were not preceded with, dismissed or withdrawn.[103] Similarly, in NSW from 2004 to 2006, there were 793 charges for sexual assault and other related offences against adults. Of these, 28% pleaded guilty, 42% went to trial and 30% had other outcomes. Across Australia from 1970 to 2005, Daly and Bouhous show that the average conviction rate is 13% of all reported sexual offences, while the conviction rate to the original offence charged by the police is 10.5%.[104] In each of these statistical sets, there was a considerable attrition through dismissal, not proceeding with the charge, or withdrawal. As Joanna Bourke concluded, 'Rapists who end up being convicted in a court of law must regard themselves as exceptionally unlucky.'[105]

[101] https://www.abs.gov.au/AUSSTATS/abs@.nsf/DetailsPage/4513.02017-18?OpenDocument.

[102] Kathleen Daly and Brigitte Bouhours, 'Rape and Attrition in the Legal Process: A Comparative Analysis of Five Countries', *Crime and Justice* 39:1 (2010): 606.

[103] Daly and Bouhours, 'Rape and Attrition in the Legal Process', 583–4.

[104] Daly and Bouhours, 'Rape and Attrition in the Legal Process', 598.

[105] Bourke, *Rape*, 389.

Changing Awareness

This leads us to a final theme: tracing the changing awareness of sexual violence that occurs across this time period. By the late 1970s, sexual assault is no longer something not spoken of, at least in public (there is an irony, of course, that it remains the most private of offences). But across the 1970s and 1980s, there was an avalanche of information about sexual violence, and it is discussed in more public spaces than ever before. Feminists showed that sexual assault is common, even omnipresent, in homes, on the street, in workplaces and in institutions. There is also a growing awareness of child sexual abuse, and the specific vulnerabilities of young people. Yet I want to pose the question: Despite the growing awareness of sexual assault, the new concepts of trauma and treatment, and the increased public horror around both rape and child abuse, did anything change?

To answer this question, I draw on numerous sources and different forms of evidence, traversing multiple viewpoints, mixed ideas and diverse stakeholders. The majority of historical studies on sexual and gender violence have focused on criminal offending and trials in one jurisdiction, due to the detailed work required in archives. Many have concentrated on one crime—homosexual offences, or crimes against children, for instance. Others (including my own work) have considered the criminal trial itself in depth. In contrast, this project considers the social, cultural and legal context of violence, alongside a close examination of both crimes and trials, to more fully understand sexual violence both in and beyond the criminal justice system. I analyse mainstream and alternative feminist literature from the 1970s and 1980s, extensive media debates and responses, governmental reports and interventions including but not only important Royal Commissions, legislation and political debates, medical literature, criminology and legal reports, autobiography and life writing. Finally, I utilise court transcripts including trials, sentencing reports and compensation claims, drawn from a non-representative sample of criminal cases from the jurisdiction of NSW.[106]

[106] The cases considered in this book are drawn from a database of sexual offences developed by Andy Kaladelfos and myself, created by research in the Supreme Court and Quarter Sessions records in New South Wales (NSW), Australia's largest jurisdiction. I examined 610 full and partial court transcripts from 1970, 1975, 1980 and 1985, including trials, sentencing hearings and compensation claims. The verbatim transcripts provide records on sexual offences that span gender and age, and include rape, sodomy, acts of indecency against men,

The book starts with the most dramatic and obvious site of the problem: the court trial. I do not argue that the practice of the law was the crux of the problem; instead, we see the problems of the wider society play out at trial. Chapter 2 traces how rape trials operated in the 1970s, initially before second-wave feminism in Australia, and then as the decade progresses, and as women's liberation began to take hold. It highlights the inherent problems faced by survivors of rape, and how they were treated in the criminal justice sector. Chapters 3 and 4 turn to explore the burgeoning feminist response outside of the courtroom, and the ways feminists and other progressive groups began to argue for sociolegal, political and medical change around sexual assault of women. In Chap. 5, we turn our gaze to child sexual abuse, and the slow realisation that adult women were not the only subjects of sexual assault.

Chapter 6 marks the turning point across the 1970s and 1980s: the significant 'rape law reforms' that took place in all Australian jurisdictions. But in the following chapters, we see that rape law reform did not, and could not, solve all of the problems of sexual violence. Chapter 7 examines new ideas about child sexual abuse that emerged in the 1980s. Chapters 8 and 9 deal with child sexual abuse within institutions, drawing on the rich, detailed and highly moving testimony gathered from the Royal Commission. From this, we see that law reform itself offered little change for children subject to abusive regimes.

In the final chapter, we draw back to our starting point: the criminal trial. How did the significant social and legal change affect the trial? On the one hand, change was slow to filter through to the courtroom, and despite some advancements, witnesses still experienced the trial as a re-traumatising event. On the other hand, I uncover one significant change, in terms of the way female complainants themselves responded to the court: some women, at least, had become to assert their own understandings of social legal concepts of consent, trauma and what it meant to be a victim. This leads directly to the conclusion, which traces the continuing

indecent assault of females and child sexual assault in various forms. These transcripts do not represent all court cases of sexual crime in NSW in this time period, but rather represent cases that the court saw fit to record, possibly as they were seen as cases that might be appealed. The 610 court transcripts are imperfect sources, for the transcriptions are regularly incomplete and fragmentary, with only parts of the court proceedings recorded. Often, we do not have an outcome of the trial or a sentence, though sometimes these can be traced in media reports.

conundrums of dealing with sexual assault in Australia and other western nations.

Throughout, I trace experiences of, and responses to, sexual violence across two decades, by thinking about the social, political and legal aspects of sexual abuse. We need to understand how the law is understood, disseminated and practised in the community. More than that, we need to examine the ways that society itself interprets concepts of sexual violence. How has and how does Australian society and culture frame sexual abuse against both women and children? To begin, we now turn our gaze to the court trial, to see just what went on in the 1970s courtroom, exposing the problems of a system that was supposed to seek justice and protect the victim, but which all too often put the female victim on trial.

CHAPTER 2

The Problem of Rape

In February 1970, in the Supreme Court of New South Wales (NSW), three men pleaded 'not guilty' to the charge of rape. The complainant Olivia Pearce was aged sixteen at the time of the trial, and she was fifteen when the crime was alleged to have occurred. In court, Pearce was first to take to the stand, and she told her version of events. She had travelled with a male acquaintance from Sydney to Taree, where they had met with a gang of eighty or a hundred 'bikies' who had convened in the area. At first, Pearce had been chatting happily to some men and women she knew. Then, she was grabbed by one of the accused men and carried away. She told the jury, 'I was struggling and screaming, but I could not get away.' Pearce described her alleged assault: she was undressed, pinned down, and raped by six men, including the three accused. After the series of assaults, she was eventually helped by another man, and taken down to the beach where she slept for the night. Pearce told the jury that the accused men had threatened to come back to get her the following day. She tried to get a lift to Sydney with another biker, but he began to harass her about sex, and she abandoned him. Instead, she walked for four or five hours, and eventually hitched a ride back to the city. After staying the night with a girlfriend, the two girls hitched back up to Maitland and reported the crime to police. Initially, the police had not believed her about the sexual assault: as Pearce described it, the police thought her 'cheap' and

L. Featherstone, *Sexual Violence in Australia, 1970s–1980s*, World Histories of Crime, Culture and Violence,
https://doi.org/10.1007/978-3-030-73310-0_2

'common'. She was seen as someone who might have underage sex, but not as someone who could be raped.[1]

On the stand, Pearce was subject to a raft of questions from combative defence lawyers representing the three men. The lawyers reminded Pearce that a young woman would be initiated into a bikie gang by participating in an 'onion', where she would have sex with seven or eight members of the gang, sometimes by force. Defence constructed Pearce as a 'bikie girl' who should have known what she was in for when she agreed to go to a bikie meet. Even her mother was questioned on her attire: Why was Pearce wearing *black* slacks? The defence was hinting that the teenager wanted to be a biker girl.

Medical evidence was then presented for the Crown by Dr Joseph Malouf, government medical officer (GMO) of the Parramatta District. He recorded that there were no external bruises or marks on Pearce's body. A gynaecological examination had revealed that the complainant's hymen was lacerated and bleeding, and the lining of her vagina was flattened. She was not a virgin at the time of examination, but Malouf could not definitively say whether or not she was a virgin before the assault. This was an important issue in any rape trial in this period, for it spoke to the young woman's sexual experience and her potential promiscuity. In this case, as with many, the medical evidence was inconclusive: Dr Malouf felt that there may have been some previous sexual acts, but he could not prove or disprove prior intercourse.

Following the medical testimony, much of the trial was made up of evidence from the arresting officers who had made initial interviews with the accused men. Some of the evidence was damning. According to police testimony, the first of the accused men, David Kenneth, told officers that the young woman had not consented to sex. Further, according to the police evidence, Kenneth acknowledged that while they were having sex, other men 'were holding her arms above her head on the ground and there was a bloke holding his hand over her mouth to stop her calling out'. He claimed he had been very drunk at the time. The second of the accused men, Kevin Smithson, on the other hand, was more circumspect in his police interview, and did not outright agree that the complainant had not consented. According to the police, Smithson responded to

[1] State Records NSW: Court Reporting Branch; NRS 2713, Criminal Transcripts, Supreme Court, *R v Kenneth, Smithson, Lewis and Watkins*, 1970 (hereafter 'Criminal Transcripts').

questions in a way that was suggestive of a lack of consent from the victim, and considerable violence from the men.

Lastly, the police evidence suggested that the third defendant, Jason Lewis, also told of non-consensual sex. Detective Sergeant Black recorded the following interview with Lewis:

> Q. What do you mean by the word 'onion'? A. An onion means a gang bang. It is when a lot of blokes decide to rape a girl....
>
> Q. What happened then? A. I don't know who first started to have intercourse with this girl but a couple of blokes had a go and when they got off I got on and had intercourse and another bloke came after me.
>
> Q. Did you have consent to have intercourse with this girl...? A. No. Like I said, it was an onion.
>
> Q. What was this girl doing at the time you were having intercourse with her? A. She was crying, I remember that. I think she called out something, but I don't remember. She could not do much because of the blokes standing around.

After the police evidence was completed, the three accused men spoke, each giving an unsworn statement from the dock. Their statements could not be cross-examined, owing to a historic law in NSW that exempted unsworn statements from the rules of evidence. David Kenneth spoke first:

> I thought she was just one of the bikie girls that hang around with the mob and she was—you know—did the same things that all the other girls did.

Here, he admitted sex with the complainant, but claimed he believed it to be consensual, based largely on her perceived affiliation with the bikie gang. Foreshadowing the possibility of a charge of carnal knowledge with a girl under the age of sixteen, Kenneth also addressed the issue of her age: 'As far as I thought, she was over sixteen. She looks well over sixteen, and I had seen her, she had been in the pub with the bikies and drinking, so I naturally assumed she was well over sixteen.'

Kevin Smithson then took to the dock. He told the court the young woman had undressed herself and told the men that she was menstruating. He explained that while she was restrained, it was only a 'hand ... over her mouth a couple of times because I thought she was doing some laughing in between the incident'. Smithson, like Kenneth, spoke to her age, suggesting, 'I thought she was over sixteen. She looked it and she used to drink at the hotels.' Then, in the final unsworn speech, Lewis gave a statement that was considerably different from the police records. He denied being present at the time of the sex, claiming he was at the hospital at the time of the 'onion'. There was a sizeable difference between the police testimony presented and Lewis' own statement. As we will see, this would play out in the final outcomes of the trial.

At the summing up of the trial, Justice Taylor explained the technical, legal meanings of the charge of rape:

> Rape is carnal knowledge of a woman without her consent. Carnal knowledge is the physical act of penetration.... Consent of a woman in a case of rape means her permission to the man to have that intercourse, freely and consciensly [*sic*] given.

But, Justice Taylor continued,

> a woman who is attacked does not have to struggle, to resist to the end of her strength. If by reason of the number of her assailants, the place where she is assailed, the absence of persons to whom she might appeal, she abandons resistance and submits to what is taking place that is not consent.

The commentary by the judge reflects directly on this trial: the young woman found herself in a vulnerable situation, where active resistance was difficult, if not impossible. Then, there was a final directive from Taylor J. To be convicted of rape, the jury had to be convinced that the complainant did not consent to sex, but that the defendants *knew she did not consent*. This was a particular problem in this case, where all agreed that at least some sex took place, but the issue was whether the young woman had consented or not and whether the men had understood this. Two of the defendants argued in their dockside statements that they believed she had consented, and that she was just another bikie girl willing to participate in an 'onion'.

The jury was unable to agree on the outcome for all three accused men. Kenneth and Smithson were found guilty of rape. But the jury could not concur on a verdict for Lewis, presumably due to the inconsistencies in testimony regarding his whereabouts on the night. He was remanded in custody. Then, the judge moved to the sentencing of the two prisoners. Kenneth had no prior criminal convictions. According to police inquiries, Kenneth was regularly employed, not generally a heavy drinker and not usually an associate of the criminal class. Detective Senior Constable

Mervyn Brazel concluded at the sentencing hearing that Kenneth had committed an 'awful thing .... But apart from this I formed the opinion that he was quite a decent type of individual'. He was, in other words, somewhat of a 'good bloke'. Justice Taylor sentenced him to five years in gaol, with a non-parole period of two years.

Smithson, however, had two prior convictions: the first, in Children's Court for breaking and entering, and the second for rape. For the rape conviction, he had been sentenced to seven years hard labour, with a non-parole period of four years. The conviction was for an offence against another young woman on the same night as the rape of Pearce. Smithson had now been found guilty of two separate charges of rape, against two different women, with both crimes committed within a couple of hours of each other. Justice Taylor saw him as the ringleader of Pearce's rape. At sentencing, Taylor J condemned Smithson:

> You and this motley section of humanity that accompanied you that night, (which must have been composed of those who are not only degenerate but depraved,) seem to regard this as some form of spectator sport. This child—she is little more than a child—had these indignities inflicted upon her as a spectacle for you and those with whom you associated.

Smithson was sentenced to eight years: for the two rapes that night, he faced fifteen years in gaol, with a non-parole period of seven years.

Though two of the men were ultimately convicted, the trial for the gang-rape of Olivia Pearce is illustrative of many of the inherent challenges of prosecuting sexual assaults in the 1970s. We have a young woman (in this case under the age of consent) who was doggedly questioned by multiple defence lawyers on her sexual past, dress and previous sexual practices. We have police reports of initial questioning that were subject to much scrutiny. There was a lack of corroborative evidence, and medical evidence proved inconclusive. There was little evidence provided by witnesses, despite the crowd at the rape itself. In the case of the accused man Lewis, it could not even be proven whether he was present at the sexual assault or not. All three men had the opportunity to speak from the dock. This was unsworn testimony and was not subject to cross-examination: the defendants were not interrogated on the stand in the same way as the female complainant. In particular, as we have seen Lewis gave a prior inconsistent statement. Under NSW laws, he still could not be cross-examined: the legal process in this instance was clearly skewed towards the accused. We can conclude that the probable reason for conviction was that two men had spoken frankly with police and admitted or hinted that the complainant had not consented. Without the police testimony, would there have been a conviction?

This trial is one example of the gendered operations of the courtroom, but it is not exceptional or unusual. This chapter explores the problem of rape, and how it was dealt with in the microcosm of the law court, at trial. Here, I do not argue that the court was the core of the problem of sexual violence: far from it. The court however acts a powerful dossier of the problem of rape in wider society. The trial is used here as a case study of the broader difficulties of dealing with sexual violence in Australian society. Pearce, like other complainants, entered the courtroom to face the legacies of several centuries of jurisprudence and courtroom practice that placed her at a substantial social and legal disadvantage. This chapter focuses on trials before law reform, drawing on a range of sources including transcripts of rape cases from Australia's largest jurisdiction, New South Wales in the early-to-mid 1970s.[2] It highlights many of the profound problems that precipitated law reform, including challenges in law, society, medicine and, most importantly, gendered relationships within Australian culture.

The chapter opens with a consideration of the issue of sexual consent, and how this was managed within the trial process. Court processes reveal just how muddy ideas of consent were, and that ideas about male sexual privilege and female consent still operated in the community and in the courtroom. Tied to ideas of consent, the chapter then offers a substantial examination of the ways female complainants were treated on the stand, including close and sustained scrutiny of their sexual history, behaviour and dress. I also consider the kinds of evidence that were acceptable to the courtroom, and how this was influenced by both legal requirements and gendered norms. I examine the ways accused men shaped their own identities in an unsworn statement, while female complainants were left to simply respond to allegations over dress, behaviour and bodily comportment. The rumblings of the social and sexual revolutions of the 1960s and 1970s had not yet challenged the norms of the courtroom. As this chapter

[2] For more on these sources, see this volume, 'Introduction', and Lisa Featherstone and Andy Kaladelfos, *Sex Crimes in the Fifties* (Carlton: Melbourne University Publishing, 2016), 8–10.

will show, all too often it was the female victim who felt that it was she, rather than the offender, who was on trial.

To Consent

Historically, physical force was an important aspect in the definition of rape. In Britain, the United States and Australia, eighteenth-century legal authorities classified rape as 'carnal connection with a woman forcibly and against her will.[3] Yet from the mid-nineteenth century, challenged by instances of sexual assault when the complaint was drugged, drunk, sleeping or otherwise incapacitated, judicial decisions moved away from concepts of force to a newer idea of consent. Slowly, 'force' as the defining factor of rape was written out of statutes and undermined in common law. A woman no longer had to 'resist to the utmost of her strength', and physical violence was no longer the primary factor of a sexual assault.[4]

Instead, in theory at least, issues of consent were rendered central to definitions of rape in modern Western cultures.[5] To prove a sexual assault, it had to be shown that the sexual act took place, and that the complainant did not consent to the act. The onus was on the prosecution, to prove the lack of consent.[6] Further, to be found guilty, it had to be shown that the accused knew the complainant did not consent to the act. Substantiating non-consent was at the very core of the rape trial, yet there was no legally agreed way to prove or disprove consent. Despite its long tradition in both statutes and common law, classifying and legally articulating 'consent' was troubling. Consent proved to be a slippery and culturally malleable concept.

[3] David Hume, 'Of Rape', in *Commentaries on the Law of Scotland Respecting Crimes, vol. I*, 4th edition, ed. Benjamin Robert Bell (Edinburgh: Law Society of Scotland, 1986), 301.

[4] Montgomerie H. Hamilton and G. C. Addison, *Criminal Law and Procedure, New South Wales: Containing the Crimes Act, 1900, the Criminal Appeal Act of 1912 and Other Statues, vol. 2*, 5th edition, ed. C. E. Weigall (Sydney: Law Book Co., 1947), 80; Victor Tadros, 'No Consent: A Historical Critique of the Actus Reus of Rape', *Edinburgh Law Review* 3:3 (September 1999): 321–6.

[5] Estelle B. Freedman, *Redefining Rape: Sexual Violence in the Era of Suffrage and Segregation* (Cambridge, Massachusetts: Harvard University Press, 2013), 3–4. On the blurred line between coercion and consent in earlier periods, see Sharon Block, *Rape and Sexual Power in Early America* (Chapel Hill: University of North Carolina Press, 2006), 16–52.

[6] Hamilton and G. C. Addison, *Criminal Law and Procedure*, 80.

In practice, though physical resistance was not technically seen as essential to a successful prosecution, 'force' and physical violence remained the primary way prosecutors framed non-consent. Paradoxically, physical violence and physical resistance were not deemed necessary for rape, and yet both made rape far simpler to successfully prosecute—and the absence of both rendered a prosecution difficult and unlikely. Arguing that the complainant had consented to sex was a common tactic of the accused, as we saw in the opening trial of the three bikies. It allowed the defendant to agree that *sex* had taken place (which was particularly important if there was physical or other evidence), but to argue that it was not *rape*. Lack of consent was difficult to prove, and the argument that the complainant voluntarily had sex continued to be the most common—and successful—defence to charges of rape in the 1970s, as it had been in earlier periods.[7]

In Australia in the 1970s, a complainant's physical resistance remained a core interest of the court when prosecuting sexual crimes against adult women. How had the alleged victim resisted her attacker? Had she *really* fought back, actively and physically? Women and girls were expected to be able to give positive evidence of considerable resistance to sex. In one rape trial in 1970 in NSW, for instance, a teenage girl accused two men of dragging into a car and raping her. Dealing with the first attack, the Crown Prosecutor's questions and her testimony was as follows:

> Q. Anything said? A. He kept on saying, "Open your legs" and I kept on closing them and he said, "Open them" and he punched me and I eventually had to open them.
>
> Q. Why? A. Because he punched me.

In asking why she had to open her legs, the prosecutor was attempting to highlight the physical assault, to counter any defence strategy that she had either consented, or perhaps not resisted 'enough'.[8] The key medical jurisprudence texts of the nineteenth century had suggested a healthy adult woman could not be raped: she would have enough strength and determination to resist.[9] The idea that a woman could repel her rapist were long lasting in the twentieth century. Here, the complainant's sharp answer,

[7] See Featherstone and Kaladelfos, *Sex Crimes in the Fifties*, 34.

[8] Criminal Transcripts, Supreme Court, *R v Gray and Davies*, 1970, 42.

[9] Stephen Robertson, 'Signs, Marks, and Private Parts: Doctors, Legal Discourses, and Evidence of Rape in the United States, 1823–1930', *Journal of the History of Sexuality* 8:3 (January 1998): 346.

'Because he punched me', served to highlight the violence of the attack, but also emphasised her opposition to sex.[10] That such intrusive, forceful questioning was necessary from the prosecution only serves to show just how important it was to the trial to show both physical harm and fierce resistance to an attack.

Complainants who did not actively and aggressively resist sex came under sharp scrutiny in the courtroom. Examples from another trial for rape in 1970 illustrate the ways violence was understood in the court. Three men had allegedly attacked an eighteen-year-old woman: one man was charged with rape, while the other two were charged with attempted rape. There was intense questioning over the level of the complainant's resistance. A witness was called to the stand, who had overheard the sexual assault taking place. The testimony described the woman calling out 'stop', but 'it was not soft but it was not, you know, absolutely screaming, sort of thing… It was not [a] real boisterous type of voice saying "Stop,"—or anything like that'.[11] Despite her verbal opposition—explicitly using the word 'stop'—the witness did not necessarily see her resistance as a strong refusal of consent. Cases such as this indicate that verbal resistance was not considered a definitive form of resistance: it was enough to bring doubt that a woman might still consent while saying 'no'.

In the same trial, the complainant's body also came under scrutiny. The young woman was questioned on the stand about the precise positioning of her body during sex. After an intensive interrogation into the exact placement of her head, limbs, buttocks and feet, the defence suggested that the woman had *participated* in sex, by lifting up her body to allow the defendant better access to her.[12] By downplaying her struggle and stating she had moved to allow penetration, defence was suggesting that the sex was consensual, not rape. Here, the argument pivoted not merely on her verbal consent, but that she had not resisted in the correct and appropriate form, denying her attacker access to her body in any way.

A woman's behaviour was thus closely scrutinised for signs of willingness, acquiescence and resistance. Alcohol was regularly raised as a problem for the giving or refusing of consent: Was a complainant or defendant who was drunk able to fully conceptualise legal definitions of consent? It would appear that in practice, a victim who was drinking was often assumed

[10] Criminal Transcripts, Supreme Court, *R v Gray and Davies*, 1970, 42.
[11] Criminal Transcripts, Supreme Court, *R v Martin, Goff and Daniels*, 1970.
[12] Criminal Transcripts, Supreme Court, *R v Martin, Goff and Daniels*, 1970.

to have given consent for sex. As Justice McClemens told his jury in summing up at this trial, 'There is drunken consent; a woman who is under the influence of liquor gives her consent under conditions where she might not otherwise do so. That is consent.'[13]

I would argue, therefore, that while 'consent' should be a simple concept to grasp, the way it was utilised in the community and the courtroom was far more complex. Evidence presented in court reveals a strong sense of masculine privilege in the testimony by and about accused men. In some instances, the accused men simply did not care about the concept of consent. In other cases, consent was expected, and men anticipated a woman would acquiesce to sex because of the way she looked, dressed or behaved. For example, in one rape trial, a teenage girl told that she had met the accused man at a Newcastle beach. In her testimony, she claimed that she had gone back to his shop with him and a group of others, and the accused man was alleged to have separated her from her friend and pushed her to the floor. According to her testimony:

> [He said] 'You know I am going to root you, don't you.' And I said, 'No, you are not.' And he said, 'Do you play around?' And I said, "no, a boy's never touched me before.' He said, 'You're a liar, you're a natural Australian girl and all girls like it." He said, 'Why won't you, are you frightened of getting pregnant?' I said, 'No, it's not that; I just don't want to.' And he said, 'Not much of an excuse;' and I started to get up and he started to get up too and he pulled me down on top of the mats and he started to undo my swimmers.

As retold in her testimony, an older man assumed that she would agree to sex—he had already told her that she went to a rough high school, where all the girls would have sex. When she categorically told him no, she was told that she did not have an adequate 'excuse' to refuse him, and, according to the complainant, proceeded to physically restrain her, to threaten her and, finally, to rape her.[14]

In arguing for consent, defence established a particular trope that women were ready and eager to have casual sex—often with multiple partners. Judging by trial transcripts, it was seen to be a reasonable argument that a young woman might allow a line of men to have sex with her in a public space. Gang bangs or 'onions' were imagined to be common, and

[13] Criminal Transcripts, Supreme Court, *R v Martin, Goff and Daniels*, 1970.
[14] Criminal Transcripts, Supreme Court, *R v Payne*, 1970.

women were thought to engage in them willingly, even when they were combined with physical violence or derogatory verbal abuse. There was no proper explanation why a teenage girl might willingly engage in rough sex with a group of bikies, for example. This set up a conundrum within the courtroom, where women were ideally to be pure and virginal, yet where it was not unexpected to have them represented as wildly sexual participants in violent forms of sexual intercourse.

This is not to suggest, of course, that some women did not engage in (and enjoy) group encounters and rough sex. Yet concepts of female pleasure were almost always left out of the courtroom discussion. In most trials it was unclear just why a woman might consent to group sex, outside, with a line of unknown men. Perhaps it was for her own pleasure and independence, or for money or drugs, or perhaps to be accepted as part of a gang? Yet these ideas were left without discussion or illumination. The argument that a woman was promiscuous or over-sexualised defaulted to much older, simpler ideas of a woman's uncontrolled and rapacious sexuality. Her willingness to engage in sexual situations was an easy default within the artillery of the defence lawyer. In the 1970s, defence commonly utilised the argument that a woman consented, even when the sexual encounter seemed from the outside to be degrading to her—and Crown Prosecutors never seemed to effectively counter this. Consent was used as a simplistic explanation for even the most complicated sexual encounters.

The issue of consent became even more thorny when a defendant claimed he *believed* the woman had consented to sex. As we have seen, common law across Australian jurisdictions dictated that rape occurred while the offender was 'aware that the person is not consenting or might not be consenting'.[15] *Mens rea* effectively meant an accused person had to be guilty of the assault itself, but also had criminal intent or a 'guilty mind'. In rape trials in the 1970s, *his* guilty mind was generally interrogated through *her* actions at the time of the assault. To give an example, in 1970 three men were charged with the gang-rape of an eighteen-year-old woman. The group had been drinking, and the complainant was questioned on her demeanour, clothing and sexual history. The defence was built on the argument that the woman had consented, and the three accused men all gave unsworn testimony claiming that the complainant had consented to sexual intercourse, with one man claiming she had

[15] This was also represented in some state legislation, for example in Victoria, *Crimes Act 1958*, S. 38(2)(a).

agreed to sex 'not only with words but by the way she acted and carried on'. Early in the trial, McClemens J was asked by defence to clarify the legal meaning of rape. Justice McClemens gave a direction to the jury that: 'The crime of rape takes place when a man has sexual intercourse with a woman without her consent.' This seemed simple enough, and McClemens J clarified that any kind of penetration was enough for a charge of rape. But then, his directions became more complex. He told the jury:

> under our criminal law no one can be found guilty unless they have a guilty mind. If a person believes a woman is consenting and she is in fact not, but he believes she is then it cannot be said he has a guilty mind which could justify the ingredient which is necessary in any criminal case.[16]

In his second attempt to refine the meaning of 'consent', McClemens J accurately reflected the legal definition of rape in NSW in this period. Yet it considerably muddied the waters in popular understandings of rape. A defendant who successfully argued he had believed a woman consented to sex would not be found guilty of rape. Similar patterns excusing men's actions, based on their 'mistaken' beliefs about consent occurred across Australian jurisdictions.[17]

A final and enduring problem with defining consent was how consent might be articulated: Was it verbal or otherwise? In the 1970s, 'consent' could be interpreted in the courts very liberally—so much so that a woman might not even know a man thought she was consenting to sex. In one trial in 1970, a man was charged with five offences: rape, attempted rape, attempted sodomy, sodomy and assault of an adult woman. During their deliberations, the jury had requested clarification on the idea of consent. Isaacs J noted that in rare cases, consent could be explicit, for instance if a man asked a woman, 'How about it', she might reply 'okay'. More often, however, he felt consent was implicit, and her consent might take a number of forms. Consent by implication, he stated:

> can take the form, for instance, of just a passionate kiss. It can take the form of a squeeze of a hand, it can take the form of a coy 'No', but a meaning in

[16] Criminal Transcripts, Supreme Court, *R v Martin, Goff and Daniels*, 1970.

[17] Beverley Scholz, 'Profile of a Gang Rape', in *Delinquency in Australia: A Critical Appraisal*, ed. Paul R. Wilson (St. Lucia, QLD: University of Queensland Press, 1977), 125.

> reality, 'Yes'. It can take the form of simply doing things without a word spoken.[18]

Here, Justice Isaacs illuminates many aspects of ordinary courtship or even friendship: on a date, a woman might kiss or hold hands, and by this measure, she may have given a man reason to think she consented to sex. Justice Isaacs' continued:

> a girl may expressly or by implication at one stage consent, but before the act is commenced to be attempted changed her mind. Well, then the consent can withdrawn and there is no longer any consent. But whether that situation ever arises is a matter for you to determine.[19]

Thus, in Justice Isaacs' model, there is a very broad concept of consent, that might be indicated even by a kiss. Isaacs J was also not confident that a woman or girl might 'change her mind' during a sexual encounter, suggesting that a woman's consent was codified and solidified almost at the start of an encounter, through her body language and demenour, and through her willingness to hold hands or kiss.

Even more alarmingly, Isaacs J drew on ideas of man's hydraulic sexuality to explain the parameters of consent. Hydraulic sexuality was a concept developed in the Victorian period by medical authorities to explain that once aroused, a normal man would not be able to control or stop his sexual impetus: once sexual activity had begun, he would need to see the process through to ejaculation.[20] Isaacs J explained that if she had impliedly consented, but then 'changed her mind' (or indeed, we may argue, have never given consent to sex in the first place), there were three options. Most obviously, a man might stop pursuit, or he might continue, knowing there was no consent. The third option had more complex outcomes, in terms of the charges in a trial. As Isaacs J stated:

[18] Criminal Transcripts, Supreme Court, *R v Paige*, 1970.

[19] Criminal Transcripts, Supreme Court, *R v Paige*, 1970.

[20] On Victorian ideas on hydraulic sexuality and rape, see Carolyn A. Conley, 'Rape and Justice in Victorian England', *Victorian Studies* 29:4 (July 1986): 525–6; Joanna Bourke, *Rape: A History from 1860 to the Present Day* (London: Virago, 2007), 24–28. For ideas on hydraulic sexuality in Australia, see Lisa Featherstone, 'Pathologising White Male Sexuality in Late Nineteenth Century Australia Through the Medical Prism of Excess and Constraint', *Australian Historical Studies* 41:3 (2010): 337–351.

> if there was no time left for him to make up his mind as to whether he was going to obey her final decision or not, if it was all for instance simultaneous, you might find it very difficult to say that the Crown has established that she did not consent to his attempt. Once she consents, then the withdrawal of consent must always be a matter of degree.[21]

In effect, Justice Isaacs' conceptualisation of consent—presented to the jury during a trial that included charges of serious crimes including rape and sodomy—meant that once a woman consented, even by oblique means, it was difficult or even impossible for her to withdraw that consent. Once aroused, a man's hydraulic sexuality meant that sex must begin or continue, especially once a certain, unnamed 'time' had passed.

A Sexual Past

Male sexual access to women was rarely questioned within the courtroom: men's heterosexual needs were understood as active, even naturally aggressive. It was quite the opposite, however, when women's sexuality came under scrutiny. Though the 1960s has been remembered somewhat nostalgically as 'the swinging sixties', in Australia, both sexual politics and sexual relationships remained largely conservative and heteronormative.[22] Despite the liberations that were slowly emerging in the United States and the United Kingdom, in Australia and particularly within the courtroom, women were expected to remain sexually pure prior to marriage and to have experienced sex only within the boundaries of marriage. What did this mean for victims of sexual assault, who had sex outside of marriage?

With consent at the centre of the courtroom trial, defence would attempt to prove that the complainant had acquiesced to sex, often relying on an examination of her prior sexual actions. The legal history of questioning the complainant about her sexual history was founded in nineteenth-century views about a woman's chastity and moral virtue. The

21 Criminal Transcripts, Supreme Court, *R v Paige*, 1970.

22 Yorick Smaal, 'Sex in the Sixties', in *Australia in the 1960s: People, Power and Politics*, eds. Julie Ustinoff and Shirleene Robinson (Cambridge: Cambridge Scholars Publishing, 2012), 69–94; Frank Bongiorno, 'January 1961 The Release of the Pill: Contraceptive Technology and the "Sexual Revolution"', in *Turning Points in Australian History*, eds. Martin Crotty and David Andrew Roberts (Sydney: UNSW Press, 2009), 157–170; Lisa Featherstone, *Let's Talk About Sex: Histories of Sexuality in Australia from Federation to the Pill* (Newcastle Upon Tyne: Cambridge Scholars Publishing, 2011), 287–292.

focus on her past was supposedly to determine a number of points. Was she moral, and hence a reliable witness? Had she had a previous relationship with the defendant, and previously consented to sex? Was she a loose woman, or a so-called 'common prostitute'?[23] These issues, it was argued, might affect both a notion of consent and her reliability in the stand.

Ideas about female morality were always problematic for sexual assault trials: in modern Western societies, cultural expectations of women's sexual purity permeated the courtroom, and indeed broader society.[24] By the 1970s, however, it was clear that many women did have a sexual 'history', either before or outside of marriage.[25] Lines of questioning over her virginity, chastity and 'respectability' were both troubling and unrealistic. Under laws of evidence, a female complainant could be cross-examined on multiple points: her previous social or sexual relationship with the accused; her previous sexual experiences with other men or boys; and on her 'general sexual reputation'.[26] Yet as the Report of the Royal Commission into Human Relationships argued in 1977, 'A defence counsel who questions a rape victim on her past sexual history is not doing so for the purpose of convincing the jury that she is a person of dubious veracity. Clearly he is trying to show that, having consented before, she is more likely to have consented on this occasion.'[27] Though such a position was increasingly untenable by the late 1970s, and key legislators increasingly saw it as out of step with community standards,[28] it remained a prime defence strategy until law reform (and, as we will see later in this book, arguably after).

[23] On sex workers and consent, see B. Sullivan, 'Rape, Prostitution and Consent', *Australian & New Zealand Journal of Criminology* 40:2 (2007): 127–142.

[24] Shani D'Cruze, 'Sexual violence since 1750', in *The Routledge History of Sex and the Body, 1500 to the Present*, eds. S. Toulalan & K. Fisher (London: Routledge, 2013), 448; Conley, 'Rape and Justice in Victorian England', 519–36.

[25] Frank Bongiorno, *Sex Lives of Australians: A History* (Collingwood, Vic: Black, 2012), 226–227, 232–240; Michelle Arrow, *The Seventies: The Personal, the Political and the Making of Modern Australia* (Sydney: NewSouth, 2019), 20–22, 65–70.

[26] NSW Parliament, *Report of the Criminal Law Review Division of the Department of the Attorney-General and of Justice into Rape and Other Sexual Offences* (Sydney: Government Printer, 1977), 27.

[27] Royal Commission on Human Relationships (hereafter RCHR), *Final Report vol. 5* (Canberra: Government Printer, 1977), 190.

[28] Mr Bryan, NSW Parliament, *Report of the Criminal Law Review Division of the Department of the Attorney-General and of Justice into Rape and Other Sexual Offences* (Sydney: Government Printer, 1977), 65.

Across the 1970s, bold questions could and would be asked of a woman's sexual past, her behaviour, and even her desires. In a trial in 1970, a woman had accused two men of raping her in her own apartment, where she was living after separating from her husband. The woman had been friends with one of the men, and had allowed him to sleep over at her flat on one previous occasion, though she claimed they had not had sex before the assault. In cross-examination, the woman was asked a series of intrusive questions about her prior sexual life, to suggest that she was promiscuous. She was also asked questions about her sexual relationship with her now-separated husband, including how often they had sex during their marriage. The woman was even questioned on her sexual pleasure during marriage: 'Did you enjoy the sexual intercourse', asked the defence. The questioning continued, suggesting that her 'sometimes' desire in sex rendered her 'passionate', and that this passion might lead to sex involving violence and bruising.[29] This was part of the defence—that sex had been consensual with both men.

Similarly, at the trial of twelve young men for the gang-rape of a young woman, it was the young woman who spent a full day in the stand, defending not only her choice on the night to go with a young man to a party, but her reputation more broadly. As one commentator noted, 'the verbal degradation inflicted on her in the Court was no less than the sexual degradation inflicted on her at the party.'[30] In contrast, the defendants were painted as exemplary young men, despite their status as bikies. Under questioning, one revealed he was a soldier who had seen active service in Vietnam, and had been a volunteer in the clean-up after the Brisbane floods.[31]

Many interrogations of a woman's sexual history included a microscopic investigation of her actions just before the alleged rape. In the trial of a gang-rape where three men were accused of raping and assaulting an eighteen-year-old woman, defence asked the complainant a series of questions regarding her own culpability. Drawing on questions and answers given at the lower court hearing, defence tested her:

[29] Criminal Transcripts, Supreme Court, *R v Clarke and Minter*, 1970.
[30] Scholz, 'Profile of a Gang Rape', 121.
[31] Scholz, 'Profile of a Gang Rape', 121

> I asked you this question: "That by going to the hotel and drinking with them you put yourself in a position where this sort of thing could easily happen, is that right?" and you answered "Yes" to that.

Here, Defence was suggesting that the woman had knowingly placed herself in a position where sex might be expected, by drinking in a hotel with men. The lawyer then took this one step further, suggesting that the young woman's actions may have 'led these boys to believe that you were a girl who was available for sex even though you did not mean it to'.[32] This is a familiar defence, reminding us of the case of Olivia Pearce, who had been seen to invite gang-rape by hanging out with bikies.

Cross-examination could be ruthless. Detective Sergeant Brian Doyle (who would later become an inspector and the assistant commissioner of NSW Police) told of the trauma suffered by young women in the stand:

> there is the cross-examination by from one to ten barristers; her past life, her association with males, the late nights, the milk bars, "the strawberry malteds" (Haven't you been sleeping in the park)?' and so on, even though she and the G.M.O. both swore that she had been a virgin up to this point, and then the old question of, "Haven't I seen you giving evidence in court somewhere before?"[33]

It could be particularly difficult in cases of gang-rape, where multiple defence lawyers could question a complainant.

In the case of one young woman who claimed she had been raped by an acquaintance, the defence asked a series of belligerent questions, which led to her collapse on the stand. It is worth considering this at length, as an example of what a complainant could be subject to in court:

> Q. Do you say at no time did you sit on the bed with him? A. Only when he threw me there.
>
> HIS HONOUR: Q. I beg your pardon? A. Only when he threw me there.
>
> MR GREGORY: Q. Did you sit there or lie there? A. I lay down.
>
> Q. I put it to you that you sat down on the bed with him for quite a long time? A. I am sorry, you are wrong.

[32] Criminal Transcripts, Supreme Court, *R v Martin, Goff and Daniels*, 1970.

[33] Cited in NSW Parliament, *Report of the Criminal Law Review Division of the Department of the Attorney-General and of Justice into Rape and Other Sexual Offences*, 63 [errors in original punctuation].

Q. And that he kissed you? A. He did not.
Q. And that he was stroking you on the back and legs? A. He did not.
Q. And on the breasts? A. He did not.
Q. And you were enjoying it? A. He did not.
Q. You mean you did not? A. I said he did not.
Q. You were not enjoying it? You say it did not happen, is that right? (Witness becomes distressed).
HIS HONOUR: Q: Would you like to sit down for a while? A. I want to get it over.
[At this stage the witness appearing distressed, left the Court].[34]

After the young woman returned to the courtroom, her interrogation continued, unaltered in pattern. Though it was legally acceptable to grill a complainant about her sexual history, the cross-examination of women on the stand threw up a raft of problems for women in the courtroom, including emotional distress.

Further, the cross-examination process allowed court officials including judges an opportunity to make substantial moral judgements about women's behaviour, comparing and contrasting her to the 'ideal victim'.[35] For example, Justice Maguire, in his summing up of a rape trial in the Supreme Court in 1970, commented on the young complainant's previous sexual experience: she was unmarried and had previously had a small number of partners. Maguire J commented:

> Speaking for myself and, prima facie at any rate, it is an improper thing for a girl to have intercourse outside marriage—that is the view that I understand.[36]

In another trial, Maguire J, clearly frustrated by a teenage complainant's inability to enumerate her past relationships, spoke sharply to her: 'Listen, did your virginity mean anything to you?' The Justice assumed her confusion on the stand stemmed from her lack of morality, rather than from the very long and arduous cross-examination she had endured in the court.[37]

[34] Criminal Transcripts, Supreme Court, *R v Pillon*, 1970, 20.
[35] Wendy Larcombe, 'The "Ideal" Victim v. Successful Rape Complainants: Not What You Would Expect', *Feminist Legal Studies* 10:2 (2002): 131–148.
[36] Criminal Transcripts, Supreme Court, *R v Pillon*, 1970.
[37] Criminal Transcripts, Supreme Court, *R v Wayne, Painter and Advent*, 1970.

A Woman's Dress

Like her sexual past, a woman's clothes and even her body could come under serious inquiry during the trial. Women's behaviour, or her clothing, was imagined as stimulating male desires to the point that a man might not be able to control himself. For instance, in one trial it was alleged that a seventeen-year-old youth had sexually assaulted a forty-one-year-old woman, just after he had moved into the boarding house she managed. Thinking no one was at home, he was ransacking rooms for money, but was discovered by the female manager. He turned on her, and allegedly raped her. Defence questioned the woman about her perceived role in the assault:

> Q. I suppose your experience as a residential proprietress would bring you in contact with young men? A. Yes, lots of young men, lots of young boys.
>
> Q. Lots of young boys and you would know that young boys of this age—well—are—they react rather readily in sexual matters. You would realize that? A. I guess they do, outside, you know.
>
> Q. They get moved very easily. You know that, don't you? A. I guess they do.[38]

Here, the defence was effectively suggesting that the women had stimulated the teenage boy beyond reason, by wearing a dressing gown around the house, inciting him so that he sexually assaulted her.

At trial, it was not only a woman's clothing that was scrutinised, but her body as well. In one rape trial, a young woman who had been consuming alcohol was taken to the home of a friend of the defendants. She was feeling a little sick, and had lain down on the couch to rest. The defence lawyer claimed that in lying on the lounge, she was 'exposing' her 'figure' to the men. The complainant retorted rather tartly that she had not been exposing anything, as she was wearing trousers. But still defence pressed her, questioning her on the position of her arms—were they above her head, presumably highlighting her breasts? And what was she wearing on her top half? Even in her seemingly modest attire of a coat and trousers, the woman's clothing and her body were both under scrutiny.[39]

Similarly, in another trial, the body of a sixteen-year-old girl and alleged victim of rape became the object of legal and medical scrutiny in the

[38] Criminal Transcripts, Supreme Court, *R v Kite*, 1970.

[39] Criminal Transcripts, Supreme Court, *R v Martin, Goff and Daniels*, 1970.

witness box. The defence lawyer asked of the GMO: 'Would you agree she is, for a girl of her age, sixteen, well developed in the bust?' The doctor answered simply 'Yes'. This was not enough, and the defence persisted, 'It is more than for an average girl of her age now? She is well developed in the bust, isn't she? A. Yes. Well, possibly more, yes.' Given that the girl was over the age of consent, it is unclear why the lawyer pursued this line of questioning: he did not legally need to show she looked older than she was. It seems that he was arguing that her body itself was a form of invitation, or perhaps even a form of consent, to the sexual intercourse that had taken place.[40]

Gender, Class, Race

The 1970s courtroom showed a pattern where some women found it hard to prove they had not consented to sexual intercourse, due to appearance, behaviour or past sexual experiences. The troubling reduction of the complainant to a series of sexualised problems was only intensified when she was not white and middle class. Race in particular played a powerful role in how both women and men were constructed in broader society, and cultural historians, legal scholars and criminologists have all shown the profound ways that race impacted on the policing and prosecution of crimes, including sexual assault.[41] In Australia, from the first moments of colonisation, white men routinely expected to have sexual access to

[40] Criminal Transcripts, Supreme Court, *R v Traitor and Smithers*, 1970.

[41] On race, see Anne McClintock, *Imperial Leather: Race, Gender and Sexuality in the Colonial Conquest* (New York: Routledge, 1995); Ann Laura Stoler, *Carnal Knowledge and Imperial Power: Race and the Intimate in Colonial Rule* (Berkeley: University of California Press, 2002); Lisa Lindquist Dorr, White Women, *Rape and the Power of Race in Virginia, 1900–1960* (Chapel Hill: University of North Carolina Press, 2004); Freedman, *Redefining Rape*; Block, *Rape and Sexual Power in Early America*, especially 163–209; Bourke, *Rape*, 76–78, 89–118; Ann McGrath, *Illicit Love: Interracial Sex and Marriage in the United States and Australia* (Lincoln, Nebraska and London: University of Nebraska Press, 2015). In race and law in Australia, see Mark Finnane and Fiona Paisley, 'Policing on a Colonial Frontier: The "Borroloola Case" and the Limits of Rule of Law in 1930s Australia', *Law and History Review* 28:1 (2010): 141–171; Mark Finnane, 'The Limits of Jurisdiction: Law, Governance and Indigenous Peoples in Colonized Australia', in *Law and Politics in British Colonial Thought: Transpositions of Empire*, eds. S. Dorsett and I. Hunter, (New York: Palgrave Macmillan, 2010), 149–168. Heather Douglas and Mark Finnane, *Indigenous Crimes and Settler Law: White Sovereignty After Empire* (Hampshire, United Kingdom: Palgrave Macmillan, 2012).

Indigenous women: this was part of the colonial process.[42] As the frontier extended, the exploitation of Indigenous women was ever-present, and expectations of the sexual availability of Aboriginal women lingered through the colonial period, and remained for much of the twentieth century.[43]

The idea that Indigenous women were sexually available had a profound impact on the way victims were imagined: it rendered black women licentious, promiscuous and free to be had. Under such circumstances, it was seemingly impossible to rape a black woman. How could she ever be a complainant? This was compounded by the general reluctance of Aboriginal women, as colonised people, to trust police and the law: it is expected that reporting of sexual crimes was and is low.[44] The combination of low reporting, unenthusiastic or antagonistic policing, suspicious juries and racism experienced within and across the criminal justice sector meant that few cases of sexual assault went to court. This is a stark contrast to the overwhelming work in law, in criminology and by Indigenous

[42] Ann McGrath, 'The White Man's Looking Glass: Aboriginal-Colonial Gender Relations at Port Jackson', *Australian Historical Studies* 24:95 (October 1990): 189–206.

[43] Larissa Behrendt, 'Consent in a (Neo)Colonial Society: Aboriginal Women as Sexual and Legal 'Other'', *Australian Feminist Studies* 15:33 (2000): 353–367; Tess Ryan, 'This Black Body is Not Yours for the Taking', in *#MeToo and the Politics of Social Change*, eds. Bianca Fileborn and Rachel Loney-Howes (London: Palgrave Macmillan 2019), 117–132; Eugenia Flynn, 'This Place', in *#MeToo: Stories from the Australian Movement*, eds. Miriam Sved, Christie Nieman, Maggie Scott, Natalie Kon-yu (Sydney: Pan Macmillan, 2019), 17–28; Raymond Evans, 'Don't You Remember Black Alice, Sam Holt: Aboriginal women in Queensland history', *Hecate* 8: 2 (1982): 6–21; Victoria Haskins, '"A Troublesome Gin Like Annie": Masculinity, Race and Intimate Violence in Federation-Era North Queensland', *Law & History* 4 (2017): 125–150; Victoria Haskins, '"Down in the gully & just outside the garden walk": White Women and the Sexual Abuse of Aboriginal Women on a Colonial Australian frontier', *History Australia* 10 (2013): 11–34; Victoria Haskins, 'A Better Chance? Sexual Abuse and the Apprenticeship of Aboriginal Girls Under the NSW Aborigines Protection Board', *Aboriginal History* 28 (2004): 33–58; Featherstone, *Let's Talk About Sex*, 71–92. On ethnicity in Australia, see also Andy Kaladelfos and Lisa Featherstone, 'Race and Ethnicity in Sex Crimes Trials from 1950s Australia', in *Legacies of Violence: Rendering the Unspeakable Past in Modern Australia*, ed. Robert Mason (Oxford, United Kingdom: Berghahn, 2017), 217–232.

[44] Judy Atkinson, 'Violence Against Aboriginal Women: Reconstitution of Community Law: The Way Forward', *Indigenous Law Bulletin* 6:27 (May 2007): 13–14; Melissa Lucashenko, 'Violence Against Indigenous Women: Public and Private Dimensions', *Violence Against Women* 2:4 (1996): 378–390.

women writers that suggests Indigenous women were vulnerable to sexual abuse in multiple forms.[45]

To highlight the complexities of prosecution when the complainant was Indigenous, I will focus on one trial from NSW in 1970. *R v Evans* illustrates many of the problems faced by Indigenous complainants in sexual assault trials: when Aboriginal women were readily imagined as sexualised and immoral, it became very difficult to prove that a complainant had not consented to sexual intercourse. Morris Evans was charged with the rape of Kerry Vaughn and with assaulting and causing actual bodily harm to her husband Keith Vaughn. He pleaded 'not guilty' to both charges.[46] In this trial, both the complainants and the accused were Aboriginal, as were some of the other witnesses. Rather unusually, the complainant was not called to the stand first. Instead, some legal matters regarding the admission of written medical evidence were attended to, as it appeared the doctor was out of the country. Then, Raymond Perry was called to the stand. He was a labourer from Griffith, and he had witnessed a physical fight between the accused and Keith Vaughn. According to his testimony, Evans left the scene, and then later returned, with the two men then seeming to be friendly. They decided to go into town to get more wine, and the two complainants left in the car of the defendant. The next time he saw any of them was two hours later, when Kerry Vaughn walked back to the house. Perry took her to call a taxi, and they went together back to the Vaughn's house. When they arrived, Perry saw Keith Vaughn, who had a bloodied face and a black eye.

A number of other Indigenous and white witnesses were called to the stand. Some told of seeing Keith Vaughn's beaten, bloody face; others told of the 'fresh complaint' where the alleged victim had told someone straight after the rape. All parties had been drinking, and were questioned by the court about their level of drunkenness. It was only after all the bystanders gave evidence—and a pathologist had reported spermatozoa in

[45] Australian Institute of Health and Welfare, *Family, Domestic and Sexual Violence in Australia: Continuing the National Story*, Category no. FDV 3. (Canberra: Australian Institute of Health and Welfare, 2019); Janet Phillips and Malcolm Park, 'Measuring Domestic Violence and Sexual Assault Against Women: A Review of the Literature and Statistics', E-Brief, updated 12 December 2006, https://www.aph.gov.au/about_parliament/parliamentary_departments/parliamentary_library/publications_archive/archive/violenceagainstwomen#top.

[46] Criminal Transcripts, Supreme Court, *R v Evans*, 1970.

the sample provided by the local doctor—that the female complainant was brought to the stand.

The Crown questioned Kerry Vaughn about her drinking, her clothing and the immediate lead-up to the assault. Her testimony described getting into the car with her husband and the accused, who then took them to a deserted area and beat her husband. The defendant took some money from her and threatened to rape her. Her evidence also told that the accused had punched her in the face, and hit her with a stick on the body: under fear of further violence, she got in the car with him. He took her up the road and raped her. She claimed she did not consent, but did not physically try to fight him off, because she was too frightened. When asked by the Crown about her feelings immediately after the assault, she spoke of the trauma: 'I was feeling shocked and feeling terrible. I don't know really how I was feeling.' Her main concerns were threefold: to find her husband, to ask if her husband wanted her to report the crimes to the police and to get more wine.[47]

It was the complainant's interest in alcohol that came under scrutiny in the courtroom in the cross-examination by defence. She was also questioned intently on her relationship with her husband, in particular on the domestic violence she had at times suffered. The defence wondered if she had in fact been hit by her partner, not the defendant, on the night of the alleged assault. She was also questioned on her past and current sexual relationships, including the naming of a long list of potential partners, all of which had to be denied by the complainant. Defence then claimed she had been convicted of sex work in South Australia, under a different name. The defence weaved questions that called upon a raft of stereotypes of Indigenous women.

Finally, Keith Vaughn took the stand to tell his story. He too was questioned about drinking, domestic violence and his wife's sexual fidelity. Slowly the defence built the case, culminating in the following exchange:

> Q. 'I put to you ... that you were drunk on that day, 8th May, there was a drunken brawl of which you got the worst, that is right, is it not? That your wife went off with the man who had beaten you and you were determined to get even with him at all costs? A. That is entirely wrong.

[47] Criminal Transcripts, Supreme Court, *R v Evans*, 1970.

At this point, Justice Brereton interjected, noting the question was in fact a speech, stating, 'I must express my disapproval.'[48] Meanwhile, the jury was left to ponder the broader question: Had the complainant been raped, or was the sex a consensual act by a promiscuous woman?

The accused man finally gave a dockside statement, admitting to sexual intercourse with Kerry Vaughn, but suggesting it was consensual. He claimed they had sex on a number of previous occasions, including when she was both drunk and sober. He reiterated the idea that Keith Vaughn was angry with him, and had trumped up the rape charge. Then, the jury deliberated. The final verdict acquitted Evans of the rape of Kerry Vaughn, but found him guilty of assaulting her husband: physical violence and strong corroborative evidence of assault made it easier to convict on the latter crime, while it was difficult to prove non-consent.[49] While the legal concept of consent was a core issue of this trial, race was also a simmering presence throughout. The trial was embedded with fixed beliefs about Indigenous Australians. It illustrates the intersections of race and gender, where Aboriginal defendants and complainants were imagined in stereotypes of abuse, alcoholism and sexual impropriety.

Gender and the Rules of Evidence

As the Evans trial shows, the complainant came under particular pressure due to specific expectations about how a 'legitimate' rape victim would act. The idea of a rational, respectable, authentic victim meant women were required to act in an established, lucid and cogent manner if they were sexually assaulted. One of the most common expectations was that a victim of a rape would make an urgent 'complaint', that is, she would tell of her trauma to another person immediately afterwards. If a woman was assaulted and immediately sought assistance from police, this was seen as a validation of her story. A woman might knock on the door of a house after a rape and ask for help; or, a child might tell a mother immediately after he or she had been assaulted. In these cases, the person who had been told of the attack would be able to give evidence in court, under guise of 'early complaint'. This was in contrast to other crimes, where such evidence would be inadmissible under hearsay rules. Yet in rape cases, it could be used to consider the victim's actions at the time of the assault, to decide

[48] Criminal Transcripts, Supreme Court, *R v Evans*, 1970.

[49] 'Acquitted of Rape Charge', *Sydney Morning Herald*, 15 September 1970, 14.

whether or not she was a credible witness in the stand.[50] It was not evidence in and itself of rape, but it was used to back up other forms of evidence, and counted towards her 'reliability', including her character, consistency and believability.

The flip side of this, of course, was that a victim who did not immediately report a crime to family, friends or police was deemed less trustworthy. So powerful was the belief in early complaint that judges might warn that its absence made a victim seem inconsistent. At most, a lack of complaint might be linked to a lack of crime. As Justice Begg told his jury in summing up for a rape case in 1970, 'You could imagine that if the girl six months later went along to a police station and said, "Six months ago I was raped", well nobody would think that was a very consistent sort of story or conduct.' In his example, a time lapse between assault and reporting was not explained by trauma, shock, fear or an attempt to ignore the attack. Instead, he suggested that no crime had taken place at all.[51]

The early complaint could also come under considerable scrutiny for its accuracy and delivery. For instance, at one rape trial, a teenage girl alleged that she had been sexually assaulted by two men, one of whom had threatened her with a gun. He told her that she would not 'last long' if she went to the police. After her release from their captivity, she had seen a police officer at the fairground, but was hesitant to approach him, fearing the offender might see her. She had eventually arranged to meet the police officer out of sight, telling him she feared she would be shot. The defence lawyer argued, therefore, that her initial complaint was about the threat on her life—not about the rape. The defence twisted the young woman's police report and attacked the very form of her immediate complaint. It was not, argued the defence, precise enough in complaining of sexual violence, and he sought to have the police officer's testimony excluded from the trial, on the grounds it would be prejudicial.[52] Justice Herron determined it could be included, but the issue of her slow and 'incorrect' form of complaint was raised during the trial in an attempt to show a lack of believability about her story.

There were other structural, institutionalised ways that gender operated within the courtroom, to throw doubt on the complainant and to undermine her version of events. Before law reform in some Australian

[50] RCHR Report, *Final Report vol. 5*, 194.

[51] Criminal Transcripts, Supreme Court, *R v Ranger*, 1970.

[52] Criminal Transcripts, Supreme Court, *R v Wotherford and Porter*, 1970.

jurisdictions, a judge had to give a jury a warning, stating that it was dangerous to convict on the uncorroborated evidence of a victim alone. The process of corroboration meant a judge was encouraging the jury to accept at least two forms of evidence of sex, two forms of evidence that consent had not been given and two forms of evidence that the defendant was in fact the assaulter. Though a judge's warning was designed to protect the accused man in case of false complaint, it had the potential to impact upon the juror's engagement with the complainant's testimony: indeed, the instruction on corroboration might be read as a warning that the complainant was unreliable.[53] Further, it was often impossible to gain a significant amount of corroborative evidence. Sexual assault was generally a private crime, so it was difficult to corroborate, as there was so rarely a witness.[54]

Another way to throw doubt on the morality or honesty of the complainant was through an unsworn statement, given by the defendant. This opportunity was not available in other Australian jurisdictions, but it was widely utilised in NSW. The accused man did not take the stand per se and was not subject to the rigours of cross-examination. But he was allowed to give a statement, explaining his case in his own voice, albeit in words that could be highly shaped by his defence lawyer. In rape trials, men regularly explained that the complainant had consented to sex, or that he believed that she had consented. For instance, in a sexual case involving three men in 1970, one of the men explained that he had thought the young woman was interested in a sexual encounter:

> She told me that when she lived in Newcastle she used to sneak out at night when her mother was asleep, to meet her boyfriend. She gave me the impression that she was a girl who liked boys… [on the night of the assault] she lay on the lounge in a very unladylike manner.[55]

Through her actions on the night of the assault, and on previous occasions, this young man had felt the complainant would acquiesce to sex,

[53] Irving Younger, 'The Requirement of Corroboration in Prosecutions for Sex Offenders in New York', *Fordham Law Review* 40:2 (1971): 268; Valerie P. Hans and Neil Brooks, 'Effects of Corroboration Instruction in a Rape Case on Experimental Juries', *Cornell Law Faculty Publications* Paper 363 (1977): 702.

[54] 'The Law as it is Now', *Sydney Women's Liberation Newsletter*, July 1977, 5; 'Women Against Rape', *Sydney Women's Liberation Newsletter*, May 1976, 8.

[55] Criminal Transcripts, Supreme Court, *R v Martin, Goff and Daniels*, 1970.

regardless of her protests at the time. Similarly, his co-accused gave unsworn testimony that the girl had acted provocatively while lying fully clothed on a lounge: 'it didn't leave much to the imagination to see what an attractive figure she had.' He also suggested, 'I know when I went there I firmly believed she knew she was expecting to have sex when she went into the car, and I believed she was not a good girl.'[56]

An unsworn statement could be used to make suggestions about the 'type' of woman the complainant might be. The defendant could draw on real or fictitious indicators of her moral values. In a trial for rape, for example, a defendant described the young female complainant and her friend as 'easy': 'I thought they were easy go sort of things and they were knockabouts and all that, you know, swearing and carrying on.' Their behaviour, he argue, convinced him that she was available for consensual sex.[57] This was especially compelling as the woman in question had already been shown to be of dubious moral character—she was rough in her speech; she knew swear words such as 'cunt' and 'prick' to describe the genitals; and she had previously been arrested as a delinquent child. Positioned at the end of the trial—with no chance of rebuttal—the unsworn statement could thus be used as a powerful commentary on a woman's moral values.

When a complainant was denigrated in these ways—either through assertions about her moral character and her previous sexual activity, or comments on her behaviour at the time of the assault—neither the complainant nor the Crown Prosecutor had effective mechanisms to counter the unsworn testimony. The defendants could not be questioned, nor could the complainant make a written or verbal response. So too, a defendant could also use the unsworn statement to show his own general respectability: a man might state that he had not been involved with the police before, and that he had a good job and came from a responsible family. None of this could be directly challenged in the courtroom. Effectively, the unsworn statement gave the accused a platform to tell his side of the story, unencumbered by cross-examination about his behaviour or sexual past. It was a distinct contrast to the complainant, who gave sworn testimony that was shaped by legal professionals, and subject to the most rigorous of investigations. The rules of evidence, then, were shaped by gendered expectations, and allowed accused men to redefine themselves as a 'good bloke', while female complainants were left to defend attacks on their looks, behaviour, dress and habits.

[56] Criminal Transcripts, Supreme Court, *R v Martin, Goff and Daniels*, 1970.
[57] Criminal Transcripts, Supreme Court, *R v Gray and Davies*, 1970.

Conclusions

This chapter has considered a range of gendered practices within the courtroom, many of which were long standing in the criminal justice system. In the midst of social, cultural and political change, the court proved remarkably resilient, and in many ways attitudes towards the complainant had seemingly changed little, despite the slow beginnings of social and sexual revolutions across the 1960s.

The court room may seem a strange place to begin a story of sexual violence. After all, it is the culmination of months and even years of struggle: the attack itself; interaction with police, medicine and other authorities; engagement with prosecution; and, finally, the brief moment of the court trial. The wait and hope for justice was long and slow. Further, only a minority of victims followed this trajectory. As we have seen, women did not always report sexual assault; and even when they did, reports were not always actioned by police and prosecutors. We know that the cases of sexual assault that reached trial were a small minority of the total instances of sexual violence. So why focus on trial, as a starting point?

I have argued that the trial is a microcosm of wider attitudes towards sexual assault: it is a convenient package of assumptions about gender, power, violence and suffering that tells us much about how Australians understood sexual violence. But it is more than this, too. Before the 1960s, sexual assault was spoken of in the public sphere largely in newspapers reports, which often focused on the scandal and horror of sexual crime. Outside of this, victims were silent and silenced. Families spoke little of sexual assault; communities were mute. The victim was voiceless, ensconced in shame.

The trial was a rare space where the victim spoke. Her voice was managed and packaged within the legal theatre: it was a highly directed, even manipulated voice. Nonetheless, there was action, and a search for reparation. Silence was momentarily broken, for the victim herself, and in terms of a wider awareness of sexual assault: this act had taken place; this act had caused harm. The court then is one of the few spaces where we have a detailed, if imperfect, report of sexual violence before the 1970s. It was not until the mid-1970s that we begin to see a wider discourse about the horrors of sexual violence, largely led by feminist commentators. The next chapter will explore the feminist intervention, and the opening up of spaces to speak about sexual assaults.

CHAPTER 3

Rape, Feminism and Culture in the 1970s

In 1978, the *Australian Women's Weekly* published a substantial three-page article on rape: it was the first time the mainstream magazine had published a major commentary on sexual violence. The article opened in a sensationalised fashion, describing rape as 'sick, savage, often fatal'. While much of the language was inflated, the article had a very serious intent: to draw attention to the ordeal of the victim. The piece began with some of the broad problems for a rape victim, including the lack of supporting resources and the issues with reporting, policing and medical care. The author then interviewed three experts on sexual assault, including a doctor, a criminologist and a police officer. All offered detailed information on what happened to the victim in the hours, days and months after the assault, including what could occur during a criminal trial. Personal examples were provided, to give the sense of immediacy, and to show how an individual woman might experience rape and its aftermath.

The prioritising of the *victim* was a significant shift in thinking. For much of the twentieth century, the social and legal focus had been on the criminal and the crime. The victim was more often silenced and invisibilsed, and when she was considered, she was regularly doubted, beleaguered and constructed as a woman of dubious morals. The 1970s, however, saw substantial shifts in the ways rape was discussed, through the new focus on the victim and her suffering. Second-wave feminism was central to the reconceptualisation of rape as a crime and a social problem.

L. Featherstone, *Sexual Violence in Australia, 1970s–1980s*, World Histories of Crime, Culture and Violence,
https://doi.org/10.1007/978-3-030-73310-0_3

Many feminist ideas slowly permeated the broader culture, from mainstream media such as the *Weekly*, to medical services, to legal authorities.

This chapter will explore the extensive, often profound shifts that occurred in public and community considerations of rape across the decade. We have seen already how gendered attitudes towards sexual violence played out in the 1970s courtroom, to make it seem as if the victim herself was on trial. In this chapter, we begin to see the response to this: the ways women in the community were beginning to speak out and back about the multiple and complex problems of sexual assault in Australian culture. We will see, at a most basic level, that there was an increase in public discussions about sexual assault. While sexual assault had never been an entirely private crime, across the 1970s the public discussion about rape had expanded notably.

But the shifts were not merely in terms of scope: there were significant changes to the way sexual violence was understood, both clinically in medicine and psychology, and more broadly within the community. Beginning with emerging feminist views of sexual assault, this chapter will analyse the ways that second-wave feminism challenged formative ideas on rape in Australia. Confronting a series of rape myths, women's liberationists effectively forced the broader community to rethink ideas about sexual violence. By 1977, the *Report* of the Royal Commission on Human Relationships stated that rape had become one of society's most controversial crimes, mainly because feminist groups had exposed it as a serious sociolegal problem.[1] This chapter charts this shift, beginning with an analysis of the ways feminists defined and undermined multiple 'rape myths'. We then turn to the idea of 'victim blaming', considering how feminists exposed the ways victims were held responsible for their own sexual assault. The chapter then explores the feminist-driven change to thinking about rape as a traumatic event with long-lasting psychological impacts. Finally, the chapter concludes with analysis of the ways feminists changed thinking about the perpetrators of sexual crime, moving discussion away from simple 'stranger danger' to thinking about violence in intimate relationships. Read together, this chapter explores the significant impact of feminism on thinking about sexual violence against adult white women.

[1] Royal Commission on Human Relationships (hereafter RCHR), *Final Report vol. 5* (Canberra: Government Printer, 1977), 159.

Feminists and Rape

The 1970s was a period of re-evaluation of traditional ideas of gender, sexuality, race and class. The rethinking of attitudes towards sexual violence was clearly part of a much wider recalibration of social norms.[2] Feminist activism around domestic violence and sexual assault was not entirely new: from the beginnings of modern Western feminism, women had raised issues of men's violence against women.[3] But from the mid-1960s, second-wave feminism developed a finely attuned critique of gendered power, ultimately suggesting that rape was at the extreme end of a continuum of violence and degradation of women by men.

The feminist view of rape in the 1970s was epitomised by the American scholar Susan Brownmiller, who published her manifesto *Against Our Will: Men, Women and Rape* in 1976. *Against Our Will* had and continues to have a profound impact on feminist thinking about rape. Brownmiller famously argued that rape was a 'deliberate, hostile, violent act of degradation and possession… designed to intimidate and inspire fear.'[4] While Brownmiller was not the first or the only feminist to think about rape, her work consolidated feminist thinking about sexual violence and was widely utilised by women's liberation in Australia. It was even reviewed positively in the mainstream press.[5]

In Australia, local feminist writings on rape and violence had begun to appear regularly in feminist newsletters and journals by 1974 (predating Brownmiller's work). An anonymous author writing in that year for the

[2] Michelle Arrow, *The Seventies: The Personal, the Political and the Making of Modern Australia* (Sydney: NewSouth Publishing, 2019).

[3] See for example: Lucy Bland, *Banishing the Beast: English Feminism and Sexual Morality, 1885–1914* (Harmondsworth: Penguin, 1995); Sheila Jeffreys, *The Spinster and Her Enemies: Feminism and Sexuality 1880–1930* (Melbourne: Spinifex Press, 1997), 54–85; Marilyn Lake, *Getting Equal: The History of Australian Feminism* (Sydney: Allen and Unwin, 1999), 19–24; Susan Magarey, *Passions of the First Wave Feminists* (Sydney: UNSW, 2001), 83–116. For an excellent overview of the Australian literature, see Zora Simic, 'Historicising a "national disgrace": Towards a feminist history of domestic violence since 1788' in *Gender Violence in Australia: Historical Perspectives*, eds Alana Piper and Ana Stevenson (Melbourne: Monash Publishing, 2019), 3–19.

[4] Susan Brownmiller, *Against Our Will: Men, Women and Rape* (Harmondsworth: Penguin, 1975), 391.

[5] 'Constant State of Fear', *The Mercury* (Tasmania), 17 December 1976; Tess Lawrence, 'The blame and the shame of rape' *Herald* (Melbourne) 13 November 1976, also reprinted in *The West Australian*, 18 November 1976; Barbara Hooks, 'A new analysis of the history of rape,' *The Age*, 9 November 1976.

feminist newspaper *Vashti's Voice* highlighted the links between power, chauvinism and sexual assault, noting that 'The rapist is the policeman of the patriarchy. Men who would never offer any kind of violence to a woman get the benefits of his activity.'[6] This was an early articulation of an idea that would become common in the women's liberation movement: that men who did not rape nonetheless drew benefits from a social order where women lived in fear. The author argued, too, that normative gender roles were seen as at the core of the problem of rape. She argued that in Western culture, men were imagined as aggressive, and women as passive: rape, she suggested, was 'just an extreme version of this'.[7]

Second-wave feminists powerfully argued that rape needed to be understood as one part of a wider social patriarchal context, where women were seen as inferior. As feminist Jenny Pausacker told the Royal Commission into Human Relationships, 'I think the main cause of rape is precisely the existing relationship between men and women in our society. A changing of that attitude is the only way rape will be stopped.'[8] The problem of rape was formed, not by an individual man's sexual assault on one victim, but rather represented a wider culture that saw men as having rights over women's bodies. This 'right' extended not just to rape but operated in myriad and sometimes subtle ways. As one feminist pointed out, women 'are subjected to quite petty types of sexual abuse like being touched up on the bus and being grabbed in a sexual way, touched in a sexual way.... I have a strong impression some degree of sexual abuse is just a natural part of the average women's life'.[9]

By positioning rape in the broader concept of patriarchy, *all* women were seen as potential victims of gendered violence. On International Women's Day in 1974 in Sydney, feminist groups held a rally, 'Women Against the Violent Society', to highlight various forms of violence against women and children, including the plight of teenagers held in institutions such as the Hay Girls Prison. Similar ideas about widespread gendered violence were expressed in feminist journals, with commentators

[6] 'Rape crisis', *Vashti's Voice*, March 1974, 1.

[7] 'Rape crisis', *Vashti's Voice*, March 1974, 1.

[8] Jenny Pausacker, representing 'Women Against Rape', Interview, *Royal Commission on Human Relationships: Official transcript of proceedings* (Sydney: Commonwealth Reporting Service, 1974–1976), 499.

[9] Alicia Lee, 'Rape Crisis Centre', Interview, *Royal Commission on Human Relationships: Official transcript*, 78–9; see also Germaine Greer, *The Female Eunuch* (London: Paladin, 1971), 252.

suggesting that 'No woman is free from sexual terror'.[10] As the *Sydney Women's Liberation Newsletter* recorded, 'all women are victims, or potential victims', of sexual assault and domestic violence. By March 1979, the first 'Take Back the Night' event was held in Sydney, where 100 women marched in King's Cross, protesting against aggression towards women. As they walked, they chanted, 'Women are not sexual commodities' and 'Women will Reclaim the Night'.[11]

There were, however, distinct limits to feminist critiques of gendered violence, in particular the invisibility of Indigenous women. White feminists assumed and prioritised a universal female experience. This focus concealed and obscured the abuse of Aboriginal and Torres Strait Islander women, who, after 200 years of colonisation, were most vulnerable to sexual assault. For most of the twentieth century, life under various 'Protection' acts meant that Indigenous girls could be removed from their family and community and sent out to work as domestic servants, where they were susceptible to sexual violence.[12] This reflected the broader logic of colonial regimes, where violence was central to the imperial process of invasion. Across the twentieth century, white Australian society saw Aboriginal people as fringe dwellers, a dying race, undesirable or expendable. Policing and legal systems did not shield Aboriginal women from sexual assault.[13] Recent criminological work suggests Indigenous women were and remain victims of violent crime at higher rates than the non-Indigenous population.[14]

[10] 'Rape crisis', *Vashti's Voice*, March 1974, 1; see also 'False Complaint—A Liscence [*sic*] to Rape', *Sydney Women's Liberation Newsletter*, May 1976, 6.

[11] 'Women March Against Rape and Pornography', *Sydney Women's Liberation Newsletter*, Feb/March 1973, 3.

[12] See examples in Human Rights and Equal Opportunity Commission, *Bringing Them Home: Report of the National Inquiry into the Separation of Aboriginal and Torres Strait Islander Children from their Families* (Sydney, HREOC, 1997); Victoria Haskins, 'A Better Chance? Sexual Abuse and the Apprenticeship of Aboriginal Girls under the NSW Aborigines Protection Board', *Aboriginal History* 28 (2004): 33–58.

[13] On legal protections, see Heather Douglas and Mark Finnane, *Indigenous Crime and Settler Law: White Sovereignty after Empire* (Basingstoke: Palgrave Macmillan, 2012), 183–213.

[14] There are particular problems with reporting and identifying Indigenous victims. Even so, there is considerable evidence to suggest that Aboriginal and Torres Strait Islander women suffer sexual and domestic violence at higher rates than non-Indigenous women. See, Aboriginal and Torres Strait Islander Women's Task Force on Violence, *The Aboriginal and Torres Strait Islander Women's Task Force on Violence Report*, Department of Aboriginal and Torres Strait Islander Policy and Development, Queensland, 2000; Monique Keel,

Yet in the 1970s, white feminists failed to regularly comment on the particular problems faced by Aboriginal women, and Women's Liberation focused on white women's experiences and treatments.[15] This was a decade that saw the emergence of Black Power and calls for Aboriginal rights by black activists and sections of the New Left. There were considerable leaps in Indigenous rights, especially under the Whitlam government.[16] Black women were powerful leaders within families and communities. Yet Aboriginal women remained largely silent on matters of sexual violence, at least openly. This was an act of agency, with individual women electing non-disclosure to protect Indigenous families living in the shadow of colonisation and dispossession.[17] Further, many Indigenous women did not think that discussions about sexual assault were culturally appropriate.[18] But there was also a lack of public space for Aboriginal women to discuss violence, based on their exclusion from feminist debates, and their marginalisation from mainstream concerns. It is perhaps then unsurprising that the sexual abuse of Aboriginal women was rarely discussed in (white) public spaces in Australia in the 1970s, even amongst feminists.

Family Violence and Sexual Assault in Indigenous Communities: "Walking the Talk", Australian Institute of Family Studies, Australian Centre for the Study of Sexual Assault, Series Briefing No 4, 2004; Judy Atkinson, *Trauma Trails, Recreating Song Lines: The Transgenerational Effects of Trauma in Indigenous Australia* (Melbourne: Spinifex Press, 2002); Jacqueline Fitzgerald and Don Weatherburn, 'Aboriginal Victimisation and Offending: The Picture from Police Records' Crime and Justice Statistics, *Bureau Brief, Issue paper no. 17*, December 2001, 2; Anastasia Hardman, 'The Not-So Standard Indigenous Question: Identifying Aboriginal and Torres Strait Islander Victims', *Indigenous Law Bulletin* 7:16 (2010): 17–19; Lorana Bartels, 'Violent Offending By and Against Indigenous Women', *Indigenous Law Bulletin* 8:1 (2012): 12–22. On child victims, see Hannah McGlade, *Our Greatest Challenge: Aboriginal Children and Human Rights*, (Canberra: Aboriginal Studies Press, 2012).

[15] On the exclusion of Indigenous women from feminist analysis, see Pat O'Shane, 'Is There Any Relevance in the Women's Movement for Aboriginal Women?', *Refractory Girl* 12 (1976): 32–34; Melissa Lucashenko, 'No Other Truth?: Aboriginal Women and Australian Feminism', *Social Alternatives* 12:4 (1994): 21–24; Adele Murdolo, 'Warmth and Unity with All Women? Historicizing Racism in the Australian Women's Movement', *Feminist Review* 52 (1996): 69–86.

[16] See amongst others Jennifer Clark, *Aborigines and Activism: Race, Aborigines and the Coming of the 1960s to Australia* (Perth: UWA Press, 2008); Bain Attwood, *Rights for Aborigines* (Sydney: Allen & Unwin, 2003).

[17] See Matthew Willis, 'Non-Disclosure of Violence in Australian Indigenous Communities', *Trends and Issues in Crime and Criminal Justice*, 405 (2011): 1–11.

[18] Keel, Family Violence and Sexual Assault in Indigenous Communities: "Walking the Talk", np.

White Women Challenging Rape Myths

If many white feminists saw rape as only one aspect of a culture that oppressed women, there was nonetheless a specific feminist attack on the politics of sexual assault. Most notably, feminists attempted to undercut a series of rape myths. As has been shown in the Introduction to this volume, rape myths were a range of (mis)beliefs about sexual assault, listed by the *Sydney Women's Liberation Newsletter* as follows: 'women enjoy being raped/it is impossible to rape a woman/rapists are psychopaths/women attract rape by the way they dress/rapists are strangers/having intercourse with your wife or girlfriend when she says no isn't rape/submission is consent/etc.'[19] First, and foremost, feminists attempted to address the idea that women provoked rape. Common forms of victim blaming included the following: '"She asked for it"—"What did she do to get herself into that situation?"'[20] Often officials recommended that girls should not be out at night: women's movements, rather than men's, were to be controlled.[21] Similarly, women who hitch-hiked could be blamed for rape: as one New South Wales judge observed, women who caught lifts with strangers 'invite sex attacks'.[22] This idea of an 'invitation' to assault was common—the head of one of the units in the Criminal Investigation Bureau in Melbourne told the press that 'Some women take no precautions and are an open invitation to rape'.[23]

Women's dress was another way that victims were imagined to provoke sexual assault, as we saw in the courtroom machinations in Chap. 2. Such ideas about clothing and seduction permeated the broader Australian society too. To give just one example, a Brisbane resident wrote a letter to the editor of a local newspaper, telling scathingly of 'immodest young women' who 'persist in cheapening themselves' so that 'men can easily get the impression that casual sex is their divine right, and see no reason not to take it when they can if their supply is cut off'. The letter was quite a

[19] 'Rape Crisis Centre', *Sydney Women's Liberation Newsletter*, February 1975, 17; see also 'Stop Rape', *Sydney Women's Liberation Newsletter*, July 1977, 7.

[20] Alicia Lee, 'Rape Crisis Centre', Interview, *Royal Commission on Human Relationships: Official transcript of proceedings*, 75.

[21] See, for example, the comments of South Australian Liberal Shadow Chief Secretary, who recommended a tightening of family control so girls would not be on the streets. 'Rape Laws should be Tougher', *News* (Adelaide) 19 June 1978.

[22] Untitled, *Mirror* (Sydney), 6 July 1978.

[23] 'Police Warn on Rape Attacks', *Sun*, 2 September 1977.

diatribe: 'Women! Don't pass the buck… Take realistic steps to minimize rape and you may be pleasantly surprised at the results.'[24] Here, rape was seen as something to be controlled by women, and not only an individual victim, but all women, who were seen as responsible for controlling the temptation of men. The idea of women as moral compasses had a long history, but the new freedoms of the 1970s—including changing fashions and increased independence for women—meant that it remained easy to blame the victim for inviting sexual assault.

In the mid-to-late 1970s, feminists began to unstitch these attitudes, suggesting that it was both unfair and unreasonable to blame the victim of the crime. As one representative of the Women's Electoral Lobby noted, this not only placed the responsibility for their own safety on women, but just as insidiously, 'it is telling men that if women do behave or dress in certain ways, it is OK to rape them'.[25] Further, feminists noted that men and masculinity were the core problems, not the victims.[26] They showed that victim blaming acted to displace attention away from the offender, who could then be read as passive and even blameless, while reverting responsibility to women.[27] As feminists pointed out, 'Rape is the only crime where the victim is made to feel guilty.'[28]

Feminists had some success in mainstreaming ideas that women were not to blame for sexual assault. In 1976, even the conservative monthly the *Reader's Digest* critiqued the belief that 'nice girls don't get raped' and 'bad girls shouldn't complain if they do'.[29] Yet, for many, these ideas about a victim's liability did continue. Recent studies show that victim blaming was and is common, especially when the woman is not an 'ideal victim'. Some women were seen as less likely to be authentic victims than others. Women can be rendered 'inauthentic' or non-genuine complainants when their 'lives, backgrounds, and characteristics depart from the narrow

[24] Ken Hood, 'Rape Argument "Illogical"', *Telegraph* (Brisbane), 28 February 1977.

[25] See June Rankin-Wilson (WEL) cited in Alison Fox, 'Rape', *News* (Perth), 13 September 1978.

[26] RCHR, *Final Report vol. 5*, 163.

[27] June Rankin-Wilson (WEL) cited in Alison Fox, 'Rape', *News* (Perth), 13 September 1978; 'Message from the Rape Crisis Centre', *Sydney Women's Liberation Newsletter*, July 1977, 4.

[28] 'Sexual Intercourse—A Woman's Right to Choose?', *Sydney Women's Liberation Newsletter*, April 1975, 3.

[29] Liv O'Hanlon, 'The terrible trauma of rape', *The Reader's Digest*, July 1976, 127.

confines of "ideal victims"'.[30] Women who had been drinking or taking drugs; Indigenous women; women who engaged in sex work; women with prior criminal records; women who behaved in ways contrary to the common expectations: these were all women who might more readily be blamed for their own assaults.[31] Victim blaming often began during the rape itself, when offenders told their victims that they had wanted sex. The criminologist Paul Wilson found offenders made comments such as: 'Everyone knows you want it'; 'A girl like you doesn't go out alone unless she's asking for it'; 'I saw you looking at me. You wanted me to fuck you; I can tell'.[32] These views were internalised by victims, who heard them not just at the time of the assault, but in subsequent discussions about sexual violence.[33]

Feminists also worked hard to undermine a raft of other misogynistic ideas about sexual violence, including the surprisingly common idea that women enjoyed rape.[34] For much of the twentieth century, post-Freudian psychoanalysis and its popular renditions hinted that women's sexual desires included violence, and there were still some people who believed that women wanted to be raped.[35] It was not uncommon to hear people

[30] Melanie Randall, 'Sexual Assault Law, Credibility, and "Ideal Victims": Consent, Resistance, and Victim Blaming', *Canadian Journal of Women and the Law* 22:2 (2010): 409. Wendy Larcombe has written intriguing work on the ideal victim in the successful prosecution. Importantly, her research in trials found that the complainant in trials that were successful in gaining a guilty verdict did not necessarily meet the profile of an 'ideal' victim. In my sample, this did not stop defence strategies that attempted to discredit a complainant: trials that were successful generally had corroborating evidence that meant a complainant might be successful, whether she was an 'ideal' victim or not. Nonetheless, similar strategies were almost always enacted to try to undermine the complainant throughout the court process. I would argue that many complainants who would not stand up to this process would suffer attrition before the trial itself. See Wendy Larcombe, 'The "Ideal" Victim v Successful Rape Complainants: Not What You Might Expect', *Feminist Legal Studies* 10:2 (2002): 131–148.

[31] Randall, 'Sexual Assault Law, Credibility, and "Ideal Victims"', 410–414. On Indigenous women as complainants, see Anne Cossins, 'Saints, Sluts and Sexual Assault: Rethinking the Relationship Between Sex, Race, and Gender', *Social Legal Studies* 12:1 (2003): 77–81.

[32] Paul R. Wilson, 'Victims of Rape: The Social Context of Degradation', *Australian and New Zealand Journal of Criminology* 9 (1976): 251.

[33] Wilson, 'Victims of Rape', 251

[34] 'Rape crisis', *Vashti's Voice*, March 1974, 1; 'What every woman should know about rape', *Women's Day*, 13 August 1979.

[35] Dr J Peter Bush, *Rape In Australia; An Appraisal of Attitudes, Victims, Assailants, Medicine and the Law* (Melbourne: Sun Books, 1977), 3, 113–14; RCHR, *Final Report vol. 5*, 163.

argue that a woman must have been 'co-operating with her attacker',[36] or that a woman 'contributed' to her own rape.[37] One woman who worked at the Sydney Rape Crisis Centre noted that victims would often be told: 'But you enjoyed it.' This belief in women's pleasure at rape was vehemently denied by workers in the field. As one noted, 'In my experience with rape victims I have never come across a woman who enjoyed being raped. Is there enjoyment in being totally objectified, dehumanized and being treated like a whole [*sic*] in the ground?'[38]

Feminists also disputed the commonly held idea that women fabricated rape, making up the crime and accusing a hapless man.[39] False claims were largely imagined as defensive: a woman needed to explain her lateness home, or her pregnancy, or she was found in an otherwise compromising position.[40] Or, it was suggested, women might say they were raped when they changed their mind during sex or foreplay.[41] Even authors who were broadly sympathetic to women victims of rape were still concerned about the possibility of false accusations. The Victorian Police Surgeon, for instance, claimed that of fifty consecutive examinations he performed on women, four were, he felt, unfounded, and a further four cases were not entirely believable.[42] In contrast, feminists argued that women had little to gain from a false accusation, and even less from a rape trial. As the sociologist Beverley Scholz noted, 'It would be difficult to imagine any woman voluntarily submitting herself to the trauma of a rape trial out of vindictiveness or mischief.'[43] Yet the idea that rape would be regularly fabricated remained a serious threat to the policing and prosecution of the crime, as

[36] RCHR, *Final Report vol. 5*, 161.

[37] Bush, *Rape In Australia*, 147.

[38] 'Stop Rape', *Sydney Women's Liberation Newsletter*, July 1977, 7; 'Rape crisis', *Vashti's Voice*, March 1974, 1; Alicia Lee, 'Rape Crisis Centre', Interview, *Royal Commission on Human Relationships: Official transcript*, 76; 'Message from the Rape Crisis Centre', *Sydney Women's Liberation Newsletter*, July 1977, 4.

[39] 'False Complaint—A Liscence [*sic*] to Rape', *Sydney Women's Liberation Newsletter*, May 1976, 6. See for example, Mr Purnell, NSW Parliament, *Report of the Criminal Law Review Division of the Department of the Attorney-General and of Justice into Rape and Other Sexual Offences* (Sydney: Governmentt Printer, 1977), Appendix 1, 86.

[40] Defence counsel, State Records NSW: Court Reporting Branch; NRS 2713, Criminal Transcripts, Supreme Court, *R v Wotherford and Porter*, 1970.

[41] Bush, *Rape In Australia*, 113–14.

[42] Bush, *Rape In Australia*, 118.

[43] Beverley Scholz, 'Profile of a Gang Rape', in *Delinquency in Australia: A Critical Appraisal*, ed Paul R. Wilson (St. Lucia, QLD: University of Queensland Press, 1977), 132.

well as to community responses, and permeated multiple levels of social and legal responses to sexual violence.

In many ways, feminist attitudes did not always filter through to the broader culture, or were slow to do so. Toxic forms of masculinity remained. As the Victorian Police Surgeon Peter Bush argued, rape was often interpreted by men as an 'understandable outlet for the release of those passionate desires contained in the male psyche which for one reason or another have failed to find legitimate outlet'.[44] This meant that men could see unwanted sex as simply another form of sexual release, rather than as a crime. As one lawyer (a victim of rape herself) explained, 'Many rapists don't see themselves as rapists. They simply think they're getting their dues.'[45]

'Getting their dues' meant men and women often had different expectations of social and sexual encounters. In a study of convicted rapists in the late 1970s, the Pentridge gaol psychiatrist William Reynolds found that men in his sample could expect sex after the simplest of interactions: going to a party, going for a drive, drinking at a pub. In the mind of these men, women had acquiesced to sex in advance, through their general behaviour, appearance, dress or availability in public spaces, and the men who had raped often saw resistance as a 'token gesture' rather than a firm 'no' or a fundamental rejection.[46] With this rationale, sex was commonly reinterpreted as consensual, or at least a reasonable expectation or a masculine right.

Other men saw rape as something that certain women deserved. For example, during a gang-rape trial in Brisbane in the mid-1970s, sociologists recorded chat in the public gallery. The audience called the victim a 'tart', and she was maligned for going to a party with bikie men; it was suggested that she 'tried to take the count then cried rape'. There was an assumption from the crowd that the woman had somehow wanted to have sex, or to be raped. One young man in the public gallery whispered to his friend, 'look at that piece of cunt. She wanted it for sure and I'd bet she'd give it to me.'[47] The dehumanisation of the complainant meant that she was not treated as a woman who might consent or not consent, but as a receptacle for a man's uncontrolled sexual urges. Even criminologists and

[44] Cited in 'Not Enough Research', *Morning Herald* (Sydney), 4 October 1977.
[45] 'Do We Give a Rapist Too Much of a Fair Go' *Telegraph* (Brisbane) 18 January 1977.
[46] Bill Birnbauer, 'Anatomy of the rapist', *Herald* (Melbourne) 14 January 1978.
[47] Cited in Wilson, 'Victims of Rape', 252.

some feminists agreed that in sexual play 'there comes a point where the girl can't expect to say no'.[48] As the Royal Commission suggested, many saw rape as a moment when the offender gave 'vent to his uncontrollable sexual lusts in a way that cannot wholly be condemned'.[49]

Rape might also be understood as part of a masculinist bonding exercise between men, rather than as a crime.[50] One eighteen-year-old told of his part in a gang-rape: 'The boys began to have a go at me, so I did it.... She had got a bit anyhow, so I might as well be in it.... I rode her in front of the boys.'[51] As he described it, the assault was less about desire or pleasure or even about the satisfaction of power over the victim, and more about proving masculinity in front of other men. In these descriptions, victims were reduced and invisibilised. The needs and rights of men were prioritised, with the woman unseen. As one study in Victoria suggested, men who raped had 'little or no moral motivation towards abstinence'. Instead, they considered women's consent peripheral, for the convicted men could think of no reason a woman might abstain, other than fear of pregnancy.[52] This meant that in the most radical and patriarchal ways of thinking of sex, rape could not really exist.[53] Or, if it did, the victim was to blame.

In the 1970s, victim blaming could occur even by the closest of family members. Examples of victim blaming abound. In one case discussed by the NSW Task Force, a young woman was gang-raped by four strangers. The men had all pleaded guilty to the charge and been imprisoned. Nonetheless, the victim's mother treated her as if she was to blame; she was made to go to church, which she had never done before, and no one else in her family was expected to do so. As the Task Force noted, it was as if the victim herself was guilty of the crime.[54] Similarly, there were reports of schoolgirls who had been raped and were then ostracised at school,

[48] Dr Art Veno, cited in 'Rape—A Complex Crime', *Telegraph* (Brisbane), 19 January 1977. See also Beatrice Faust, cited in 'Women to Blame Also', *Gippsland Times*, 9 March 1978.

[49] RCHR, *Final Report vol. 5*, 161. See also Bush, Rape In Australia, 3.

[50] 'Rape Crisis', *Vashti's voice*, 1.

[51] Scholz, 'Profile of a Gang Rape', 119.

[52] RCHR, *Final Report vol. 5*, 175.

[53] Quote from the Victorian Police Surgeon, Peter Bush, quoted in 'Not Enough Research', *Morning Herald* (Sydney), 4 October 1977; RCHR, *Final Report vol. 5*, 161; Bush, *Rape In Australia*, 3.

[54] Report by the Inter-Departmental Task Force, *Care for Victims of Sexual Offences*, Premiers Office, NSW, February 1978, 10.

often driven by parents of other students.[55] In another shocking case, a judge complained that a mother had pleaded with her daughter to confess sex was consensual so that the accused—her friend—would not be gaoled. The mother ostracised her child and even threatened to commit suicide if her daughter did not protect her attacker.[56]

Even women who more broadly identified as feminist could engage in victim blaming. In 1977, journalist and feminist Beatrice Faust was quoted as writing:

> the ladies act as if they want to be raped. They shorten their dresses to fanny pelmets and lead with their nipples through see-thru's. They drift calmly into situations that are throbbing with sexual possibilities, typically drinking with a man or getting into a car.[57]

Faust went on to say that women wanted and needed sexual activity, but they could not do so freely, so they entered situations where they might be 'forced into it'. Despite advocating a pro-sex feminist attitude, Faust's analysis still blamed the victim for sexual assault: it was her dress, and her inability to either actively consent or reject sexual activity, that rendered her, not a man, the problem. Feminism was, of course, a diverse movement, with many differences in opinion, but Faust's analysis highlights that even social commentators who were interested in both gender dynamics and feminism, and who were aware of issues of power and authority, could still critique or even persecute the victims of sexual abuse.

Concepts of Harm and Trauma

The final rape myth that feminists disputed was that rape caused little long-term harm to adult victims. Across the nineteenth and twentieth centuries, it had been common to acknowledge that rape impacted victims in specific ways. These were considered in terms of property rights, harm to the victim's future prospects, or, perhaps most importantly, physical violence.[58] The focus on physical wounds meant that certain forms of rape were widely regarded as more serious than others. Assaults where the

[55] 'Harsher Penalties for Rape Opposed', *News* (Perth), 23 July 1976.

[56] 'Young Girl Shunned by Mum after Rape', *Telegraph*, 24 December 1976.

[57] Cited in Bush, *Rape In Australia*, 2–3.

[58] Lisa Featherstone and Andy Kaladelfos, *Sex Crimes in the Fifties* (Carlton: Melbourne University Publishing, 2016), 27, 29–31.

victim suffered beatings, head injuries or permanent physical damage were regularly regarded as more substantial crimes, both within the courts and in the community. Assaults that included anal sex and other acts considered transgressive or particularly degrading were also seen as more serious than vaginal sex. The focus on physical violence and immorality meant that some forms of sexual violence, especially non-penetrative acts, were not considered as serious as others.

If certain forms of sexual assault were invisible or trivialised, the psychological harm of sexual violence was also only beginning to be recognised. Some continued to view rape as something that was not especially traumatic to women. For instance, in 1977 a NSW Public Prosecutor, a man with much experience in prosecuting sexual offences, told other members of a NSW Inquiry into rape that many cases were merely 'forcible seduction', leaving little or no physical or mental injury.[59] But he was increasingly an exception, and the 1970s was a turning point in thinking about the *psychological* impacts of rape. Feminists were the essential players who would initially articulate the mental distress and trauma a victim could suffer—more so than doctors, psychiatrists and social workers. Feminist activists working in domestic violence refuges and rape crises centres showed that shock occurred not only in the immediate moments after assault but could be long lasting.[60] These ideas were reiterated by doctors and other experts who worked with rape victims. As the Victorian Police Surgeon Dr J Peter Bush noted in 1977, 'The scars and distress of a rape attack last for days, weeks and even years.'[61]

In part, the new understandings of the physical and psychological harm of rape were brought to the fore by victims themselves stepping forward to tell of their suffering. Within feminist spaces, the telling of rape stories had become more common: this was part of the broader project of consciousness raising, which aimed to show and share the various injustices faced by women as a 'class'.[62] Rape was a shared experience amongst many

[59] NSW Parliament, *Report of the Criminal Law Review Division of the Department of the Attorney-General and of Justice into Rape and Other Sexual Offences*, 16.

[60] Alicia Lee, 'Rape Crisis Centre', Interview, *Royal Commission on Human Relationships: Official transcript*, 69.

[61] Bush, *Rape In Australia*, 3.

[62] On consciousness raising, see Arrow, *The Seventies*, 31–47. On the links between anti-rape, feminism and consciousness raising, see Rachel Loney-Howes, 'The Politics of the Personal: The Evolution of Anti-Rape Activism from Second-Wave Feminism to #MeToo',

women, who spoke up in small groups and at larger public events.[63] In feminist print media, women used their stories of survival to show gender inequities and the powerlessness of victims.[64]

Individual stories of sexual violence also hit mainstream media outlets, including the *Readers Digest*, *Woman's Day* and, as we have seen, the *Australian Women's Weekly*. Newspapers regularly reported on sexual assaults, including interviews, opinion pieces, commentaries and letters to the editor. Women began to write in to news outlets describing their experiences of rape and other forms of sexual violence.[65] Survivors told their stories to reporters, while some women spoke out at public meetings, which could be reported by the press.[66] Journalists increasingly wrote shocked exposés of what might happen to a victim.[67]

Discussing sexual violence, especially in terms of victims' suffering, was one important step away from a model of silence about rape. The focus on the intimate individual stories of victims was a significant shift in the way sexual crime had been discussed. There had long been stories of sexual crimes in newspapers and print media that focused on the assault and then the trial. In the 1970s, in contrast, we begin to see the inclusion of a victim's voice: women were increasingly able to speak of and to their trauma, in the telling of deeply personal stories in a public space. I suggest that this shift to include a survivor's perspective slowly helped reshape cultural attitudes towards victims and offenders.

It took time, however, for ideas about trauma to filter through to state responses, public practice and community understanding. In NSW in

in *#MeToo and the Politics of Social Change*, eds. Bianca Fileborn and Rachel Loney-Howes (Cham: Palgrave Macmillan, 2019), 22–28.

[63] 'Forum Women Against the Violent Society', *Sydney Women's Liberation Newsletter*, April 1974, 8.

[64] 'Stop Rape', *Sydney Women's Liberation Newsletter*, July 1977, 7; Drusilla Modjeska, 'Review: Against Our Will: Men, Women and Rape', *Refractory Girl*, March 1977, 61.

[65] Yvonne Sullivan, 'Fear, the Paralyser', Letter to the Editor, *The Age*, 27 November 1976.

[66] Liv O'Hanlon, 'The Terrible Trauma of Rape', *The Reader's Digest*, July 1976, 126; Cecily Davis, 'I've GOT to Talk About It', *Pix-People*, 2 December 1976; 'Girls Tell of Terror and Abuse', *News* (Adelaide), 28 June 1977; 'Mother of 2 Driven to Suicide Attempt' *Sunday Mail* (Adelaide), 19 June 1977; 'Teenage Virgin Pack-Raped', *Sunday Observer*, 8 May 1977; Ann Pilmer, 'Night of Terror', *Herald* (Melbourne) 30 January 1978; Helen O'Neil, 'The Threat of Rape', *The Age*, 18 April 1977.

[67] Eve Dixon, 'Rape Leaves Tragic Scars', *Sunday Observer*, 5 December 1976; 'Girls Say Pack Rapes Common in QLD Town', *The West Australian*, 1 December 1976; Anne Summers, 'How Women are Trained', *National Times*, 29 November 1976, 6.

1978, an Interdepartmental Task Force in NSW, made up of six representatives working in policing, crime and health, reported to the Premier.[68] The Task Force concluded that there 'was no general appreciation of the social-psychological trauma' of sexual assault, in either the general public or the agencies that dealt with the victims. In a damning claim, their Report suggested that 'there is no adequate system for caring for victims of sexual assault in New South Wales'.[69] One outcome of the lack of understandings of psychological harm was a lack of services, as we will see in Chap. 4.

The problem, however, was deeper and more complex than the simple provision of resources. Women who had been raped were often told to minimise their experience. As one woman who worked at the rape crisis centre noted:

> We have had women reporting to us that a psychiatrist will say to a woman, "But you should not feel so angry towards this man; didn't you realize he was sick? You have got to live with it." There is the attitude a woman is not entitled to feel anger.[70]

While the mood was shifting across this period, there remained a stubborn unwillingness amongst many to accept that a woman might be deeply emotionally wounded by rape.

Gender and Power

The reluctance to deal with the emotional aspects of rape was intertwined with an unwillingness to consider the issue of power, masculinity and sexual offending. Just as there was a certain blindness to the damage caused by rape—even as feminists attempted to highlight the trauma it caused—there was also a general unwillingness to consider the complex reasons why men might choose to rape. Concepts of 'stranger danger' and the psychopathic rapist had inured the public to the idea that the sexual

[68] The members were Roseanne Bonney, of the NSW Bureau of Crime Statistics and Research; Det. Sen. Const. Dennis Gilligan, NSW Police Force; Det. Sen. Const. Merilyn Wood, NSW Police Force; Dr T.H.G. Oettle, Health Commission of NSW; Peter Rath, Premiers Department; Richard E. Howell, Task Force Co-ordinator Premier's Department.

[69] Report by the Inter-Departmental Task Force, *Care for Victims*, 1.

[70] Alicia Lee, 'Rape Crisis Centre', Interview, *Royal Commission on Human Relationships: Official transcript*, 78.

predator was a sick man who attacked random women in darkened streets. In North America, a series of legislation had been enacted in the mid-twentieth century, linking sexual violence with psychiatric disorders. Men charged with sexual assault were understood as diseased, and were treated within a therapeutic model. Most notably, offenders could be institutionalised in psychiatric care, rather than in jail.[71] In contrast, Australian jurisdictions continued to understand sexual violence within the criminal justice model, and psychiatric care for offenders was spasmodic and underfunded. Nonetheless, the idea that a sexual offender was an exceptional man—a sick man—remained. As the Women's Electoral Lobby noted, 'The excuse is given that the rapist is sick, he is of unsound mind or he wasn't aware of what he was doing.'[72]

Across the 1970s, feminists attempted to unpack the cliché of offenders as deviant: 'A rapist can't be spotted by the insane glint in his eyes', as one author reminded readers.[73] Women's groups stated over and over that men who raped were not psychologically abnormal, but rather ordinary or 'normal' men. Any man, they suggested, might be a rapist.[74] Feminists argued that rape was an extension of other forms of a gendered hierarchy that saw women as inferior to men. In a culture where men's demands were prioritised, men felt they had ownership over the bodies of women.[75] In *The Female Eunuch*, Germaine Greer explored rape within the context of misogyny in a chapter titled 'Loathing and disgust', beginning her argument with the statement, 'Women have little idea of how much men hate them'.[76] Greer violently denied that rape was a result of uncontrolled desire. Instead, she explained rape was an act of 'murderous aggression, spawned in self-loathing and enacted upon the hated other. Men do not

[71] See George Chauncey, 'The Postwar Sex Crime Panic' in *True Stories from the American Past*, ed. W. Graebner (New York: McGraw Hill, 1993), 160–178; Estelle Freedman, '"Uncontrolled Desires": The Response to the Sexual Psychopath, 1920–1960', in *Passion and Power: Sexuality in History*, eds. K. Peiss and C. Simmons (Philadelphia: Temple University Press, 1989), 199–225.

[72] 'Sexual Intercourse—A Woman's Right to Choose?', *Sydney Women's Liberation Newsletter*, April 1975, 4.

[73] 'Rape crisis', *Vashti's Voice*, March 1974, 1.

[74] 'Rape crisis', *Vashti's Voice*, March 1974, 1; 'Rape Crisis Centre', *Sydney Women's Liberation Newsletter*, February 1975, 17; 'Stop Rape', *Sydney Women's Liberation Newsletter*, July 1977, 7; WAR quoted in 'War Against Rape', *Herald* (Melbourne), 12 June 1978.

[75] RCHR, *Final Report vol. 5*, 163.

[76] Greer, *The Female Eunuch*, 249.

themselves know the depth of their hatred'.[77] This hatred was conceptualised by Greer as ordinary and banal, rather than something psychopathic or exceptional.

What was significant was the shift in thinking about rape as something driven by power and violence, rather than sexual desire, and this idea was mainstreamed, appearing in popular media as well as more explicitly feminist writing.[78] Alerting women to the 'normality' of the rapist acted as a warning to young women. A man might be a predator, but also publicly respectable. As Jenny Pausacker of the Melbourne Rape Crisis Centre told the Royal Commission into Human Relationships:

> everybody knows they should not get into cars with strange men … It is always strange men—you do not get the idea that the 21-year-old captain of the football team taking you out to the commencement ball, might be able to get you into a car.[79]

In the 1970s, feminist commentaries foreshadowed debates that would be highlighted in the coming decade: a rapist might also be known, an intimate partner, a husband, boyfriend or a lover. The threat came not necessarily from the stranger, but from men known to the victim, even from within the 'confines of a normal heterosexual relationship'.[80]

[77] Greer, *The Female Eunuch*, 251.

[78] See for example, 'Defence Against Rapists', *Advertiser*, 14 September 1977; Margot Lang, 'Perth Women Angry', *West Australian*, 7 April 1977; Letter to the Editor, 'Breasts and Rape', *Advertiser*, 7 March 1978.

[79] RCHR, *Final Report vol. 5*, 164.

[80] 'Women Against Rape', *Sydney Women's Liberation Newsletter*, May 1976, 8. A survey of clients using sexual assault services in Sydney public hospitals showed that 54% of offenders were strangers to the victim, followed by acquaintances (20%), friends (6%) and fathers or stepfathers (4%). A further 3% were listed as boyfriend or ex-boyfriend, and 2% were a husband or an ex-husband. NSW Health Commission, *Help Centres for Victims of Sexual Assault: A Summary of Three years of Service July 1978–June 1981* (Sydney: NSW Health Commission, 1982), 15. Other surveys in Sydney and Brisbane suggested that between 22% and 33% of women were assaulted by strangers. See Rape Crisis Centre 'Progress Report', *Sydney Women's Liberation Newsletter*, April 1975, 4; Rosemary Munday, 'Rape The Victims', *Australian Women's Weekly (AWW)*, 3 May 1978, 18; Paul Wilson, *The Other Side of Rape, Commission Research Report*, Annexe VII.c; RCHR, *Final Report vol. 5*, 271; 'News From Rape Crisis Collective', *Sydney Women's Liberation Newsletter*, November–December 1976, 9–10.

Conclusions: Rape/Culture

Feminists were involved in debunking a series of 'rape myths' around victims, offenders, power and trauma. These included the idea that a woman could not be raped, that women found pleasure in rape and that women tempted rapists through their clothing, flirtations or drinking. Feminists also sought to revise ideas that rape caused little harm to women; instead, they talked about the ways that sexual violence could have a long-term impact on women's psychological wellbeing.

As feminists showed, these conceptual misunderstandings of rape had profound impacts on the ways the victim could deal with the crime. Feminists had outlined a series of ideological and practical problems for female victims, which needed to be addressed in tangible ways. And they did so very persuasively, meaning that the debates about rape and community standards had moved beyond feminists into the mainstream. It was no longer possible to ignore sexual crime, or the victims of sexual crimes, and many in the community began to demand better services at all levels including policing, health care, crisis care and through the law itself. Just how this might be done, was, however, a significant problem, as will be explored in the following chapters.

CHAPTER 4

What to Do with the Victims?

In late 1974, a group of women set up a rape crisis centre at Women's House in Sydney, including an emergency telephone hotline, where victims could call twenty-four hours a day. Funded initially by donations, activists would answer the phones on a roster system, to assist women in a 'constructive and sympathetic' way. The centre was, from the outset, designed as a counter to the 'ruthless and suspicious treatment which the police so often deal out'.[1] Volunteers would accompany women to medical examinations and could help them to decide whether or not they wanted to report the assault to the police.[2] In cases that went to court, volunteers might accompany the victim. The activists were untrained, though they could call on psychologists, psychiatrists and social workers, if needed.[3] Alongside the support and help it provided to women who had been raped, the centre also aimed to change the laws surrounding sexual assault, including the admissibility of evidence regarding a woman's sexual past, and the need for corroborative evidence.[4]

[1] 'Rape Crisis Centre', *Sydney Women's Liberation Newsletter*, June 1974, 11.
[2] 'Rape Crisis Centre', *Sydney Women's Liberation Newsletter*, June 1974, 11.
[3] Royal Commission on Human Relationships (hereafter RCHR), *Final Report vol. 5* (Canberra: Government Printer, 1977), 184. See also 'RAPE "The Epitome of Sexual Oppression"– A Crisis Centre Opens,' *Tribune*, 4 March 1975, 5.
[4] 'Rape Crisis Centre', *Sydney Women's Liberation Newsletter*, February 1975, 17.

L. Featherstone, *Sexual Violence in Australia, 1970s–1980s*, World Histories of Crime, Culture and Violence,
https://doi.org/10.1007/978-3-030-73310-0_4

In the first three months of operation, the Sydney centre supported fifty women and children, many of whom had suffered through horrific sexual assaults.[5] As feminist Anne Summers would later write, 'The truth was far worse than we had imagined.'[6] Yet despite the constant calls for assistance, funding remained a critical problem. In late 1974, the Rape Crisis Centre was denied state assistance through a large round of grants in celebration of International Women's Year. While the arts, film and television were well funded under the new scheme, practical initiatives such as the Sydney Rape Crisis Centre and Elsie, the Sydney women's refuge, would go unrecognised. Though the centre would go on to receive funding from the Whitlam government in 1975 under their new Community Health Program, they continued to be plagued by money concerns, with promised state and federal grants slow to flow through to the services.[7] In the face of such high demand for women in crisis, why was funding so difficult to gain?

The chapter will explore some of the practical problems in providing services for victims of sexual assault in the 1970s, including a lack of initial reporting of crime, problematic policing and the nascent forms of medical care and other services that emerged in this period. Even in the midst of far-reaching changes traced in the previous chapter, many pre-feminist or anti-feminist ideas and issues endured. Dealing with sexual assault—across policing, health care and welfare services—was far more intractable than it appeared on the surface. As this chapter will show, there was substantial and significant change—and more would come in the following decade. Yet so many aspects of public and state thinking remained static. Therein lay perhaps the most significant problem with rape reform: change could not and did not come quickly or radically enough.

Impacts of Rape Culture: Reporting Crime

By the 1970s, it was clear that many, if not most, women chose not to report sexual assaults to police. Alicia Lee, a psychologist working with a rape crisis centre, suggested that the number of women who reported rape

[5] 'Rape Crisis Centre', *Sydney Women's Liberation Newsletter*, February 1975, 17.

[6] Anne Summers, *Ducks on the Pond: An Autobiography 1945–1976* (Ringwood, Victoria: Viking, 1999), 357.

[7] 'Rape Crisis Centre', *Tharunka*, 30 July 1975, 7.

to the police was 'infinitesimal'.[8] This was perhaps an exaggeration, but rape is commonly acknowledged as an under-reported crime, both in the past and the present. In the 1970s, evidence that rape was an under-reported crime came from many frontline services. In their study of the first eighty-three cases through their doors, the Rape Crisis Centre in Sydney found that most sexual assaults were not reported—only eleven of the eighty-three victims (13%) contacted police.[9] Of victims who attended sexual assault HELP centres in Sydney public hospitals in the late 1970s, around 53% of the clients intended to make a complaint to police, while 38% claimed they would not.[10] More broadly, estimates of reporting suggested from 5% to 20% of sexual assaults were reported to the police. This was lower than estimates in other Western nations.[11]

Women chose not to report rape for many reasons. The Queensland sociologist Paul Wilson produced a comprehensive study on unreported rape, which revealed most women did not inform authorities because they simply wanted to 'forget' the assault.[12] As one woman recorded, 'reporting brings in my family and friends whereas now I have only had to cope with it myself.'[13] Given the considerable stigma and shame associated with sexual violence, some women did not want to report, discuss and prove

[8] Alicia Lee, 'Rape Crisis Centre', Interview, *Royal Commission on Human Relationships: Official transcript of proceedings* (Sydney: Commonwealth Reporting Service, 1974–1976), 69.

[9] Rape Crisis Centre 'Progress Report', *Sydney Women's Liberation Newsletter*, April 1975, 4.

[10] The rest were unsure, or did not state. NSW Health Commission, *Help Centres for Victims of Sexual Assault: A Summary of Three years of Service July 1978-June 1981* (Sydney: NSW Health Commission, 1982), 16–17.

[11] Rosemary Munday, 'Rape The Victims', *Australian Women's Weekly (AWW)*, 3 May 1978, 18; Beverley Scholz, 'Profile of a Gang Rape' in *Delinquency in Australia: A Critical Appraisal*, ed. Paul R. Wilson (St. Lucia, QLD: University of Queensland Press, 1977), 118; 'Rape Crisis Issue', *Sydney Women's Liberation Newsletter*, April 1975, 2. In contrast, the London Rape Crisis Centre recorded 25% of women reported their rape to the police, in the years 1976–1980. See John H Biebel, 'I Thought She Said Yes: Sexual Assault in England and America', *Suffolk Transnational Law Review* 19 (1995): 156.

[12] Paul R. Wilson, *The Other Side of Rape* (St. Lucia, Qld: University of Queensland Press, 1978); *Commission Research Report*, Annexe VII.c, RCHR, *Final Report vol. 5*, 273.

[13] Paul R. Wilson, 'Victims of Rape: The Social Context of Degradation', *Australian and New Zealand Journal of Criminology* 9 (1976): 251.

the crime.[14] Women feared upsetting husbands, parents or friends.[15] One married woman with six children did not want to report her rape, because she was concerned it would bring embarrassment to her children.[16] In a sign of their own agency, many women explicitly refused to report. When one victim was asked by a reporter if she would go to the police, she retorted:

> No way. I'd been through enough without sticking my neck out for more. As far as I know, police and court procedures are still pretty primitive, and I was in no shape to give them the benefit of the doubt. What I needed was a shoulder to cry on, not a doctor examining me.[17]

Women knew what they were capable of, and if they wanted to endure the long and arduous formal prosecution process.[18]

Others were frightened of further consequences. Some victims who were single mothers were scared their children might be removed. At least some women did not want to go to the police because they were frightened of further violence from the rapist or rapists.[19] Victims may have been explicitly threatened: one woman who had been repeatedly raped by three men told the courtroom she was warned, 'We'll let you go, but if you go to the Police you can consider yourself dead.'[20] Other women were probably too scared to report assaults, in particular when the violence had been gang related. At one Brisbane trial for the gang-rape of a young woman by twelve men who identified as 'bikies', a detective testified that one of the accused told him that the complainant was the first woman who had stepped forward to tell the police. It left commentators wondering how many girls and women had been victims of the same group.[21] The law was not necessarily able to protect women under these circumstances, and at worst, the potential for violence spilled over even into the court system.

[14] Munday, 'Rape the Victims', 18; Paul Wilson, 'Interview', *Royal Commission on Human Relationships: Official transcript*, 1664.

[15] 'Victims of Rape Don't Report It', *Telegraph* (Sydney), 2 September 1978.

[16] State Records NSW: Court Reporting Branch; NRS 2713, Criminal Transcripts, Supreme Court, *R v Hillstrand*, 1970 (hereafter 'Criminal Transcripts').

[17] Cecily Davis, 'I've GOT to Talk About It', *Pix-People*, 2 December 1976.

[18] Cecily Davis, 'I've GOT to Talk About It'.

[19] This was mentioned in court cases, including Criminal Transcripts, Supreme Court, *R v Pillon*, 1970; Criminal Transcripts, Supreme Court, *R v Wayne, Painter and Advent*, 1970.

[20] Criminal Transcripts, *Supreme Court, R v Royce*, 1970, 9.

[21] Scholz, 'Profile of a Gang Rape', 117.

A seventeen-year-old man was accused of raping a woman who had come home while he was breaking into her house. On indictment, he was recorded as saying, 'I didn't rape her. She gave her consent. If I go away for this, when I get out I will kill her. That is not a threat, that is a promise.'[22]

Other girls and women did not report rapes because they did not think the authorities would believe them. Many women did not have tangible evidence of assault, and as the Sydney Rape Crisis Centre noted, 'unless she has been beaten within an inch of her life she bears no marks which would "prove" her resistance so therefore she has cooperated.'[23] Five years after 'Jane' was raped, she told a social worker that she had not gone to the police because she was scared of being interrogated about her morals and sexual past. Even when she sought medical advice, she did not tell the doctor that she had been raped. At the core, she assumed she would be disbelieved, because of broader cultural attitudes towards sexual violence. As she explained: 'I feel that men, every man, or most men that I know, don't really believe that there is such a thing as rape.'[24] Other women did not report the crime, to 'avoid the court assuming that she "probably asked for it anyway"'.[25] Women are often reproached by husbands, boyfriends or parents, and victims internalised this, 'blaming herself for being in a situation in which she could be raped'.[26] As women at one feminist forum in 1974 told the group, they felt that 'it would be futile to report the crime—Who would believe them anyway, or say it was not their fault?'[27]

There could be profound community pressures for girls and women not to report crimes, and there were strong incentives for certain groups to protect men. In 1976, Anne Summers broke a media exposé over gang-rapes in the Queensland town of Ingham, a sugar community with a high population of Italian migrants. Young feminists claimed that girls were being gang-raped several times a week in an organised process known as 'training'. Few of the girls complained to police, and it was speculated in

[22] Criminal Transcripts, Supreme Court, *R v Kite*, 1970, 1.

[23] 'Sexual Intercourse—A Woman's Right to Choose?', *Sydney Women's Liberation Newsletter*, April 1975, 3.

[24] Cited in Dr J. Peter Bush, *Rape In Australia: An Appraisal of Attitudes, Victims, Assailants, Medicine and the Law* (Melbourne: Sun Books 1977), 57.

[25] 'Rape Crisis Centre', *Sydney Women's Liberation Newsletter*, February 1975, 17.

[26] 'Rape Crisis Centre', *Sydney Women's Liberation Newsletter*, February 1975, 17.

[27] 'Forum Women Against the Violent Society', *Sydney Women's Liberation Newsletter*, April 1974, 8.

the press that Italian families did not want daughters to prosecute offenders, particularly if the victim was not a virgin, or had agreed to sex with one of the men. But there were also elements of coercion and threats of violence. As the Inspector of the Ingham CIB noted, 'It's a physical intimidation. Force is applied and they are threatened with more of the same if they go to the police.' He also noted that the men involved were well educated, with good legal counsel.[28] One fifteen- year-old who did report the crime told reporters that few girls did, and she regretted doing so:

> If it happened to me again I wouldn't report it. Because I know I can't win. What's the use of going [to court]? I nearly went insane in those court cases, you know, asking me questions that really made me sick. About what they did to me, and I didn't like talking about it. I nearly had a nervous breakdown… I'd go through the agony again but I wouldn't report it.[29]

The men, charged first with rape and then prosecuted on charges of carnal knowledge, were found guilty but released on a good behaviour bond.[30] It is not surprising, then, that the survivor felt the additional trauma of reporting and prosecuting had not been worthwhile.

The Problems with Police and Policing

There were twofold concerns over the policing of sexual violence in the 1970s: first, that police were unsympathetic or even cruel to women who reported rape and second, that police did not adequately investigate alleged sexual assaults. A key part of the reluctance to engage with policing authorities was the feeling that the police would not take up rape cases, even when they were genuine. This was drawn from evidence of low levels of charges against men accused of rape. For instance, of women seeking assistance from the Sydney Rape Crisis Centre, only 34% of victims reported the assault to the police. Of these cases that were reported, 30% had no charge pressed, 3% had charges withdrawn and 50% had charges pressed against an accused man, while the outcome was unknown in the final cases. In the end, there was a guilty verdict in 14% of cases reported

[28] 'How Women are Trained', *National Times*, 29 November 1976, 1–2.
[29] 'How Women are Trained', *National Times*, 5.
[30] 'How Women are Trained', *National Times*, 5.

The Architecture of Rights

David Frydrych

The Architecture of Rights

Models and Theories

palgrave
macmillan

David Frydrych
Faculty of Law
Monash University
Melbourne, VIC, Australia

ISBN 978-3-030-76038-0 ISBN 978-3-030-76039-7 (eBook)
https://doi.org/10.1007/978-3-030-76039-7

This Palgrave Macmillan imprint is published by the registered company Springer Nature Switzerland AG.
The registered company address is: Gewerbestrasse 11, 6330 Cham, Switzerland

Abstract

This book concerns concepts of rights and philosophical accounts thereof. It distinguishes between two kinds of philosophical accounts of rights: models and theories. Models outline the 'conceptually basic' types of rights and their relationships with other kinds of 'normative positions' (e.g., duties, liabilities, etc.). Theories of rights offer criteria for the concept of a right, or some subset thereof, including an ultimate purpose they all supposedly serve.

Chapter 2 criticises monistic models (ones positing only a single basic kind) for being under-inclusive and a subset of pluralistic ones (those positing several basic kinds) as over-inclusive. Chapter 3 identifies and analyses different conceptions of rights correlativity and shows how they motivate features of certain rights models. Chapter 4 helps to clarify the concepts of rights claiming, exercise, enforcement, remedying, and vindication. Chapter 5 explains the theories of rights debate, whilst Chapter 6 argues that such theories and their very debate are irredeemably flawed and should be abandoned. Chapter 7 further analyses rights enforceability, showing why legal rights are not invariably enforceable via legal powers. Chapter 8 nonetheless explains why wholly unenforceable legal rights constitute 'imperfect' cases. Chapter 9 shows why there are more ways to use legal rights than just via enforcement powers, elucidating two such modes: legal liberty-based claims and invocations of right. Chapter 10 then shows what is defective with rights that are not claimable or invocable.

- Chapter 1 includes portions of 'Down the Methodological Rabbit Hole' 49 (147) Crítica 41

- A version of Chapter 2 was published as 'Rights Modelling' 30(1) Canadian Journal of Law and Jurisprudence 125 (Cambridge University Press, February 2017).
- A version of Chapter 3 appears in *Wesley Hohfeld A Century Later: Edited Work, Select Personal Papers, and Original Commentaries* (Shyam Balganesh, Ted Sichelman, & Henry Smith eds., (Cambridge University Press 2021).
- Portions of Chapter 4 were published as 'Kramer's Delimiting Test for Legal Rights' (2017) 62 American Journal of Jurisprudence 197; 'The Theories of Rights Debate' (2018) 9 Jurisprudence: An International Journal of Legal and Political Thought 566; and 'What Is the Will Theory of Rights?' (2019) 32 Ratio Juris 455.
- A version of Chapter 5 was published as 'The Case Against the Theories of Rights' (2020) 40(2) Oxford Journal of Legal Studies 320.

This book was born out of a deep puzzlement over the—often contradictory or contrary—claims of 'fundamental', 'human', or 'basic' rights that inundate this age's legal and political discourses. Is this nothing more than 'metaphysic sophistry', as Edmund Burke would say? This led to more basic questions. What is 'a right'? What makes something count as a bona fide instance? What, if anything, is distinctive about rights?

The philosophy of rights offered hope for illumination. This is a rich body of literature on the (contested) concept(s) of a right, some related 'normative positions' (e.g., duties, liabilities, etc.), and their role in helping to structure legal, moral, and political worlds. Like many before me, it was initially wondered whether this area of philosophy might show that form informed substance; that, somehow, the structure of the concept(s) might delimit what can be rendered into rights. Alas, this is not so.

This book aims to contribute to, and advance, the philosophy of rights. The field is beholden not only to analytic legal philosophy and 'metaphilosophy', but equally to the scholarship of extremely clever jurists and lawyers who have noted important conceptual and verbal distinctions over the centuries. It is an honour to add a link, howsoever small, in this great chain.

The work would have been impossible without the support of a great many people. Thanks are due first and foremost to my family: Seymour and Rochelle Frydrych, and my siblings, Paul, Karen, and Eric. My friends also went above and beyond the call of duty. I am particularly indebted to Hamish Bridges, Jacques Schumacher, and Jonathan Ward for reading and editing older versions of certain chapters. Pavlos Eleftheriadis, my DPhil supervisor, along with Andrew Halpin and James Penner, my postdoctoral fellow mentors, were of tremendous help. Further, the Oxford Law Faculty's Jurisprudence Discussion Group proved to be a wonderful source of friendship, intellectual stimulation, and critical feedback.

John Gardner opened my eyes to Sanction theories of law, which helped to reorient my thinking about rights (particularly vis-à-vis the merits—and demerits—of the 'method of hypothetical cases'). John Finnis and Tony Honoré were also very kind to indulge me in discussions about their work on rights. As this book has benefited tremendously from Matthew Kramer's scholarship on rights, I also wish to express my thanks to him (howsoever much he might disagree with its content).

Thanks also to PMS Hacker for opening my mind to Wittgenstein and for reading and discussing my DPhil thesis' methodology chapter. His lectures and conversations improved my understanding of what philosophy can accomplish, especially regarding actual and hypothetical counterexamples.

Contents

CHAPTER 1

Introduction: The Philosophy of Rights

§ I. Introduction

This book falls within a long tradition of philosophising about the structure, purposes, and uses of rights. It has proven quite tempting to ask, and to try to answer, the following sorts of questions. What is a right? What, if anything, makes rights different from other features of the normative world, such as duties, standards, rules, and principles? What are the necessary conditions of A RIGHT, if any?[1] Do all rights, or at least certain subsets thereof, serve some *ultimate* purpose?

Philosophers and jurists have long been aware that different senses of the term 'a right' abound in legal, moral, and political practices and discourses. To help make sense of this diversity, they developed two different kinds of accounts of rights' 'formal' features: models and theories.[2]

[1] The contemporary philosophical convention is to use all capitals to mark concepts. This is done to distinguish them from denotations of words, phrases, and terms (for which quotation marks are used instead), e.g., 'a right'.

[2] Although the model/theory characterisation is novel, identifying two different kinds of philosophical explanations of rights is not. Instead of 'models' and 'theories', Leif Wenar styles the difference in terms of 'forms' and 'functions' Wenar (2020). That distinction is unhelpful, though, because both terms work equally well in either category. For example, one could say it is the function of a power to change parties' normative positions, whilst it is the function of all rights to protect right-holders' interests. Alon Harel distinguishes two kinds of accounts that govern the 'nature' and 'role' of rights respectively. Harel (2007:

D. Frydrych, *The Architecture of Rights*,
https://doi.org/10.1007/978-3-030-76039-7_1

Most lawyers and the general public nevertheless ignore these elucidations and continue to speak as though 'a right' was a univocal term.

Even so, many scholars believe that these models and theories are important not only to make sense of our discourses, but also because of the mass proliferation of claims of rights in the last few decades, coupled with ubiquitous disputes over what counts as genuine cases, given the pervasive disagreements about what people's rights are and should be. There is a wariness and fear that the exponential growth in (both legitimate and dubious) claims of right will devalue the concept(s).[3]

Indeed, this era is also witnessing a sizeable increase in the amount of moral, social, and political disputes *being framed in* the language of rights. One might call this the 'rightsification' of our normative discourses. For example, instead of either just arguing in favour of their policy preferences or in terms of what (they believe) justice requires, people now more regularly frame their concerns in terms of 'rights'. They might claim to 'have' a 'fundamental' right to *X*—where *X* stands for some good or service, one which, typically, is to be provided or secured by the state. By this, speakers are often not referring to established, undisputed cases of legal norms and simply debating their proper scopes or extensions. Nor, frequently, are such remarks mere expressions of aspirations for positing new legal rights in the future. Instead, people frequently speak as though such putative entitlements are already in force, that they are valid norms of a legal system, without bothering to query whether this is so and being unperturbed by evidence that it is not actually the case. By framing their concerns as though there is already an—indisputable—entitlement, an already existing norm, proponents then treat the putative right as a reason for deeming those who take opposing stances on the policy question at hand to either be mistaken or to simply be outranked ('trumped'). Opponents, in turn, may frame *their own* preferences in terms of rights, and so adjudge the other side's claim of right to be spurious and disingenuous.[4]

192). This too is unhelpful because either category can be labelled 'role'. We could say that each Hohfeldian kind of a right serves a distinct role, whilst the Interest theory posits that a right's role is to protect some interest or other.

[3] E.g., Sumner (1987: 1); Wellman (1995: 11, 176); Steiner (1998: 233); Rainbolt (2006: 147).

[4] E.g., Sumner (1987: 8). Edmund Burke foresaw this sort of development long ago, in the context of the French Revolution. Framed in today's nomenclature, Burke believed that French government officials lacked a shared paradigm for determining what the new legal system's rights should be. Even if they could agree on the *names* of certain rights for the

Even without these developments it would be helpful to be able to appeal to a definitive standard or test by which to resolve all disputes about: (i) what rights are; (ii) what can legitimately be rendered into a right (or what a right may credibly protect); and (iii) where genuine instances obtain. (It would furthermore be of great assistance to have credible, universally shared criteria of fundamentality by which to determine what can and ought to constitute constitutional and human rights.[5])

Lofty aspirations though these might be, the philosophy of rights cannot satisfy all of those things. It was not its original goal to do so, either; models and theories of rights did not start out, and indeed today generally still do not have, any such grandiose political objectives. Rights modellers' aims were predominantly clarificatory—and without bearing some crypto-normative or overt political or moral agenda necessarily driving their constructions or promotion. They simply wished to dispel ambiguity and to evidence technical differences in normative positions that are all labelled 'a right'.

To understand what rights models and theories are and do, it will first prove helpful to roughly distinguish between a thing, a concept, and a term, phrase, or word. A *thing* (which, for better or ill, some philosophers treat synonymously with 'phenomenon') includes a person, place, object, and state of affairs.[6] *Words*, *terms*, and *phrases* are symbols used in a language. These can be used to express a concept. (Note that more than one word may nevertheless be available by which to express a given concept.) The *concept*, A CONCEPT, is contested. One popular view construes concepts to be mental representations (of a thing, say), which involve beliefs and propositional attitudes, and which bear internal structures containing more basic representational elements.[7] Observe the difference between

system (e.g., 'freedom of speech', 'right of association', 'freedom of conscience', etc.), the revolutionary government had no *shared* basis for determining those rights' contents. Burke (1987).

[5] If, that is, all people and societies were even inclined to frame such matters in terms of the normative grammar of rights. This, rather than perceive that very framing to be a tool of legal and political imperialism, let alone the imposition of a great many international legal rights upon them counting as such too.

[6] Although not simply concepts or terms, rights (duties, liabilities, etc.) are not 'things' in the sense of being physical objects in the universe. Whilst some people are inclined to treat rights as 'abstract objects', 'abstract entities', or artefacts, these first two at least are also misguided efforts (but not of reification exactly).

[7] See, e.g., Laurence and Margolis (2019). The view of concepts being beliefs is said to generate a regress problem, as the constituent 'representations' themselves require explanation. Ibid.

the word 'right' (often meaning good or correct), the term 'a right', the concept A RIGHT, and a given right, such as the right to free speech.

A few philosophers additionally carve a concept/conception distinction. On this view, a *concept* covers a whole category (or an entire field of enquiry), whilst a *conception* refers to particular viewpoints about that concept.[8] For example, in a tradition tracing from (at least) Jeremy Bentham to Wesley Hohfeld and beyond, philosophers and jurists have argued about whether the term 'a right' refers to different *concepts*. Hohfeld identified five: a claim, a privilege, a power, an immunity, and a 'right complex'.[9] (A complex is a larger, unified normative construct composed of various instances of Hohfeld's more basic kinds, e.g., a claim + an enforcement power + a liberty to exercise that power, etc.[10]) There are also various *conceptions* of the kind of a right that correlates to a duty, which I shall style throughout the book as 'an RCTD'.[11] Unlike Hohfeld's A

[8] E.g., White (1975: 113–4). Some scholars nevertheless doubt the distinction's worth, holding instead that people merely harbour different beliefs about one concept. Others believe the distinction is misleading because there may not even be 'a' concept to which the various 'conceptions' refer. See Halpin (1997: 11).

[9] Hohfeld (1913a); Hohfeld (1917).

[10] E.g., Terry (1884: 386); Hohfeld (1913a: 35 n.39, 38 n.48).

[11] The differences amongst the various conceptions of an RCTD are not as great as sometimes made out to be. Even so, here are some of the salient ones. First, despite my 'RCTD' label, some modellers deny that rights always bear correlatives because they posit that a right is conceptually, and even sometimes temporally, prior to duties. (They nonetheless believe that duties can always be affixed to rights). E.g., MacCormick (1977). Cf. Terry (1884: 93). Second, rights are sometimes treated as reasons, not just normative positions. E.g., Raz (1986). Third and fourth, it is debated whether certain such conceptions, such as Hohfeld's A CLAIM, are able to account for pro tanto rights (and duties) and the qualities of 'force' or 'weight'. See MS Green (2007). Fifth, some scholars argue that rights are not claims, but rather (sometimes) defended by claims. E.g., Honoré (1960: 456–7). (Matthew Kramer shows that Hohfeld's *schema* is compatible with the first four views. Kramer (1998: 23–9, 36–49)).

My label, 'an RCTD', suffices to cover all of the various conceptions, with the caveat that: certain ones deem enforcement powers to be features of an RCTD; others hold an RCTD to simply be constituted by such powers; whilst still others treat enforcement powers as being conceptually distinct from an RCTD, but insist that both serve as components within a right complex. Furthermore, as shall be discussed in Chapter 5, despite my label, some Interest and Will theorists may deny that all tokens of this type of normative position actually count as rights if the instances fail to meet their specified theoretical criteria. In other words, for such theorists, not all Hohfeldian claims are necessarily rights. Additionally, some scholars explain many legal and moral rights in terms of right complexes.

There are also various conceptions of powers, liberties, and immunities. Consider A LIBERTY. On certain conceptions, a liberty must be an express permission; on others it can simply be the mere absence of a duty. Second, on some conceptions there can be *unilateral*

CLAIM,[12] which is probably the most popular conception of an RCTD, HLA Hart's conception of a (private law) right-correlative-to-an-obligation is a composite of powers and liberties: the capacity to enforce or waive a correlative duty plus permissions to undertake either option.[13] Joseph Raz's conception of an RCTD is similar to Hohfeld's insofar as it marks its holder as the intended beneficiary of a correlative duty-bearer's action or forbearance, but differs insofar as the right (i) is a reason, predicated upon some interest or other of the right-holder, which has the qualities of force or weight, and (ii) is *justificatorily* prior to its correlatives (*A*'s right is the reason for *B*'s duty).[14]

Whether understood as presenting conceptions of a concept, rivalrous concepts, or various accounts of the same concept, modellers' (and theorists') products are often presented as being 'conceptual clarifications'. As words and/or concepts can admit of ambiguity, vagueness, etc., many philosophers believe they can tidy up this messiness by either: (a) rendering the concept's features more perspicuous (so that it might be better understood),[15] or (b) by replacing the concept with a more precise one.[16] Others may then employ the refurbished concept in their philosophical, scientific, social scientific, or legal work.[17]

liberties: you can have a liberty to do φ even if you lack the liberty not to do it. Others reject that notion because, for them, a true liberty must be *bilateral*, i.e., one must be free to both do φ and not to do φ. Third, on certain conceptions a liberty can correlate directly with a duty, whilst others reject that as a 'conceptual error'. See, e.g., Hohfeld (1913a); Hart (1982: 166–7, 171–4); Robinson et al. (1983).

[12] Hohfeld (1913a: 30–2).

[13] Hart (1982: 180–91).

[14] Raz (1986: Chapter 7 'The Nature of Rights'); Raz (1996: particularly Chapter 12 'Legal Rights'). Hart and Raz also see their conceptions as being criticisms of, and improvements upon, Hohfeld's. See Hart (1982: 162); Raz (1996: 254–5).

[15] For example, PMS Hacker suggests that we clarify a concept, expressed by means of a word (the usage of which we as language users have relatively mastered), by examining its uses to make explicit its combinatorial possibilities, its entailments and incompatibilities, the presuppositions of its use, its purposes, etc., Meeting with Dr. Peter Hacker, University of Oxford (Oxford UK, March 7, 2016). See also Baker and Hacker (2005: 246–7) on 'necessary propositions', but which, in conversation, Hacker agreed applies equally to concepts' features.

[16] E.g., Jackson (2000: 38, 46–7). See also Stoljar (2013: 237), *citing* Rudolph Carnap and Willard Van Orman Quine on 'explicative definitions', which 'make more exact a vague or not quite exact concept used in everyday life … or rather of replacing it by a newly constructed more exact concept' (Carnap (1956: 7–8)), or 'improve upon the definiendum by refining or supplementing its meaning' (Quine (1951: 25)).

[17] E.g., Leiter (2007: 134). See *infra* § IV for further discussion of conceptual clarifications.

§ II. Models of Rights

With this in mind, we can begin to distinguish models and theories of rights. (More in-depth explanations will be provided in Chapters 2 and 5 respectively.) A *model* provides a typology of conceptually basic types of rights, explains how rights and other kinds of normative positions (e.g., duties, liabilities, etc.) can relate to one another, and shows if and how instances thereof can be packaged together in a 'right complex'.[18]

Some further terminology will prove helpful here. For one thing, 'basic' and 'fundamental' will generally be used throughout this book to mean being irreducible, conceptually speaking, rather than marking a judgment about which rights are morally or politically essential for persons, justice, a political order, etc.[19] Second, the philosophy of rights literature often refers to rights and their correlatives (e.g., duties, liabilities, etc.) as 'normative positions'. This suggests people's and institutions' identities and/or statuses within a normative system or domain: a legal system, a community's positive morality, a corporation, etc.[20] It is also a slightly controversial term, as some scholars deny that certain positions (e.g., liberties and powers) constitute norms on the grounds that they do not guide or

[18] Why style these as 'models'? Aside from the fact that 'theories' is the well-established label for the—quite different—second kind of explanation of A RIGHT (ones which provide criteria for the concept), rights models offer representations of real-world normative positions.

[19] A popular idea in analytic philosophy is that concepts are (often) complex and decomposable into more basic ones. I take no stance on whether this is true of most concepts, and only employ 'basic' and 'fundamental' as a putative description of certain concepts within rights models.

[20] Hart distinguished between the conventional morality of a particular society and a different set of normative standards an individual may harbour that can be used to adjudge the former. '…I would revive the terminology much favoured by the Utilitarians of the [19th] century, which distinguished "positive morality," the morality actually accepted and shared by a given social group, from the general moral principles used in the criticism of actual social institutions including positive morality. We may call such general principles "critical morality"…'. Hart (1963: 20). See also Hart (1982: 84); Hart (1983: 52–3).

One might be able to cogently speak of normative positions derived from an ethical theory (Deontology, Utilitarianism, etc.). It is less clear whether the idea of normative positions is even sensible if one's critical morality is not predicated upon any such system; instead, one simply seems to have *reasons* for criticising or praising aspects of a given conventional morality.

regulate behaviour.[21] Third, rights are generally held to have 'correlatives'. For example, a Hohfeldian claim perforce correlates with a duty,[22] whilst a Hohfeldian power correlates with someone else's 'liability' (meaning susceptibility to having one's normative positions changed). Fourth, some models, but not all, posit more than one basic kind of a right. The generic term for the basic kinds, and for complexes, is 'rights'. Moreover, each basic kind of a right correlates with a specific kind of normative position. However, there is no commonly established term for these latter correlative positions. For want of a better term, I shall style them 'ligations'.[23]

There are several models of rights. Appendix 1 provides some examples and elucidates some of their features. Certain models also admit of their own set of scholarly interpretations and suggested modifications. It is not within a model's purview to explain whether rights ought to exist, or if they all serve some singular, ultimate purpose. (The latter is ostensibly a *theory*'s job.)

Rights models can also be divided into monistic and pluralistic varieties.[24] Pluralistic models identify different basic types of normative

[21] E.g., Wellman (1995: 8). Throughout this book, *legal* rights, duties, powers, liabilities, etc., shall frequently be referred to as 'legal positions'.

[22] Some people insist upon a difference between duties and obligations. E.g., Brandt (1964); Beran (1972); White (1984: 51–3). The supposed differences are mostly unconvincing. The book will generally stick with 'duty', but otherwise uses the two words interchangeably. Cf. Hart (1994: 284).

[23] The term 'ligation' comes from Albert Kocourek. (1923: 26). Years before Hohfeld, John Salmond, who posited four basic kinds of rights, noted the lack of a generic term for his four correlatives (duty, liability, etc.). Salmond (1902: 236). He failed to coin one, though. Whilst there is still no common term, 'ligation' remains the least bad option. Pavlos Eleftheriadis calls them 'legal negations'. Eleftheriadis (2008: 123). However, this seems to miss some of the positions' affirmative qualities, e.g., a duty's requirement to act, a liability's susceptibility to having one's position changed, etc. The same problem applies to Pierre Schlag's entitlements/disablements distinction. Schlag (2015: 188). Other scholars divide Hohfeld's eight positions into four 'advantages' and four 'burdens', but he himself shows why many liabilities are actually desirable and even sometimes advantageous. Hohfeld (1913a: 54 n.90). The same might be said for Hohfeld's other three kinds of ligations.

Kocourek is an Imperatival (aka Command) theorist, erroneously holding that all legal relations involve some form of legal constraint. However, one can just employ 'ligation' as a technical term which excises that element: not all ligations are duties, borne of legal officials' commands, let alone ones that are subject to sanction for non-conformity. Kocourek's terminology of 'dominant' and 'servient' parties (***dominus*** and ***servus***) may also be a good way to distinguish rights and ligations. Kocourek (1920a: 49).

[24] Sumner (1987: 32–3). For further discussion, see Chapter 2 note 2 and the accompanying text.

positions as kinds of rights. They posit that expressions such as 'I have a right to say that', 'I have a right to sell my property', and 'I have a right to be paid for my work' contain subtle differences, ones evidencing the existence of different kinds of normative positions being in play here, despite the shared label of 'a right'. The first concerns what you *may* do, the second what you *can* do, and the third what someone else *must* do for you.[25] Pluralists believe, in other words, that these are not simply the diverse operations of one and the same normative position made manifest in different contexts, but rather distinct kinds of rights which do different kinds of things: permitting you act, empowering you to change things, entitling you to something from another person, etc.

The most famous rights model is Hohfeld's *schema of jural relations.* Again, it is usually taken to register different senses of the term 'a right', four of which in turn refer to distinct fundamental conceptions of four normative positions: a claim, a privilege, a power, and an immunity. (Remember, too, his fifth type: a complex.[26]) Each of the four basic kinds of a right perforce correlates with one—only one, and always the same—kind of ligation: a duty, a 'no-right', a liability, or a disability.[27] ('Jural' is meant to cover both legal and equitable positions. Many scholars nonetheless deem the *schema* to be equally applicable to moral rights, game rights, other institutional rights, etc.)

By contrast, monistic models posit that there is only one kind of a right. Almost all modern-day Monists deem that one to be a right-correlative-to-a-duty, 'an RCTD'. For them, it is inappropriate to count other basic normative positions, e.g., liberties, powers, or immunities, as kinds of 'rights'. Of course, those others constitute bona fide normative positions in law, morality, etc.; Monists simply deny that those count as 'rights'. Similarly, there are monistic *interpretations* of pluralistic models, whereby one kind of position is deemed to be a real right whilst the rest are re-characterised as being something else.

[25] See Salmond (1902: 238).

[26] Hohfeld (1913a); Hohfeld (1917). Hohfeld preferred the term 'privilege' over 'liberty' to label his conception. For better or ill, it has nevertheless become fairly standard for Hohfeldians to use 'liberty' instead.

[27] See Appendix 1 for Hohfeld's *schema*. Chapter 3 § III addresses the confusion generated by Hohfeld's contradictory remarks about a claim; particularly, whether it is an 'active' or 'passive' kind of normative position. Some Hohfeldians and anti-Hohfeldians nevertheless reject the idea that a given right can only correlate with just one ligation. E.g., Chapter 3 note 14 and the accompanying text.

As already seen, be it monistic or pluralistic, no model is concerned exclusively with rights. Each addresses other related basic kinds of normative positions: duties, liabilities, etc. Generally, models aim to explain the relationships between: (I) the various basic kinds of rights (if the model posits more than one); (II) rights and other kinds of normative positions (e.g., a right and a correlative duty); and (III) those other related kinds of positions, e.g., between a duty and a liability. What makes them 'rights' models, then, rather than accounts of normative positions more generally? (Hohfeld's, for instance, is called the '*schema of jural relations*'.) Rights are given a central role in almost every such model whilst elucidations of (certain of) the non-right normative positions are often left underdeveloped—to say the least.

Now, some models are presented as being system or domain specific, i.e., as accounts of *legal* rights exclusively, or just of *institutional* rights, of only *moral* ones, etc. This can leave open the nature of the relationships between legal, moral, institutional, and other rights.

Certain modellers take an explicit stance on those relationships, though. This latter group in turn divides over whether rights are functional or modal kinds.[28] *Modalists* deny that there are conceptual differences amongst legal, social, and moral rights. For them, such rights do not do anything differently from one another. The only significant difference is being housed in different normative domains.[29] *Functionalists*, by contrast, posit that legal, moral, social, etc., rights differ in structure. As examples, some hold that legal rights are always enforceable whilst moral rights are not (or vice versa), or that moral rights are bona fide reasons for action whilst legal ones need not be.[30] Though Functionalists need not go so far, some additionally believe that, because of these differences, legal, moral, and institutional rights are mere homonyms.

There are nevertheless reasons to doubt the appropriateness of these stipulated domain limitations. One is that this might lead to a distorted

[28] The functional/modal distinction is adopted here from Leslie Green. He argues that law is a modal, not a functional, kind of normative domain: it has no unique function by which to distinguish it from morality, custom, religion, etc. L Green (1995–6: 1711).

[29] E.g., Raz (2009b: 158–9; Raz (1996: 255–8, 269–74).

[30] E.g., Hart (1982: 157–60, 266–8). Cf. Waldron (1981: 23).

picture of rights.[31] Second, the stipulations seem to rely on underlying conceptual commonalities in order to mark supposed functional differences in the first place. Particularly, modellers rely upon the same basic components in order to even express the supposed functional differences. Take, for example, a functionalist version of Hohfeld's *schema* that professes to apply only to legal rights, not moral ones. A typical reason why functionalist modellers hold that legal rights differ from moral ones is because they believe that bona fide legal rights are really enforceable complexes (composites of Hohfeldian claims and powers, say) whilst moral rights are not. Regardless of whether that is true, *we must already know* what each fundamental concept is about in order to explain that purported functional difference. You must know what Hohfeldian claims and powers are, to understand what it is to have a claim coupled with an associated power (the latter being the mechanism by which to enforce the overall right complex) as opposed to a solitary claim, in order to even establish the supposed difference between legal and moral rights for your functionalist model. Hence, professing a limited application or range itself (ostensibly) relies upon a conceptually more basic toolkit for all normative domains.

§ II.1. The Primary/Secondary/Tertiary Rights Distinction

Before turning to *theories*, some further distinctions and concepts will prove helpful, as they show how normative positions may interrelate and, in part, what enforcement involves (which is integral to the theories of rights debate). Consider first the primary/secondary/tertiary distinction [hereinafter the 'PST distinction']. It construes the different stages of enforcement to be the function of distinct rights. Although commonplace in jurisprudence, scholars divide over the distinction's accuracy and utility (let alone how best to carve it).

The distinction, concerning legal rights at least, is this. *Primary* rights are substantive entitlements, e.g., to engage in free speech, to purchase some land, etc. *Secondary* (or 'procedural') rights do several things. Some authorise their holders to initiate dispute resolution proceedings

[31] On the other hand, there are grounds for the opposite concern. For example, Raz is bothered by (what he takes to be) a dubious inclination to seek moral and social analogues to legal rights enforcement mechanisms, which may not obtain—even for certain legal rights. Raz (1996: 255–7).

(litigation, arbitration, mediation, etc.) when primary rights seem to have been, or are threatened to be, violated. They also authorise right-holders to waive such processes. Other secondary rights are those afforded and utilised within official proceedings, e.g., to file certain motions. Still others are employed outside of institutional settings, e.g., entitlements to undertake self-help remedies. *Tertiary* rights are the 'remedial' entitlements provided in dispute resolution proceedings.

For example, *A* and *B* enter into a contract. *A*, for $100, will buy 10 widgets from *B*. Both have created *primary* legal rights and duties. *A* holds (1) a primary right to receive 10 widgets from *B* and (2) a primary duty to pay *B* the money. In turn, *B* has (1) a primary right to be paid the money and (2) a duty to provide *A* with the widgets. If *B* either threatens not to deliver the goods, or simply fails to do so, then *A* may be able to employ *secondary* rights to sue *B*. If the court decides in *A*'s favour, then *A* gains a *tertiary* legal right to the court-granted remedy (which may in turn have to be enforced), whilst *B* is assigned a new duty to provide said remedy.

Some scholars insist that tertiary rights additionally include the means by which to enforce or waive the remedial entitlements, e.g., the right to secure a writ of execution. Others nonetheless argue that those enforcement mechanisms are better understood as (further) 'procedural' rights. For example, Hohfeld suggests that these constitute 'adjective' rights.[32] In turn, I suggest adopting the term 'quaternary rights'.

As shall be discussed in greater detail in Chapters 4 and 7, even on the PST distinction, rights enforcement is not restricted to secondary and tertiary rights. There are cases of being able to waive or extinguish an RCTD—which the philosophy of rights literature treats as modes of enforcement, for better or ill—even without (threatened) breach of correlative duty. The capacities to do so are either be considered to be features of the primary right itself, or as associated normative positions.

There are two kinds of critics of the PST distinction. The first holds that it misidentifies mere components of a single right complex as being distinct 'secondary' or 'tertiary' rights.[33] Instead of distinct rights, one and

[32] Hohfeld (1913b).

[33] Hart's 'later' model of a private law RCTD seems to waver on this point. For whilst he suggests that an RCTD can admit of 'fuller' or 'lesser' measures of control, he also notes that 'secondary' duties arise in other parties upon violation of their primary duties. Hart (1982: 183–4, 186). Other rights modellers who appear to reject the PST distinction include Kant (1996); Weinrib (1995).

the same right obtains throughout the entire enforcement process of ensuring duty compliance, of seeking a remedy for a breach of duty, etc. The second kind of critic believes that there are distinct, separate normative positions, but denies that secondary and tertiary rights constitute 'rights', regardless of legal and ordinary linguistic practices suggesting otherwise. The reason being that, unlike 'primary' ones, 'secondary' and 'tertiary rights' are really just powers (where, on this sort of critic's view, a power is not actually a kind of a right).[34]

PST distinction apologists disagree with the second kind of critic, but not necessarily with the first (strongly, at any rate). They, too, could conceivably just characterise the normative components within a unified right model as serving in different stages of the enforcement process of a given right. Proponents may also dispute amongst themselves whether duty violations necessarily give rise to, or are invariably associated with, secondary and/or tertiary rights. Some are happy to admit that not all primary rights give rise to secondary rights and that the latter can also be rendered 'ineffective'.

§ II.2. *Perimeters of Protection*

A second helpful concept for understanding how normative positions can interrelate is A PERIMETER OF PROTECTION. Before explicating it, though, note that normative positions can relate to one another in a variety of ways. Here is just a sampling. First, two positions may be connected if one entails a second's existence. For example, as it affects two or more parties' positions, there is no exercise of a power without other *pre-existing* or *resulting* rights and ligations also obtaining or being created.[35] *A*'s using a power to gift a watch to *B* concerns *A*'s RCTDs, duties, and liberties regarding that personal chattel (bestowing normative positions on *B*, divesting them from *A*). Powers are therefore logically related to (a not necessarily determinate set of) other positions. A second and third way of relating are correlativity and logically contradictory relationships. A fourth way is when two or more positions serve as components in a larger construct, e.g., a right complex.

[34] E.g., Kramer (1998: 13–4, 34).
[35] See Rainbolt (2006: 12–3).

A fifth way that normative positions can relate to one another is due to the overlapping application of various rules governing a given situation, transaction, or state of affairs. For example, RCTDs and duties often provide the exercise of a liberty with a modicum of protection. Your liberty to do something may be *indirectly* protected by someone else's duty not to otherwise interfere with you, which therefore helps to secure your so acting. (Despite this overlap, this neither entails that the liberties necessarily gain comprehensive protection nor that they are inviolable.) HLA Hart calls an RCTD's guardianship of the exercise of liberties 'perimeters of protection'.[36]

Hart's discussion of the matter arises in his explication of Jeremy Bentham's Vested/Naked distinction,[37] which concerns whether a given normative position benefits from a perimeter of protection or not. 'Vested' liberties are those that, however weakly, are directly or indirectly protected by at least one legal RCTD. For example, you have the liberties to eat or not eat, to stand or sit down, to go inside your house or to refrain from doing so. These liberties are protected because it is a legal offence for others to criminally or tortiously prevent you from so acting.[38] Hart deems protected cases to be 'liberty-*rights*'.[39]

Here is an example. Oxford law students have the legal liberty (not merely an institutional or moral one) to park their bicycles at the law faculty's bicycle lot. They are not guaranteed a spot, and it may be that on any given day a student cannot park there because the lot is full. Even so, the liberty to park there is protected by legal RCTDs against: a bicycle's wrongful removal; its theft; others trying to assault a student in order to lock their own bikes in a spot before the student can; etc.[40]

'Naked' liberties, by contrast, are not protected by any RCTDs.[41] Hart does not seem to deny their existence—or, at least their conceivability. He

[36] The idea has long been recognised. Hart asserts that Bentham presents it. Hart (1982: 171–3). See also Salmond (1902: 231–2); Hohfeld (1917: 748). As opposed to protecting the exercise of liberties, there can also be a relationship wherein a claim helps to protect a liberty's very obtaining, e.g., an RCTD correlating with another party's duty not to use his or her power to nullify the liberty in question.

[37] Hart (1982: 172–4). See also Appendix 1.

[38] Ibid 172–3.

[39] Ibid 171.

[40] This is a modified example adopted from Rainbolt (2006: 7), which quotes Carl Wellman, *Welfare Rights* (Rowman and Allenheld 1983) 8–9.

[41] Hart (1982: 172).

merely rejects the idea that they, unlike vested liberties, count as rights; neither lawyers nor anyone else, he suggests, would consider naked liberties to be 'rights' precisely because they are unprotected by RCTDs and correlative duties.[42]

Whether invariably obtaining in all normative domains or not,[43] the idea of a perimeter of protection raises the following question. Would it matter if all explanations of such perimeters are, and/or must be, content-dependent or circumstantial? For example, Bob has a legal right (liberty) to cross the street. He also has a legal right (an RCTD) against being assaulted. Hence, one may not impinge upon Bob's exercise of his right to cross the street *by* assaulting him. What does *that* RCTD have to do with the exercise of *that* liberty, though? In other words, just because the RCTD concerns a given person why believe that it must also apply to the use of his or her other normative positions?

The relationship between an RCTD and the exercise of a liberty does not seem to be one of logical entailment. The relationship arises simply by virtue of both positions being (contingent) members of the same normative system. Perimeters of protection, moreover, reflect an important feature of *legal* rights modelling: their concern for the aggregative effect of all legal materials (norms, rules, etc.) upon a particular relationship between parties, even if garnered from diverse areas of the system, e.g., from both tort and contract law.[44] The protection afforded to Bob's exercise of his liberty to cross the street by his RCTD against being assaulted arises given the totality of legal norms governing a particular person and situation. Further, Bob's ability or willingness to exercise his legal liberty to cross the street might be hindered or deterred if those sorts of RCTDs

[42] Ibid 173–4. For Hart, then, the set of liberties is larger than the set of all liberties that qualify as rights.

[43] Whilst Hart prefaces his discussion of perimeters of protection by stating that the exercise of all *legal* liberties is protected in some such fashion (Ibid 171), his account wavers over whether some such perimeters *perforce* obtain. He may simply have thought it to be the case that 'naked' legal liberties are a mere conceptual possibility, but which never obtain in any actual legal system. If so, it would be unfair to attribute to him an 'invariable protection' view of all legal RCTDs over the exercise of all legal liberties. For various reasons, though, certain scholars insist that such legal perimeters of protection do invariably obtain, i.e., that in any actual legal system, at least some RCTDs will partially protect (i.e., perhaps not comprehensively) the exercise of any liberty. E.g., Halpin (1997: 37–41); Kramer (1999: 316); Kramer (1998: 12 & n.3).

[44] See Halpin (1997: 39). Cf. Raz (2009b: 33).

did not also obtain or were legally ineffective. Whilst inessential to establishing the liberty's legal validity (i.e., its status as a bona fide normative position of the system), a right against being assaulted nevertheless seems to facilitate the liberty's effective utilisation.

§ III. Theories of Rights

In contrast to a model, a rights *theory* aims to provide the criteria for A RIGHT, or for some specified subset of rights. Each theory's criteria include: (I) an ***ultimate*** purpose all (designated) rights purportedly serve; (II) means of protecting or effectuating that purpose, e.g., by ***imposing*** duties on other parties, by ***including*** means of enforcement, etc.; and (III) specifying which types of normative positions (e.g., Hohfeldian claims, liberties, etc.) and which tokens of those types (e.g., what subset of Hohfeldian claims) qualify as rights—not all might.[45]

The first criterion is an ultimate purpose that all rights (or at least that subset of rights covered by a particular version of a theory) purportedly serve, their raison d'être. Rights are said to advance, protect, justify, promote, or serve some ultimate value or activity. Why an ***ultimate*** purpose? It could be said that both models and theories explain rights' purposes. For example, a power's purpose is to modify normative relationships; an immunity's purpose is to prevent changes to normative positions; etc. If, however, more than one of those types of positions count as rights, then what is their common purpose? If they are all kinds of rights, then what is it that they all do *qua* rights? This notion of an ***ultimate*** purpose shall be explained further in Chapter 5.

The theories of rights debate has carried on for a long time. Its dominant candidates are, and remain, the Interest and Will theories. The Interest theory holds that rights perforce advance, serve, or protect their holders' interests. The Will theory posits that rights necessarily protect their holders' wills and provide some modicum of control. The theories' rivalrous criteria are also used to determine which normative positions within an existing model actually count as rights and which do not.

To be clear , not all models are constructed by relying on such 'theoretical' criteria. Hohfeld's *schema* is an example. Indeed, his is often said to

[45] 'Tokens of a type' here simply means instances of a class.

be neutral between the Interest and Will theories.[46] Some theorists also employ Hohfeld's *schema* to help explain and advance their respective theoretical stances.[47] Let us style those models constructed without relying upon theories as 'theory-independent' ones.

By contrast, some theorists construct their own models instead of relying on existing ones. As they are influenced by their designers' 'theoretical' commitments, these will be styled 'theory-driven' models. (Additionally, there are theory-based interpretations of, and modifications made to, 'theory-independent' models. A theorist might start with a theory-independent model like Hohfeld's and then alter some of its components in order for it to better conform to his or her preferred 'theoretical' commitments, thereby producing a theory-driven iteration of the model.[48])

Many accounts of rights are composed of both a theory and model.[49] Whilst there are theory-independent models, all rights theorists either rely upon or create a model. Further, although any scholar's theory and theory-driven model are conceivably severable, it is possible that there could be information loss were this to be done. Specifically, the motivations behind positing a model's propositions (rather than understanding the propositions themselves) may be indiscernible without appreciating that its designer was heavily influenced by a particular theory of rights.

Whilst the theories offer rivalrous criteria for the concept, modellers, too, disagree about what makes something a right. Some rely on a theory to defend their typologies ('theory-driven' ones). Others do not ('theory-independent' ones, such as Hohfeld's). Either way, both rights modellers and theorists lack shared criteria and shared paradigms by which to assess

[46] E.g., Kramer (1998: 61); Halpin (2017: 19–22). 1998's *A Debate Over Rights* was the most extensive treatment to date of the theories till 2017's *New Essays on the Nature of Rights*. To date, there has been no extensive treatment of the various models. For some introductory treatments, see Simmonds (2013); Wenar (2020); Rainbolt (2006).

[47] Hohfeld himself probably had no such theory in mind when constructing his *schema*. But cf. Finnis (2011: 202–3, 465 n.32); Kramer (1998: 61 n.23, 62).

[48] To clarify, not all modifications made to models are based on 'theoretical' considerations. For example, as suggested above, there is an intra-Hohfeldian dispute about whether to use the label 'liberty' or 'privilege' for Hohfeld's basic position, or whether to treat these as being two different concepts and normative positions. This disagreement does not rest on the disputants' commitments to the theories of rights, if any.

[49] 'Account' will often be used throughout this book to refer to a model-theory combination.

each other's identifications. Are such 'theoretical' criteria indispensable starting points for understanding A RIGHT though? Chapter 6 will argue they are not. Indeed, the philosophy of rights would do well to leave these sorts of theories behind; and this book aims to show, by example, how the field can carry on just fine without them.

§ IV. Methodological Matters

The models and theories of rights' connections to the philosophy of law (and other areas of philosophy) have largely been neglected.[50] To make sense of what modellers and theorists aim to accomplish, and to ascertain if their work constitutes credible enterprises, therefore requires making a foray down the methodological rabbit hole. This will involve a brief exploration of philosophical views about concepts, conceptual clarifications, and the methods of producing philosophical explanations of concepts and things.

Whilst, amongst other things, philosophy aims to help us better understand concepts and the 'things' our concepts are concepts of (if of anything), there is obviously no established set of universally endorsed or preferred philosophical procedures. Consider even the above-mentioned notion of offering 'conceptual clarifications'. The techniques for generating them are not uniform.

One (set of) method(s) for their production is called conceptual analysis. This approach, which is of some provenance, retains a lingering appeal in legal philosophy, if not as much in other areas of philosophy.[51] On the assumption that concepts bear internal structures, a conceptual analysis explains a given concept in terms of its more basic components. The concept is decomposed into its constituent parts until one is left with more (if not irreducibly) basic concepts.[52] A conceptual analysis generally proceeds by trying to distinguish what is necessary to a concept from that which is

[50] Cf. Halpin (1997: 4).

[51] E.g., Huemer (2015: 52).

[52] In the words of its most famous contemporary apologist, 'conceptual analysis is the very business of addressing when and whether a story told in one vocabulary is made true by one told in some allegedly more fundamental vocabulary'. Jackson (2000: 28). Conceptual analyses are said to admit of immodest and modest versions. 'Immodest' analyses purport to be able to tell us something about the very things our concepts of. By contrast, 'modest' ones merely aim to elucidate a concept *qua* concept; it does not purport to describe 'the world' itself. Ibid 42. But see Leiter (2011: 512) on whether conceptual analyses of 'hermeneutic' concepts can yield knowledge about the world.

merely contingently associated with it. Being 'necessary' means that a given feature (i) is constitutive of the concept and (ii) is exemplified in every token of the type.[53] In other words, a necessary feature's failure to obtain in a given instance is deemed to be inconceivable.[54]

Whether for the sake of rendering a concept more perspicuous, or as part of an effort to promote its replacement with a 'more precise' one, conceptual analyses often levy definitions. Not only are there different kinds of definition, but some philosophers also claim to be able to define words, concepts, and things.[55] Many analytic philosophers—used to—strive to provide *philosophical* aka 'analytic' definitions.[56] These aim to provide a set of necessary and sufficient conditions for a concept, specifying its (as opposed to a word or term's) extension.[57]

The idea of providing conceptual analyses and analytic definitions rests upon several assumptions. Amongst them are these. First, that it is possible to 'capture precise, informative, tractably specifiable, noncircular necessary and sufficient conditions for the application of [concepts]'; second,

[53] This book will use 'essential' and 'necessary' interchangeably. Some scholars nevertheless treat essential properties as a subset of necessary ones: those which are specific or unique to a particular concept. E.g., Patterson (2012: 52 n.8). Historically, essential or accidental properties were predicated of things, not concepts. Bix (2003: 541 n.17).

[54] This is not to say that conceptual analysts assume that a concept, in contrast to one or more of its features, is itself indispensable. (For some legal philosophers' defences of the notion of continent-concepts-bearing-necessary-features, see, e.g., Bix (2003); Raz (2009a); Giudice (2015)). Furthermore, not all philosophical analyses aim to focus on, let alone capture, concepts' necessary features. Sometimes there is value in examining the contingent-yet-important features. E.g., Giudice (2011); Schauer (2012).

[55] E.g., Gupta (2015).

[56] In contrast to *analytic* definitions, philosophers also sometimes present stipulative and real definitions. *Stipulative* definitions are rules for the usage of a word or term, along the lines a definer will design. Stipulations ostensibly aim to help elucidate (by suggesting particular usages), rather than try to police word usage pe se. (Being concerned with word usage, moreover, such definitions need not aim to include all of the cognate concept's relevant features. E.g., Raz (2009b: 41). Space does not allow further elucidation here, but some philosophers also claim to present *real* definitions: definitions of 'things' (as opposed to words or concepts). E.g., Rosen (2015).

[57] See Laurence and Margolis (2019). For an excellent summary of the history of analytic definitions, see Baker and Hacker (2005: 201–8).

'that statements expressing these analyses are analytic truths'; and third that these analyses can be produced via a priori reflection.[58]

Philosophers test an analytic definition by subjecting it to actual or hypothetical cases to see if it can cover them.[59] Two or three kinds of cases can be employed to do the falsifying. First, imagine that a candidate analytic definition of X construes feature φ to be necessary to the concept. To test this, just present or imagine a plausible case of X that lacks phi. The counterexample's existence is taken to show that, *contra* the definition,

[58] Graham and Hogan (1998: 271–2). Do analytic definitions suffice for *identificatory* purposes, i.e., for locating instances of things that the concept represents? Some philosophers suggest as such. See, e.g., Putnam (1979: 67):

> Although sufficient conditions, necessary conditions, etc., are sometimes called 'criteria'... the sense of 'criterion' in which an analytic definition provides a criterion for something's being the sort of thing to which a term applies is a very strong one: (a) the 'criteria' I am speaking of are necessary *and* sufficient conditions of something's being an *A*; and (b) by means of them people *can and do determine* that something is an *A*.

[59] E.g., Daly (2010: 48–9); Jackson (2000: 28–9, 35–6). Philosophers often claim to use their intuitions to make these categorisation judgments. However, they disagree about what they mean by 'intuitions'. It is also unclear whether intuitions are even reliable tools. See, e.g., *Rethinking Intuition* (1998); Jenkins (2014: 92–7). Additionally, quite a few philosophers treat 'ordinary' or 'folk' linguistic usages, patterns, or understandings as the data to be employed in such analyses—at least for certain sorts of concepts. Jackson (2000). For example, HLA Hart ostensibly does so when inquiring into what any educated person would be able to identify vis-à-vis the salient features of legal systems. Hart (1994: 3, 240). Sometimes, though, the data is restricted to technical discourses, e.g., lawyers' talk for the purposes of a legal theory. Philosophers then 'test' their intuitions about cases using this linguistic data.

A famous legal philosophical example is Joseph Raz's Community of Angels case. He suggests that angels would need laws to coordinate and structure their social order. Being highly virtuous, though, their legal system would not require (the utilisation of) coercive measures in order to establish conformity with given laws or for the system as a whole to be effective. Raz (1999: 156–61). This *seems* to be a case of law without coercion. Coercion, Raz concludes, is therefore not a necessary feature of 'our' concept, LAW. Conceptually, coercion is only contingently related, even if it is present in all *human* legal systems. Raz's argument reflects his judgment that the example constitutes a bona fide case of a legal system (albeit a hypothetical one), and not of something else. Others disagree, and thus deny that the angels case constitutes a bona fide counterexample to the view that law is necessarily coercive. E.g., Himma (2001: 308). In the Christian narrative, I would add, God punished Satan by expelling him from Heaven. So, depending upon your conception of AN ANGEL, there might still be the need to exercise coercive liability for rule violation in the angel case anyway.

feature φ is not *necessary* to the concept after all. Alternatively, present a case that is *not* thought to be an example of *X*, but which nevertheless satisfies the analytic definition's conditions. This kind of counterexample is taken to show that the definition's features are *insufficient* for *X*.

However, analyses and conceptual clarifications need not always involve levying analytic definitions in efforts to capture concepts' necessary and sufficient conditions. One alternative approach is via (soft) methodological naturalism. This calls for philosophers to employ or emulate the methods of the hard and social sciences.[60] Another alternative method, suggested by John Finnis, involves utilising central cases, selecting the appropriate point of view from which to adjudge matters (i.e., the appropriate sort of person's internal point of view), and utilising a teleological understanding of the 'objects' of inquiry. Throughout, a scholar's 'normative' (i.e., morally or politically evaluative) judgments drive the process, i.e., determining which constitute the 'central' cases, the most apt point of view, the true teleology, etc.[61] Neither of these alternative approaches must lead to clarifications presenting a concept's putative necessary and sufficient conditions.

Additionally, some philosophers follow Wittgenstein in rejecting the idea that some or all concepts even possess necessary features. That is to say, they deny that the various things falling under a given concept must exhibit some common feature or group of features, which obtain in every token of the type. Instead, those various things relate to each other in diverse, overlapping ways. A concept presents 'a complicated network of similarities overlapping and criss-crossing',[62] where there is 'no one thing in common in virtue of which we use the same word for all—but there are many different kinds of *affinity*...[63] This is called a *family resemblance* concept. For just as members of a biological family can exhibit shared physical characteristics, (e.g., certain members having the same nose shape, the same eyebrows, etc.) without there being one that is common to the entire

[60] Leiter (2017). This method comes with two caveats. First, some modicum of conceptual analysis *may* be necessary to get a naturalised jurisprudential inquiry off the ground. E.g., Leiter (2007: 65). See *supra* note 52 for the second caveat: the potential value of conceptually analysing 'hermeneutic' concepts.

[61] Finnis (2011: 14–9, 426, 434 n.14). On the use of central cases seemingly without relying upon morally or politically evaluative judgments to drive the process, see, e.g., Hart (1994).

[62] Wittgenstein (2009: § 66 pg 36^{e}).

[63] Ibid § 65 pg 35^{e}.

family (e.g., everyone having the same eye colour), so too the things falling under a given concept may exhibit overlapping features without there being features that are common to all of them.[64]

Wittgenstein's famous example of a family resemblance concept is that of GAME (and thus the multifarious things we call games).[65] Here is a legal example, though. Hohfeld claimed to have identified four conceptually basic types of rights. Many have since asked, what makes these all types or examples of 'the' concept, A RIGHT? Is it that they are all entitlements? That they are all normative advantages? Do they all protect the right-holder's will or interests? *If* A RIGHT is a family resemblance concept, then there simply is no common necessary feature that all rights exhibit. Instead, they are just related to one another in distinct, overlapping ways.

To the best of my knowledge, although some legal philosophers express fidelity to Wittgenstein, no rights modeller or theorist adopts this view of A RIGHT. (Moreover, it would probably only be available to modellers, not theorists; for, whether they be normative or analytic,[66] rights theorists offer necessary conditions for the concept.[67]) Even if they are not Wittgensteinians, it is nevertheless worth bearing in mind that rights

[64] Ibid § 67 pg 36–7ᵉ. Wittgenstein also analogises the extension of a concept to the spinning of a thread by twisting different fibres. 'And the strength of the thread resides not in the fact that some one fibre runs through its whole, but in the overlapping of many fibres'. Ibid § 67 pg 36ᵉ.

[65] Ibid §§ 69–71 pg 37–8ᵉ.

[66] There are both analytic and normative theories in legal philosophy. Roughly speaking, *Analytic* theories aim to provide morally and politically neutral explanations of a legal concept or legal 'phenomenon'. *Normative* theories are morally or politically evaluative accounts of what those concepts or 'things' ought to be. On analytic and normative versions of the theories of rights, see Chapter 5 § II.

[67] Some Hohfeldians would insist that, because Hohfeld thought you must understand each of his eight basic conceptions via its specific correlative and 'opposite' (logical contradictory), it would be impossible to understand his four basic kinds of rights solely in terms of family resemblance. For example, to understand a claim as a being owed a duty and a 'no-right' (the absence of a claim), which correlates with a liberty (the absence of a duty) *entails* that the relationship between claims and liberties is something more than mere family resemblance. The same can be said for the relationship between powers and immunities. However, this still does not explain the relationship between claims and powers (on the one hand, and thus between liberties and immunities on the other). *That* relationship, a claim and power both being 'rights', could, at least conceivably, be deemed due to A RIGHT's simply being a family resemblance concept.

modellers can be agnostic about whether A RIGHT bears necessary and sufficient conditions. For example, Hohfeld never offered these.

There are more ways to understand and explain concepts than as bearing necessary and sufficient features (and so are subject to analytic definitions) or as family resemblances. An alternative, or supplementary, basis is the central case method (aka the paradigm case or focal case method) mentioned above.

> A central case analysis of some phenomenon identifies some subset of possible or actual instances of that phenomenon as explanatorily privileged. The members of this subset are the paradigm or *central cases* of the phenomenon, and they are privileged in two respects. First, the central cases are privileged insofar as a theory of the phenomenon is primarily concerned with explaining the important features of these cases. Second, the central cases are explanatorily prior to those instances of the phenomenon that are not members of the set of central cases. These are the peripheral cases of the phenomenon, and they are explanatorily posterior in that they can only be understood as defective, failed, or "watered-down"... versions of the central cases.[68]

I have argued elsewhere that philosophers actually use central cases in at least two ways.[69] The first is well known. It is as a tool to explain other cases (and the things of which they are cases) and as a basis for determining whether a candidate case really is a genuine token of the type in the first place. A second usage, though, is this: deeming the case to be part of an adequacy condition for a theory. In being treated as an incontestably genuine token of type *X*, the central case's being covered by (explained by) a theory of *X* is deemed to be a *sine qua non* for any viable candidate theory of *X*. Thus, a given theory of *X*'s inability to cover that case is a ground for adjudging it to be a failure, and not merely deficient in some way (unlike, perhaps, 'peripheral' cases of *X*, which might also be served up as counterexamples to that theory of *X*). Both analytic and normative legal philosophers employ the central case method in these two ways—often in conjunction with other methods, and generally without affording much consideration to whether all of their methods are compatible or not.

[68] Langlinais and Leiter (2016: 682), discussing Finnis (2011: 11).
[69] Frydrych (2017a: 49–53).

Like a family resemblance concept, a central case is not, or at least need not be 'essentialist': it need not be said to be composed of necessary properties.[70] A central case contains important features, but not all must obtain in every instance of *X*. For example, Anthony Honoré presents 'the' central case of ownership in a modern 'liberal' legal system. The case includes eleven standard incidents.[71] However, it is debatable whether all eleven must obtain in every instance of (full) ownership within a liberal legal order.

The selection method, or criteria for selection and designation of a candidate as a 'central' case, is an undeveloped methodological issue. Indeed, there seems to be no 'shared paradigm', in the Kuhnian sense, for case selection. Philosophers may at least be becoming more aware of the extent to which the selection and employment of such cases is reliant on—methodologically suspect—'intuition pumping'. *Normative* legal philosophers may be unperturbed by this, however. For example, John Finnis believes that, when legal theorising, the selection process for central cases is a predominantly normative affair.[72]

Another methodological issue which arises in the contexts of assessing analytic definitions and the use of central cases is this. What does the presentation of a genuine counterexample accomplish? Does it show that a theory or definition is:

[70] E.g., Stich (1998: 104); Ramsey (1998: 168–72). Some socio-legal pluralists nevertheless reject the central case method, claiming that it is essentialist after all. E.g., Tamanaha (2001: 149–51). Presumably, they believe that the most important features of a central case are essential to it. However, it is unclear that this *must* be so. (Even so, it does raise the question of whether, if true, this renders the method redundant insofar as conceptual analysts are concerned).

At any rate, Wittgenstein's family resemblance concept may also be distinguishable from Aristotle's focal meaning on the grounds that, whilst the former includes 'paradigms' (tied together by a 'similarity rider') by which we compare to peripheral cases, it has 'no *single* centre of variation', as a focal case does. Baker and Hacker (2005: 215).

[71] Honoré's standard incidents of ownership are: (1) a right to possess; (2) a right to use; (3) a right to manage; (4) a right to the income of the thing; (5) a right to the capital; (6) a right to security; (7) an incident of transmissibility; (8) an incident of absence of term; (9) a duty [to prevent] harm; (10) a liability to execution; 11, an incident of residuarity. Honoré (1961).

[72] Meeting with John Finnis, Emeritus Professor, University of Oxford Faculty of Law (Oxford UK, February 12, 2014). See also Finnis (2011: 418, 429–31).

A. wholly mistaken;
B. under-inclusive but salvageable; or
C. that it faces a pro tanto challenge but is otherwise unaffected?

When does a counterexample constitute a mere exception to a theory, when does it suffice to falsify the theory, and when is it simply not impactful?[73] Further, if more than one counterexample is required for falsification, then how many are needed? What is the threshold? (And by what criteria was *that* determined?) Philosophers, and perhaps everyone else, appear to lack a shared paradigm governing a counterexample's effect. Some scholars believe that counterexamples can be used to examine a concept's extension and can serve as (at least prima facie) reasons for disbelieving claims about certain features being 'necessary' to a concept. They take either single counterexample, or some—unspecified—number of them, to be sufficient grounds to falsify a theory, an analytic definition, an account of a concept, or a proposition. Other philosophers treat counterexamples differently. They either (a) propose 'error' theories instead; (b) believe that counterexamples merely circumscribe or delimit a theory (or constitute exceptions to it); or (c) are not bothered by such cases at all.[74]

Importantly for this book's purposes, scholars lack a shared paradigm within and by which to weigh rights 'theories' respective faults and virtues. Furthermore, as shall be discussed in Chapter 5, many scholars remain stalwart defenders of their theories even in the face of putative counterexamples, ones which they themselves nonetheless consider—correctly or otherwise—to be bona fide cases.

In a similar vein, some analytic philosophers tend to appeal in vain to certain metatheoretical desiderata—e.g., consilience, extensional adequacy, simplicity, conservativism, etc.—as tools for assessing and comparing jurisprudential theories.[75] How a *legal* theory can be shown to *meet* any of the desiderata is nevertheless left unexplained. (In other words, there is no shared paradigm governing which metatheoretical desiderata even count, what their respective weights are, or how to establish that a

[73] It is at least conceivable that some putative counterexamples to a theory of *X* could be rejected as spurious by deeming them to constitute 'peripheral' or 'degenerate' cases of *X* instead.

[74] Brian Weatherson believes that the effects of a given counterexample are treated differently in the various branches of philosophy (but seems to believe there is a correct answer to this methodological matter, at least in the field of epistemology). Weatherson (2003: 1–2, 8).

[75] E.g., Dickson (2001: 32–3); Leiter (2009: 1239); Sumner (1987: 49–50, 96–7).

candidate theory better meets them than does its rivals.) For it is uncertain: what weight to affix to each desideratum in order to show which matters are of greater concern when comparing two or more theories; how to apply the desiderata; how to prove that theory *A better* meets a given desideratum than theory *B* does. The problem is not just being unable to show whether theory *A* or theory *B* better meets desideratum φ. Even if could be credibly established that *A* better meets φ than does *B*, if *B* better meets desideratum ψ than *A* does, then which of the two desiderata is weightier for the overall comparative evaluation, φ or ψ? This is not to insist upon the impossibility of settling such matters; it is merely to note that such efforts have not even been attempted. It also raises the fact that the entire process of theorisation involves a great many more judgment calls than could easily be enumerated here.[76]

Moreover, whatever their view of concepts, many philosophers believe themselves to be adept at conceptual clarification (by whichever of their preferred methods). An under-discussed concern is nonetheless whether attempts to recraft concepts are even worthwhile—especially if the reformed product does not track the usual ways people employ the unreconstructed concept. It is also possible that adopting conceptual clarifications for usage in social scientific research projects may deleteriously affect what researchers actually get out of their enquiries.[77] For example, some Hohfeldians

[76] As Andrew Halpin puts it:

> [I]n too many ways the judgment of the theorist rather than the imperative of methodology will be a determining factor, in shaping what feature of the subject matter is regarded as worthy of theoretical inquiry, or in shaping the theoretical construct that is regarded as offering greatest illumination on the subject matter as the theorist perceives it. Even at the low level methodology of metatheoretical precepts there remains room for the theorist's judgment to influence the impact those precepts will have upon the construction of theory. And in recognizing technical semantic or philosophically sophisticated analytical approaches, the pervasive influence of the theorist's judgment is still to be found: in selecting a particular type of semantics; or in discerning an essential property and elaborating its quality in the tension between its recognition and the basis for its selection. Even where the apparent strictures of methodology are the strongest, in directing the theorist to one side or another of the normative/descriptive divide, we have seen that the particular position adopted here is influenced by the choice of the theorist over how to focus on the subject matter of the theory. Halpin (2010: 617)

[77] See, e.g., Leiter (2011: 516).

favour restricting A RIGHT to just a Hohfeldian claim.[78] However, as they admit that A CLAIM is itself a clarification or 'correction' to lawyerly (if not also ordinary) discourse, why believe that we can get to the truth about rights by restricting our focus to Hohfeld's conception?

On the other hand, bald faith in empirical work is no escape from the difficulties regarding how best to determine what a concept is, let alone if and how it should be clarified. Additionally, if (at least some) counterexamples do not suffice to distinguish what is necessary to a concept from that which is merely contingently associated with it, yet legal philosophers continue to present concepts (of LAW or A RIGHT, say) containing only those purportedly necessary features, might the theories not just be distortions as well?[79]

This book is not the place to resolve long-standing debates over A CONCEPT (e.g., whether (all) concepts admit of necessary features and what the means of their discernment are) and regarding the rivalrous techniques for philosophising. Still, it is worthwhile to put one's methodological cards on the table.

To that end, doubts about the viability of conceptual analysis and analytic definitions are nothing new.[80] Although Chapter 6 will argue against the very enterprise of rights theorisation (as opposed to modelling), it will not simply rely on those fairly standard general critiques; for there are more particular reasons to be incredulous of rights theories—including those proffered by normative theorists (who generally eschew analytic definitions). However, it does not follow that all conceptual clarifications must follow that route, or even endeavour to provide a concept's necessary features. Rights models need not. Again, Hohfeld's *schema* is an example of that.

An additional methodological issue warrants mention here. A staple dispute amongst legal philosophers is whether they must make normative—once more, in the sense of being morally or politically evaluative—judgments when (re-)forming (clarifying) or selecting concepts. Is it possible to describe or interpret the concept *X* without engaging in normative judgments about (i) what *X* is, or (ii) its value, worth,

[78] Kramer & Steiner (2007: 295–9).

[79] For example, could critics of Raz's conception of LAW not argue that it is in part the product of his 'community of angels' hypothetical (which aims to function as a counterexample to the proposition that law perforce includes, and must deploy, coercive sanctions)?

[80] See, e.g., Frydrych (2017a: 59–62).

or goodness? What about for legal concepts? What about for A RIGHT, which is not exclusively a legal concept?

No legal philosopher believes that data can just be identified and described 'as is'. Each must judge what count as such and how to interpret them. Now, contemporary Legal Positivists come closest to the 'as is' view. However, some of them claim only to defend the following proposition: 'the existence and content of law depends on social facts and not on its merits'.[81] This is false to the extent that, generally, Positivists are *additionally* committed to the idea that one can come to know, analyse, and present accounts of the features of a legal system (and of legal concepts) without having to (first) adjudge them to be morally or politically good or bad, valuable or valueless.

Pace Positivists, 'Normativist' legal philosophers, i.e., Interpretivists and Natural lawyers, seemingly believe that it is impossible to know what a legal concept or institution is without making 'normative' judgments about what it is. These include assessments of *X*'s point or purpose. To their minds, every concept that can serve as the subject of a legal theory is inseparably entwined with, and shaped by, evaluative features and judgments about its 'nature'. Hence, the process of determining (and clarifying) a concept's content and contours is an inherently moral/political enterprise.[82] The challenge Normativists pose to Legal Positivists is whether concepts can really either be selected or clarified/reformed without making morally or politically charged evaluations. The debate over this issue has dominated analytic legal philosophy for over forty years (at least).

[81] L. Green & Adams (2019). See also Gardner (2012: 33). Contemporary Legal Positivism posits the existence of a rule of recognition: (a) master *social* rule(s), held by officials, which contain overarching criteria for determining whether something counts as a valid legal norm of their legal system. E.g., Hart (1994: 94–5, 292–3). However, they divide over what may form the content of the master rule(s). *Exclusive* Positivists insist that a rule of recognition can never include moral criteria. E.g., Raz (2009b: 47–8); Raz (1996: Chapter 10); Gardner (2012: Chapter 2). *Inclusive* Positivists, by contrast, believe that the master social rule(s) can, but need not, include moral criteria. E.g., Hart (1994: Postscript).

[82] Normativists nonetheless disagree about why this must be so. Interpretivists rely upon Ronald Dworkin's method of 'Constructive Interpretation': provide an account of *X* that fits most of the facts of a practice and that shows it in its best light vis-à-vis its point or purpose. Dworkin (1986: 47–53, 65–8, 90). On Interpretivism as a methodology and theory of law more generally, see Stavropolous (2021). By contrast, Natural Lawyers generally present teleological accounts that rely upon the central case method. See Finnis (2011: Chapter 1, Postscript).

This book generally adopts a Legal Positivist stance. Your author believes there are generally no compelling reasons to adopt Normativists' respective methodological approaches.[83] In the context of rights modelling and theorisation, a simple defence of this position is this: Normativists' methodologies, which they hold out as being indispensable for theorising about LAW, have gone unutilised in, and are unnecessary for, *their own accounts* of A RIGHT. This is not simply a case of their merely failing to comply with their own stated methods. There is simply no need for them to do so here.

For example, John Finnis, Natural Law theory's leading present-day proponent, does not employ its methods when either endorsing Hohfeld's *schema* or advancing his version of the Interest theory of rights.[84] Nor does any other Natural lawyer, so far as I am aware. Moreover, you do not need the central case method (let alone the putative central case of the internal point of view: the *spoudaios*)[85] to either distinguish between liberties, RCTDs, and powers, or to ascertain whether or not rights perforce afford control (Will theory) or protect interests (Interest theory). Whilst that method could be used to distinguish certain interests from others as being more worthy of rights protection than others, it will not help you to determine whether the 'paradigmatic' legal right is enforceable in some way or not.[86] (For further discussion, see Chapter 6 § III.)

In turn, despite his famous arguments about (certain) rights being trumps and the need to take them 'seriously',[87] Ronald Dworkin, the father of Interpretivism, generally eschewed both models and theories of

[83] Frydrych (2017a: 65–7).

[84] See Chapter 6 notes 92–4 and the accompanying text on Finnis on theorisation. In is most important work on the topic, *Natural Law and Natural Rights*, he claims it is not even necessary to resolve the theories of rights debate, at least as regarding strictly legal rights at any rate. Finnis (2011: 205). On the supposed need to nonetheless employ natural law's methods when theorising about law and rights, see also ibid 417, 428–31, 434–5, 437.

[85] See Finnis (2011: 14–9, 431, 437); Frydrych (2017a: 64, 67).

[86] In his postscript to *Natural Law and Natural Rights*, Finnis implies that Hohfeld's claim is the paradigmatic case of a right *vis-à-vis* Hohfeld's four basic kinds. Finnis (2011: 423). However, he does not explain the basis for his selection (even if it is based upon some value judgment or other) and is silent as to whether the paradigmatic Hohfeldian claim is *enforceable* or not. As Chapter 8 shows, it would nevertheless be odd if the paradigm of a claim were unenforceable, as even quite a few Interest theorists (and others) believe there to be something defective about unenforceable cases.

[87] Dworkin (1977).

rights.[88] His methodology, Constructive Interpretation, is unneeded for modelling at any rate; it is unnecessary for distinguishing amongst the basic types of rights (or determining whether there is indeed more than one type), for showing how they relate to other normative positions, etc.[89]

§ V. Outline

This book aims to advance the philosophy of rights. Chapter 2 defends the idea that the term 'a right' refers to different basic concepts. It does so by showing that the bases for monistic models (those positing there to be only one kind of a right) are unmotivated or unsound—based upon Monists' own methodological commitments. However, certain pluralistic models are shown to be over-inclusive for treating 'ligations' as (the cores of) rights.

Chapter 3 addresses RIGHTS CORRELATIVITY. Modellers' and theorists' views of correlativity colour their entire projects. Three implicit debates about the concept(s) in the philosophy of rights will be explicated, along with how some of these issues impact interpretations of the most famous conception of the kind of a right which correlates with a duty. Chapter 4 then provides working conceptions of RIGHTS EXERCISE, ENFORCEMENT, REMEDYING, and VINDICATION. This involves showing how various normative positions may relate and interact. It shall be argued that rights enforcement constitutes a subset of modes of rights exercise, and that not all rights vindication concerns remedy procurement. These clarifications aim to open the literature's horizons to many more aspects of rights and their usage. They are also important because much of the theories of rights debate hinges on rights enforcement. The chapter additionally explores rights claiming and its relationship to rights exercise and enforcement.

Chapter 5 more fully explicates the theories. It will show how characterisations of the debate has gone awry in several ways of late and why existing so-called hybrid and alternative theories are no such things.

[88] For his few remarks on the models and theories, see Dworkin's replies in Cohen (1983). Pavlos Eleftheriadis, a Hohfeldian Will theorist and Interpretivist, who denies that Hohfeld's *schema* is really about rights and instead concerns (downstream) 'legal relations' (See Chapter 3 note 32), also does not utilise constructive interpretation when endorsing or presenting Hohfeld.

[89] It is also doubtful that a moral or political evaluation, the internal point of view of the *spoudaios*, or a constructive interpretation, is required to assess whether or not A DUTY is, or contains, a second-order exclusionary reason, as Joseph Raz suggests. See Raz (1999: 58–9).

Chapter 6 then argues that the very debate ought to be abandoned: any such 'theoretical criteria' for A RIGHT (or even just some subset of rights) are of questionable construction and are superfluous anyway.

Chapter 7 further analyses RIGHTS ENFORCEMENT. Enforcement involves many more features than previous accounts suggest. It also advances the literature beyond the theories of rights to tackle the issue of whether legal rights are invariably enforceable. Chapter 8 nonetheless shows why unenforceable rights constitute 'imperfect' cases. Chapter 10 continues in this vein, demonstrating why 'uninvocable' or 'unclaimable' legal rights are also imperfect.

In between, Chapter 9 argues that there are ways to enforce legal rights other than by simply utilising third-party dispute resolution mechanisms or institutional bodies such as courts. There are ways to lawfully claim or invoke rights in private or social circumstances, ones that are best understood as the use of legal *liberties* (rather than *powers*) in support of legal RCTDs. This analysis also helps show why there is actually a greater array of means by which to 'support' or 'control' a legal right than just by using enforcement and waiver powers.

CHAPTER 2

Rights Modelling

§ I. Introduction

Philosophers and jurists try to make sense of rights by constructing models and theories of them. Models can be divided into monistic and pluralistic varieties. Pluralist modellers believe the different senses of *the term* 'a right' found in ordinary and technical discourses reflect the existence of different *concepts* of A RIGHT and distinct basic kinds of normative positions. By contrast, Monists either believe that there really is only one basic kind of a right, or that the term 'a right' ought to be reserved for just one basic type of normative position.

This chapter argues that Monistic models (those positing only a single basic type of a right) are under-inclusive. They wrongly exclude, and cannot explain, relevant data, i.e., ordinary and legal linguistic practices. Monistic modellers will herein be criticised on their own terms—particularly, their assumptions and methodological commitments—by showing why their delimitation efforts are unmotivated and unsound. The chapter also impugns Monists' stated desiderata or bases for nonetheless circumscribing 'a right' to just one basic kind of normative position. (In doing so, the chapter does not necessarily defend a particular pluralistic model (one presenting multiple basic types of rights); demonstrate how many

D. Frydrych, *The Architecture of Rights*,
https://doi.org/10.1007/978-3-030-76039-7_2

different basic types of rights there are; or champion particular conceptions of those basic normative positions.[1])

Whilst Monists provide under-inclusive models, certain pluralistic models are over-inclusive: those that count duties, liabilities, and/or comparable positions as (the cores of) rights. This chapter argues that advocates cannot square A LIGATION-RIGHT with their own stated methodological commitments and theories of rights.

§ II. Modelling

Rights models can be divided into monistic and pluralistic varieties. Wayne Sumner provides a helpful typology of how models differ in this regard.

> Here we can broadly distinguish two hypotheses. [I] One is that rights are simple, thus that every right consists of just one position. [II] The other is that rights are complex, thus that every right consists of some bundle of different positions. [III] These two hypotheses do not exhaust the possibilities; some rights might be simple while others are complex. Further, we can easily distinguish between monistic and pluralistic versions of each hypothesis. **[Ia]** A monistic version of the first hypothesis would hold that every right consists in the same normative position, while **[Ib]** a pluralistic version would allow different rights to consist of different positions (though only one in each case). Likewise, **[IIa]** a monistic version of the second hypothesis would hold that every right consists of the same bundle of positions, while **[IIb]** a pluralistic version would allow different rights to consist of different bundles.[2]

Let us use various interpretations of Wesley Hohfeld's model to flesh out Sumner's typology. (Presenting some intra-Hohfeldian disagreements also helps to show how diverse scholarly views about a given model can be.) Matthew Kramer posits that only Hohfeld's claim is really 'a legal right'. Liberties, powers, and immunities are not, even though ordinary

[1] A positive defence of pluralistic modelling is nonetheless feasible. For example, it seems perfectly reasonable to believe that the phrase 'a right to do' (e.g., a right to speak) reflects one or more additional basic kinds of rights, and that, in law, the normative abilities to buy and sell property, and to solicit people to enter into contracts, constitute bona fide examples of legal rights. Such rights cannot simply be identified with RCTDs—at least if the latter are understood as being 'passive' normative positions. Monistic models are therefore explanatorily inadequate for excluding these cases.

[2] Sumner (1987: 32–3, numbering added).

and legal parlance suggests otherwise. As shall be discussed in greater detail below, talking about legal rights as entitlements *to do* things is therefore erroneous and unhelpful.[3] Kramer thus represents view **Ia**: a monistic view (only singular claims are rights) where a right is simple (as opposed to being 'a complex': a unified normative construct composed of various instances of the Hohfeld's basic kinds).

Carl Wellman represents view **IIb**. He believes that all rights are complexes.[4] Hence, a singular claim, liberty, power, or immunity is not a basic right; each such normative position either just serves as a component within a right, or is simply an independent, non-right position.

George Rainbolt's stance represents view **III**: a pluralistic model allowing for rights to be either single positions or complexes. Rainbolt believes that, whilst Hohfeld's basic positions can serve as components of a complex, two of them—namely, a claim and an immunity—also count as rights in their own right.[5] To provide an example of view III which Rainbolt would nevertheless disapprove of, a liberty can serve as part of a complex, such as the right (liberty) to enter your own land, which is but one part of your property right complex. A liberty can also be a right on its own, e.g., the right to pick up abandoned money off of the street.[6]

§ III. Under-Inclusivity: Monistic Modelling

Monists' reasons for restricting rights to just one type are mistaken and their methodological priorities are skewed. This section's purpose is not to defend any given conception of the various normative positions.[7] It is merely to defend the idea that there is more than one basic type of a right. Particularly, a right-correlative-to-a-duty ('an RCTD') is not the only one.

[3] Kramer (1998: 13–4); Kramer & Steiner (2007: 295–9).

[4] E.g., Wellman (1985: 59–60, 80, 92); Wellman (1995: 7–8).

[5] Specifically, Rainbolt believes that claims and immunities are rights, whilst powers and liberties are not. He also thinks there are many kinds of rights complexes, including power-rights and liberty-rights, but only so long as a claim and/or immunity is a component in each one. Rainbolt (2006: xi–xii, 30–9).

[6] Again, Rainbolt denies that singular liberties count as rights.

[7] Much ink has been spilled trying to show errors in the Hohfeldian conceptions of A LIBERTY, A POWER, etc. Even granting that such arguments evidence certain difficulties for Hohfeldians, they do not *ipso facto* also constitute good arguments against any and all conceptions of those normative positions, or in favour of the view that liberties, powers, etc., do not count as distinct kinds of rights.

Now, you might be tempted to call the following endeavour mere 'intuition pumping'. If your intuitions suggest otherwise, then we may be at an impasse. However, Monists themselves do not oppose rights pluralism based on mere intuitions or their understandings of ordinary or technical (e.g., legal) linguistic practices. Instead, their stance is predicated upon various methodological assumptions or preferences, which will be elucidated below. Rather than a mere clash of intuitions, there is therefore real room for debate here about how many basic kinds of rights obtain.

Tony Honoré: Rights Are Not Claims, Powers, or Liberties

Anthony Honoré levies a series of arguments against Hohfeld's *schema*.[8] One of them offers a reason against identifying claims, liberties, or powers as rights and for instead thinking there is only one basic type. 'Ordinary legal usage certainly does treat a right as something different from a claim, power, liberty, etc. or even some aggregate of these'.[9] Rights are instead, he thinks, 'protected' by certain claims. The right is what unifies the various claims (it antedates some of them, and often outlives some too) and 'give[s] rise to' certain liberties.[10] For example, if *A* has a right to £100 from *B*, *B* might transfer that debt to *C* (who now owes £100 to *A*). *A*'s right was protected by a claim against *B*, but, post-transfer, the right survives and can be protected by a new claim to the money held against *C*.

Unfortunately, Honoré has been misled by Hohfeld's (and others') confusing and self-contradictory remarks about A CLAIM. For there are good reasons to think it denotes a 'passive' normative position.[11] In other words, you do not *make* claims using Hohfeldian claims. They simply mark you as the intended recipient of another party's (a duty-bearer's) required action or forbearance. Even if one were to adopt the rival 'active' interpretation of claims, though, Honoré has not shown why they—let alone liberties or powers—fail to constitute different kinds of rights, be they non-*stricto sensu* cases or otherwise.

[8] Honoré (1960: 456).

[9] Ibid. Cf. White (1982a: 323–36).

[10] Honoré (1960: 457).

[11] For further explanation of the active/passive distinction and of Hohfeld's A CLAIM, see Chapter 3 § III.

Joseph Raz: 'Rights to do' are Really Just Rights Against Interference

Joseph Raz characterises his account of rights (a model plus a theory) as a 'partisan' one based on moral, political, and legal philosophical discourse, and not as an analysis of legal practice or ordinary usage.[12] He nevertheless offers an analytic definition of A RIGHT,[13] according to which a right is a weighty interest-reason that, perhaps in combination with additional interests, suffices to ground duties in other people.[14]

Raz only briefly touches upon liberty-rights and rights exercise. Reconciling his various remarks on the topic nevertheless suggests that he

[12] Raz (1986: 165–6, certain internal citations embedded into the quote):

> [A] philosophical definition of 'a right', like those of coercion, authority, and many other terms, is not an explanation of the ordinary meaning of a term. It follows the usage of writers on law, politics and morality who typically use the term to refer to a subclass of all the cases to which it can be applied with linguistic propriety. Philosophical definitions of rights attempt to capture the way the term is used in legal, political and moral writing and discourse. (I refer of course to what philosophers commonly do, whether they know it or not. I do not wish to deny that some understand their enterprise in other ways). They both explain the existing tradition of moral and political debate and declare the author's intention of carrying on the debate within the boundaries of that tradition. At the same time, they further that debate by singling out certain features, as traditionally understood, for special attention, on the grounds that they are the features which best explain the role of rights in moral, political, and legal discourse. It follows that while a philosophical definition may well be based on a particular moral or political theory (the theory dictates which features of rights, traditionally understood, best explain their role in political, legal and moral discourse), it should not make that theory the only one which recognizes rights. To do so is to try to win by verbal legislation.

These remarks cannot be squared with Raz's presentation elsewhere of legal officials' reasoning processes using rights. Raz (1996: See especially Chapter 12). He also does not even adhere to his own stated methodology: his most important writings on rights are devoid of citations to moral, political, and legal philosophical works, let alone citations to legal texts. Ibid; Raz (1986: Chapter 7). Even if he had complied, why should moral and political philosophical conceptions predominate over examples of rights found in legal practice? What is the point of modelling rights and theorising about them if not to help explain real-world legal, moral, and institutional practices, and lay linguistic usages and practices? Why do those data/*explananda* not take priority over, say, a possibly obscure and possibly misguided moral philosopher from 1850?

[13] For Raz's analytic definition and further discussion thereof, see Chapter 5 note 33 and the accompanying text.

[14] Raz (1986: 166); Raz (1996: 254).

does not really believe there to be 'rights' to do, e.g., liberty-rights, after all. Such cases are instead to be explained thus: the real right is the reason for other parties' non-interference (i.e., it is an RCTD), whilst the liberty to act (which is not a right) is merely the right-against-interference's referent.

> The issue of so-called liberty rights is a complex one… The absence of duty does not amount to a right. A person who says to another 'I have a right to do it' is not saying that he has no duty not to or that it is not wrong to do it. He is claiming that the other has a duty not to interfere'… [a] right to *x* is not the same as to have no duty to *x* or not to *x*.[15]

Raz's point is not merely directed against a certain conception of A LIBERTY. For example, some scholars attack the Hohfeldian conception for being (a) the mere absence of a duty and/or (b) an unenforceable position. For them, a genuine liberty must instead be an express permission (as opposed to the mere absence of a duty), or it must (also) always be protected by another position, e.g., a Hohfeldian claim or power.[16] This is not Raz's (only) point. His is rather that the right in question is the entitlement to another's non-interference, and that the related express permission to act or not is not itself a right.

Pace Raz, there is a long-standing practice in moral, political, and legal philosophical discourse, let alone legal discourse and practice, of treating—at least a certain subset of—liberties as being (kinds of) rights. Further, Raz's reduction of 'a right to do *X*' to a right against interference by others simply begs the question; some reason must be offered to show *why* the relevant liberty to act, which Raz deems to be the right's referent, is not itself also a right.

Imagine that Bob the law student wants to park his bicycle in front of his university's law building. A staff member approaches Bob, telling him that the bike racks are for the law faculty's exclusive usage. Bob, the budding lawyer, knows better about the relevant regulations. 'I have a right to park here', he says in reply. He does not simply mean that he has a right

[15] Raz (1996: 275). Cf. Raz (1986: 167); Kramer (1998: 13–4). See also Williams (1956: 1145).

[16] E.g., Robinson et al. (1983: 269): '[n]o person can be said to have a right to do that which he can always be prevented from doing or forced to do. The mere negation of a duty to do and not to do is a necessary, but not a sufficient, condition of a right to do. The other person must also have a duty not to interfere with you in doing it'.

against the staff member's interference with his parking there. Bob's primary intention is to convey the fact that he is permitted to undertake the very act of parking there, let alone being entitled to do so without interference.

In response, a Razian might say: forget 'interference'. Bob's real right just concerns the staff's duty to allow him to park there; it is not a liberty to act plus a claim against interference per se when doing so. The liberty is wholly separate from the right itself. However, this still does not explain why Bob's liberty to act itself is not a right. Further, the contrast between a right to act and a right against interference (a right to someone else's forbearance or action) is also made clear in situations where one has a right to park one's vehicle, but certain other persons lack duties against interference with the parking (within certain bounds), e.g., competitors for a parking spot where one party arrives there first. If the party who arrives second nonetheless manoeuvres her vehicle into the spot before the first party can park there (without hitting the other's vehicle), then, whilst doing so might be rude and socially impermissible, it is not legally impermissible per se. Here, it still makes sense to say, even vis-à-vis the non-duty-bound parties that one has a right to park there, even if others have no duty to acquiesce if they get there first.[17]

Neil MacCormick: Rights Must Be Rightful

Neil MacCormick thinks powers do not count as rights because their exercise can be valid but wrongful. He suggests that, to count as a right, even a legal one, a position must enable actions the system deems to be rightful. If it involves or entails an action that is not 'rightful', then the normative position in question cannot count as a right.

> [As] example[s], [**1**] *A* having validly contracted to sell a piece of land to *B*, proceeds to convey the same piece of land to *C* under a subsequent contract of sale, *C* acting in good faith and with no notice of *B*'s prior right. Here *A* acts wrongfully towards *B*; but the conveyance, albeit not rightfully executed, is valid and effectual in *C*'s favour. [**2**] There can be other cases in the sale of goods where a person has a power to transfer property in goods without having the right to sell them, eg, on account of having acquired them by fraud, and thus under voidable title. This sufficiently indicates that powers are not themselves rights, although one can only have *a right to*

[17] For similar arguments against Raz on liberty-rights, see Campbell (1997: 27–9).

exercise a given power provided one has that power, and provided that the exercise in question is not on some ground a wrongful one.[18]

Pace MacCormick, the connections between rights, rights exercise, and rightfulness are not necessary ones, at least for legal positions (let alone of rights in games, institutions, etc.). There can be trivial legal rights, immoral ones, others predicated upon governmental corruption or incompetence, ones born out of favouritism, etc.[19]

Second, MacCormick's argument does not establish that *all* powers are, or should be, disqualified from counting as rights. Requiring a demonstration that all tokens of the type are to be excluded also hoists MacCormick with his own petard, as it were; for his own assertion incorrectly delimits the *right to exercise* a power (using legal liberties) to situations wherein the uses of the power would not be wrongful.

Kenneth Campbell: Rights Must Be Entitlements or Permissions

Kenneth Campbell denies that powers and immunities are rights on the grounds that powers are capacities, not entitlements or permissions, whilst immunities are simply the absence of powers in others.[20] (Technically, Campbell is not a Monist, just a more restrictive Pluralist, as he deems both liberties and RCTDs to be kinds of rights.[21]) One of Campbell's reasons for denying that powers count as rights is because legal ones can be used to do things which one has no legal right to do, e.g., a thief's dishonest transfer in market overt. (Here, 'right to do' concerns a legal

[18] MacCormick (2007: 127, numbering and emphasis added). His stance is distinct from a similar view, held by Raz and Carl Wellman, that certain legally valid but wrongful actions ought not to even count as bona fide powers, let alone as rights. Raz (1996: 267); Wellman (1985: 44–6, 50). Although perhaps criminally and civilly liable to the wronged parties, the agents in the examples above can create legally valid contracts and exchanges. For both a Hohfeldian and MacCormick, this involves a power: the capacity to change the parties' normative positions.

[19] See, e.g., Chapter 6 notes 35–7 and the accompanying text. Conceivably, even if you treat powers as a type of a right, not all tokens of that type must count as such. For a more general discussion of rights *theories* delimiting which tokens of which types of positions count as rights, see Chapter 5 § II. As examples, on only certain Hohfeldian claims counting as rights see, e.g., Cruft (2004: 347, 356); Wenar (2005: 243–6). On only certain powers counting as rights, see, e.g., Kramer (1998: 103); Finnis (2011: 226–7). On only some but not all immunities counting as legal rights, see, e.g., Hart (1982: 191).

[20] Campbell (2001: 884). Cf. Campbell (1997: 26–7).

[21] Campbell (1997: 24, 27–9).

liberty to so act.) The legal power to transfer here involves a bona fide legal position, the impermissible exercise of which nonetheless yields legally valid results. The thief has no legal right to exercise the power, though; so, by exercising it anyway, the thief commits the tort of conversion of goods—something one is duty-bound not to do.[22] (Whereas MacCormick focusses on the rightfulness of the act, Campbell is concerned with the right to do the act independently of the power to do so.) As some powers can be used to accomplish illegal-yet-legally-valid ends, their holders possess the capacity to do that which is impermissible. Campbell concludes that '[i]f one can have a power without a right, then powers are not a species of right'.[23]

Campbell's reliance on a capacity/entitlement distinction equally fails to show how or why all tokens of a type of normative position should be disqualified from counting as rights. Granted that a power is a capacity, it has not been shown that capacities cannot also be entitlements; why capacities are not rights; and why all rights must be entitlements. Lawyers would be happy to say that we are generally 'entitled' to gift our property to those whom we choose, or that we are 'entitled' to buy a house or to sell it. We are also entitled to enter contracts so long as they are for legal purposes and we are legally competent consenting persons. Why ignore, discount, or exclude this data? Campbell would also have to provide reasons for thinking that *all* powers (not just some) cannot be both entitlements and capacities. To do so, it would help to know what makes something an entitlement in the first place.

Matthew Kramer and Hillel Steiner

Matthew Kramer and Hillel Steiner present the most sophisticated case to date for delimiting rights to one basic kind, a Hohfeldian claim.[24] They co-authored a paper to rebut Gopal Sreenivasan's and Leif Wenar's

[22] Campbell (1997: 27); Campbell (2001: 884). He furthermore (correctly) notes that the power and right by which to exercise it are only contingently connected. 'To be sure, the lawmaker generally confers a right to exercise a power at the same time as granting the power itself. But the two are quite distinct and are related only pragmatically, not conceptually'. Campbell (2001: 884).

[23] Campbell (1997: 27). For his second—question begging—reason to deny that powers are kinds of rights, see ibid 26–7.

[24] This seems to diverge from Steiner's earlier view that only complexes containing claims or immunities (plus enforcement powers) are rights. E.g., Steiner (1994: 61 & n.9). The

respective works, which claim to present alternatives to the Interest and Will theories of rights.[25] In so doing, Kramer and Steiner also outline some of their own views about rights modelling.

To understand Kramer and Steiner's monistic stance, though, we must first briefly address Wenar's interpretation of Hohfeld. Wenar believes that certain (but not all) tokens of Hohfeldian claims, liberties, powers, and immunities count as rights because everyday discourse reflects these different basic types. For Wenar, a good way to test an account of rights is to see how well it captures our ordinary understanding of what rights there are.[26] One that narrowed down the number of basic types would therefore be incorrect as measured against common understanding.[27]

Kramer and Steiner disagree. They provide several arguments aiming to show why 'a right' should be restricted to a Hohfeldian claim and for disregarding Wenar's proposed test. Mostly paraphrased, their arguments are:

(I) There is no single ordinary understanding of what rights are. There are instead multiple ordinary understandings, which conflict with one another in a number of respects. Hohfeld himself notes that even professional jurists employ the language in confusedly inconsistent ways.[28]
(II) Wenar acknowledges the systematic ambiguity of ordinary usage but attempts to defuse it via assurances that ordinary rights-talk can be entirely rigorous and error-free, provided speakers understand how assertions of rights map on to the Hohfeldian incidents. However, his assurances are uninformative and carry a patently unsatisfied proviso.[29]
(III) Moreover, his proviso can be countered with an alternative one: that ordinary rights talk can be error free so long as speakers restrict 'a right' to a Hohfeldian claim.[30]

stance presented in the 2007 article, at least in this regard, might therefore only reflect Kramer's views.

[25] Kramer & Steiner (2007); Sreenivasan (2005); Wenar (2005).
[26] Wenar (2005: 238).
[27] Ibid 243.
[28] Kramer & Steiner (2007: 295).
[29] Ibid 295–6.
[30] Ibid 296.

(IV) When Hohfeldians frown upon the looseness of the terminology of 'rights' in quotidian discourse, they are actually ***distancing*** themselves from the ways in which lay people and professional jurists ***do*** discuss various legal entitlements.[31]

(V) A major reason for their distancing themselves thus is that the indiscriminate use of 'a right' to cover each of the Hohfeldian entitlements (i.e., claims, powers, liberties, and immunities) is strongly conducive to muddled thinking and argumentation. Indeed, Hohfeld's investigations into jurists' paralogisms were intended to demonstrate as much.[32]

(VI) Hohfeldians are not seeking to lay down terminological prescriptions for everyday communications and contexts. Any such prescriptions would be futile and misconceived. Rather, they have striven to devise an intricately precise vocabulary from which *philosophical disputes* about the basic nature of rights can be conducted rigorously and perspicuously. (Whilst ordinary usage is an essential point of departure of the development of that specialised philosophical parlance, it is only an initial point of reference. Some regimentation/purification is inevitable if the requisite degree of precision for philosophical disputation is to be attained. Indeed, Wenar himself has had to do so, albeit obliquely.[33])

(VII) The foremost reason for limiting rights to claim-rights—ones accompanied by protective immunities, at any rate—is itself grounded in the presuppositions of ordinary usage. As Hohfeld's investigations tended to reveal, an assumption ordinarily underlying the invocation of 'a right' is that the holder of an entitlement denoted by that term is owed a duty with some specified content by somebody else. An assumption to that effect will be fully apt when the entitlement under consideration is a claim—since every claim is correlative to a duty—but will otherwise be prone to be false. Hence, reserving the term 'rights' for claims is singularly appropriate. Such a limitation departs from the prevailing regularities of juristic discourse in a superficial respect, but it pays heed to them in a deeper respect.[34]

[31] Ibid.

[32] Ibid.

[33] Ibid.

[34] Ibid 296–7.

(VIII) A chief factor behind the tendency of both ordinary speakers and professional jurists to refer to Hohfeldian powers and liberties as 'rights' is that nearly all such entitlements in any civilized society are accompanied by claims against many forms of interference with the exercise thereof. No liberty or power would ordinarily be designated as 'a right' if it were wholly unaccompanied by claims against interference with the exercise of it. What is carrying the burden of earning the label 'right' among those speakers is the protective ambit of the claims, rather than the liberty or power in itself. *By contrast, a claim does not need such supplementation to be ordinarily classifiable as a right.* It is itself an instance of legal protection against interference or uncooperativeness, and it is itself thus correctly regarded as a right by ordinary speakers and Hohfeldian theorists alike… When powers and liberties consort with claims that protect the power-holders' and liberty-holders' abilities to exercise their respective entitlements, the presence of those claims is what commonly elicits the application of the term 'rights' to the powers and liberties. Because claims are unique in performing that particular function, the singling out of them as right is hardly an arbitrary stipulation.[35]

Kramer and Steiner agree with Wenar that, in everyday discourse, people would call (what Hohfeldians style) powers and liberties 'rights'.[36] In turn, I agree with Kramer and Steiner that Hohfeld's *schema* is a corrective to both ordinary and legal usage[37] and that people (in both ordinary and technical discourses) use the term equivocally. Hence, one cannot lean *too heavily* on provisos about usage, per the second argument above. That is where we part company, however.

[35] Ibid 297–8. The following portions of their argument were omitted for brevity's sake. 'To be sure, a claim must be accompanied by immunities against most types of divestiture if it is to count as a genuine right at all… However, the lesson to be drawn here is not so much that concomitant immunities against divestiture are necessary for a claim's status as a genuine *right*; instead, the presence of such immunities is necessary for a claim's status as a genuine *entitlement or legal position* of any sort. Any entitlement that is wholly unaccompanied by immunities against termination will be purely nominal rather than genuine.' Ibid 297. Both genuine and nominal entitlements nevertheless seem to count as valid positions within a legal system in his view. See Chapter 5 note 38 on the evolution in Kramer's thought on what makes legal positions 'nominal' and 'genuine'.

[36] Kramer & Steiner (2007: 295).

[37] See also Kramer (1998: 22–3).

Whilst muddled thinking is a genuine worry, it is not so weighty as to warrant restricting the term (and the cognate concept) to one basic kind of a right. The *schema* provides distinct terms to help philosophers, lawyers, and others avoid ambiguous thinking and argumentation. Hohfeld's adoption of the term 'a claim' is itself a form of philosophical correction and clarification; depending upon how it is understood, it is not something ordinary folk (as opposed, perhaps, to lawyers) would always recognise as being identical with a right readily.[38]

It not simply that Kramer and Steiner harbour divergent methodological desiderata from both Wenar and your author; there is also something mistaken about their stated aims and priorities. Instead of constructing a model that *balances* (i) an effort to best track the data of ordinary and technical (e.g., legal) usage and (ii) meeting the stated desiderata of a precise vocabulary that helps to avoid muddled thinking in philosophical discussions of rights, Kramer and Steiner simply concern themselves with the latter. Even if treating a Hohfeldian claim as the sole type of a right (rather than just deeming it to be the *stricto sensu* case, which other Hohfeldians tend to do) achieved that latter end, it is so unrepresentative of the data the model is meant to represent as to constitute a distortion. Thus, it is also unacceptably under-inclusive.

Moreover, Kramer and Steiner's approach may even defeat the very purpose of having a model altogether *as they themselves construe it*. Hohfeld was trying to make sense of existing rights discourse. One does not do so by denying that much of it is about rights at all, especially when it is admitted that the *explananda* strongly suggests otherwise. Again, Kramer and Steiner even concede that ordinary usage is 'an essential point of departure for the development of [a] specialized philosophical parlance' about rights[39] and the ordinary users would consider cases of what Hohfeldians call liberties and powers to be 'rights'.

Additionally, what is the value of, philosophical disputes about A RIGHT, or even just A LEGAL RIGHT, if interlocutors are restricted to using one *philosophically constructed*, *corrective* conception, e.g., Hohfeld's A CLAIM? If concepts do indeed have discernible, relatively fixed, internal structures, and what we want is an account of A RIGHT displaying those features, why believe that Hohfeld's conception, alone, is going to get us

[38] For some of the questionable Hohfeldian propositions that help to shape A CLAIM, see Chapter 3 note 18.

[39] Kramer & Steiner (2007: 296).

to an adequate understanding thereof? All we will get is the 'nature' of Hohfeldian claims. Is it by approximation or abduction, then, to the 'nature' of real-world rights (or, at least, real-world RCTDs)? If so, then that approximation is quite off the mark for discounting other kinds of normative positions that can count as rights.

Hohfeld was adamant that the *schema* aimed to provide practical guidance to lawyers and judges.[40] It was not strictly meant for employment in philosophical debate. If rights modelling is not directed towards explaining real-world practices in a way that aims to clarify the concept(s) or practice(s) to the practitioners, and is simply for philosophers to pursue their own ends, then something has gone awry with the very enterprise—at least insofar as Hohfeld and other modelers are concerned.

Kramer and Steiner also assume a right/entitlement distinction, whereby four of Hohfeld's kinds (claims, liberties, powers, and immunities) are entitlements, but only one (claims) counts as rights. What would they say to someone who believes that all entitlements are rights? The closest they come to a possible response can be found in their seventh argument: a presupposition that ordinary usage establishes a relationship between rights and duties. However, Hohfeld's investigations do *not* actually reveal that most people believe duties to be invariably tethered to rights. He just baldly states this assumption. He also fails to explain or justify why claims ought to constitute the *stricto sensu* case, save to say that it is *because* they correlate with duties…[41] for which he then proceeds to cite just three cases as evidence.[42] This is, of course, no answer at all. For why should the mere fact of that correlation render 'a claim' the strict sense? In fact, his *Fundamental Legal Conceptions* articles do not even try to demonstrate that that assumption is held by most people. Whilst it might nonetheless be true, Hohfeld, Kramer, and Steiner do not even begin to provide real evidence for it.

Kramer and Steiner's last argument also presumes, rather than demonstrates, why liberties and powers are ordinarily counted as rights (because they are accompanied by claims against interference with their exercise). Counterexamples also abound. One was already mentioned in the

[40] Hohfeld (1913a: 20).

[41] Ibid 31: 'Recognizing, as we must, the very broad and indiscriminate use of the term, "right," what clue do we find, in ordinary legal discourse, toward limiting the word in question to a definite and appropriate meaning. That clue lies in the correlative "duty," for it is certain that even those who use the word and the conception "right" in the broadest possible way are accustomed to thinking of "duty" as the invariable correlative'.

[42] Ibid 31–2.

argument against Raz vis-à-vis the law student parking his bicycle. Others are ordinary and legal usage of 'rights' to buy and sell property, and to make contract offers. Jurists and others style these as 'rights', which in Hohfeldian terms can be understood as either Hohfeldian powers or as complexes containing powers. Jurists and ordinary people would call each of these 'a right to do' (which cannot be explained in terms of a 'passive' Hohfeldian claim—more on which in Chapter 3). Holders are entitled and authorised *to do* these thing; these are said to be rights, but not because of any associated claim against interference when so doing.

Similarly, Kramer posits that a 'right of action' (i.e., a secondary right)[43] is simply a Hohfeldian power.[44] Hohfeld himself, however, insists that rights of action are, or include, claims.[45] Regardless, it begs the question to insist that a 'right of action' would constitute a bona fide right only because of some direct or indirect protection against non-interference afforded to it by another party's correlative duty—if there even is one. (Here, the relevant duty against non-interference would have to concern the secondary/'remedial' right of action itself, not the underlying primary right.) A right of action entitles you to commence legal proceedings, say, against the holder of a primary duty. Lest one think that ENTITLEMENT is doing all the work here, the idea can be reiterated without it. Imagine that *A* owes *B* money for goods delivered according to a contract. *A* refuses to pay. *B* then commences a lawsuit. Is *B*'s right of action considered to be 'a right' by lawyers and ordinary folk because *B* can legally commence institutional proceedings, or is it a right (if at all) because the capacity to do so is protected by *A* or other parties being duty-bound to refrain from interference with the commencement process? Although ultimately an empirical query, it seems implausible to your author that most people, let alone lawyers and judges, would choose the latter option. More importantly, no good reason is on offer for believing that *that* is why it is considered to be a right.

Kramer and Steiner also beg the question that most people would consider a 'naked' claim, i.e., one unprotected or supported by liberties or

[43] On the primary/secondary/tertiary rights distinction, see Chapter 1 § II.1.

[44] Kramer (1998: 34 n.14).

[45] Hohfeld (1913a: 35 n.39); Hohfeld (1913b: 554, 556); Hohfeld (1917: 753, 760). Officials are duty-bound to initiate institutional dispute resolution processes and not merely liable to do so. Furthermore, the idea of a *tertiary* right being a claim (or a complex containing one) makes better sense of the idea of a judgment creditor being entitled to a judgment debtor's duty to pay a court-imposed damages award, and not just the mechanisms by which to enforce the court order (which may concern *quaternary* rights instead).

power to exercise or enforce it to be a right.[46] It is yet another empirical question as to whether most people believe—correctly or otherwise—that (1) rights are perforce claimable and (2) that an unclaimable or unenforceable right is no right at all. Even so, many of those scholars who insist that there exist unenforceable rights nevertheless tend to mark them off as constituting 'degenerate' cases.[47] Kramer and Steiner's view being based on an appeal to ordinary linguistic usage for the purportedly unique function of a claim (against interference) being able to elicit the application of the term 'a right' when powers and liberties are in play is thus at least open to empirical challenge, if not simply false.

Now, the two scholars may nevertheless be unmoved by all of this. They might just reply that, absent the protection afforded by claims against interference, i.e., whereby others may interfere with any attempted exercise of any of the above-listed powers or liberties, people might be disinclined to call the latter rights because they would be practically ineffectual.[48]

If so, this would constitute a 'Kelsenian twist',[49] i.e., a turn towards the view of enforceability being more closely connected with A RIGHT (and perhaps also the further view of duties being identified with, or invariably tied to, sanctions) than Kramer, at least, would like.[50] For he (but not Steiner) denies that legal RCTDs are perforce enforceable.[51] Still, what if claims against interference (and correlative duties to forbear) abounded, but *their* violation was generally or systematically ignored? Would we then have to say the claims themselves are not rights, absent effective, regular enforcement?

Furthermore, the two scholars overemphasise the direct or indirect security that duties and immunities can afford as a potential criterion for a (different) normative position's rights status.[52] Think of cases of liberties

[46] On the vested/naked distinction, see Chapter 1 § II.2.

[47] See Chapter 8 for further treatment of this issue.

[48] Kramer & Steiner (2007: 297).

[49] Raz (1984: 131). Raz uses this phrase to criticize HLA Hart's account of private law RCTDs and duties. See also Chapter 4 note 113.

[50] For further discussion of these views, see Chapter 5 and Chapter 7 § III. 'Argument 4'. See further Frydrych (2018a: 307–8).

[51] For some explications of Kramer's *theory* of rights, see Chapter 5 §§ II.1—II.2, especially notes 36–9 and the accompanying text.

[52] Again, this is somewhat ironic, given Kramer's opposition to the Will theory, which holds that an RCTD is either a complex (a Hohfeldian claim plus some number of enforcement powers), or is itself a kind of enforcement power. See Chapter 5.

regarding activities that were previously forbidden. As examples, the Charter of the Forest granted certain English people rights to hunt and gather; the English Parliament granted to its members freedom of speech; etc. It is not that people were insecure in their entitlements or capacities to do such things beforehand; they were not allowed to do (duty-bound not to do) them at all.[53]

Still, Kramer and Steiner could additionally offer the following rebuttal. In terms of conceptual resources, it makes sense to focus on Hohfeldian claims. 'Liberties' and 'powers' are established terms, one which can be distinguished from 'rights'. Change its label to 'a right' (and abandon the '*stricto sensu*' label if you wish), a claim nevertheless does a distinct job from the other Hohfeldian positions. ('Immunity' might also be a poor label, but it serves a different role, and not one that most people would consider to be the paradigmatic usage of legal rights.)

In response, *Hohfeld's* 'claim' is, again, a technical term, one with which ordinary speakers may not be familiar, if not also legal practitioners.[54] More importantly, the would-be rebuttal takes the philosophy of rights literature for granted as having a greater foothold in ordinary and legal consciousness and discourse than it in fact does. In 1915 Roscoe Pound lauded the addition of 'a power' as a distinct label from an RCTD as a great *jurisprudential* contribution.[55] Has it caught on with judges and lawyers en masse? Have they ceased to use the language of 'a right' to buy or sell property, and restricted their vocabulary to that of 'powers'? Not at all. *Should* they, simply because a different technical term is available? Howsoever one chooses to answer that question, it will not change the fact that most, if not all, people continue to think and talk of such matters in terms of rights. It is that, moreover, which an account of rights must take seriously.

[53] For a different set of responses to Kramer & Steiner's arguments, see Wenar (2008).

[54] It is also a somewhat unhelpful label, as it is has led to 'active' and 'passive' interpretations. Again, see Chapter 3 § III.

[55] Pound (1915: 95): '[r]ights in this sense, or powers, as we are now coming to call them…'.

§ IV. Over-Inclusivity: 'Ligation-Rights'

The last section showed why certain models are under-inclusive because of their proponents' unwarranted assumptions and/or methodological commitments. This section shows the opposite: other scholars present over-inclusive models by deeming some or all ligations to be types of rights. Their general argument is as follows. Ligations are indispensable for structuring our social, legal, moral, and political relations. We need duties and liabilities to even have contracts, property, etc., at all. It is thus desirable and advantageous to possess ligations in many situations. Therefore, it seems fitting to treat (at least certain) ligations to be basic kinds of rights: duty-rights, liability-rights, etc.

The idea of a ligation-right is not completely farfetched. Ligations are often thought to serve as components within right complexes, or as parts of larger legal concepts and doctrines. For example, Anthony Honoré construes OWNERSHIP to be a bundle of *sticks* (rather than a bundle of *rights*, because not all of its components are rights), which includes ligations amongst its eleven incidents.[56] The idea of a ligation-right goes farther, though, by making the ligation the defining feature, or 'core', of a right complex.[57] .

For example, Carl Wellman reports that HLA Hart suggested to him the idea of a (Hohfeldian) liability-right. Hart's examples were the legal right to inherit property and a right to be given something.[58] However, Hart's *theory* of a private law right (and certain other legal ones) posits that it necessarily affords some modicum of control in terms of bilateral liberties by which to exercise the right (and, specifically in the case of RCTDs, enforcement capacities plus liberties by which to exercise those capacities).[59] Liabilities, however, cannot be controlled in these ways. How, then, could liabilities count as (the core of) rights per Hart's own 'theoretical' criteria for the concept?

Wellman may nonetheless proclaim to be able to bypass Hart's difficulty. Explaining how, though, first requires an understanding of his account of rights, which we will divide into its 'model' and 'theory'

[56] See Chapter 1 note 71.

[57] On the idea of a right complex's core, see Wellman (1985: 81); Sumner (1987: 48–9, 98–9).

[58] Wellman (1985: 86).

[59] Hart (1982: 183–5). See further discussion of Hart's model in Appendix 1 and his theory in Chapter 5 § II and Chapter 7 § III 'Argument 1'.

aspects. On Wellman's *model*, real rights are all complexes composed of the more basic Hohfeldian positions.[60] (Again, a single or 'atomic' position, such as a particular Hohfeldian claim or liberty, in his view, is never a right.[61]) The right's components either constitute its 'core' (always a singular Hohfeldian position) or its 'associated' elements.[62] For example, if *A* and *B* enter a contract for widgets, *A*'s right against *B* is a complex containing a Hohfeldian claim (correlating with *B*'s duty to pay) at its core whilst other positions constitute ancillary positions which service that claim (e.g., enforcement powers, liberties to enforce those powers, immunities from the claim's divestment, etc.).

Wellman furthermore thinks that legal rights are advantages.[63] Hohfeldian claims, immunities, powers, and liberties, and even liabilities (i.e., susceptibility to having one's legal relations changed), can serve as the core of a legal right.[64] Hohfeldian liabilities, such as the susceptibility of being rendered into a contract offeree or the recipient of a gift, can constitute a right's core because it is sometimes advantageous to have a liability.[65]

Moreover, a right is said to be dynamic: its associated elements (but not its core) can vary over time.[66] Despite the dynamism, Wellman holds that every right contains at least one liberty and one power.[67] This conceptual minimum, he thinks, is true of rights in all normative domains: moral rights, legal ones, institutional ones, etc. (However, most rights are said to typically contain *multiple* liberties, powers, and immunities.[68]) Indeed, all rights are said to contain an 'active' element, i.e., an entitlement or authorisation for the right-holder to act on behalf of the right. Rights speak with an 'active voice'; even their component 'passive' positions can contribute to a right's active nature.[69] Such activity is possible predominantly due to a right's component liberty(ies) and power(s), regardless of

[60] Wellman (1985: 59, 81); Wellman (1995: 8, 24–5, 30, 100, 108, 178, 181–2).
[61] *Supra* note 4.
[62] Wellman (1985: 81–95); Wellman (1995: 8, 25).
[63] E.g., Wellman (1995, 7–8).
[64] Wellman (1985: 85–9); Wellman (1995: 190).
[65] Wellman (1985: 85–9).
[66] Wellman (1995: 7–9, 24, 190–5).
[67] Wellman (1995: 108–12, 123, 140, 186–7); Wellman (1985: 93, 95–6, 204–11).
[68] Wellman (1995: 140, 178).
[69] Wellman (1995: 110).

whether one of them serves as the core, or if both (or more) are simply associated elements.[70]

On Wellman's *theory*, moreover, all rights afford their holders 'dominion' in potential conflicts with other parties.[71] This 'essential function', of affording dominion status is to be understood in terms of providing freedom *and* control.[72] A right's containing at least one liberty plus one power appears to constitute that minimal level of freedom and control.[73] That Wellman takes the relevant sort of 'control' to be a function of *enforcement* powers is evidenced by his view that a Hohfeldian claim-right (a complex with a claim serving as its core) perforce includes this kind of power.[74] Indeed, his most common example of the most basic sort of a claim-right includes a power to claim performance of a correlative duty.[75] (The 'freedom' component of his theory concerns liberties, such as those by which to exercise the powers to claim or not.[76]) Rights in all normative

[70] He suggests there are two aspects for identifying the core of a right. Aspect 1: look at the language of legal rights and interpret its meaning (plain meaning, legislative intent, etc.). Aspect 2: look at the matter through the lens of an actual or hypothetical confrontation between two parties under the law. Identify and define the way in which the law might favour a party alleging some right in the face of the contending party. Wellman (1985: 89–90). There are also two stipulated limiting conditions: (1) the core must be a legal advantage. (2) it must be the sort of legal advantage whereby *X* can have 'dominion'. Ibid 85.

[71] Wellman (1985: 95–6).

[72] Wellman (1985: 7, 81, 95–102); Wellman (1995: 8, 25, 107, 110–1). 'The dominion conferred upon a right-holder by a respected legal right… is a two-sided freedom-control concerning a limited domain defined by the core of the right and in the face of the second party or parties to that right. To the extent that it is realized, this dominion enables the will of the right-holder to prevail over the will or wills of the second parties in any confrontation to which the right is relevant'. Wellman (1985: 96). Although not always consistent on the matter, Wellman insists that rights-based dominion requires *both* freedom and control.

[73] Whilst Wellman frequently styles his own account as a Dominion theory (e.g., Wellman, (1985: 95–102); Wellman 2000), he also identifies it as a version of the Will theory, e.g., Wellman (1995: 123); Wellman (2000: 954).

[74] Wellman (1985: 39); Wellman (1995: 187).

[75] E.g., Wellman (1995: 80, 87, 89, 95, 119, 131, 184–5). Wellman identifies a Hohfeldian claim as a kind of power. This, not only because he rejects the idea of strict 'logical correlativity', which (he believes) would reduce A CLAIM to A DUTY (e.g., Wellman (1995: 100, 123)), but also because he insists that *the act of claiming* changes the meaning of the recipient duty-bearer's subsequent actions and position: it increases the duty's stringency and adds force to the reasons others have to react negatively to the duty-bearer's non-compliance. Ibid 80–1, 87, 95.

[76] E.g., Wellman (1995: 80–1, 90, 95).

domains, and all kinds of rights (i.e., claim-rights, liberty-rights, etc.) contain freedom-affording and control-affording liberty and power.[77]

Others have already shown that Wellman's suggested tools for determining what constitutes a complex's core are wanting.[78] Take as an example the famous case of the right of African Americans to sit on juries.[79] A state law barring Black people from jury selection was held to violate the Fourteenth Amendment. Wellman's criteria do not help to determine whether the core of the right to sit on a jury is: (a) a Hohfeldian liability, i.e., susceptibility to a change in your status from non-participant to that of a candidate juror in a particular jury pool; (b) the duty(ies) to attend the court and participate in the jury pool and to serve *qua* juror if selected; (c) a liberty to so serve; (d) claims correlating with a duty to be considered as a candidate and/or not to be removed from the role for certain reasons; or something else.

Wellman's own example of a liability-right, though, is the right to be married. Certain people are legally eligible to marry. He identifies this eligibility with a Hohfeldian liability, which, in turn, is held to form the core of the right to marry.

> [T]he eligible couple have legal dominion concerning its enjoyment. Thus, they acquire this legal liability to be married only if they first freely consent to be married to each other; no minister or magistrate has the legal power to marry reluctant couples dragged in off the streets, or even out of the bedrooms. And presumably the couple retain the legal power to withdraw their consent at any time during the marriage ceremony before the declaration has been completed. And individuals have the legal power to take legal action… to establish their liability to be married or their lack of it.[80]

Whatever one thinks of Wellman's theory of A RIGHT, the notion of a right complex with a liability at its core fails to meet it. The work of establishing dominion is accomplished by a complex's liberties, powers, and immunities. A liability does the opposite of establishing a right-holder's

[77] E.g., ibid 190. See Chapter 5 § II.1's discussion of Wellman's insistence that his theory is actually about vindication of the will, rather than control over enforcement matters, and why it is nonetheless about both.

[78] E.g., Campbell (2001); Rainbolt (2006: 105–9, 242). They also show why Wellman's DOMINION conception is underdeveloped. Even so, one could try to show how certain positions are dependent upon others within a complex through alternative means.

[79] *Strauder v. West Virginia*, 100 U.S. 303 (1880).

[80] Wellman (1985: 89).

dominion over others: it marks its bearer's susceptibility to a change in his or her normative position(s). In other words, if Wellman's theory relies either on the would-be marrying parties' effectuating their consent, or their power to establish their status as marriageable, then their dominion cannot be explained in terms of a liability serving *as the core*. On the other hand, if Wellman wants to say that the right to marry has a Hohfeldian liability as its core because of the dominion that *a liability* somehow affords, then that stance is either circular or incomplete.

Now, he might want to reply that a right's dominion can be afforded by its associated elements, rather than the core. However, as he believes that the 'core' defines the entire right complex, it remains to be explained why the core need not be the sort of advantage that can itself afford dominion. Consider the right to marry. To be sure, eligibility is a *sine qua non* for being able to marry. Still, there is a difference between a legal status of being married, being compelled to marry, and *the right(s) to* (gaining and/or maintaining) that status. It also unnecessary that those rights/positions form a unity, i.e., serve as components within a right complex.

Moreover, an oft-neglected feature of Hohfeldian and other conceptions of A POWER is that a power changes *both* the power-holder's and at least one other party's normative positions.[81] For Hohfeldians like Wellman, a liability always correlates with a power. Nonetheless, Hohfeldians either deny, or fail to adequately address the issue of whether, a liability is itself inherent in a power. For exercising a power changes both its holder's and the correlative liability-bearer's statuses, e.g., from owner and non-owner to the reverse, from non-relations to contract offeror and offeree, etc. Even so, the power-holder is seemingly not 'self-liable' simply by virtue of possessing that power—though he or she may be render liable by its usage—as no one bears a correlative power.

With this in mind, and returning to Wellman's marriage example, an authoritative third party (a government official, a religious figure, etc.) is usually required to marry people. The marrying couple must be competent and eligible to trigger that process. As Wellman notes, at least in many modern Western societies, one cannot legally be compelled to marry. Thus, one must make oneself susceptible to a legal official's marriage

[81] Not all changes in people's normative positions are the function of powers, however. The operation of law and changes in facts can effectuate such modifications too. E.g., Hohfeld (1913a: 44).

ceremony. This requires exercising a power that in turn renders oneself liable. This power correlates with the official's liability to having a duty created in him or herself to use his or her own legal power to marry the couple.

Pace Wellman, the *right to* marry is better understood as a complex with a power at its core. True, there is no marriage without being eligible. Hence, eligibility is logically prior to *making oneself* marriable to a particular person. Even so, marriageability is itself partially established via a change in one's own position: by applying to the state, say, to get a marriage certificate, a ceremony, etc. Thus, the power to get married is more basic, or 'core', to *a right to* marry than is the liability (if eligibility is indeed to be identified exclusively with that type of Hohfeldian position) to being married.[82]

If one nevertheless denies that a power forms the core of the right to marry, then the only plausible alternatives cores are a Hohfeldian claim or liberty. (The claim correlating with an official's duty to marry the parties.) Regardless, whether a claim or power constitutes the 'core' of the right, and even if a liability forms part of that right, that still does not render it sensible to deem the complex to be a 'liability-right'.

As evidence, consider arranged marriages and child marriages. There are of course jurisdictions authorising such marriages, wherein the parties' parents arrange them and/or the regime allows for legal subjects of any age to marry. In this case, one might say that the marrying parties are liable to be married, but perhaps not that they had the right to be married—even if the marrying parties possess some relevant powers and liberties (say, the power and liberty to veto a certain number of candidates for marriage selected by their parents).

Now, imagine a jurisdiction wherein the government arranges all of its legal subjects' marriages, of any age and without their consent. In this regime, compliance is mandatory. Further, people can only marry at the government's direction and discretion. So, perhaps not everyone gets married. Here, it would make sense to say that people are liable to be married but lack any right to marry.

[82] For a different argument that a 'power-right' forms the core of the 'the right to marry', see Strauss (2016: 1694, 1696, 1724–41). However, Strauss conflates (I) the right to marry with the rights of marriage (e.g., ibid 1724–5), and (II) Hohfeld's A CLAIM with A POWER when deeming the core 'power-right' in the right to marry as correlating with a state duty (rather than a liability). Ibid 1740.

Even in real-world arranged and child marriage cases, however, the *right to* marry primarily seems to concern the capacity to trigger a change in the parties' legal statuses, and/or a claim in the child to be married off, rather than mere susceptibility (a Hohfeldian liability) to such changes. Perhaps only Hegelians might defend the notion that there is a right to being liable to being sentenced for one's crimes;[83] still, even they might dispute that a Hohfeldian liability forms the core of such a right.

These considerations also help to explain the jury right case too. Jury duty in a given American state is a civic responsibility, constitutive of citizenship. Just as in the case of ownership being understood as a bundle of *sticks*, the same may be said in the case of citizenship. The *right to* qualify/sit for jury duty, especially as discussed in the context of The US Constitution's Fourteenth Amendment Equal Protection Clause, is better understood as grounding an RCTD not to be discriminated against by legal officials considering someone's eligibility to serve in the role, rather than either the liability to serve in that role or the duty to comply.[84]

Rainbolt, another ligation-right proponent, believes that all four basic types of Hohfeldian ligations (duties, no-rights, liabilities, and disabilities) can form the core of a right complex. This, so long as each such complex includes at least one (ancillary) claim and/or an immunity.[85] For on Rainbolt's *theory*, all rights justifiably affix a normative constraint upon others; some feature or other of the right-holder *qua* person (any feature really, not a specific one or set thereof) is the *reason/justification for* another party's bearing correlative duties or disabilities.[86] Amongst the Hohfeldian basic types, only a Hohfeldian claim and—purportedly—an

[83] See Hegel (2008: 126 § 100).

[84] What about a right to be a contractual offeree, or the right to be the donee of a gift? What happens if some people in a legal system are denied the legal status to be contracting parties or property owners? The same sort of answer applies: these rights are a function of citizenship/being treated as a certain level of legal subject. Hence, the *rights to* those statuses are better understood in terms of having RCTDs at their core.

[85] Rainbolt (2006: xii, 34–9).

[86] Ibid xi, xiii, 118–9.

immunity can normatively constrain another person.[87] Hence, any complex must contain at least one of those two basic positions as a component.[88]

How can A LIGATION-RIGHT be squared with Rainbolt's own 'theoretical' criteria for A RIGHT, though? According to his *theory*, rights are reasons to *impose* normative constraints on other parties. If this is what rights really do, then this seems to speak to its primary purpose, not to auxiliary ones which support or advance the right (and which are perhaps only contingent associated elements, let alone possibly fungible ones). Although he himself challenges the very notion of complexes even having 'cores',[89] just like Wellman, Rainbolt would need to better defend the idea that the requisite constraining component, imposed on another in order to advance some feature of the right-holder, need not constitute a right's core. For, again, there are grounds for differentiating between a normative

[87] *Pace* Rainbolt, Hohfeldian disabilities are not normative constraints per se. They simply mark the lack of normative power. Hence, immunities do not normatively constrain. There is thus an important difference between being obligated (not) to act in certain ways and lacking the capacity to so act. In the latter case, one may act despite being normatively disempowered to do so. Such an act may be 'wrongful' or 'invalid', but it is not constraining per se. As examples, a legislature may pass laws that are *ultra vires* its constitutional competencies and a person may create a will that is not witnessed by the required number of parties. The effect is either that their acts are legally ineffectual, or they nonetheless changed parties' statuses (citizens, beneficiaries, etc.) in invalid-yet-valid ways (ones that may get validated downstream by other legal agents such as courts). Rainbolt may reply that a legislature's disability leads it to circumscribe its decisions about what sort of laws it should try to pass. However, it is instead that body's *duty* to abide by the constitution/higher-order laws and to operate within its delimited set of powers which does that constraining work, not the disability as such. No one, moreover, would say that legislators bear disability-rights not to pass *ultra vires* laws in a jurisdiction lacking judicial review to overturn legislation, i.e., where the legislature is also immune from having its actions reversed. For further elucidation and criticism of Rainbolt's view, see Chapter 5 § V.

A more general concern is how exactly RCTDs actually constrain. This is generally left unexplained by scholars who advance this sort of view. Is the constraint different from, or identical to, the constraint imposed by, the correlative duty? For Max Radin, the answer is that the Hohfeldian claim-duty jural relation is what matters, and so it is a mistake to focus on two distinct normative positions. See Chapter 3 notes 8–9 and the accompanying text. For those who reject Radin's interpretation, how does a Hohfeldian claim itself constrain? For Joseph Raz (a non-Hohfeldian), a right is a reason to impose duties and other normative positions upon others. For him, duties are (or include) exclusionary reasons that constrain their bearers' deliberations. See Chapter 3 notes 13–16 and the accompanying text. Razian rights, however, are not identical to duties. So, how can a Razian right itself constrain?

[88] Ibid 25, 30.

[89] Rainbolt (2006: 107–9).

role (marriage, citizenship, etc.) that includes a ligation on the one hand, and *the right to* adopt or bear that role on the other.

Rainbolt also misidentifies what counts as the cores of would-be ligation-rights. Take his example of the so-called duty-right to vote.[90] Certain countries, such as Australia, impose a duty to vote. That duty qualifies or shapes the right to vote, e.g., by eliminating the freedom not to participate. *Pace* Rainbolt, that duty is not itself a right, let alone the core of the right to vote. If anything, the core is either the legal capacity to vote, or the holder's authorisation/permission to undertake the relevant actions that constitute voting. (These legal positions may or may not be protected by claims against interference with voting and immunities against their nullification.) As another example, if there is 'a right to create contracts' (and thus be eligible to bear contractual duties) it does not follow that *A*'s contractual duty to pay *B* is a right, or forms part of a right complex, even if it is accompanied by an immunity from nullification or a claim against interference with its fulfilment.

The idea of a ligation-right is dubious. Rights allow and help people to enter into social, legal, and political relations (contracts, citizenship, etc.). Some such rights may correlate with other people's duties not to deprive us of our personhood, e.g., to enslave us, to denigrate our reputation, etc. It may be quite valuable to be able to bear the duties that come with citizenship, contracts, etc., but that alone does not render them into types of rights. Further, advocates of ligation-rights cannot square the concept with their own theoretical criteria for A RIGHT. This is not to deny that ligations can form ('associate') components of right complexes or other larger legal constructs (e.g., property). It is simply to note that ligations are not themselves basic kinds of rights, and nor do they constitute the 'cores' of right complexes.

[90] Ibid 35.

CHAPTER 3

Rights Correlativity

§ I. Introduction

Scholars deem RIGHTS CORRELATIVITY to be indispensable for understanding rights. However, there has never been a comprehensive treatment of the concept(s).[1] Indeed, some of the issues the concept(s) raise have hitherto gone unnoticed. As they are indispensable to all rights models (let alone for assessing their merits), it is vital to address them.

There are actually three core disputes about correlativity in the philosophy of rights—though the first and third ones tend to be implicit in the literature. The first concerns the structures of the tethered normative positions: does correlativity mean that rights and duties must be *symmetrical*? Are correlatives the 'mirror images' of one another, or not? A second dispute is over 'existential' correlativity: must the correlated positions perforce co-obtain, or can one exist without the other(s)? For example, can there be a right without a correlative duty, or vice versa? The third regards 'justificational' correlativity: *must* all correlative relationships be explained in terms of one position grounding the other(s)? Is it necessarily the case that, when a right and a duty correlate, the right was the reason for the duty, the basis for imposing a duty on its bearer in the first place?

[1] For some partial treatments, see Radin (1929); Lyons (1970); Donnelly (1982); Kramer (1998); Gorman (2003: 83–99); Halpin (2019a, 2019b).

D. Frydrych, *The Architecture of Rights*,
https://doi.org/10.1007/978-3-030-76039-7_3

Section II explicates and assesses those three issues and the various concepts. Section III then shows how these issues affect interpretations of Hohfeld's A CLAIM, which is perhaps the most famous conception of a right-correlative-to-a-duty ('an RCTD').[2]

§ II. Disagreements About Correlativity

§ II.1. Symmetrical Versus Asymmetrical Views of Correlativity

Is CORRELATIVITY best understood as a relationship wherein (View A) two or more connected normative positions are the 'mirror images' of one another, or (View B) one or more of the positions bears features that are not reflected in the other(s)? Whilst scholars have discerned the difference between these two before,[3] no one seems to have noticed that A and B are in fact ranges of views.

Commencing with View A, it is often said that the correlatives are 'two sides of the same coin',[4] or, again, mirror images of one another.[5] I will style this the '*symmetrical view*' of correlativity. It actually admits of different versions because adherents (implicitly) disagree about whether it denotes: an *identity* or *logical equivalency*[6] of the connected positions; a relationship of *mutual entailment*; one of *logical converses*[7]; or something else.

For example, Max Radin endorses an *identity version* of the *symmetrical view*. He rejects the idea that a Hohfeldian claim and duty constitute two united but distinct positions. Instead, they are deemed to be merely two names that express the same thing: 'a relation'.[8] 'They are not even two aspects of the same thing. They are two absolutely equivalent statements

[2] See Chapter 1 note 11 on AN RCTD.

[3] E.g., Radin (1929); Anderson (1962: 43 n.3); Mullock (1971: 159).

[4] Feinberg (1980: 148–9); Donnelly (1982: 290). Both scholars deny that the metaphor fully covers matters, though. In part, this is because they seem to hold that rights are perforce claimable. Feinberg at 149–50; Donnelly at 290. They nonetheless fail to see that, if A DUTY includes the feature of being subject to claims of right, then the metaphor remains apt—as far as the claimability charge is concerned, at any rate. (But see Rainbolt (2005) on Feinberg's account). (Typically, of course, each side of a coin contains distinct images…).

[5] E.g., Radin (1929: 903).

[6] E.g., Mullock (1971: 159).

[7] E.g. Fitch (1967).

[8] Radin (1929: 903–4).

of the same thing'.[9] In part, Matthew Kramer's account of Hohfeld also reflects that stance:

> [Hohfeld] posited the correlativity for rights and duties as a definitional fundament of his theory, by explicating the concepts of 'right' and 'duty' in such a way that each *entails* the other; each *is* the other from a different perspective, in much the same way that an upward slope viewed from below is a downward slope viewed from above.[10]

The identity version is nevertheless erroneous. The positions in a correlative relationship are not the same, so it is a mistake to deny that they consitute distinct components of a jural relation. My requirement to act or forbear vis-à-vis you is not the same thing as your entitlement to my action or forbearance; that I must do something for you is not the same thing as your being entitled to my action. My power to make you a trustee is not the same thing as your being liable to being designated as such (especially as the exercise of my power changes both my status and rights in addition to yours). Take 'parent' and 'child' as a further example of correlatives. One cannot be a parent without the existence of a child, and (at least till now, technologically speaking) vice versa. This pair does not involve identical concepts, and nor is one reducible to the other; being a parent is neither the same thing as, nor reducible to, being a child, simply viewed from the vantage of one position rather than the other.[11]

Many rights scholars also ignore (potential) differences between (i) logical equivalency and entailment and (ii) between mutual (two-way) and one-way entailment. From *X*'s entailing *Y* it neither follows that *X* is strictly identical with *Y* nor that *Y* in turn necessarily entails *X*. For example, many jurists acknowledge the existence of 'absolute' duties: duties that do not correlate with rights, such as self-regarding ones. The existence of such duties undermines the *mutual equivalence* version of the

[9] Radin (1938: 1149–50). Whilst acknowledging that Hohfeld's own view is of a relationship between two united 'things', Radin believes that to be erroneous. He prefers to instead construe rights and duties as being logical converses, on the grounds that that better explains what happens when one term is replaced with the other in a given proposition. Radin (1929: 904–5). Hohfeld himself says the two positions are mere 'phases' of one jural relation, as viewed from two different angles. Hohfeld (1917: 719). Cf. Hohfeld (1917: 749–50).

[10] Kramer (1998: 24, emphases added). Cf. Ibid 33, 39, 43. Kramer conflates different possible understandings of correlativity here: mutual entailment and identity.

[11] See Stepanians (2005: 68–9). Cf. Ibid 53.

symmetrical view of correlativity, because they show that a duty is not necessarily equivalent with, or identical to, a right. Absolute duties also serve as a counterexample to the idea that duties and rights must mutually entail one another; a right may entail a duty, but not necessarily vice versa.[12] As a second example, people are sometimes susceptible to having their legal positions changed by operations of law, rather than because someone used a legal power to do so. Regardless of what Hohfeld thought of the matter, some people might believe that A LIABILITY is apt here yet deny that a liability bears a correlative in such circumstances. Hence, they would think that a power entails a liability, but not necessarily vice versa. (Absolute duties and any liabilities triggered solely by operations of law (and thus not by Hohfeldian powers), if real, would also serve as counterexamples to the idea that jural positions perforce bear correlatives, thus marking a deficit in Hohfeld's *schema*).

View B, by contrast, holds that correlatives can bear distinct features. In other words, the connected positions are neither equivalent nor identical because one or more of them might include features not borne by the other(s); they therefore need not 'mirror' each other in structure. For simplicity's sake, this shall be styled the '*asymmetrical view*' of correlativity.

Joseph Raz's account of normative positions is a good example of the *asymmetrical view*. For Raz, rights are reasons, ones that are sufficient but unnecessary grounds for imposing duties and other normative positions on (the right-holder and) others.[13] In contrast to Hohfeld, Raz also believes that a right can correlate with any number of, and different types of, normative positions, e.g., with multiple duties, liabilities, disabilities, etc.[14] These correlatives, however, are not the same reasons. Further, Raz's A DUTY is not equivalent to A RIGHT in either its content or structure. For one thing, a duty is a reason to act or forbear, rather than a reason *for another party to bear* a normative position in the first place. For another, a Razian duty is an *exclusionary* reason: in addition to the first-order normative requirement to act or forbear, it also includes a second-order normative requirement to exclude from consideration certain matters that would

[12] E.g., Wellman (1985: 57). Wellman treats the biconditional stance and its rejection as being 'weak' versus 'strong' correlativity theses. Ibid.

[13] Raz (1986: 176, 180–1, 183–4, 188, 192, 193, 202, 249); Raz (1996: 3, 41). Raz thinks rights are merely sufficient grounds because other sorts of reasons can also ground duties, e.g., those which ground absolute ones. Raz (1986: 170, 183–4, 186, 201).

[14] Ibid 167–8, 170–1; Raz (1996: 31, 46, 268). He therefore rejects what I call the Strict Bilaterality thesis, *infra* note 18.

weigh against fulfilling the duty's requirements.[15] This (purported) exclusionary feature of a duty, however, is not reflected in a Razian right.[16]

Albert Kocourek's work provides a second example of the *asymmetrical view* of correlativity. He lambastes Hohfeld on the grounds that AN IMMUNITY is insusceptibility from nothing: it merely marks someone else's lack of power.[17] Wittingly or otherwise, Kocourek is hereby criticising a *symmetrical view* of immunities and disabilities. It is a separate question whether or not his criticism is actually on target. That will depend on whether you think it accurately captures Hohfeld's view. For, as shall be discussed presently, one possible *asymmetrical view* of AN IMMUNITY is as a trump over someone else's power.

As his is the most famous model, it is worthwhile utilising Hohfeld's *schema* to further explore this issue. In fact, each one of the *schema*'s novel features is a product of Hohfeld's views about correlativity.[18] Now, in his

[15] Raz (1986: 168); Raz (1999: 58–9). Exclusionary reasons are nevertheless said to have scope: they only exclude some, but perhaps not all, of the countervailing considerations. Raz (1999: 46–7). Whether duty-bearers can easily ascertain what that scope might be is a different matter.

[16] Some Razians might disagree with this interpretation, as Raz claims that rights possess a special force, one that is reflected in the fact that they are sometimes the grounds of duties, which are peremptory reasons for action. Raz (1986: 249). However, Raz himself cannot really believe this about *legal* or *institutional* rights because he thinks there are: trivial ones, ones granted by officials by mistake, rights that are the product of corruption, morally invalid ones, etc. Ibid 180–1, 261–2; Raz (1996: 45–9). See also Chapter 6 notes 33–7 and the accompanying text.

[17] Kocourek (1920b: 32).

[18] For one thing, Hohfeld appears committed to the idea that rights and ligations only obtain as components of jural relations. (Hohfeld (1917: 722 n.30). This could be interpreted as his rejection of absolute duties. (He is certainly not unaware of their possibility. See ibid 744 n.71). I will style this the **Exclusively Jural Relations thesis**. For another, Hohfeld deems jural relationships to be solely *interpersonal*, thus rejecting the possibility of person-object relationships. Ibid 720–33. We can all this the **Interpersonal thesis.** (Both of these propositions had been defended and attacked in the rights literature for nearly a century prior to Hohfeld. A JURAL RELATION can be traced back to Savigny, at least. See Savigny (1867: 6–7, 269–80). Pound claims that Savigny got it from medieval works. Pound (1959: 65–6)). Third, what appears to be novel to Hohfeld's *schema* is his commitment to what I shall call the **Strict Bilaterality thesis**: the proposition that all jural relations only ever obtain between two parties, never more. Whilst never articulated expressly, this thesis is nonetheless implicit in his *Fundamental Legal Conceptions* articles. Strict bilaterality also adds a further specification to Hohfeld's conception of CORRELATIVITY: it requires that any given right (or ligation) have a determinate normative position tethered to it, wielded by a determinate, or potentially determinable, second party. See Hohfeld (1917: 718, 742–5). Cf. Radin (1938: 1155–6); Kramer (1998: 10 n.1). Whilst CORRELATIVITY also drives Hohfeld's deeming a unilateral liberty to form part of a jural relation, some of his predecessors had already established this idea. For a more in-depth explication of these developments, see Frydrych (2021); Frydrych (2018a).

first *Fundamental Legal Conceptions* article, he states that the basic rights and ligations are incapable of formal definition. Instead, each is to be comprehended via its relationships with its specific correlative and 'opposite' (i.e., logical contradictory) positions.[19] Despite this methodological proclamation, he nevertheless proceeds to define the four basic rights:

> A right is one's affirmative claim against another, and a privilege is one's freedom from the right or claim of another. Similarly, a power is one's affirmative "control" over a given legal relation as against another; whereas an immunity is one's freedom from the legal power or "control" of another as regards some legal relation.[20]

Notice Hohfeld's slippage between *symmetrical* and *asymmetrical views* of correlativity here. (These definitions should also be contrasted with his explications of the various correlative and 'opposite' relationships.) Consider first A LIBERTY. Is it: (A) the non-existence of a duty (not) to φ and a second party's lack of a claim to that effect, or (B) a permission to (not do) φ that outweighs, or trumps, a second party's claim that the liberty-holder must (not) φ? In *Fundamental Legal Conceptions #1* of 1913, Hohfeld tells us that the liberty of entering some land is the 'negation' of a duty to stay off.[21] It is one thing to say that *A* has a claim but *B* is nonetheless free from it (for some reason or other), and quite another to say that *A* has no claim whatsoever vis-à-vis *B*. The former (suggested by Hohfeld's definition, quoted above) means that the liberty surmounts a countervailing duty; the latter entails that there is no duty the liberty-holder requires 'freedom from' in the first place.

As already touched upon, there are bases for disagreement over AN IMMUNITY too. Hohfeld tells us that an immunity is the opposite, or 'negation' of, a liability,[22] and that a disability is the equivalent of the negation of a power.[23] On one *symmetrical view*, a Hohfeldian liability is simply susceptibility to another party's power, and an immunity is not 'freedom

[19] Hohfeld (1913a: 30).
[20] Ibid 55.
[21] Ibid 32.
[22] Ibid 55.
[23] Ibid 58 n.99.

from' a power: the correlative disability simply marks the absence of any such power (as Kocourek complained). On an *asymmetrical view*, by contrast, a liability-bearer may have an immunity that is nevertheless surmounted or trumped by the other party's power.[24]

The relationship between Hohfeldian claims and duties, which is heavily contested in the philosophy of rights literature, also serves as a good example for contrasting the *symmetrical* and *asymmetrical views* of correlativity. Compounding issues, Hohfeld also never clarifies what the modifier 'affirmative' does vis-à-vis a claim or power in his definitions above. For example, can you (performatively) *make a claim* using a Hohfeldian claim, or is the position instead simply an inert one that marks its holder as the recipient of another party's duty-required act or forbearance?

On a *symmetrical view*, a claim can be understood as an entitlement to a second party's required action or forbearance, whilst a duty is a normatively required action or forbearance owed to the entitled first party. There is nothing more to A CLAIM than the idea of being entitled to another's duty-bound action or forbearance; you need not, and do not, 'do' anything with a bona fide claim.[25]

On an *asymmetrical view*, by contrast, in addition to being an entitlement to another party's action or forbearance, a claim authorises *claiming* the required action or forbearance from the duty-bearer. However, even if claimability is a necessary feature of A CLAIM, the liability to being claimed, through some means or other, might not be a feature of A DUTY. Instead, that susceptibility is the function of separate liabilities (e.g., to compelled participation in dispute resolution processes). In other words, under this view the capacity to claim is a feature of A CLAIM, whilst liabilities to being claimed are exogenous to A DUTY. Hence, claims and duties are asymmetrical in structure.

Now, some people hold that the liability to being claimed is a feature of A DUTY itself.[26] True or not, if this is coupled with the idea that a

[24] Elsewhere, Hohfeld explains 'affirmative' in contrast to 'negative' as being the distinction between an act and a forbearance. Hohfeld (1917: 719). However, that cannot be what he means in this context.

[25] E.g., *infra* notes 55–6 and accompanying text (Finnis and Williams on Hohfeldian claims).

[26] E.g., Hart (1982: 159–60, 266) Cf. Ibid 183–4; Simmonds (1998: 223); John Stuart Mill (1863: 71). See also Appendix 1 note 65 and the accompanying text.

Hohfeldian claim bears the capacity to make claims, then that is an example of a *symmetrical view*. It also entails that claims and duties are not conceptually basic. For each position then bears at least two features. Specifically, A CLAIM would be composed of (i) being entitled to another's duty-based action or forbearance and (ii) a (set of) capacity(ies) by which to make claims of right. In turn, A DUTY includes (i) the requirement to undertake a particular action or forbearance and (ii) a (set of) liability(ies) to having the required activity or forbearance claimed of the duty-bearer in some manner.

The consequences of giving preference to one of these two vying views of correlativity are substantial. As will be shown in § III, (i) picking either the *symmetrical* or *asymmetrical views* and (ii) also deciding whether the conceptions of the normative positions can bear one or more features (i.e., whether they are 'fundamental' or not), leads to significantly different interpretations of Hohfeld's *schema*—and of A RIGHT and A DUTY more generally.

§ II.2. Existential Correlativity

A second scholarly disagreement concerns 'existential' correlativity. This is the view that certain normative positions perforce co-obtain.[27] As already seen in terms of duties and liabilities, scholars dispute which basic normative positions must bear correlatives, i.e., which must form parts of a jural relation, and which positions, if any, are capable of being freestanding.

The strongest interpretation of existential correlativity is that rights are always tied to duties *and* vice versa. Few scholars actually adhere to that biconditional stance, though. Most, including many contemporary Hohfeldians, happily acknowledge that certain duties do not correlate with rights.[28] This leaves a narrower, or 'weaker', view of existential correlativity: that all rights correlate with duties, but not vice versa.[29]

[27] The terms 'existential' and 'justificational' in reference to rights correlativity (the latter of which is discussed below in § II.3) are taken from Kramer (1998: 40).

[28] John Salmond and Kramer are notable exceptions. By rejecting the idea of absolute duties, Kramer suggests that all troublesome cases, wherein a duty-bearer is discernible, but a correlative right-holder is hard to find, can be explained in terms of a *collective* right held by the state or the community. Kramer (1998: 58–9). Cf. Salmond (1902: 224).

[29] See Wellman (1985: 57).

A handful of scholars nevertheless reject even that narrower stance. Neil MacCormick, for example, argues that rights are 'logically', and sometimes also temporally, prior to duties. For him, rights not only ground duties but can sometimes also exist without them.[30] (He nevertheless seems to believe that (i) a second party must eventually be assigned the role of duty-bearer and (ii) that unenforceable legal rights constitute 'imperfect' cases.[31])

Inspired by Raz and Hohfeld, Pavlos Eleftheriadis distinguishes between 'rights' and 'legal relations'. The former are general weighty reasons that figure into practical (including legal) reasoning, whilst the latter, identified with Hohfeld's eight fundamental normative positions, are what help to protect and effectuate a right.[32] Eleftheriadis does not himself seem to say so, but it could be thought that, *qua* general reasons, rights lack correlatives.[33]

Whilst the case may still be out on 'uncorrelated' rights, the bases for subscription to the notion are quite weak. MacCormick's particular efforts to provide examples are unsuccessful. One of his most important is a Scottish intestate statute affirming a surviving child's right to inherit. The child, he argues, has the right even without a correlative duty-bearer yet being to provide what is owed; and there is no such duty-bearer till an executor is appointed.[34] Kramer nevertheless shows that the case in question does in fact include correlative rights: the first being an immediate *in rem* right against interference with the proper distribution of the estate, and a second *in personam* right once an executor is appointed.[35] I, in turn,

[30] E.g., MacCormick (1977: 200–1).

[31] MacCormick (2007: 129). The idea of rights grounding duties does not necessarily entail a given conceptual or 'logical' priority between the two concepts thereof. For example, Joseph Raz's view of a right as a sufficient but unnecessary ground for duties entails that, whilst rights are *justificationally* prior to some duties, conceptually speaking, A DUTY is prior to A RIGHT. Raz (1986: 170–1, 180–1, 196); Raz (1996: 33, 35–6). In other words, because on Raz's view a right is a sufficient reason for grounding duties, one must first have the concept A DUTY in order to even understand the concept A RIGHT.

[32] Eleftheriadis (2008: 1, 123–8, 168). For Raz on rights as reasons, see, e.g., Raz (1986: 169, 181); Raz (1996: 46).

[33] Raz himself might reject that idea (along with Eleftheriadis' right/relation distinction). 'Nothing, however, can legitimize the notion of rights against oneself. The very idea is self-contradictory, for rights are essentially interpersonal. Their existence entails consequences to others'. Raz (1996: 33).

[34] MacCormick (1977: 200–1).

[35] Kramer (1998: 27–9). Cf. Ibid 23–4.

suggest that MacCormick's example fails to establish the lack of a correlative because the child's right is *to the legal status of being* an heir (which entails a claim to an equal share in the residue, not to particular assets per se—if there are any, that is). This right includes, amongst other things, an immunity from being divested of that status (to which others bear correlative Hohfeldian disabilities), which obtains before an executor is appointed.[36]

Raz and Eleftheriadis' bases for deeming general reasons to be rights, rather than *reasons for* rights, are also debatable. It is furthermore difficult to make sense of a Razian right *qua* legal position. For once the weighty reason is adopted by legal officials it is not, or is no longer, just a reason for grounding a duty (per Raz's analytic definition). Following August Thon and Ernst Bierling (who criticise Rudolph von Jhering's conception, which deems a legal right to be a protected interest), Roscoe Pound notes the importance of distinguishing between an interest and something conferred by law which renders that interest effective.[37] That 'something' is an entitlement, a normative position—over and above the typical modes of protection (e.g., court enforcement).

[36] Cf. MacCormick (1989: 24). Almost all Hohfeldians, moreover, reject the possibility of uncorrelated rights on conceptual grounds. E.g., Kramer (1998: 22, 31). MacCormick further argues that the heirship right's being a ground for one of the children to serve as the executor shows that the right is *logically*, and not just *temporally*, prior to the correlative duty. MacCormick (1977: 201). However, this argument seems to conflate the right to be an heir with the right to be (serve in the role of) an executor and the rights an heir has against an executor. For a similar argument, see Paulson (1979: 500–1: the right to be appointed to the office of executor does not correlate with the executor's duties. The former right *does* have existing correlative duties).

[37] Pound (1959: 70). Hohfeld agrees. Hohfeld (1917: 726 n.34). On Jhering's conception of a legal right being composed of a 'core' (the interest) plus a 'protective shell' (*die klage*: entitlement to sue), see Chapter 6 note 14.

Joel Feinberg, who otherwise seems to think that a right is a claimable claim, nevertheless extends an olive branch to what he calls 'manifesto' rights: cases where people invoke morally valid concerns about human needs that nonetheless cannot (yet) suffice to practically ground (legal?) duties in anyone. He deems this to be acceptable 'rhetorical license': people who invoke such matters are not really talking about 'rights', but merely saying that there *ought to be* rights. Feinberg (1980: 153).

§ II.3. *Justificational Correlativity*

A third—implicit—disagreement in the philosophy of rights literature is over 'justificational' correlativity. This is the idea that one normative position justifies another's existence. For example, *A*'s right is the reason for, the ground of, *B*'s duty; it is the reason why the duty was imposed upon *B* in the first place. The implied disagreement is this: is justificational correlativity a *conceptually/logically necessary* feature of: any right-duty relationship, all jural relations, and any sound account of rights?

According to Raz it is—if rights are involved, that is (for he believes there are absolute duties). Whilst Raz deems a right to be a reason that is sufficient but unnecessary ground for a duty,[38] he seems to deny that justificational correlativity ever obtains without existential correlativity.[39] Thus, my right can be the basis for your duty (and liability, and disability, etc.) even if both normative positions are (and must be) generated at the same time.

Here, then, are the various possible relationships between existential and justificational correlativity. Option A: existential correlativity can obtain without justificational correlativity and vice versa.[40] Option B: no existential correlativity without justificational correlativity. Option C: no justificational correlativity without existential correlativity. Option D: no existential without justificational and vice versa.[41]

To my mind, justificational correlativity is not a necessary feature of normative (e.g., jural) relations. Here is an example to that effect: a vehicle's right-of-way at a traffic intersection. When two roads intersect there are four (legal) ways by which a vehicle might approach the intersection. In most technologically and legally advanced countries, such intersections are governed by streetlights or stop signs. This example concerns instances governed by the latter. The general rule at such intersections is that, if

[38] Raz (1986: 166–8).

[39] See Raz (1996: 33, 34–5). Further, the right may later ground new positions in either the existing duty-holder or other parties. Raz (1986: 171).

[40] MacCormick's view, restated, allows for the possibility of justificational correlativity without existential correlativity: my already-existing right can come to serve as the grounds for imposing a duty on someone at some point.

[41] Kramer convincingly argues that existential and justificational correlativity are wholly compatible, at any rate. Kramer (1998: 38–44).

multiple vehicles are approaching the intersection, the one that arrives first has the right-of-way. This means that others must let the first vehicle to arrive traverse the intersection before they themselves may start to do so (in some legally governed sequence). There is also another common legal rule that, if two cars arrive at this sort of intersection at the same time, the one that approaches from the right side of the other has the right-of-way. Let us focus on this latter, more specific right-of-way. This rule solves a simple coordination problem. The legal right and duty created by it are temporally and justificatorily equal: one position does not ground the other. Duty-bearers have reason to comply because of the other parties' rights of way, but those rights are not the reason for the creation or existence of their correlative duties to wait. No drivers have personal interests in having such rights either. Whilst you may prefer to be able to go first in order to expedite your own journey, your arrival at the intersection from the right (direction) relative to the other driver is a mere coincidence.[42] Nor is it a role-based or kind-based right: what is the role of the 'accidentally-arriving-first-at-an-intersection-vehicle-driver'?

§ III. What Is an Hohfeldian Claim?

Hohfeld's A CLAIM, which is the most famous conception of the kind of a right that correlates with a duty, helps to further explicate certain conceptions of CORRELATIVITY, because interpretations of the former turn in part upon one's understanding the latter. Despite deeming a claim to be the 'strictest sense' of 'a right', Hohfeld, again, also proclaims all of his basic normative positions to be indefinable (formally).[43] Instead, each

[42] Nor is this right grounded in the driver's *personal* interest (itself insufficient to do the grounding) as *buttressed by* the community's interest in the driver having that right. For, again, there is no personal interest in this case that requires or warrants buttressing. This buttressing notion comes from Raz. He suggests that certain individual interests are insufficient to ground a right and must be buttressed by those of others', or the whole community's, in order for such persons to have rights. One example is that of a journalist's interest in protecting her sources; it is *the community's* interest in news reporting that adds the additional weight requisite for *the journalist* to have a right to keep her sources secret. A second example is that of parent's right to child support. It is *the child's* interest that provides much of the weight for warranting the *parent's* right to child support. Raz (1986: 247–9); Raz (1996: 49–51). Raz's buttressing approach has nonetheless been deemed fatal to his Interest theory. Sreenivasan (2005: 265–7); Leif Wenar (2008: 255).

[43] *Supra* note 19. There is also a long history of attributing a 'strict sense' of term 'a right'. Hugo Grotius, for example, did so in the seventeenth century for a right as a kind of normative power. Grotius (1625: 1.5). English and German nineteenth century Pluralist modellers who distinguished amongst the different basic types of normative positions they adjudged to

is to be comprehended through its relationships with its specific correlative and 'opposite' (i.e., logical contradictory) position, all within a scheme of two tables or matrices. Understanding A CLAIM via both its correlative (A DUTY: a normative required action or forbearance) and 'opposite' (A LIBERTY: the absence of a duty to act or forbear) suggests that a claim is an 'inert' normative position: you are simply entitled to another party's (in)action. On the other hand, in the very same work, Hohfeld also offers a definition and examples, ones suggesting that a claim does something more.[44]

Hohfeld therefore left us with a contested concept of A CLAIM. Again, this is in no small part additionally due to his inconsistency about CORRELATIVITY and how it shapes normative positions. To this day, Hohfeldians disagree about whether it is merely an entitlement to another party's action or forbearance, or if it additionally authorises its holder to *make* claims of right. Is a claim therefore 'inert', or is it instead self-exercisable or self-enforceable? Sometimes Hohfeld seems to support a *symmetrical view*, other times an *asymmetrical* one. Compounding the problem, many of the two *Fundamental Legal Conceptions* articles' examples of claims are quotations from judges and scholars. Whether Hohfeld actually endorses what each person states, or is instead using it as an example of what he considers to be fallacious reasoning, is often debatable.[45] To better understand this interpretive dispute it will help to introduce a common heuristic in the philosophy of rights: the active/passive distinction.

The Active/Passive Distinction

The philosophy of rights has long employed an active/passive distinction to help explain different kinds of normative positions.[46] (This is not the same thing as the difference between *symmetrical* and *asymmetrical views* of correlativity.) The distinction carves up the various fundamental types of rights and ligations as being either 'active' or 'passive'. More specifically, it identifies the position as: authorising or requiring a certain action, or the forbearance from an action; marking the (in)competency to act; or

be 'rights' (e.g., a claim, a liberty, a power, etc.) tended to deem one to constitute the strict sense thereof. See, e.g., Pound (1959: Chapter 21); Salmond (1902: 219–36).

[44] *Supra* note 20 and the accompanying text.

[45] See, e.g., *infra* note 53.

[46] Whatever its true provenance, the distinction certainly predates the twentieth century. E.g., Salmond (1902: 225), who cites to earlier authors discussing it.

as marking its holder as the person towards whom a different person's action or forbearance is to be directed or to affect.[47]

Bear in mind that 'active' and 'passive' are misleading labels. Normative positions mark out what each party is entitled to, able to do, required to do, unable to do, etc. An active right, though, is neither an action, nor the physical basis by which, or through which, someone acts. Rights may authorise actions, but the physical acts thereby authorised are events, not normative positions.[48] Take the right to self-defence as an example: the act of kicking an attacker is not itself a right; a right is rather what entitles you to kick the attacker.

The distinction is best explained in terms of two agents, be they individuals or groups, and one normatively guided or authorised action. An active right renders its holder competent or entitled to act. A second party, the ligation-bearer, is directly affected by that act.[49] Further, a right is 'active' even if it is not being exercised at a given moment; it suffices that it be potentially exercisable.

For example, assume ***arguendo*** that (at least certain) powers count as rights and that the power to give a gift is a token of the type. The right to gift something to a friend enables the owner (the power-holder) to alter

[47] E.g., White (1984: 13). Leif Wenar explains the distinction thus: 'Active rights are signalled by statements of the form "A has a right to φ"; while passive rights are signalled by statements of the form "A has a right that B φ" (in both of these formulas, "φ" is an active verb)'. Wenar (2020). The active/passive distinction applies to all rights models, even monistic ones (i.e., those positing only a single conceptually basic kind of right); for it still makes sense to say that that one kind of right is 'active' or 'passive'.

[48] For a discussion of the difference between facts and normative positions, see Hohfeld (1913a: 20, 21, 24, 43, 52). Andrew Halpin thinks Hohfeld's rigid fact/position distinction is problematic. It is a mistake, he thinks, to treat normative positions as being wholly abstract and thus disconnected from the facts comprising human action. See Halpin (1997: 29–30). It is nonetheless unclear whether Hohfeld's division between facts and positions is as firm as Halpin suggests.

[49] The right-holder's action affects the ligation-bearer directly, even if the latter is not cognisant of it. For example, *A* exercises a liberty to park a car in a public parking spot. This directly affects *B* because *B* cannot park there in the interim. However, *A* need not have acted with *B* in mind, and nor must *B* even be aware of the fact that *A* has acted.

the friend's legal status from non-owner to owner of the gifted item by undertaking some legally valid performative act.

By contrast, a 'passive' right marks its holder as the intended recipient or beneficiary of a second party's action, forbearance, or incompetency. It is the second party, the ligation-bearer, who must, must not, or cannot act vis-à-vis the right-holder. Here, the ligation is 'active', whilst the correlative right is 'passive'. However, even if the ligation is active it does not follow that the ligation-bearer is entitled to act—even if he or she *must* so act; for whilst the duty ought to be fulfilled, whether the duty-bearer is entitled to act in any of the myriad ways that would enable him or her to do so is a distinct matter. For example, you may bear a duty to deliver flowers to a particular office at a particular time, but due to the building being locked, you have no authority to enter and complete the delivery.[50]

Scholars dispute which basic types of normative positions are active or passive. Regarding Hohfeld's *schema*, for example, the majority interpretation is that liberties and powers are active, whilst claims and immunities are passive.[51] The minority holds that claims and/or immunities are, or can also be, active rights.[52] (All would probably agree, though, that a duty-to-act is the only active kind of ligation.)

Hohfeldians particularly disagree amongst themselves about claims. On the active interpretation, a claim not only entitles its holder to another party's duty-based action or forbearance; it also enables the holder to *make* a claim of right—where 'claiming' usually means being able to

[50] Cf. Kramer (1998: 17–8); Simmonds (1998: 184 n.91); Steiner (1994: 74–85).

[51] E.g., Kocourek (1920b: 25); Williams (1956); Finnis (1972); Wellman (1985: 70–1, but cf. ibid 39); Halpin (1991: 293); Kramer (1998: 13–4, 22 n.8); Brown (2005); Rainbolt (2006: 32–3).

[52] E.g., Simmonds (1998: 223 & n.137); Eleftheriadis (2008); Cf. Stewart (2012: 339); Gilbert (2018: 27 n 48, 56–7). American Legal Realists interpreted Hohfeldian claims as not being only active, but also invariably enforceable. E.g., Radin (1938: 1148, 1152); Llewellyn (1951: 96). On the Legal Realists on rights, see Frydrych (2018a).

initiate legal proceedings.[53] Those who interpret a claim thus sometimes deem it to be a species of normative power.[54]

On the passive interpretation, by contrast, a claim simply marks a party as the intended recipient of a duty-required action or forbearance. Hohfeldian claims do not entitle or authorise their holders to act. You therefore cannot make claims using a claim. John Finnis' and Glanville Williams' understandings reflect the passive view:

> *A Hohfeldian claim-right can never be to do or omit something: it always is a claim that somebody else do or omit something*. A's claim-right is always to B's action or omission, never to A's.[55]

[53] The most conspicuous active view examples in Hohfeld's works are probably the quotes from Justices Jackson and Sneed in Hohfeld (1913a: 30–1) 'a legal claim to do', 'whatever may be lawfully claimed', from Justice Stayton in Hohfeld (1917: 717 n.16) an 'enforceable claim', and from the book edition edited by Cook:

> [Compare the following passage from Holmes, *The Common Law*, 214: 'A legal right is nothing but a permission to exercise certain natural powers, and upon certain conditions to obtain protection, restitution, or compensation by the aid of the public force.']

Hohfeld (1919: 42 n.39).

At least some of the relevant quotes and text, such as the one just provided, are not found in Hohfeld's essays as originally published. They made their way into the posthumously published book versions. Whether they are all really Hohfeld's own amendments (ones based upon recommendations for changes derived from his notes: he was planning to publish the essays in a book), or instead unscrupulous insertions by his editor, Walter Wheeler Cook, may be impossible to discover. The 1919 book's first *Fundamental Legal Conceptions* chapter notes that it is reprinted with permission from the Yale Law Journal and 'with manuscript changes by the author'. Hohfeld (1919: 23). The 1923 version includes a preface noting that all of the changes and additions to the text, aside from some purely typographical ones, are indicated in Hohfeld's manuscript notes. This new material, the preface states, is noted in the text either by being enclosed in square brackets or, in the case of a new footnote, indicated by the letter 'a', e.g., '32a'. Hohfeld (1923). There may be reason to doubt that all of the square bracketed material originates with Hohfeld rather than Cook, though. Unfortunately, the preface's caveat and/or the letters marking new footnotes and the square brackets were dropped in some of the later editions. See, e.g., Hohfeld (1964); Hohfeld (2001). These additions certainly influenced certain scholars' 'active' interpretations of a claim and their endorsement of the Will theory. E.g., Wellman (1985: 35, 39); Steiner (1998: 244 n.19).

[54] E.g., Simmonds (1998: 223).

[55] Finnis (1972: 380). Finnis also says that '[a] claim-right is always either, positively, a right to be given something (or assisted in a certain way) by someone else, or, negatively, a right *not* to be interfered with or dealt with or treated in a certain way, by someone else.

> No one ever has a [claim-]right to do something; he only has a right that some one [sic] else shall do (or refrain from doing) something. In other words, every right in the strict sense relates to the conduct of another, while a liberty and a power relate to the conduct of the holder of the liberty or power.[56]

It may be tempting to interpret these scholars as suggesting here that, whilst the content of a claim is the duty-based action, the claim nevertheless authorises the making of a claim of right. For example, *B* owes *A* ten dollars. Whilst *B* must transfer the funds, *A* may also claim the money from *B*. On the passive view, this suggestion is erroneous. Claiming a right is a normatively permitted act. Yet a *Hohfeldian* claim, interpreted as a passive position, concerns a second party's conduct: the duty-bearer's requirement to act or forbear from action (here, to transfer the ten dollars).

The dispute between the active and passive interpretations is not merely terminological. Furthermore, the use of the term 'a claim' for a (kind of a) right, and its active interpretation, has roots in the nineteenth-century German jurisprudential concept *ANSPRUCH*, which was often taken to mean both an entitlement to another's duty and the capacity to claim, if not still older ideas.[57] However, the dispute about whether A RIGHT is necessarily self-enforceable, and hence an active normative position, dates back—at least—to the middle ages.[58]

As noted in § II.1 above, were the ability to claim a feature of a Hohfeldian claim, then the latter would not be conceptually basic—a

When the subject matter of one's claim of right is one's own act(s), forbearance(s), or omission(s), that claim cannot be to a claim-right, but can only be to a liberty or, in the case of juridical acts, to a power'. Finnis (2011: 200).

Finnis furthermore asserts that a claim of right concerning the claimant's own behaviour cannot be 'to a' Hohfeldian claim. Ibid. Instead, he should have said that such claims of right are neither made by utilising Hohfeldian claims, nor undertaken simply for the sake of procuring for oneself a Hohfeldian claim. For, to build upon Feinberg's point, claimants want not only the liberty or power to act, but probably also to be granted Hohfeldian claims against non-interference by others. See Feinberg (1980: 149–52) and Chapter 4 § V on Feinberg's notion of 'making claim to' being granted a right.

56 Williams (1956: 1145).

57 E.g., Brinz (1857: 49–50, 52); Bierling (1877: 39–40); Thon (1878: chapters 5–7). See also Pound (1915: 105–11) and Pound (1959: 62–6, 69–70) discussing (amongst others) the views of rights of nineteenth century German legal scholars such as Alois Brinz, Bernhard Windscheid, August Thon, and Ernst Bierling. Cf. Hart (1982: 183–4, 188, 194, 159–60, 266).

58 See, e.g., Tierney (1997: 36, 55–68, 117–8, 189).

metatheoretical desideratum Hohfeld believes his conceptions ought to meet. That, I think, is the best reason to endorse the passive interpretation over the active one. Adding the capacity to claim as a feature of A CLAIM renders the concept subject to decomposition into more basic components. On the active interpretation, it is: (i) an entitlement to someone else's act or forbearance and (ii) a normative capacity or permission, or set of them, to act oneself, i.e., to performatively claim. Furthermore, the capacity to claim is better explained in terms of other normative positions, i.e., liberties, powers, and complexes thereof.

The same holds for AN IMMUNITY. It is better understood as marking a disability-bearer's powerlessness (incompetence) to alter certain of the immunity-holder's other normative positions. On the passive interpretation, in other words, you do not 'exercise' an immunity either. Again, on the active interpretation, an immunity is a trump over another's power that is somehow utilised by its holder. However, the capacity (and permission) to exercise the position would not only make AN IMMUNITY conceptually complex, but also any such 'utilisation' would be better explained in terms of other positions (i.e., powers, liberties, etc.).

Notice, however, that the same argument cannot be used to champion a *symmetrical view* of AN IMMUNITY over an *asymmetrical* rival; for it need not be the case that, on the latter interpretation, one must exercise the immunity in order for it to trump another party's power. In other words, on an *asymmetrical view*, AN IMMUNITY could trump another's power without the immunity-holder having to act to make it do so. Thus, the position need not be conceptually complex.[59]

[59] Whilst it is valuable for flagging the fact that normatively authorised, entitled, or required actions are features of many if not all rights and ligations, the active/passive distinction cannot accurately or fully account for what normative positions do and require. Indeed, passive understandings of immunity/disability relations and claim/duty-to-forbear relations mark the breakdown of the distinction's soundness and utility. For where is the relevant 'action'? Further, how are we to understand duties of the following sort: the duty to obey a commander's orders? (This, rather than the duty to obey a commander's particular order, e.g., to go over the trench.) Is a duty to adhere to a state of affairs (e.g., an authoritative command structure), or to adhere to future orders, really best described as a normative requirement to act or forbear? Third, powers affect *both* the power-holder and liability-bearer's positions concurrently. *A*'s gift-giving to *B* changes both parties' statuses vis-à-vis the chattel. Is the power-holder's position *both* active and passive, then? Does the power correlate with liabilities in both a second party and the power-holder?.

CHAPTER 4

Rights Exercise and Enforcement

§ I. Introduction

This chapter provides working conceptions of RIGHTS EXERCISE, RIGHTS ENFORCEMENT, REMEDYING RIGHTS, and RIGHTS VINDICATION.[1] Despite their ubiquitous employment, to the best of my knowledge, there has never been a significant attempt to distinguish (and clarify) all of these concepts. This may partly be due to the fact that the *terms* 'rights exercise', 'enforcement', 'remedying' etc., are frequently used interchangeably, which masks pertinent differences amongst the concepts.

To summarise, rights *exercise* concerns authorised or permitted actions or omissions that advance a right's content, regardless of the right-holder's subjective motivation for acting. Rights *enforcement*, in turn, is a subset of modes of rights exercise. It involves attempts to vindicate a right or to procure remedies for its violation. Rights remedying and vindication also differ, as the former is a subset of the latter. Vindication sometimes merely concerns status recognition, as opposed to procuring or imposing some form of compensation from, or a sanction upon, another party. The chapter then addresses the literature on claims of right.

[1] Not analytic definitions thereof.

D. Frydrych, *The Architecture of Rights*,
https://doi.org/10.1007/978-3-030-76039-7_4

§ II. Exercisable Rights Versus Active Rights

The active/passive distinction governs an individual normative position—a conceptually basic type of right or ligation—understood exclusively vis-à-vis its specific correlative, e.g., a Hohfeldian claim vis-à-vis a duty. The distinction therefore cannot explain the *interplay* amongst normative positions outside of their correlative pairings, i.e., how one (e.g., a claim) can be used in conjunction with another (e.g., a power). Hence, it cannot account for all the ways rights can be exercised.

Whilst the active/passive distinction helps to show how some kinds of rights are exercisable, it would be wrong to assume that only active rights are so. On the contrary, this section posits that active rights can be used to exercise 'right complexes' containing passive positions as components, if not also the passive position component directly. In other words, 'passive' rights are potentially exercisable *qua* components of a complex, even if they are not self-exercisable. Thus, the set of exercisable rights is larger than the set of active rights.

Here are two examples. The first is a right to a contract option. This is a complex composed of: a right-correlative-to-a-duty ('an RCTD') correlating with my duty to let you call in the option whenever you please; liberties (and a power) to call in the option or not; a power to modify the contract; etc. The liberties (and power) by which to call in the option exercise the entire right complex, not just themselves. In ordinary and legal parlance, it makes sense to say that you exercised your option right, and not just that you had a power and accompanying liberties which were exercised. Consider as a second example the calling in of a debt. You owe me 100 pounds, collectable at will. Amongst other things, you have a duty to pay, whilst I have an RCTD to the money. You call me on the telephone and say, 'come collect the money whenever you please'. I show up at your office next week. I thereby exercise my right to claim the debt, i.e., I exercised the right complex.

It is also important to note that RIGHTS EXERCISE does not require that one and the same person possess both the passive position (e.g., an RCTD or an immunity) and the means of the overall complex's exercise. In other words, to count as exercisable, analytically (but perhaps not morally or politically), it is irrelevant whether right-holders exercise their rights personally, or other authorised parties do so on their behalf, e.g., a legal guardian for a child, a trustee for a beneficiary, an agent for a principal, a state official for a citizen, etc.

§ III. Rights Exercise, Enforcement, Remedying, and Vindication

§ III.1. Exercise Versus Enforcement

How can one proclaim that the set of exercisable rights is larger than the set of active ones without already knowing what rights exercise is? This section provides the beginnings of clarification of that concept. Here is a preliminary suggestion. RIGHTS EXERCISE is *a normatively authorised or permitted action or omission, undertaken either in furtherance of a right's content.* There are two parts to this conception: (i) an entitlement to act; and (ii) acting in a way that advances a right's content.

What does it mean to 'advance' the content, and why is it a feature? Take the right to park a vehicle in a public parking spot as an example. That right's features might include: the authorisation to park; being able to assert to others that they ought to refrain from acting in certain ways (e.g., from moving your vehicle, touching it); etc. The right's content, though, is about parking. You exercise your right *by parking* your vehicle in a parking spot.

Must rights *solely* be used to further their contents, though? No. People can and often do use their rights for ulterior purposes: to extort or punish others, to gain publicity, etc. Here are some examples. First, *A* sues *B*, who has infringed *A*'s right, simply because *A* knows it will hurt *B* financially to go through a costly litigation process. *A*'s real aim is this sadistic undertaking, not vindicating the right as such.[2] Second, lawyers sometimes exploit procedural rights just to drag out proceedings (by filing genuine

[2] Even so, it makes sense to say that *A* 'enforced' the right (which, it will be argued below, is a way to exercise it), despite *A*'s being somewhat indifferent to the right *qua* right. Alternatively, we might say that *A exercised* a secondary right in order to *enforce* the primary one, not because *A* cares about the secondary right as such, but rather because of the fear and anger its use might instil in *B*.

Civil law jurisdictions have the doctrine of 'abuse of rights'. *Black's Law Dictionary* (11th edn, 2019) defines it thus. 'The principle that a person may be liable for harm caused by doing something the person has a right to do, if the right is exercised (1) for the purpose or primary motive of causing harm, (2) without a serious and legitimate interest that is deserving of judicial protection, (3) against morality, good faith, or elementary fairness, or (4) for a purpose other than its intended legal purpose'. However, the example here, and those that follow, concern legally permissible actions in common law systems, ones which are not impugned or voided because of the right-holder's subjective motivation for exercising their rights.

but unnecessary motions, say), which in turn puts financial pressure on opponents, giving them an incentive to settle or drop a lawsuit. Third, people are usually motivated to sell their houses for the monetary gain, rather than out of a special concern with their right to alienate *qua* right, e.g., to vindicate their property-holding status. Fourth, you generally solicit others to enter into contracts in order to engage in mutually (or individually) profitable exchanges, not out of concern with the right to solicit as such. Fifth, people can also sometimes exercise their rights without even being aware of doing so, such as when parties make a legal contract despite believing that they merely have an informal agreement.

Therefore, the initial suggestion about RIGHTS EXERCISE requires further specification. Particularly, the idea of normative actions 'undertaken in furtherance of a right's content' need not concern the right-holder's subjective motivations for so acting. Exercising a 'right to φ' by undertaking action X furthers that right's content (φ-ing), even if the holder's ulterior motive for so acting is really to accomplish outcome ψ.

With this modification, our conception ought to be able to cover the cases mentioned in the penultimate paragraph: *A* exercises his right to sue *B* by commencing litigation, even though all *A* personally cares about is thereby hurting *B* financially. *C* furthers the content of her right to alienate her property by soliciting and finalising a sale to *D*, even though all *C* really cares about is the financial bottom line.[3] It makes sense to say that *A*

[3] It might further be objected that not all normatively authorised actions count as rights exercise. Two candidate counterexamples are adverse possession and dishonest transferring, i.e., the exception to the *Nemo Dat* rule. (These two are also often taken to be examples of legal powers that are not rights).

Adverse possession is easier to counter: it simply does not concern (*ex ante*) normative authorisation. You breach duties by trespassing on *A*'s land. The law holds that, after a given statutory period, and after meeting all the statutory requirements, your actions entitle you to gain relatively superior title to the property. More accurately, meeting all the statutory requirements *bestows* rights upon you. You did not exercise a right (or a non-right power—if there even are any valid legal powers that do not count as legal rights, that is) to adversely possess the land. What you did was simply unauthorised, and you were not—directly—entitled to so act. In Hohfeldian terms, adverse possession is best explained in terms of meeting all the relevant 'operative facts' (Hohfeld (1913a: 25–7)) for the legal doctrine, which converts the tortfeasor into a party with relatively superior title. (Prior to the limitation period being met the adverse possessor may have 'inchoate' possessory rights vis-à-vis third parties, including powers, but not powers or RCTDs as against the original owner. Cf. Moore, Grattan, and Griggs (2020: 181–2)).

What about the dishonest transferor? *A* steals *B*'s television, and then sells it to *C*, a third-party purchaser for value without notice, i.e., someone who genuinely did not know the item

and *C* exercised their rights, even if the parties were indifferent to their rights *qua* rights.

Not all forms of rights exercise are positive acts: omissions can count too. For example, you can exercise your right against self-incrimination by not taking the stand in a legal proceeding. (At least conceptually this need not depend on some assertion, gesture, or performance on the right-holder's part, such as orally refusing to take the stand.) Whilst it is beyond this chapter's purview to give a comprehensive account of what constitutes 'an action', cases involving neither performative utterances nor actions are nevertheless often spoken of as being 'acts of omission'. Furthermore, the working conception here is not restricted to self-exercise. *A* can be authorised or permitted to exercise *B*'s right.

What, then, is rights enforcement? What is its relationship to rights exercise? Are they distinct, is one a subset of another, or are they just the same? There may be no shared criteria amongst ordinary folks, lawyers, and/or philosophers about what counts as rights enforcement. Indeed, legal, philosophical, and ordinary discourse about it is ambiguous amongst:

Sense A: a capacity or set of capacities enabling efforts *to try* to ensure that a correlative duty-bearer complies with the duty;

Sense B: a capacity or set of capacities enabling efforts *to try* to obtain a remedy or other form of vindication for (threatened) rights violations;

Sense C: *successfully* securing duty compliance;

was stolen. Irrespective of *A*'s criminal and civil liability, in some jurisdictions still, *C* gains superior title to *B*, the original owner. This means that, whilst *A* was under a duty not to steal or transfer the television, the subsequent exchange was nonetheless capable of creating legally valid rights in *C*, directly or indirectly. How could *A* have been 'normatively authorised' to so act despite bearing a duty to forbear from doing so? The dark options are two-fold. Option 1: the law treats the 'exchange' as mere operative facts, rather the dishonest transferor's use of a power to create a valid contract, which creates rights in *C*. Option 2: *A* *is* legally authorised to do so—in a way. The power to contract is not actually rendered invalid or impotent by an associated duty not to exercise it. *A* is thus legally capable of doing that which is not permitted (creating a contract to sell a thief's title). See, e.g., Hart (1982: 212). The dishonest transfer rule might therefore be said to contain a paradox ('you are empowered to do what you must not do, let alone that doing so will render you liable to punishment and rectificatory action'). Cf. Terry (1884: 90–1). The question then becomes whether 'authorisation' is better associated with a power or a liberty (or a complex containing both)—but note the disjunction in the working conception (i.e., 'authorised or permitted').

Sense D: being awarded (the tertiary right to) a remedy, or some other means of vindication.

Sense E: successful effectuation/procurement of the remedy or alternative means of vindication.

Clearer distinctions in philosophical and legal rights vocabulary may nevertheless be warranted to mark these differences. For example, many scholars treat certain sorts of normative positions as instruments of rights enforcement, but almost no lawyer or jurist believes that enforcement efforts must be successful. How can a failed effort count as 'enforcement', then? It is odd, but perhaps not nonsensical, to say that 'Suzy enforced her rights by going to court, but the judge decided against her'. One might therefore be inclined to replace 'enforced' with 'tried to enforce'. Thus, despite being commonly considered as such (particularly in terms of secondary rights) in the philosophy of rights literature and elsewhere, one could object to Senses A and B's being included as features of RIGHTS ENFORCEMENT. On the other hand, as the term 'enforcement' is commonly employed for both efforts and successes, its usage ought not to be limited to one subset or the other.

In the literature, moreover, 'enforcement' typically concerns certain normative powers—those enabling right-holders: to try to ensure duty compliance; to try to seek a remedy for (anticipated) breaches of ligations; to try to vindicate the right in other ways; or to secure a third-party-ordered remedy. In legal contexts, this often means commencing and prosecuting authoritative, institutional dispute resolution processes such as litigation.[4]

'Enforcement' is also generally used therein as a synecdoche for enforcement and waiver. In other words, waiver (a capacity to forego undertaking remedy- or vindication-seeking activities or proceedings, despite being entitled to do so) is counted as a subset of enforcement mechanisms. (In legal contexts, officials or authorised agents generally preside over dispute resolution processes in order to provide determinative, binding resolutions to disputes.) Whilst a given morality or a set of social conventions need not have analogous dispute resolution mechanisms, it may nevertheless contain other ways by which to enforce rights (sometimes).

[4] See Chapter 7 § III for discussions of the legal versions of these powers. For HLA Hart's famous list of such private law ones, see Hart (1982: 183–4) and Chapter 5 § II note 16 and the accompanying text.

Even so, why *should* waiver be deemed to be a form of enforcement?[5] It is difficult to square with enforcement's being a way to protect or defend a right. Would it not be better to construe waiver instead as a way of 'controlling' a right?[6] As shall be discussed in Chapter 7, for example, there are possible disconnects between controlling and enforcing rights. Several candidate ways of controlling rights can also help to distinguish exercise from enforcement, such as alienation (through sale, gifting, transfer, etc.) and nullification.

There have been few efforts to analyse enforcement as such. Let us address three, starting with John Salmond's. Initially, his appears to be under-inclusive in being restricted to legal proceedings.[7] Salmond nevertheless posits a direct/indirect enforcement distinction, which greatly expands his account's scope of coverage. Indirect enforcement helps to explain how rights can continue to be legally valid even if they cannot (any longer) *ground* legal proceedings, e.g., being time-barred by a statute of limitations. Even so, these 'imperfect rights' retain legal recognition and protection in most circumstances.[8] Here are some of his examples of indirect enforcement.

> [By way of defence:] An imperfect right is good as a ground of defence, though not as a ground of action. I cannot sue for a chattel belonging to me, which has been in the possession of another person for six years; but if by any means it comes back into my possession, I can defend myself on the strength of my ownership against the claim of the prior possessor. Similarly I cannot sue on an informal contract, but if money is paid or property delivered to me in pursuance of it, I can successfully defend any claim for its recovery... [By way of security:] An imperfect right is sufficient to support any security that has been given for it. A mortgage or pledge remains perfectly valid, although the debt secured by it has ceased to be directly enforceable.[9]

[5] Cf. Wellman (1985: 72–3).

[6] Cf. Hart (1982: 183–4).

[7] 'The term enforcement is here used in a wide sense to include the maintenance of a right or duty by any term of compulsory legal process, whether civil or criminal. There is a narrower use of the term, in which it includes only the case of civil proceedings'. Salmond (1902: 239 n.1).

[8] Ibid 240. See Chapter 8 for further discussion of imperfect rights.

[9] Salmond (1902: 241–2, 266). An imperfect right may nevertheless become perfect later. Ibid 242.

Salmond therefore suggests that indirect enforcement obtains even if the right-holder remains passive throughout the process. His account nonetheless accounts for private enforcement efforts, ones undertaken by the right-holder personally, inadequately.

A second account is Joshua Kleinfeld's. Building upon and criticising Oona Hathaway and Scott Shapiro's work, he provides one of the few efforts to provide a conception of enforcement in law generally.[10] For him, enforcement is an activity in which a legally constituted power is applied (by legal officials or those legally deputised to so act) to make the law's dictates actual, via specified, authorised legal mechanisms.[11]

There are several components to Kleinfeld's 'enforcement-as-efficacy' conception.[12] First, enforcement is a means to an end: it makes legal norms 'actual', i.e., obtain in the world.[13] Second, those norms are made to obtain because they are backed by the law's power.[14] However, the exercise of such power must itself be *legally* constituted,[15] whilst the imposition of costs for violating the law, and the authority to determine those costs, must be specified by the law or the law's agents.[16]

His conception also includes a test for distinguishing *legal* enforcement from other kinds of sanctions, costs, or consequences (e.g., moral or social ones),[17] including informal enforcers and mechanisms that might be legally authorised.[18] To qualify, an exercise of power must be grounded in a (legally valid) secondary enforcement rule.[19] Kleinfeld's test thus aims to '[limit] the range of *legal* enforcement from all mechanisms of efficacious power whatsoever to only those properly attribut[able] to the law'.[20] Accordingly, it must involve specified, authorised legal mechanisms.[21]

[10] Kleinfeld (2011); Hathaway and Shapiro (2011).
[11] Kleinfeld (2011: 293, 300–1).
[12] Ibid 300–1, 302.
[13] Ibid 296.
[14] Ibid 296, 298.
[15] Ibid 298.
[16] Ibid 299.
[17] Ibid 302.
[18] Ibid 300 n.14.
[19] Ibid 300. For applications thereof, see ibid 303–5.
[20] Kleinfeld (2011: 303).
[21] E.g., ibid 304.

What is an enforcement rule, though? 'Modifying' Oona Hathaway and Scott Shapiro's distinction,[22] Kleinfeld distinguishes 'primary enforcement rules', which are addressed to conduct rule violators and require them to perform a duty or to 'forgo some beneficial right', from 'secondary enforcement rules', which are addressed to third parties, who are affixed with rights/permissions (more on this below) and/or duties by which to act against a conduct rule violator in order to enforce the law.[23] Per Hathaway and Shapiro, '[s]econdary enforcement rules come into play when the conduct rule violator fails to follow the primary enforcement rules'.[24]

Whilst there are several bases for criticising Kleinfeld's conception,[25] let us just focus on its under-inclusivity in two ways. First, vis-à-vis legal right-holders' (discretionary, permissive) modes of enforcement, which fall (at least) under *primary* enforcement rules. Second, concerning legal modes of enforcement which are not grounded in 'enforcement rules'; for legal enforcement of legal rights (as opposed to social or moral enforcement of a legal norm) need not be predicated upon primary or secondary enforcement rules exclusively.

[22] Hathaway and Shapiro (2011: 270–1).

[23] Kleinfeld (2011: 298 n.10). The modification is to explicitly include power-conferring rules within the set. This, on the assumption that, as Hathaway and Shapiro deem the enforcement rules to just be a subset of conduct rules (rules telling people which actions they are required or permitted (not) to perform), the former would only concern duties and liberties. Ibid 299 n.11; Hathaway and Shapiro (2011: 270–1).

[24] Hathaway and Shapiro (2011) 271.

[25] For one thing, enforcement is not a matter of actualisation. It concerns existent primary rights. For another, Kleinfeld's conception appears to include the *explanandum* within the *explanans*: being grounded in a (secondary) enforcement rule does not really explain what makes something an 'enforcement' rule. More generally, his conception of EFFICACY is too circumscribed. In part, the problem of seeing enforcement as efficacy is in treating the latter in terms of actuality and power—where 'power' means enforcement power grounded in a secondary enforcement rule. This is under-inclusive both as to EFFICACY and ENFORCEMENT as there are other ways of making legal norms active and effective independent of enforcement. For example, when *A* and *B* make a contract, believe themselves to have a legal contract, and consider themselves to be bound by its terms, why have they not helped to make the relevant contract laws 'actual'? Kleinfeld thus incorrectly frames the boundaries between a norm's existence, its enforcement, and its being rendered efficacious. Enforcement is a sufficient but unnecessary means for making a legal norm 'effective'.

Regarding the primary/secondary enforcement rules distinction, the place for legal right-holders undertaking permissive, discretionary, yet formal legal enforcement is left somewhat ambiguous. Is it per primary or secondary enforcement rules? Both? Neither? Kleinfeld himself is sceptical about primary enforcement rules; he is dubious that legal systems' enforcement rules are ever directed towards duty-bearers directly.[26] It is doubtful that that fully covers Hathaway and Shapiro's account of such rules, though. They claim that primary enforcement rules are directed at 'conduct rule' violators, whilst secondary enforcement rules are 'secondary' by virtue of being directed at third parties.[27] Even so, their first example of the primary/secondary distinction is affixing a parking ticket to someone parked illegally (primary) and a rule directed at the scofflaw's employer to garnish the person's wages for not having paid the parking ticket.[28] However, the power to issue a parking ticket is with a parking enforcement officer.[29] Thus, Hathaway and Shapiro must really mean that primary enforcement rules concern both (i) conduct duty-bearers and (ii) certain legal officials.

If so, then, at least armed with Kleinfeld's modification of including power-conferring rules, primary enforcement rules would also seem to be capable of including right-holders who possess legal capacities by which to enforce their rights. (There are of course clear grounds for secondary enforcement rules engendering rights-enforcement too—particularly for tertiary rights, e.g., officials granting, and then enforcing, writs of execution.) At any rate, the law is rife with examples of enforcement by right-holders personally, or someone authorised to act on their behalf. These include both right-holders' capacity and/or entitlement to claim its performance (and to waive doing so), as it were, even before (the threat of) breach.[30] There are also right-holders' 'secondary'/'remedial' rights, such as those authorising the undertaking of self-help 'remedies'.[31] If

[26] Kleinfeld (2011: 298 n.10).

[27] Hathaway and Shapiro (2011: 271 & n.49).

[28] Ibid 271.

[29] The powers to levy fines and to declare outlawry are also held by legal officials. Ibid 288.

[30] Chapter 7 § II 'Arguments I-II' will style these 'primary enforcement powers', per the primary/secondary/tertiary distinction outlined in Chapter 1 § II.1.

[31] Examples include a landlord's personally evicting a tenant, and an owner's reclaiming stolen chattel using legal liberties and powers that perhaps need not be exclusively employed for remedial purposes.

these needed to be squeezed into one of the two categories, then they all seem to be examples of the utilisation of primary enforcement rules.

On the other hand, Hathaway and Shapiro appear to exclude 'self-help' actions from counting as cases of law enforcement. In fleshing out their own thesis about law and enforcement, they discuss medieval Icelandic law where, in addition to having public prosecutions for duty violations, ancient Icelanders also engaged in feuding and private settlements for disputes. Hathaway and Shapiro state that they assume the latter two were not forms of law enforcement because the law prioritised prosecution and afforded greater rights to prosecutors than to feuding parties.[32]

However, the existence of a priority scheme is no proof that feuding was not a mode of law enforcement, or, at least, conceptually, that it could not be. Moreover, Hathaway and Shapiro note that Iceland 'outsourced' law enforcement by relying on community members to implement it through outlawry (which included the legal authorisation of violence and killing).[33] They also tell us that, even when public prosecutions were held against conduct rule violators, parties to a dispute were 'free' to abandon the proceedings at any time in order to engage in bloody attacks on the other party.[34] Feuding's unpalatability does not mean either that it was legally prohibited at the time, or, more interestingly, that feuding fails to count as the exercise of 'primary enforcement rules' (if initiated by the right-holder whose right was violated) or 'secondary enforcement rules'.[35]

One might object that feuding (unlike, perhaps, blood avenging in the Bible) was not legally required by the Icelandic system: it was merely permitted. So, something might turn here on *permission to enforce (and discretion to enforce)* versus *being duty-bound to enforce*. Moreover, one might think that enforcement actions must be mandatory in some sense.

[32] Hathaway and Shapiro (2011: 287 n.101).

[33] Hathaway and Shapiro (2011: 289). On Icelandic outlawry, see ibid 287–8.

[34] Ibid 289 n.113. People were at liberty to do so, if they indeed were, to the extent that they were not duty-bound to forbear from doing so.

[35] Compare this with the Bible's liberty and duty of blood vengeance. Before a manslaughterer reached one of the cities of refuge, the law required, let alone permitted, atonement by blood, spilled by the 'blood avenger', i.e., the victim's family. Bamidbar/Numbers 35:6–34.

Now, Hathaway and Shapiro define secondary enforcement rules as imposing rights[36] or permissions[37] on the one hand, and/or duties on the other.[38] But this does not fully explain if the RCTDs and/or liberties (must) come coupled with duties requiring enforcement action. More importantly, those scholars are silent on permission and discretion vis-à-vis primary enforcement rules. There are nonetheless good reasons for thinking that they are included. For example, officials sometimes bear some discretion about whether to enforce the law, e.g., public prosecutors who choose not to bring a case out of uncertainty as to the outcome (and, as political actors, who do not want a case to affect their win rate and thus public perception). So too, private law right-holders, or others authorised to act on their behalf, typically have discretion about whether to enforce the rights or not, e.g., (i) waiver power over a correlative duty (ii) the choice of whether to exercise secondary rights (and thus to enforce the primary right).

More contentiously, whilst it is reasonable for Kleinfeld to want a test to distinguish *legal* enforcement from non-legal efforts,[39] legal enforcement (and actions that render the law effective) is not restricted to normative positions grounded in (secondary) enforcement rules. Such legal norms authorise actions to try to ensure a duty-bearer's conformity with his or her duty, or to seek redress for violating that duty. (One is therefore tempted to say that Kleinfeld's conception is circumscribed to *law* enforcement, rather than the broader one of *legal* enforcement.)[40]

[36] Hathaway and Shapiro (2011: 272: 'providing rights to others'). 'Rights' must be read in conjunction with their definition of primary enforcement rules on page 271).

[37] Ibid 271: '...or the rules permit people other than the conduct rule violator to perform some harmful act on... the conduct rule violator'.

[38] Ibid 271–2.

[39] Kleinfeld correctly wishes to exclude Hathaway and Shapiro's examples of political dishonour, public scorn, and voting someone out of office from counting as examples of legal enforcement. Kleinfeld (2011: 303); Hathaway and Shapiro (2011: 303). On my working conception, outlined below, something counts as *rights* enforcement if the position's content, or the very status of being a right-holder, is at stake.

[40] Cf. *infra* note 60 and the accompanying text on *legal* enforcement versus *lawful* enforcement.

Kleinfeld might be nonplussed by this. He could say that these other sorts of actions merely concern legally authorised social and moral sanction-seeking, not legal enforcement mechanisms, let alone ones *grounded in* legal enforcement rules.[41] Again, whilst there are good reasons to distinguish legal enforcement from social or moral norm enforcement, it would be a mistake to treat non-enforcement-rule-based legal positions as merely authorising or enabling social or moral enforcement efforts and thereby exclude them from the category of *legal* (or at least *lawful*) enforcement. For there are plenty of actions that legal and ordinary language would call 'rights enforcement' which are not authorised by primary or secondary enforcement rules. For example, in the face of a dispute with her next-door neighbour *B*'s trespassing and/or claiming to own a portion of her land, *A* erects a fence in order to stop *B*'s entering onto that land. It is sensible to say not only that *A exercised* her property rights, but that *A* thereby *enforced* her property rights over the land in question.

A third account of ENFORCEABILITY is Mark Reiff's. On his view, enforceability is about making restraints operative in the world.[42] The account covers all modalities, i.e., legal, social, moral, etc., forms of enforcement.[43] His preferred *definition* of 'enforceability' is this: 'the ability to employ means and measures of enforcement that are sufficient to satisfy… a standard that reflects our desire to make the restraints we have elected to impose on others operative in the world'.[44] Here, 'operative' means the restraints are likely to achieve their goals.

[41] Cf. Kleinfeld (2011: 300 n.14).

[42] Reiff (2005: 2–3). Whilst the conception concerns all norms' enforceability, Reiff's book mostly discusses legal rights. A (legal) right is 'the communal validation of a particular individual interest'. Ibid 242.

[43] Reiff sees his conception as being comprehensive and unified. It is comprehensive because: it covers pre- and post-violation of rights enforceability; it applies to all forms of restraints, not just rights; it applies to all means of enforcement, not just legal (or lawful) ones; it covers both civil and criminal law; and it incorporates deterrence and retribution *as means* to accomplish social cooperation and social (rather than antisocial) conflict. The conception is unified because it shows how all of these various elements of enforceability interrelate and influence one another. Ibid 207. However, there is some room to doubt whether it actually covers the enforcement of tertiary rights.

[44] Ibid 7.

Reiff's account is self-styled as consequentialist and normative.[45] Further, he notes two senses of 'enforceability' from which to reconstruct a conception. The first is a normative claim about whether the goals of enforcement have been, or could be, met. The second is a descriptive claim about whether some means or measure of enforcement could be, or has been, attempted, but without implying that the action would have, or has had, any particular effect. Reiff makes clear that his conception concerns the first sense.[46]

Using this normative lens, Reiff insists that there are actually different measures, or stages, of enforceability: pre-violation of rights, post-violation ones (entailing breaches of correlative duty, or at least threats thereof), and the post-enforcement stage.[47] These stages reflect enforceability's different purposes.

In the *pre-violation* state of affairs, the purpose of enforceability is to facilitate social cooperation. It provides duty-bearers ('potential violators') means by which to credibly commit themselves to act in certain ways (within certain bounds), and right-holders with the means to act without fear of interference.[48]

In a *post-violation* state of affairs, enforceability facilitates 'social (as opposed to antisocial) conflict'.[49] More specifically, the goal is to procure others' acceptance of the remedy. Via enforcement, parties to a dispute are now able to view the conflict over the breach of a right as being complete. So, even if the right-holder is not *fully* convinced that complete justice has been done, he or she is sufficiently satisfied such that the parties can resume their pre-violation level of social cooperation, i.e., without the right-holder seeking revenge, further retaliation, etc., thereafter.[50]

Reiff also provide tests, threshold requirements, to determine when those purposes are met. There are two separate and independent ones for the pre-violation state of affairs. The first is the *sufficiency of punishment* test: a right is enforceable if the threat of punishment is sufficient to make the beneficiary (the right-holder) rationally believe that potential violators

[45] Ibid 9, 45 n.1. For example, asking whether a right is enforceable is equivalent to asking whether the (expected or actual) consequences of violation will be. Ibid 10.

[46] Ibid 45 n.1.

[47] Ibid 7–9, 46. By 'post-enforcement', unfortunately, Reiff means post-grant of an officially awarded remedy, e.g., a court order, rather than the enforcement of *that* order.

[48] Ibid 67.

[49] Ibid 9.

[50] Ibid 73–4, 122, 158. The *post-enforcement* goal is the same. Ibid 75.

will prefer to remain in the pre-violation state of affairs. The second is *the sufficiency of compensation* test: a right is enforceable if the promise of compensation is sufficient to make the beneficiary rationally indifferent to the possibility that a violation might occur.[51]

Of the pre-violation state of affairs generally, Reiff also states: a right is enforceable if its holder rationally believes that the requisite probability of preference or indifference is present.[52] In other words, the test of pre-violation enforceability is reliability: if right-holders can rely on their rights to carry about their business without worry of violation, such that some quantum of alternative precautionary measures must be undertaken in order to act, then their rights are 'enforceable'.

His test for the *post*-violation state of affairs is different. Here, a right is enforceable if the amount of compensation and punishment available is morally significant.[53] Reiff offers a Goldilocks view. It is unlikely that enforcement will *fully* satisfy the demands of justice in rectifying the violation—and neither society nor the law need to do so either.[54] To succeed, enforceability need only lead the right-holder to accept the results (without seeking further means of satisfaction) in order to restore a situation of social cooperation. The problem, then, is rather of providing insufficient rectification, 'minimal redistribution'. That will not sate a right-holder's desire for further satisfaction, revenge, and compensation, and so will not even count as a remedy that restores social cooperation.[55]

The solution thus involves providing a remedy that is 'morally significant': one providing enough compensation or punishment to, although not fully satisfy right-holders, suffice for them to consider its provision to be the end of the dispute.[56] More fully:

[51] Ibid 98, 111. The two pre-violation tests are separate but not independent, because an insufficient amount realised by one does not reduce the amount required by the other. Ibid 77.

[52] Ibid 234. However, '[s]aying that a right is enforceable does not mean that the available measure of punishment is actually sufficient to deter most or even any violations. It means the probability [that] it is sufficient is high enough (and the corresponding risk of violation low enough) that a potential violator is able to make credible promises to perform and a rights beneficiary is willing to incur risks of violation he would otherwise avoid and to refrain from taking socially burdensome precautions'. Ibid 87.

[53] Ibid 234.

[54] Ibid 149.

[55] Ibid 149–50.

[56] Ibid 151.

> A right is enforceable in the post-violation sense if the amount of punishment and compensation available is equivalent to the amount due under [the] formula for retribution, discounted to moral significance [as opposed to (a) minimal redistribution or (b) full justice]. The amount of punishment and compensation available is morally significant, in turn as long as it would pass a hypothetical ultimatum test—as long as the beneficiary would not rather suffer more than see the violator [duty-bearer] suffer only that percentage of the amount otherwise due. The amount of punishment and compensation that is morally significant is accordingly determined *in reference* to the amount required by justice but is not equivalent to it.[57]

With these purposes of, and tests for, enforceability in mind, Reiff provides six categories of enforcement: the threat and use of physical force; the threat and use of strategic power; the sanction of moral condemnation and regret; the sanction of social criticism and the withdrawal of social cooperation; the threat or imposition of personal or financial injury that flows from 'automatic sanctions'; and the threat and use of legal remedies.[58]

On this view, a legal right's enforceability is not dependent upon the existence of *legal* enforcement mechanisms exclusively.[59] Furthermore, Reiff helpfully distinguishes between *legal* and *lawful* remedies, the latter being social, moral, etc., ones that are not illegal to undertake.[60]

Additionally, Reiff presents a genuine/nominal/naked distinction for legal rights.[61] *Genuine* rights are enforceable. *Nominal* ones are enforceable to some extent, but the measure of available enforcement for them is

[57] Ibid 158. An ultimate *game* is one 'developed by experimental economists to investigate whether and to what extent fairness concerns will override self-interest in human decision-making'. Ibid. 151. See generally ibid 151–8.

[58] Ibid 7, 19–44. 'Automatic sanctions' are ones that can be imposed without post-violation interventions, i.e., without anyone having to decide to take action in response to the violation. Instead, the sanction is triggered by some mechanism, one which does not depend on whether it is in anyone's interest to impose it. Ibid 35. There is some reason to doubt whether some of Reiff's examples really constitute 'sanctions' imposed on violators, e.g., spring-guns and booby traps (ibid 36)—especially if their existence is wholly unknown by others.

[59] Indeed, legal remedies are neither a necessary nor sufficient condition for enforceability. Ibid 5.

[60] Ibid 192. A *lawful* remedy is one that can be exercised without violating a legal right. Ibid 199. Reiff also proffers an enforceability/remedies distinction. E.g., ibid 5, 21 n.6, 40.

[61] E.g., ibid 9, 158 n.42, 234. The genuine/nominal distinction is adapted from Matthew Kramer. See Chapter 5 note 38.

insufficient to meet the tests for pre-violation and post-violation enforceability. A *naked* right is completely unenforceable in any way. (Reiff doubts whether any naked ones actually exist, though.) However, enforceability is deemed to be a fluid state of affairs; a change in circumstances may transform a nominal right into a genuine one, and vice versa, any number of times.[62] Furthermore, a particular right may only be nominal in a particular set of circumstances, rather than in all.[63]

Despite being presented as 'consequentialist', Reiff's conception is better understood as being teleological. For him, both rights and enforcement mechanisms serve certain purposes. Failure to meet those purposes does not merely mark a defect. For a right must meet the proposed tests of enforceability (reliability for pre-violation, acceptability for post-violation) to count as 'enforceable'; but if the candidate mechanisms fail to meet those 'tests', then a right 'protected' thereby is not simply 'unenforceable'—at least in certain regards, it is also deemed to be merely 'nominal', rather than 'genuine'.[64]

Whilst Reiff's is an intriguing teleological account of enforceability (of what it would take for enforcement mechanisms to be successful in terms of their purpose), for those seeking a 'descriptive' account instead, his is under-inclusive. For one thing, it does not account for 'defective' or deficient cases of *legal* enforcement mechanisms—as opposed to, perhaps, deeming those instances to be peripheral or degenerate cases, relative to central cases; for the former are deemed to be 'nominal', rather than genuine. Again, for Reiff, a right in such circumstances is unenforceable, at least in certain ways, rather than enforced *poorly*, *weakly*, *superficially*, etc.

For the same reason, Reiff's conception is difficult to square with Legal Positivism, i.e., treating certain enforcement mechanisms as being valid, recognised norms of a legal system, regardless of whether they satisfy the goals of enforceability (of reliability or acceptance leading to restored social cooperation). This is important in the philosophy of rights context

[62] E.g., ibid 234. Reiff's first example of such a transformation is this. 'In light of newly discovered evidence, or simply after further reflection, a beneficiary may come to realize that her initial calculation of the probability of the requisite pre-violation preference or indifference was erroneous, and she should have considered her right enforceable all along'. Ibid 235.

[63] E.g., ibid 238.

[64] Ibid 234.

regarding primary, secondary, and tertiary rights.[65] For Legal Positivists, those legal enforcement mechanisms can obtain *regardless* of whether they meet Reiff's tests. For example, a right may be said to be enforceable to the extent one can commence a legal action in a corrupt legal system based upon it, despite having little chance of getting a fair trial, let alone a remedy therein (or even if you only get awarded the minimum moral remedy, which will not stop victims from pursuing further alternative, private means of rectification.)

Both Positivists and anti-Positivists who utilise the central case method can say that those examples constitute 'peripheral' cases of enforceability (relative to the paradigms). By contrast, Reiff cannot do so, because, again, his tests of enforceability appear to treat enforcement as being effective; for, if the right is ineffective, then it is adjudged to simply be unenforceable (at least in certain regards) and thus 'nominal'.[66] His account therefore does not treat defective enforcement mechanisms, let alone ones intentionally designed by officials to be inadequate, as bona fide instances, even though Positivists and others would or could identify them as being genuine norms of a legal system (of a game, etc.), ones allowing for a modicum of enforceability howsoever unsatisfactorily. *Pace* Reiff, normative positions need not meet those tests in order to count as valid normative positions or legal rules, e.g., even if they are ineffective, insufficient, inappropriate, etc. Moreover, they can be enforceable without meeting those tests either. Positivists and their rivals could agree that the mechanisms may do so without adequate measure or effectiveness, but not that they fail to evidence a lack of enforceability. Hence, those seeking a 'descriptive' account may complain that Reiff's approach does not fully track both ordinary and legal linguistic usage of rights enforcement, because it does not cover: mere efforts; failed or inadequate enforcement efforts; or ones undertaken knowing full well that they will fail to provide legal or lawful remedies but can nonetheless help to achieve ulterior ends. (More on this last point below.) Again, Reiff is aware of this, and rejects it for his own usage.[67] Still, he does not provide sufficient reason to sub-

[65] On these constituting legal modes of rights enforcement, see Chapter 5 § II.1 (regarding Hart's elements of control) and more generally Chapter 7 §§ II–III.

[66] E.g., ibid 198: a right is unenforceable because the measure of enforcement available for it is insufficient. Ibid 199: unenforceability should also depend on our pre- and post-violation expectations. If the lawful means are of sufficient measure, then the [right] will be enforceable.

[67] Ibid 45–6 n.1.

scribe only to this type of account ('normative', rather than 'descriptive') when crafting and presenting his conception of ENFORCEABILITY.

For another thing, as Reiff knows, rights can be operative even without relying upon enforcement[68]; enforcement is but one means of making rights and rules operative. More importantly, his conception is about rendering rights operative by enforcing *restraints*. However not all rights restrain or involve correlative positions that restrain others. We can nonetheless enforce those other rights (e.g., powers, liberties, and complexes lacking component RCTDs) too. Whilst Reiff accounts for declaratory judgments and similar legal remedies, those do not involve *enforcing* restraints (e.g., other parties' views about whether to risk transgression), but rather concern *validating or recognising* a right. Any enforcement of restraint would involve violations downstream of those legal remedies.

Furthermore, you can enforce RCTDs where an individual or group, or even the legal system's own goal is not to re-establish social cooperation post-violation, but to (permit people to use the system to) catalyse social change. An example is allowing for 'test cases' to proceed through courts, which will lead to further litigation, even whilst knowing that the defendants and certain other members of society may be rendered even *less* willing to cooperate thereafter.

Indeed, you can even enforce your RCTD despite failing to procure a legal remedy—and sometimes even intentionally so. Your actions thereby make the right 'operative'. However, your aims may not be in furtherance of Reiff's articulated pre- and post-violation goals for enforceability, but rather to *vindicate* the right's content. For example, your goal might never have been to be able to rely on your right without others interfering, or about accepting a remedy that restores social cooperation, but rather concern status recognition *qua* right-holder *by* having the right violated and then getting it legally or socially (re-)recognised thereafter.

Moreover, Reiff's test/measure of pre-violation is about reliability, not enforceability. His test concerns whether the right-holder can rely on it (alone or for the most part, without having to take additional precautions), and not whether the right is enforceable or not. Reliability in turn reflects operability, but that is not the same thing as enforceability.[69] This alone constitutes grounds for rejecting his theory of enforceability.

[68] E.g., ibid 47–9, 236–7.

[69] E.g., ibid 92–3 (the right-holder's pre-violation calculation is whether to proceed to act as if no violation is likely to occur). This is to say that you can just carry on doing what you

Now, Reiff may say that the threat of punishment, or the probability of being required to provide compensation, as calculations in the potential violator's deliberations, are what make the rights (and duties) operative. Even so, he believes the tests must be run from the right-holder's perspective (what *the holder* thinks about what potential violators believe). Yet being operative, with people feeling constrained by their correlative duties, is not itself enforceability: this just speaks to (the right and the correlative duty's) effectiveness.[70] In other words, it conflates the positions being *in force* and operative with their being enforceable/*enforced*.

Last, most of Reiff's examples of nominal rights transforming into genuine ones are sensible.[71] One example, however, seems to show that he thinks enforceability is ultimately dependent upon an individual subjective judgment of whether it is or not.[72] This is understandable, given his tests for enforceability. Even so, that cannot make sense of the idea of a right being enforceable even if the right-holder is mistaken about whether it is or not. It is sensible to think that rights may or may not be enforceable irrespective of our judgments about such matters. This, especially when it comes to arcane matters such as legal enforcement of legal rights, for which lawyers will be far better placed to judge than ordinary folks. However, this also applies for other calculations Reiff would have right-holders make under his tests vis-à-vis cost-benefit analyses, and people's imperfect information and judgments about what they could do and what potential violators would do.

In light of the aforementioned considerations, here is my own working conception of RIGHTS ENFORCEMENT: *attempts to protect or defend either the content of a right or right-holding status, in the face of (threatened) challenge, infringement, or violation, by seeking to procure: (a) a remedy; (b) some other form of vindication; or (c) a correlative duty's fulfilment.*

would otherwise do, which is just being able to rely on your rights *because* they are otherwise enforceable. In other words, it is not what makes rights enforceable in the pre-violation stage, but rather evidence that they are enforceable.

[70] To reduce duties to (or to prioritise as features within them) calculations of the costs of transgression, rather than deem them to be normative requirements to forbear, constitutes a form of Sanction theory of law. See Chapter 7 notes 44–5 and the accompanying text.

[71] Ibid 235.

[72] 'In the light of newly discovered evidence, or simply after further reflection, a beneficiary may come to realize that her initial calculation of the probability of the requisite pre-violation preference or indifference was erroneous, and should have considered her right enforceable all along'. Ibid 235.

As this conception includes both efforts to secure a result (such as a court order) and remedial awards *that themselves* require enforcement, these are no guarantees that right-holders, or other parties enforcing the right on the holders' behalf, will get what they want.[73] Furthermore, this conception is not delimited to efforts undertaken within a given normative domain e.g., exclusively using legal enforcement mechanisms in order to enforce legal rights.[74]

Now, some philosophers might oppose any effort to distinguish rights exercise from enforcement. One reason would be if they are inclined to see cases of successful enforcement efforts as also constituting instances of rights exercise.[75] Moreover, some philosophical accounts take the use of enforcement and waiver powers to be either the (i) typical or (ii) exclusive ways by which to exercise rights.[76]

Both concerns are misplaced. Deeming rights enforcement to be a subset of rights exercise renders such terminology unproblematic. All rights enforcement counts as rights exercise, but not vice versa; for there are many ways by which to exercise rights that ought not to be construed as

[73] Therefore, whilst this book shall continue throughout to treat 'enforcement mechanisms' as means of rights enforcement, bear in mind that they are no guarantee that a right will be successfully (let alone adequately) enforced.

[74] Additionally, rights enforcement can be characterised as forming 'perimeters of support', whereby one or more normative position are used to try to remedy or vindicate a right. See Chapter 9 §§ II–III.

[75] For example, Hart says:

> Where infants or other persons not *sui juris* have rights, such powers and the correlative obligations are *exercised* on their behalf by appointed representatives and their *exercise* may be subject to approval by a court. But since (a) what such representatives can and cannot do by way of *exercise* of such power is determined by what those whom they represent could have done if *sui juris* and (b) when the latter become *sui juris* they can *exercise* such powers without any transfer or fresh assignment; the powers are regarded as belonging throughout to them and not to their representatives, though they are only *exercisable* by the latter during the period of disability.

Ibid 184 n.86 (emphases added). Additionally, see Raz (1996: 255–7) for a concern about searching for, wrongly positing the existence of, or overemphasising the importance of such means for *moral* rights.

[76] Hillel Steiner's view is representative: 'There are at least six features that have been attributed to rights or presupposed about them in virtually all legal and moral discussions of rights... 5. Rights are exercisable. 6. This exercisability *consists in* the capacity to control [ligation-bearers'] encumbrances by either extinguishing them or enforcing them...'. Steiner (2006: 461, emphasis added). Cf. Steiner (1994: 56–7).

modes of rights enforcement. Here are some examples: rights (powers) to create, modify, or terminate contractual relationships; rights (powers) to procure, alienate, or exchange property; and rights (liberties) to act, speak, create, or destroy, within certain boundaries. It would be odd to say that *X* 'enforced' his right to buy property by purchasing Blackacre from *Y*. It would be equally odd to say that *Y* 'enforced' her property rights by selling *X* her house. It nonetheless seems perfectly fine to say that *X* and *Y* exercised their rights to buy and alienate the property. When *A* either gifts a gold watch to *B*, or forfeits the claim to a watch he wants *B* to have, it would be odd to say that *A* thereby 'enforced' his rights. When *C* and *D* self-publish pamphlets on the finer points of neo-mercantilist economics that no one will ever read it is sensible to say that they are exercising their rights to free speech, but not that they are thereby enforcing them. When *E* sends *F* an email soliciting a contract bid, it makes sense to say that *E* is exercising rights to free speech, to associate, and solicit for contractual relations, but not that *E* is enforcing the rights to make contracts, to free speech, etc.[77]

Not everyone will agree with this account of the relationship between rights exercise and rights enforcement. One of the few (if not the only other) rights scholars to even address the matter, Henry Terry believes they are simply different things.

> A right of this sort [an RCTD] can not [sic] be exercised, but can be violated. To exercise a right means to do, or abstain from, the act which forms its content. But here *ex hypothesi* the only act is one that is to be done, if at all, not by the holder of the right but by the other party on whom the duty rests. There may be some way to enforce the right by compelling that other party to do what he ought to do or to make compensation for not doing so; but enforcement is different from exercise.[78]

[77] For each of the examples given above, there might nevertheless be circumstances where it would be apt to style their actions as constituting rights enforcement after all, but only when provided with additional information about either their rights or their right-holder status being in question or under threat. For example, *C* and *D* enforced their rights to free speech by publishing an article about a certain economic matter that a local government official dubiously claimed could not be published legally.

[78] Terry (1903: 188). See Appendix 1 for Terry's model of rights. Cf. Goudmit (1873: 227–40).

Terry appears to rely on both (i) the active/passive distinction and (ii) the idea that rights exercise is limited to a single position's capacity for self-utilisation. Yet he provides no reasons for thinking either that enforcement ought not count as modes of exercise, or that liberties or powers can only *self*-exercise, and are thus incapable of exercising right complexes containing passive positions (if not also singular passive positions).

Furthermore, even with the proffered relationship between them in mind, there is often interplay between rights exercise and enforcement. It is sometimes said that liberties are needed to *exercise* a power, whilst that power is in turn used to *enforce* an RCTD. Most of the time there are legal liberties by which to undertake the actions requisite for exercising legal powers. Occasionally there are not, i.e., when one has a power but also a duty (no liberty) not to use it.

One example is the *Nemo Dat* exception mentioned in footnote 3. The dishonest transferor may be criminally and civilly liable for, amongst other things, breach of the duty by exercising the power to sell the item to a third party. A second example is secondary rights. These are complexes composed of—at least—liberties and powers. To exercise them successfully you must not have duties proscribing the commencement and prosecution of legal proceedings *and* you must legally be competent to do so. Such duties against commencement may be the product of a contract. Now, you might breach the contractual duty by suing anyway and 'get away' with it;[79] but if the other party raises the duty in court, then, barring other factors, the case can be dismissed.[80]

Of course, not every action undertaken on behalf of rights will count as rights exercise. When someone assassinates a political leader based on the belief that the official impinged upon his or her rights, say, to free assembly or to free speech, the act of assassination is generally not taken to be a way of exercising either the right *to* speech or *to* assemble. This is at least in part because the act does not further those rights' contents.[81] Nor is the generation or destruction of a right always a matter of its having been

[79] Whilst people may invariably have the right to commence legal proceedings, wholly groundless causes of action will generally be dismissed fairly quickly.

[80] Note that this actually calls into question the first part of RIGHTS EXERCISE outlined above: is being *entitled to so act* (authorised or permitted action) actually essential to it?

[81] On the other hand, one can imagine a legal system where, not only could such acts count as 'speech', but wherein political violence is constitutionally protected, e.g., a sic semper tyrannis right.

exercised.[82] For example, a right's vesting in someone is not necessarily a function of anyone having exercised it. For example, a remainderman's interest in Blackacre *qua* trust property is the product of the settlor's powers. The former's being able to exercise the right to dwell in the trust property, say, will typically arise simply upon the life tenant's death.[83]

§ III.2. Remedy Versus Vindication

Not only should rights enforcement be distinguished from rights exercise (and be deemed a subset of the latter), but enforcement can also be distinguished from both remedying and vindicating rights. Moreover, rights remedying should be considered a mere subset of modes of rights vindication: all cases of remedying vindicate a right, at least nominally, whilst not all cases of rights vindication concern the grant or procurement of a remedy.[84]

Successful enforcement efforts *vindicate* a right. Sometimes, though, a right can be vindicated even without right-holders either being granted by

[82] Nigel Simmonds believes that a distinction ought to be made between exercise and alienation or extinguishment (Simmonds (1998: 229)). Even so, he provides no reasons for thinking the latter two are not actually varieties of exercise.

[83] Rights enforcement can also be prevented indirectly, by legal, moral, or social rules and circumstances. Right-holders may be financially incapable of initiating or sustaining a legal action, e.g., being able to pay lawyer's fees. Many legal systems have rules concerning filings, proceedings, and even minimal monetary amounts for asserted damages in order to have standing (e.g., in American federal courts for diversity cases), which make litigation sufficiently expensive and lengthy so as to be prohibitively costly for many right-holders. Additionally, for a host of reasons, right-holders may also face social pressure from friends, family, peers, etc., not to pursue a particular legal dispute. Opposition to commencing litigation could also be based upon social, religious, or moral requirements. Sometimes parties are deterred from pursuing their rights out of fear of physical or other forms of violence or retaliation. Of course, none of these exigencies proves that the person lacks either a bona fide legal right or the requisite enforcement mechanisms.

[84] Reiff distinguishes rights enforcement from remedying, deeming the latter to be a subset of means for effectuating the former. However, he does not distinguish remedying from vindication, exercise, or enforcement. Reiff (2005: 4–5, 7, 21 n.6, 40, 191–212). On neither causes of action ('secondary rights') nor what in Chapter 1 I called 'quaternary rights' (i.e., legal norms by which to enforce tertiary positions, e.g., judgment creditors' rights to secure liens in furtherance of court orders) being remedies, see Zakrzewski (2005: 50–2).

others, or their procuring for themselves, a *remedy*.[85] For example, merely by recognising its validity and another party's transgression of it in their public decisions, officials can vindicate a legal right even without granting the right-holder compensation or equitable repair.[86]

What counts as vindication nonetheless varies. It can mean procuring the remedy or award sought; obtaining *some* award; securing desired status recognition; etc. Faced with breached correlative duties, some legal RCTD-holders demand compensation and damages. Others have ulterior goals. They might seek declaratory judgments (aka 'declaratory remedies'). As Salmond says:

> A litigant may claim the assistance of a court of law, not because his rights have been violated, but because they are uncertain. What he desires may be not any remedy against an adversary for the violation of a right, but an authoritative declaration that the right exists.[87]

Again, though, a legal right can sometimes be vindicated even absent the grant or procurement of a remedy or a declaratory judgment. For example, people occasionally commence lawsuits simply to try to get officials (and perhaps the public at large) to recognise rights, even if the plaintiffs know they will lose the case. 'Success' therefore can sometimes be gauged in terms of legal, social, or political recognition of one's status.[88]

[85] In searching for a 'stable' conception, Rafal Zakrzewski identifies a remedy as the rights immediately arising from certain judicial commands [orders] and statements which aim to redress a pre-suit grievance, usually an actual or threatened infringement of a substantive (primary) right. Zakrzewski (2005: 2). He considers this to be superior to both an overly narrow understanding, e.g., as mere court orders (ibid 50) and an over-inclusive one of all means provided by the law to redress a grievance (ibid 48). Unfortunately, his conception excludes self-help remedies. Ibid 47–8.

[86] Cf. Dicey (1896: 30); Feinberg (1973: 73–5); Martin (1993: 58–9) on recognition versus enforcement (including maintenance, promotion, and protection) of a legal right in law.

[87] Salmond (1902: 95). However, he continues: 'Such a declaration may be the ground of subsequent proceedings in which the right, having been violated, receives enforcement, but in the meantime there is no enforcement or any claim to it'. Ibid. This does not seem to square with his remarks on direct and indirect enforcement (*supra* notes 8–9 and the accompanying text). Regardless, see also ibid 95–6 on judicial decrees which establish titles of right, rather than remedies.

[88] Private law scholars should take heed to distinguish the above from so-called common law 'vindicatory damages', which is a court-awarded remedy. The literature on that debated remedy tends to mention Lord Dyson's remark that all awards of compensatory damages also

Comparable efforts at rights vindication are also possible in other normative domains (moral, social, etc.). Consider the example of personally confronting duty-bearers. *E* promises to meet *F* at the park on Tuesday at 2 pm. Assume that this gives *F* a moral right and *E* a correlative duty to show up at the specified time. *E* breaches by failing to turn up. When *F* confronts *E* about this, the former may say to the latter 'apologise for breaking your promise'. Especially as the scheduled event has already passed, *F* is not simply enforcing the right that *E* keep the promise by attending; *F* is rather trying to vindicate that right by utilising an additional normative position. (See Chapter 9 for the legal analogue.)

This remedy/vindication distinction may prove unsatisfactory to some because it is commonplace to style secondary rights as 'remedial' ones, self-help actions as 'self-help remedies', and certain institutional proceedings (lawsuits, administrative tribunals, arbitration, etc.) as 'remedial proceedings'.[89] These labels might in turn reflect a certain set of prejudices: that claimants are always 'in the right', that if such third-party processes have been implemented it could only be because a wrong was done, and/or that the bestowal of a remedy is the inevitable result of any such process. These are all untrue. Frivolous lawsuits happen. Defendants sometimes win—for valid or dubious reasons. Et cetera. As they are no guarantees of securing remedies, it is therefore inapt to style secondary rights as 'remedial' ones.[90]

Summary

Some basic kinds of rights are active, whilst others are passive. Yet the set of active rights does not exhaust the set of exercisable rights. Some rights can either exercise others or can at least serve as components of complexes and are able to exercise that larger construct. There are also significant differences amongst the concepts of rights exercise, enforcement, remedying, and vindication.

Take the right against self-incrimination as an example. It is a complex that, amongst perhaps other basic positions, can include: an RCTD that

serve to vindicate a right that has been infringed. E.g., Edelman (2017: 357), citing Lord Dyson in *R (Lumba (Congo)) v Secretary of State for the Home Department* [2012] 1 AC 245, [100].

[89] But see Zakrzewski (2005: 47–53).

[90] See also ibid 50–2.

legal officials must not compel you to testify under oath; liberties to testify or not if you choose; and an immunity from legal officials changing your legal status by nullifying the right. By choosing to take the stand or not you exercise the right complex, not just its component liberties. You are, moreover, *exercising* the right against self-incrimination, but not necessarily *enforcing* it. However, if the right has been breached (say, if a corrupt judge orders the bailiff to forcefully place you into the witness box), then you may try to enforce it.

Whilst it makes sense to say that secondary rights *exercise* your primary rights, e.g., when seeking to obtain a remedy for the latter's transgression, secondary (and tertiary) rights nonetheless exist in order to *enforce* primary ones. Secondary and tertiary rights can correct a (perceived) wrong and validate right-holding status itself. That is what differentiates rights enforcement from most kinds of rights exercise. Whilst they concern the primary right, secondary rights entitle action in furtherance of their own content too (to commence a lawsuit, to file a motion, etc.). It would be odd to say that the secondary right enforces itself, but not to say that a secondary right enforces a primary one.[91]

§ IV. An Objection and Responses

A possible objection to the notion that one type of right can exercise or enforce another might take this form. Powers and liberties simply exercise themselves. Even if a given right complex contains liberties, RCTDs, powers, and immunities, all that really gets exercised is the liberty *qua* liberty or the power *qua* power. Those basic positions do not exercise a component RCTD or immunity, or the right complex itself per se. Whilst a liberty or power may *reference an RCTD or immunity as its content*,[92] that is not the same thing as exercising an RCTD, immunity, or right complex.

For example, *A* and *B* enter a contract whereby *A* owes *B* 100 widgets and *B* in turn owes *A* 10 gold coins. *A* has a right to the gold upon fulfilment of the contractual duty. If *B* does not pay, *A* may be entitled to sue.

[91] It is also commonplace to say that we 'claim' our rights, e.g., by commencing institutional proceedings. As shall be discussed below, this is a (set of) way(s) by which to enforce rights. 'Claim' is not univocal, as evidenced by the problems arising with Hohfeld's technical term. For example, 'we claim the right to be granted a claim by staking a claim in a mine'. See also Chapter 9 on making claims of right (using legal liberties) outside of institutional contexts.

[92] E.g., Finnis (2011: 200).

Even so, *A*'s 'right' to sue is really a distinct set of legal positions, a combination of (at least) powers and liberties, from *A*'s contractual right to the gold. The labels 'primary' and 'secondary' rights mark this difference. The primary right is the reason for the second's existence. The secondary right's content also *refers* to the first ('*B* owes me gold but did not pay, so I am entitled to sue for damages'). Nevertheless, the secondary right does not *exercise* the primary right simply by referring to or relying on it (remembering that enforcement is here considered to be a subset of exercise).

This objection calls into question many things lawyers, philosophers, and others typically refer to as 'rights exercise'. I offer two rejoinders. First, the notion of two or more normative positions interacting is indispensable to any adequate explanation of many cases of rights exercise. Second, *one version* of the objection leads to absurdity: it eliminates the very possibility of 'rights exercise' altogether.

The idea of one normative position exercising or enforcing, if not passive positions, then at least a right complex containing them, is required to explain many forms of rights discourse. In ordinary and legal parlance, it is often said that we 'enforce' our legal rights in legal proceedings. This includes rights that are, or complexes that include, RCTDs. Further, as the right against self-incrimination is not simply a liberty and/or power, its exercise is not simply a matter of active positions self-exercising. Additionally, specific performance is just one example of a primary right being enforced by secondary and tertiary rights. Concerning the widget-gold contract example, if *B* refuses to pay for the widgets, it is *A*'s right to the gold which gets enforced when *A*'s secondary right to commence litigation is recognised by the court and when a judge decides in *A's* favour.[93] (If instead we say that *A* only exercised a right to commence litigation, as opposed to also enforcing the primary right, then we will not be capturing what lawyers and jurists usually mean by 'enforcement'.) Furthermore, a judgment creditor enforces and exercises a *tertiary* right—but *not* neces-

[93] Zakrzewski distinguishes between two kinds of remedies: 'replicative' and 'transformative' ones. The former do, whilst the latter do not, duplicate a primary legal right's content. Zakrzewski (2005: 54–61). Further, the American Legal Realists insisted that many if not all tertiary legal rights differ in content from primary ones (and thus constitute the system's 'real' legal rights) because they are fashioned in part by officials using considerations other than just the rules 'on the books'. See, e.g., Frydrych (2018a). Regardless, note that being awarded a tertiary right with different content can still be a way to enforce and vindicate a primary right.

sarily via the tertiary right itself—if it is understood to be a passive RCTD (as opposed to a complex). *A* wins a lawsuit and becomes the judgment creditor of *B*. *A*'s tertiary right may itself nonetheless have to be enforced by a different set of legal positions, namely by exercising legal liberties and powers, e.g., getting a lien imposed on *B*'s (the judgment debtor's) property, etc.[94]

The objection also renders certain kinds of rights exercise impossible. Recall the examples from Section II about the rights to call in an option and a debt. Both are right complexes. (So too is the right against self-incrimination.) It is erroneous to posit that only these rights' component powers or liberties get exercised. Those complexes are not reducible to their liberties or powers, and nor do those liberties or powers cease to operate *as components* when utilised. To hold otherwise entails that these rights are unexercisable.

Passivism

Denying the possibility of interplay between rights might also generate a serious conceptual difficulty. The problem is this. One is free to think that: (Proposition I) all real rights are passive normative positions; (Proposition II) liberties and powers are not 'rights'; and (Proposition III) liberties and powers simply exercise themselves, not other types of basic positions or complexes. One can consistently endorse all three propositions concurrently. Let us style anyone who does a *Passivist*. Passivism is neither a far-fetched viewpoint nor a mere strawman. Although I am unaware of anyone who explicitly endorses all three propositions, many scholars advance different combinations of at least two of them.[95]

Passivism comes at a cost: it entails that the very category of 'rights exercise' is spurious, as it renders all rights 'inert'. The most Passivists can say is that, whilst liberties or powers can *refer* to rights (e.g., that RCTDs can be the content of liberties), powers and liberties do not exercise rights.

[94] Tertiary rights also require enforcement. Again, I suggest that those enforcement mechanisms be called 'quaternary rights'. There is furthermore no guarantee that these will secure for tertiary right-holders what they want or are entitled to get.

[95] On Proposition I, see, e.g., Raz (1986: 167); Kramer & Steiner (2007: 295–9). On Proposition II, see, e.g., Kramer & Steiner (2007: 295–9); Rainbolt (2006: 30, 32); Raz (1996: 275, on liberties). On Proposition III, see *supra* note 78 on Terry (1903: 188), at least per RCTDs (if not also immunities and complexes).

There is a partial escape, however. If Passivists would be willing to modify Propositions I and III, and admit that complexes can constitute rights too, then they could agree that complexes get exercised, not just their components. As suggested above, a complex is exercisable because its parts can be exercised, even if it has component RCTDs or immunities (which are themselves passive types of basic normative positions).[96] Still, the admission would be tantamount to abandoning Passivism.

Unreconstructed Passivists would therefore face a daunting prospect: they must hold that all lay and juridical linguistic practices and understandings of 'rights exercise' are mistaken. By claiming it to only really be a matter of liberties or powers' self-exercising, Passivism ends up explaining 'rights exercise' out of existence.

On the other hand, Passivists could bite the bullet and insist that 'rights exercise' is indeed a misnomer and false depiction. If all rights are passive positions that simply cannot be exercised by other types of normative positions, even just *qua* components of a complex (where it is the complex itself which gets exercised), then it would be erroneous to consider the use of powers, liberties, or anything else on a right's behalf as actually exercising the right.

If Passivists stood their ground thus, one would have to appeal to other sorts of methodological considerations to resolve the matter. This would involve, inter alia, comparing the relative costs of excising RIGHTS EXERCISE and the cognate term from accounts of rights versus the costs of 'misrepresenting' the employment of other kinds of normative positions as being involved in rights exercise. In other words, it involves weighing the costs of completely discarding ordinary and legal usages and perceptions against the supposed benefits of the demystification of the metaphor (demystified in an accurate fashion, presumably) of

[96] Obviously, any Passivists who also reject the very possibility of right complexes could not benefit from this modification. They might deny its soundness on the grounds that (a) the larger construct is an aggregation of different kinds of normative positions, only one or two of which is a right (i.e., RCTDs and, perhaps, immunities), or (b) there is really only a basic right accompanied by different kinds of positions, but in a way that does not amount to a unified larger construct warranting 'rights' status.

'exercising' rights. As no one fully endorses Passivism, that debate is best left for another time.[97]

§ V. Claims of Right

This last section touches upon the philosophy of rights' treatment of rights claiming. What is to make a claim of right? What is the relationship between claiming, demanding, and enforcing? Are they distinct, is one or more a mere subset of another, or is there an identity? How are rights claimed, and with which normative positions can they be claimed?

It has long been understood that there are different senses of rights claiming. For example, Carl Wellman says:

> There are in the recent literature two paradigms of legal claiming. Hohfeld, and probably most practicing lawyers who reflect upon the matter, take suing in a court of law as their model of claiming. Feinberg, on the other hand, takes claiming a checked umbrella by presenting a chit or demanding payment of a note payable on demand as paradigms.[98]

Let us first consider Joel Feinberg's popular account of rights claiming. He distinguishes amongst: (I) 'making claim to'; (II) 'claiming that'; and

[97] One might see Passivism as a *reductio* in the same spirit as Anthony Honoré's criticism of Hohfeld's *schema* to the effect that it cannot explain the subsistence of a right over transfers between holders. Hohfeldian rights involve interpersonal relations (between two people vis-à-vis some object, say). Honoré and others criticise this view for failing to account for the idea that there are rights in and to objects. If *A* owes *B* £100 under a contract, but *B* transfers the right to the money to *C*, then Hohfeld's model entails that there is a new duty to pay and a new right to the debt. This, instead of saying, as would seem sensible to lawyers and others, that it is the same right to £100 being *transferred* from *B* to *C*. Honoré (1960: 456–7). Coming to Hohfeld's defence, John Finnis notes that the shifting sets of Hohfeldian positions are unified by the same topic: the right to £100. Thus, the rivalrous person-object and interpersonal accounts are really just two equally valid ways of telling the same story. Finnis (2011: 201–2) and in personal conversation (Oxford, 12 February 2014). Cf. Eleftheriadis (1996: 36–9); Penner (2013).

Similarly, one could argue that parcelling out different interpersonal normative positions makes it impossible to explain how 'a right' can be *exercised* or *enforced*. This need not be the case, however. Passivists might simply deem rights to be unexercisable even if they form part of a normative relationship with an object (rather than with other persons vis-à-vis the object), obtain over time, and 'survive' transfers amongst different possessors.

[98] Wellman (1985: 204). Wellman also suggests there is a necessary connection between rights and claiming, and that claiming is the exercise of a normative power. Ibid 206–7.

(III) 'having a claim'.[99] *Making claim to* something is 'to petition or seek by virtue of *supposed* right; to demand as due'.[100] It is a legal performance (a performative utterance) with direct legal consequences. Such communications admit of two types: (Ia) to exercise a right you already possess, by requiring from another that you be given that which is already due to you ('by presenting title'); and (Ib) to be granted a right in the first place ('apply for the title itself'), by showing that you have met the rule-based conditions for it.[101]

By contrast, *claiming that* concerns assertions about something being the case, e.g., that the sky is blue. These, Feinberg thinks, are 'propositional' rather than 'performative' claims.[102] In contrast to *making claim to* something, assertions *claiming that* X are 'often' or 'characteristically' without legal consequence or force.[103] They are mere 'demands'.[104] (However, Feinberg also says that bona fide rights can be claimed, demanded, insisted upon, etc.[105]) *Having a claim* consists in being in a position to claim, that is, to *make claim to* or to *claim that*.[106]

Whilst you can either make claim to having an existent right be recognised, or to seek the grant of a right, Feinberg's rigid *making claim*

[99] Feinberg (1980: 149–51). See also Rainbolt (2006: 75–6). For an alternative account, one distinguishing *indicative*, *subjunctive*, and *possessive* senses of claims, see White (1984: 115–32). On White's account potentially being under-inclusive, see MacCormick (1982b: 350–6).

[100] Feinberg (1980: 149–50, emphasis added).

[101] Ibid. 150. Whilst seemingly discussing (Hohfeldian) 'claim-rights' and 'the conceptual linkage between personal rights and claiming [that] has long been noticed' (ibid 148. Cf. ibid 157), both types of claiming here are nevertheless said to be the function of normative powers. 'The legal power to claim (performatively) one's right or the things to which one has a right seems to be essential to the very notion of a right'. Ibid 150.

[102] Ibid. You can *claim that* you have a right, which is an assertion about possession. Ibid.

[103] Ibid.

[104] Ibid 152. Not all demands are valid claims, even if presented as such. Ibid.

[105] Ibid 151.

[106] Ibid. (emphases removed). See also ibid 155. Feinberg later revised his view, holding instead that a *having a claim* simply means being in a position to *make claim* to something. The original stance was presented in a 1970 article that was republished essentially verbatim in 1980. The revised view is from 1973. See Feinberg (1973: 65); Rainbolt (2006: 76). Feinberg also endorses the idea of a right as a valid claim, as opposed to its being a justified one. This, on the grounds that a right-holder might have a claim without ever claiming it (and without even knowing he or she has it), and because non-right-holders can advance invalid claims. Feinberg (1980: 151–2). He furthermore posits that legal claims are not just held against correlative duty-bearers, but also 'against the state to recognition and enforcement'. Feinberg (1973: 58).

to/claiming that distinction is probably unsustainable.[107] For example, it is untrue that all instances of 'claiming that' are legally ineffectual, e.g., the potential legal effects of assertions made under oath.[108] Regardless, scholars continue to debate whether having a claim and making a claim mutually entail one another, and/or if one explains or defines the other.[109]

§ V.1. Claiming, Demanding, and Enforcing

What, though, is the relationship between claiming and demanding rights? Some philosophers are adamant that demanding, referencing, discussing, requesting, or pleading for rights are not, or need not be, forms of enforcement.[110] Relatedly, Joseph Raz distinguishes between directives and requests. Directives possess a binding quality that requests lack.[111] Are legal claims made by private citizens (as opposed to officials acting *qua* officials) more like directives or requests? Raz's remarks elsewhere *seem* to suggest the latter.

> Primary organs are concerned with the *authoritative* determination of normative situations in accordance with pre-existing norms. Consider judicial bodies. Courts and tribunals have power to determine the rights and duties of individuals. But cannot any person do the same? Cannot John determine whether he owes £100 to Alan or whether Paul owes money to Jack? He may be ignorant of the law but like a court he may study it. The difference between a court and a private individual is not merely that courts are provided with better facilities to determine the facts of the case and the law applying to them. Courts have power to make an authoritative determination of people's legal situation. Private individuals may express their opinion of the subject but their views are not binding.[112]

If so, then Raz goes awry here—but only slightly. Whilst courts are often needed to provide binding determinations of normative positions' contents and scopes, it is untrue that private parties can only express mere opinions. They can create, modify, or terminate each other's legal

[107] E.g., White (1984: 116 n.8).
[108] My thanks to James Penner for this point.
[109] See White (1984: 115–32) for some of the relevant literature.
[110] E.g., Wellman (1985: 207–11).
[111] Raz (2009b: 21–3).
[112] Ibid 108.

positions in binding ways. People can make contracts; sell their property; give gifts; etc. For they are sometimes engaged in performative utterances and activities. So too when making claims of right.[113]

Even so, a stable distinction probably cannot be sustained between (i) *claiming* and *demanding* rights—as opposed to (ii) making a claim versus making a demand. Concerning the latter distinction, Neil MacCormick argues that, although they may just be a 'species' of demands, an 'imperativ[al]' claim of right presupposes legitimate entitlement to that which is claimed (even when falsely or erroneously presented), whilst mere demands need not. In other words, demands can be founded on might or on right, but claims of right can only be founded on the latter.[114]

Similarly, Wellman believes that claims of right involve demands,[115] but denies that every demand is a claim of right. The difference, to his mind, seems to be that a claim of right involves a demand based on (what the claimant takes to be) duty-imposing reasons.[116] For Wellman, making a claim of right involves a normative power (a 'power to claim').[117] Making a claim of right to a duty-bearer alters the meaning of the recipient's subsequent action and position: it (1) increases the duty's stringency and (2) adds force to the reasons third parties have to react negatively to the duty-bearer's non-compliance.[118]

Are claims of right (always) modes of rights enforcement? If the working conception of RIGHTS ENFORCEMENT provided above is accepted, then it seems so. One of the few scholars to explicitly address the

[113] Would this/Raz's view reduce all such activities to mere pro tanto cases of legal rights and duties, ones that are not binding until a court reaches a decision about them? If these legal positions (powers) are not binding until a legal official's authoritative say-so, then Raz would be guilty of the same 'Kelsenian Twist', i.e., making the same sort of Sanction theory of law error he attributes to Hart's account of private law RCTDs and duties, which explains private law RCTDs in terms of variable sets of enforcement powers. Raz (1984: 131). Cf. Hart (1982: 157–60, 266–8). On Sanction theories, again, see Chapter 7 notes 44–5 and the accompanying text.

[114] MacCormick (1982b: 351). But cf. Gilbert (2018: 57–8) on authoritative demanding versus mere demanding.

[115] E.g., Wellman (1995: 80, 87, 95).

[116] Ibid 95.

[117] E.g., ibid 80–1, 87, 90, 95, 119.

[118] Ibid 81–1. Cf. ibid 87, 90, 95. Chapter 9 will argue that right-holders can invoke their rights to third parties directly in ways that differ from direct communications to duty-bearers.

matter, though, is Onora O'Neill, who distinguishes rights claiming and enforcement. She nevertheless fails to explain the difference.

To uncover O'Neill's view, it will help to note that she also cuts a distinction between two sorts of rights.[119] The first, 'rights that demand non-interference' (i.e., 'liberty-rights'), are those that can be claimed from others without relying on institutional structures (courts, police, etc.). These are universally claimable because everyone bears duties correlating with them. Despite being perforce '*claimable* and waivable', however, rights to non-interference require institutional structures for their *enforcement*.[120]

The second, rights to 'a specific performance' (e.g., 'welfare rights') do depend on legal institutions to be both claimable and enforceable. They require the existence of institutions for their claimability because only such bodies can set and determine the identity of the relevant correlative duty-bearers.[121] The idea is this: if you do not know who the relevant duty-bearer is, then it would be useless to try to claim it. Doing so otherwise would, at best, constitute a mere rhetorical gesture.[122] So, whilst both rights to non-interference and rights to specific performance ultimately rely on the existence of institutional structures for their enforcement, the key difference is that the former are claimable (and waivable) without the existence of such bodies, whilst the latter sort of rights cannot be.[123]

O'Neill's claiming/enforcement distinction is untenable. First, it is untrue that institutional bodies are always required to determine or fix specific duty-bearers for *all* 'positive' duties, i.e., those correlating with rights to specific performance.[124] If the duty-bearer's identity is determinable, moreover, then why would *private* claims of right be impossible, save if 'claiming' exclusively means successful remedy procurement via institutional proceedings (an unduly narrow view of ENFORCEMENT)? No

[119] O'Neill (1996: 129–32, especially 130 n.4).

[120] Ibid 131 (emphasis added).

[121] Ibid 131.

[122] Ibid 129, 131, 132.

[123] Ibid 131.

[124] For a different argument against O'Neill on this point, noting the very positive/negative rights distinction's dubiousness, see Etinson (2013: 467). On the distinction itself (i.e., rights to non-interference versus rights to someone else's action or forbearance), see Salmond (1902: 245); O'Neill (1996: 131). Perhaps O'Neill's analysis is distorted by her overall focus on implementing international rights (especially so-called 'social, economic, and cultural' rights), and thereby ignoring or underplaying the run-of-the-mill rights to performance in domestic private law contexts.

argument is given as to why institutions are required to enforce all rights, let alone why claims cannot alone count as a mode thereof. More work would be needed to establish why claims of right do not themselves count as a form of rights enforcement. Second, O'Neill cannot account for self-help 'remedies'—unless, that is, she believes all such actions ultimately rely upon the implicit backing of legal officials (which, given her toleration of institution-free rights to non-interference, at any rate, does not seem to be necessary, conceptually speaking).

§ V.2. *The Structure of Claiming*

The philosophy of rights literature tends to focus on enforcement powers, to the detriment of other means of rights enforcement or exercise. As shall be further discussed in Chapter 7, HLA Hart, Neil MacCormick, and Hillel Steiner identify various ways by which to legally enforce legal rights. They explain these in terms of legal powers by which to: waive a correlative duty; commence and prosecute institutional proceedings in the face of that duty's breach (or the threat thereof); and—in a certain sense, at least—undertake self-help remedies.[125] They also posit a legal power by which to 'demand' compliance or observance with a legal right, even absent a threatened breach of the correlative duty.[126] Whilst they do not elucidate it fully, the right-holder presumably uses this power when confronting the duty-bearer personally.

Moral rights scholars' accounts of claiming and otherwise enforcing moral rights are typically explained in terms of powers as well.[127] There are a few exceptions to this, though. Stephen Darwall, for example, identifies claiming as being the function of a Hohfeldian claim.[128] As explained in

[125] Hart (1982: 183–6). 'These legal powers (for such they are) over a correlative obligation…'. Ibid 184. (However, Hart also requires liberties by which to exercise those powers. Ibid 188); MacCormick (2007: 129); Steiner (1998: 240 n.14).

[126] See Chapter 7 § III 'Argument 2'. This seems to concern a normative power which conserves the status quo, as opposed to one that changes parties' (other) normative positions, unlike Hohfeld's A POWER.

[127] E.g., James (2003); O'Neill (1996: 128–36); Skorupski (2010: 309–13). Their views therefore all count as instances of the Control View (elucidated in Chapter 7), if not also the Will theory (explained in Chapter 5).

[128] Darwall (2006: 18). Margaret Gilbert had done so too in her earlier work. Gilbert (2012: 308).

Chapter 3 § III, this requires the (sub-optimal) 'active' interpretation of Hohfeld's conception.

Cognisant of this difficulty with Hohfeld's A CLAIM, Margaret Gilbert professes to have carved out a subset of RCTDs that engender their own claimability.[129] She calls these demand-rights.[130] Whilst (most) Hohfeldian claims are passive, demand-rights—if they indeed form a subset of claims—are active insofar as they are, or include, a power to demand one's right from a correlative duty-bearer,[131] thereby enforcing the right itself.[132] This power (or power embedded in a claim) is intentionally non-Hohfeldian, though, because it cannot alter parties' legal relationships. Instead, it is a capacity to make demands which nonetheless maintain the normative status quo (e.g., it does not nullify or change the correlative duty's content).[133] Gilbert's demand-rights also come with the standing to demand action or forbearance from the correlative duty-bearer.[134]

One notable exception in the literature to this power-centricity is John Finnis. He suggests there are also certain legal *liberties* by which to enforce legal RCTDs.

> In the law, such conjunctions of a liberty with a [Hohfeldian] claim-right are often supplemented by further conjoined rights; for example, by the claim-right to compensation in the event of wrongful (i.e. duty-breaking) interference with the liberty, and/or by the ancillary liberty to resort to self-help or to approach the courts in defence of one's substantive liberty, and/or by the power to institute legal proceedings or to waive compliance with the duty, etc.[135]

[129] Gilbert seems to be inconsistent about whether these rights constitute a subset of Hohfeldian claims or are merely analogous to them. See, e.g., Gilbert (2018: 22–3, 57, 61 n.18, 76, 80, 98, 344). As Visa Kurki points out, despite presenting demands-rights as being a mere subset of RCTDs, Gilbert equally presents her account as explaining the direction of *all* directed duties (more on those in Chapter 5 § III). Kurki (2019: 533); Gilbert (2018: 70–1). This calls into question her 'thin sense' of claim (i.e., passive Hohfeldian claim)/ demand-right distinction. Ibid 80. But cf. ibid 344.

[130] Ibid v, 11. Cf. Radin (1938: 1148–9).

[131] Gilbert (2018: 22–3, 254).

[132] Ibid 23 & n.33, 77, 323.

[133] Ibid 22–3.

[134] Ibid 56, 344.

[135] Finnis (2011: 201). Cf. Ernst Bierling's (undeveloped) concept, FORDERNDÜRFEN. Bierling (1877: 39–40, the footnote on 40 (§ 141)). See also my Appendix 1.

Liberties can be used to buttress and support RCTDs. Both legal and moral rights can be claimed using liberties, powers, or combinations thereof—and in ways that differ from than any of those mentioned by Finnis. I shall present two such modes of doing so in Chapter 9. William Galbraith Miller also discusses several examples, two or more of which, I submit, ought to be understood in terms of legal liberties (rather than as powers, Hohfeldian claims, or combinations of the latter two).

> The word "claim" comes to us from "clamor" through the Normans. It signifies "a complaint," "a hue and cry," as will be seen from the authorities referred to hereafter. As "action" points to self-help, so "claim" refers to a "calling out," either to a wrongdoer to do right, or to society to help. "Stop thief" serves both purposes. So Glanvill[e] (i. 5), "Cum clamat quis Domino regi aut ejus Justiciis de feodo, ... This mode of asserting and enforcing a private right is referred to in the Twelve Tables, and, if we may coin a word from the obsolete term there used, we may describe it as "**obvagulation**," when the creditor on every second day (*tertiis diebus*) was allowed to make a disturbance before the door of his debtor. It is known in India, where sitting **dharna** before the door of a debtor until the creditor perhaps died of starvation, so that his ghost might haunt the unjust debtor, was a recognised mode of procedure until it was forbidden by the 508th section of the Criminal Code (Stokes I 281. Fn 2: Balfour's Cyclopedia of India (3rd ed, sv. Sharna; *Code of Gentoo Laws* London 1777 pg 19. **Fasting** was also known in the ancient Irish law to enforce claims particularly against persons in high position (Senchus Mor, i. 113 (Rolls Ser.)). The creditor waited before the door of his debtor for a certain time, and if he did not receive a pledge he got double the debt and double food. These modes of enforcement were an indirect appeal to public opinion.[136]

At any rate, many (but not all) philosophers conceive of legal and/or moral rights as capacities by which to make claims or demands.[137] Those who reject such accounts instead believe that claiming and otherwise enforcing rights must be explained in terms of multiple normative positions. This usually takes the form of an enforcement power(s) + an RCTD.

However, rights enforcement can also involve: a liberty + an RCTD; a liberty + a power + an RCTD; etc. Further, the liberties or powers that

[136] Miller (1903: 58–9, bolded emphases added and paragraph breaks removed). For still other senses of claiming, see ibid 59–62; Wellman (1985: 204–11); Gilbert (2012). The Glanville quote translates as '[w]henever anyone complains to the King, or to his Justices, concerning his Fee, or his Freehold, if the complaint be such as be proper for the determination of the King's Court...'. Glanville (1900: 5).

[137] E.g., Feinberg (1980: 150–1); Darwall (2006: 18); Skorupski (2010: 311–2).

underpin the making of claims of right, or by which to enforce RCTDs in other ways, can either (a) serve as components in right complexes, or (b) constitute distinct rights. Hence, if (at least certain) powers and liberties count as kinds of rights, then claims of right can also *be about* other rights.

§ V.3. Where Can Legal Rights Be Claimed?

Much of the philosophy of rights literature assumes or argues that claims of right made outside of official proceedings do not count as forms of *legal* claiming. They are instead moral or social claims, ones which are incapable of producing legal consequences or effects.[138] For example, Gilbert states:

> I take it that, *outside the legal context*, verbal acts, such as demanding performance and rebuking someone for non-performance, count as a kind of *enforcement* [of RCTDs]. Indeed, these things constitute an important special class of *non-legal* enforcement mechanisms. One of their important aspects is that they do not in and of themselves involve more than verbal address.[139]

It is important to be clear about the sense of 'legal' here, though. Bona fide legal contexts are not restricted to institutional proceedings, bodies, or officials. When a right-holder turns in a chit, a receipt, an IOU, a check, an insurance policy, or a deed, to another private party, both parties' legal positions are at play.[140] *Lawful* claims of right are performative utterances/acts, ones relying upon legal normative positions which can bear legal force and significance. They are not, or at least need not be, mere rhetorical gestures. It is perhaps also worth bearing in mind a distinction between *lawful* and *legal* rights enforcement,[141] so long as one notes that (1) the former can also create legal consequences and (2) a legal system can also render (at least some) lawful ones into legal ones. This shall prove significant when we return to liberty-based claims of right in Chapter 9.

[138] In a similar vein, Susan James suggests that, absent legal enforcement powers to back rights up, claims of right are mostly useless. James (2003: 135–6). She nonetheless acknowledges O'Neill's point that claimable-yet-unenforceable rights may still be used (by cajoling, protesting, or 'appealing') to try to convince legal officials to render those rights legally enforceable. Ibid 136.

[139] Gilbert (2012: 308, emphases added). Cf. Gilbert (2018: 22–3, 61, 77, 323) on claiming as rights enforcement.

[140] Cf. Feinberg (1980: 150).

[141] Reiff (2005: 192, 199).

CHAPTER 5

The Theories of Rights Debate

§ I. Introduction

What is a right? Do all rights serve some singular ultimate purpose? What, if anything, makes rights different from other features of the normative world, such as duties, standards, rules, and principles? What are the necessary conditions of A RIGHT? Once again, these questions have plagued philosophers, jurists, and others for centuries. Indeed, they help to form the basis of the long-standing theories of rights debate.

Chapter 1 distinguished between models and theories. This chapter explains the theories of rights as competing explanations of, and criteria for, A RIGHT. Till now, these 'theoretical' criteria have never been fully elucidated. Despite its age, moreover, the debate's terms are quite muddled. Section II clarifies these matters.

Section III then argues that some of the debate's most famous arguments are unsuccessful. They either fail to address more versatile versions of their target theory, or, relatedly, they do not account for how rights theories interact with other theories of law—particularly Legal Positivism—in ways that render the charges levied against the rights theories to be off the mark.

The chapter then shows why recent developments have not moved the debate forward. Section IV argues that efforts to (re)frame the debate as competing explanations of the direction of 'relative'/'directed' duties is mistaken. This is because the theories' respective answers to that issue *themselves depend upon* their conceptions of A RIGHT, ones which do not

D. Frydrych, *The Architecture of Rights*,
https://doi.org/10.1007/978-3-030-76039-7_5

necessitate divergent identifications of a duty's direction. (The point here is not to exclude certain issues and disputes. It is only to show why it is erroneous to characterise the *entire* debate along those lines.) Second, despite the fact that two rivals continue to dominate this dispute, the Interest and Will theories, there have been quite a few recent attempts to provide hybrid or alternative theories. Building on Matthew Kramer's work, Section V argues that these efforts are all just versions of the Interest theory. (It also points out defects in each one.) Third, some scholars try to characterise the theories as being exclusively 'normative'—in the sense of being morally or politically evaluative. This would preclude the possibility of *analytic* versions of the interest and will theories. Section VI demonstrates why that effort is misguided.

§ II. Rival Conceptions of A RIGHT

Generally, the rival theories debate the best explanation of, and criteria for, A RIGHT. (However, certain disputes merely provide criteria for some specified subset of rights.[1]) The theories' rivalrous criteria for the concept are either analytic definitions,[2] or something akin to them. The latter seems to be the better explanation for three reasons. First, some versions of each theory only claim to offer the concept's necessary conditions, not its sufficient ones.[3] Second, theorists' criteria are often not fully encapsulated within their analytic definitions (if proffered) anyway. Third, *normative*—in the sense of being morally or politically evaluative—rights theorists equally provide criteria for the concept.

Each rights theory's criteria include: (I) an ultimate purpose that all instances purportedly serve; (II) means of protecting or effectuating that purpose, e.g., by *imposing* duties on other parties, by *including* means of enforcement, etc.; and (III) specifying which types of normative positions (e.g., Hohfeldian claims, liberties, etc.) and which tokens of those types (e.g., what subset of Hohfeldian claims) qualify as rights—not all might. (The next three subsections will explicate these features.)

[1] For histories of the debate, see Pound (1915); Pound (1959); Simmonds (1998). For the idea that these are just definitions of 'a right', see, e.g., A.H. Campbell (1940: 206–7).

[2] On analytic definitions offering 'criteria' for a concept, see, Chapter 1 note 58 and the accompanying text.

[3] E.g., Kramer (2017: 54, 59). Cf. Kramer (2010: 35). See also Wenar (2008); Stewart (2012: 319–20).

Again, there are both analytic and normative versions of the theories. *Analytic* versions are said to be morally and politically neutral, in the sense of elucidating what ultimate purpose rights serve, but without judging whether rights are good, bad, or valuable things, whether people ought to have them, whether their ultimate purpose is good or evil, etc. *Normative* versions provide criteria that fit into a larger account of what role rights ought to serve within a normative system. These can be moral or political explanations of what rights ought to do and which values they ought to advance.

Whether analytic or normative, the theories also admit of (at least) two varieties: protection and justification.[4] The *protection* variety posit that all rights protect the right-holder's will or interests respectively. The *justification* variety hold that the existence or imposition of correlative normative positions (e.g., duties, liabilities, etc.) borne by other people is justified by the right-holder's interests, or by the need to buttress the right-holder's will vis-à-vis those other parties.[5]

The theories of rights debate appears to build on an earlier one dating back to (at least) the twelfth century about whether (at least some) rights were perforce enforceable and/or if a right is a kind of power or something akin to one.[6] *If* the two debates actually differ, it is because the older one does not concern theories offering detailed criteria for the concept and is instead simply a dispute over whether rights are perforce enforceable.

Regardless, although historically about A RIGHT, some versions of the theories of rights are nonetheless qualified in one or two ways: particularly, by specifying that theirs only concerns (1) the rights of a given normative domain or system and/or (2) a certain kind of a right. For example, some versions cover legal rights exclusively, not moral ones. (Some may even just concern a subset of rights within a domain, e.g., private law rights, rather than all legal rights.) Others may, additionally or alternatively, only

[4] Rainbolt (2006: 86–7). However, no one seems to have advanced a justification version of the Will theory. Ibid 87.

[5] Many theorists are nevertheless inconsistent about this. A given scholar may write about 'protection' or 'justification', but then switch to discussing the 'effectuation', 'promotion', or 'facilitation' of interests or the will within the same work. This may simply be due to his or her lack of awareness of the potentially different theoretical implications.

[6] See, e.g., Tierney (1997). This concern, and the conception of rights as powers, persisted throughout the renaissance and early modern period. See, e.g., Brett (1997); Fouta (2019). These ideas influenced nineteenth century German Will theorists considerably. See Pound (1959); Jhering (1865: § 60 pg 307–16).

profess to explain a right-correlative-to-a-duty ('an RCTD'), not liberties, powers, or immunities.[7] Even so, some versions cover moral, social, and/or institutional RCTDs,[8] whilst others concern additional basic types, e.g., RCTDs, immunities, and liberties of any sort (legal, moral, game-based, etc.).[9]

Theorists also differ over what their stated delimitations entail. Some claim that their respective version of each theory is a mere preparatory effort for more expansive accounts, i.e., more work could be done to extend it to cover other kinds of rights and/or to other normative domains. Others insist that their versions (should) extend only as far as the kind of a right and/or domain actually discussed. Hence, neither of the two types of delimitation entails a denial that other (kinds of) rights exist, ones which are ungoverned by the version of the theory presented.

§ II.1. Criterion 1: An Ultimate Purpose

Wittingly or otherwise, the theories advance the idea that rights serve some singular, ultimate purpose. They therefore have, at least in part, a teleological focus. Confusingly, though, this matter gets expressed in different ways. Sometimes, it put it thus: what makes it the case that Hohfeldian liberties, claims, powers, and immunities (or, at least some of them) are all kinds of rights?[10] Are they different 'species' of one 'genus'? Another way is by putting things is in terms of what it is to *have* or *hold* a right, or what it is to be a right-holder.[11] However, this is just a different

[7] As discussed in Chapter 1 note 11, there are various conceptions of the kind of a right that correlates to a duty.

[8] E.g., Sreenivasan (2010: 468).

[9] For example, whilst they admit that there could be more expansive versions of both theories, Matthew Kramer and Hillel Steiner, an Interest and Will theorist respectively, think it dubious to inflate the debate—as least insofar as it concerns legal rights—beyond an RCTD. In other words, the debate ought not to concern legal immunities, legal liberties, etc. Kramer & Steiner (2007: 295–9); Kramer (2010: 31–2).

[10] E.g., MacCormick (1977: 194); Martin & Nickel (1980: 172); Hart (1982: 189); Wellman (1985: 56); Kramer (1998: 1); Cruft (2004: 356 n.17); Rainbolt (2006: 25). As shall be discussed in § II.3, many theorists nevertheless deny that all four Hohfeldian types, let alone a given token of a type (e.g., a given claim), count as rights. Putting the debate in these terms is therefore problematic.

[11] E.g., Finnis (2011: 203): '[w]hat, if any, is the underlying principle, unifying the various types of relationships that are reasonably said to concern "rights"? Or, more crudely: Is there some general explanation of what it is to have a right?'; Stepanians (2005: 68); Kramer

way of asking what it is that rights *necessarily* do for their holders *qua* normative positions, which in turn falls under the analysis of A RIGHT. The debate's two main rivals answer that rights concern their holders' wills (the Will theory), or some interest of theirs (the Interest theory).[12] The theories' respective explanations are treated as being mutually exclusive.

Of late, some theorists have posited that the debate really is about right-*holding*, which is a distinct issue from the 'what is a right' question. This is incorrect: the debate is about rights. The proof is this. When presented with a candidate case wherein no one can enforce a putative right-holder's right, Will theorists simply deny that that person actually has a right. For Will theorists, the person is not a genuine right-holder *because there is no right*. Real rights, on their view, are necessarily enforceable in some way or other. Interest theorists, by contrast, believe that third-party beneficiaries, incompetents, children, and others can have rights even if they are unenforceable *because* they deny that a right must be enforceable. Hence, their respective views about A RIGHT shape what it is to have a right and who can count as bona fide right-holders.

Interest and Will are actually both families of theories. Within each family there are: nuanced differences concerning their teleological claims; analytic and normative versions; justificatory and protection varieties; and versions of varying scopes, i.e., where the theory might profess to cover only a particular normative domain (e.g., law, but not morality) or just one basic type of a right (e.g., a Hohfeldian claim, but not a liberty, immunity, etc.).

All versions of the Will theory (hereinafter '**WT**') posit that a right necessarily affords its holder (or, on some versions, also another party authorised to act on the holder's behalf) the capacity to control a correlative normative position. 'Control' here generally means using enforcement powers. Typically, it is control over a correlative duty. However, WT need not be delimited to covering RCTDs.

Concerning teleology, there is an intra-WT dispute about its ultimate locus of concern. What is most significant: that rights afford their holders

(2013: 246). This way of framing things is somewhat ambiguous, though. Is it really asking: what the right-holder *can do with* a right; what a right *does for* the right-holder; or both?

[12] For example, Kramer explains them as being in part thus. 'For the Interest Theory the essence of a right consists in the normative protection of some aspect(s) of the right-holder's well-being… For the Will Theory, the essence of a right consists in opportunities for the right-holder to make normatively significant choices relating to the behaviour of someone else…'. Kramer (2000: 473–4).

the ability to make certain kinds of choices; how rights protect their holders' wills, even if they cannot personally make those sorts of choices; or the structure of freedom and independence that rights afford?

There are also certain seeming differences in focus amongst the various versions of WT. Are there moral or political constraints on what a legal right can be posited for? Second, what is of greater relevance: the control rights provide, or the status they afford? Third, is the focus on how rights work *within* the system or domain in which they are housed, or rather on what they can effectuate *beyond* that system or domain?

Consider first HLA Hart's 'later' WT of private law (and certain other legal) RCTDs, power-rights, and liberty-rights. For him, such rights afford their holders a legally respected choice and modicum of control. In part, this is because each contains bilateral liberties by which to exercise it or not, e.g., liberties by which to choose to (not) exercise a power to waive an RCTD's correlative duty.[13] Further, a private law RCTD is held to be a set of normative powers by which to enforce or waive the correlative duty at different stages.[14] These 'measures of control' provide the (private law) right-holder a modicum of choice over other parties' actions.[15]

Given its composition, however, a particular private law RCTD may afford 'fuller' or 'lesser' measures of control. The fullest measure includes all of the following 'elements':

Element I: the right holder may (Ia) waive or (Ib) extinguish the duty or (Ic) leave it in existence.

Element II: after breach or threatened breach of a duty he may (IIa) leave it 'unenforced' or (IIb) may 'enforce' it by suing for compensation or, in certain cases, (IIc) for an injunction or (IId) mandatory order to restrain the continued or further breach of duty.

Element III: and the right-holder may (IIIa) waive or (IIIb) extinguish the obligation to pay compensation to which the breach gives rise.[16]

13 Hart (1982: 188–9).

14 'These legal powers (for such they are) over a correlative obligation…'. Hart (1982: 184). See also Appendix 1 on Hart's model.

15 Hart (1982: 183–4 & n.85). Cf. Pound (1959: 75) on conceptions of RCTDs and powers in terms of control.

16 Hart (1982: 183–4, bolded emphases, labels, and extra numerals added). Steiner adds to Element III the capacity to seek to enforce the obligation to pay. Steiner (1998: 240 n.14). Hart also notes another sub-element—at least for public law rights—that would fit under Element I: demanding compliance directly from the duty-bearer. Hart (1982: 186).

Hart also posits that private law RCTDs, power-rights, and liberty-rights (three types of right complexes) provide their holders a legally respected choice and control because each contains bilateral liberties by which to exercise it or not. As examples, liberties by which to (not) exercise one of an RCTD's component powers to waive the correlative duty; liberties by which to (not) exercise a power-right to make a contract offer; etc.[17]

Additionally, a private law RCTD's 'modicum of control' over a correlative duty is said to render the right-holder a 'private legislator'[18] or 'small-scale sovereign',[19] one who is afforded a '*locus standi*' by which to be recognised by the legal system (and by others) and through which to effectuate one's will within the law.[20] Hence, such rights provide a sort of status, recognition, and empowerment within a legal system.[21]

Certain other anti-Interest theorists nevertheless wish to either distinguish Hart's theory from WT, or their own from WT. For example, Carl Wellman classifies Hart's as a 'Choice' theory, rather than as a version of WT. 'Choice' theories are said to concern the ability to make decisions regarding a right's enforcement or waiver. By contrast, Wellman insists, WT is really about vindicating right-holders' wills and rights, not the

[17] Hart (1982: 188–9). Hart thus asserts that the sense of legal right here, at least regarding his three types, is that of 'a legally respected choice'. Ibid 189. However, bilateral liberties only count as liberty-*rights* if protected (directly or indirectly) by duties. Ibid 171–4. (This may mark (just one of) Hart's breaks with Hohfeld's view of correlativity.) Without fully elaborating on the matter, Hart suggests that the bilateral liberties at the heart of private law liberty-rights and power-rights are what afford control, unlike private law RCTDs which are identified with enforcement powers coupled with such liberties. Ibid 188. (Whilst for power-rights the relevant sort of control concerns changing people's legal positions, for liberty-rights the relevant sort of control is vis-à-vis oneself, not over others per se). On the limits of Hart's theory vis-à-vis other kinds of legal rights, see ibid 185, 186 & n.90, 189–90, 192–3.

[18] Hart (1994: 41).

[19] Hart (1982: 183, emphasis added): '[t]he idea is that of one individual being given by the law exclusive control, more or less extensive, over another person's duty *so that* in the area of conduct covered by that duty the individual who has the right is a small-scale sovereign to whom the duty is owed'. Cf. Savigny (1867: 6, 271).

[20] Hart (1982: 183, 186). Joel Feinberg discusses the dignity that rights possession affords to holders. Like Hart, he also presents the idea of a right giving people 'something to stand on' in terms of being able to assert oneself in the world, etc. Feinberg (1980: 151).

[21] Will theorists' stances on the merits of the primary/secondary/tertiary rights distinction, i.e., whether these are distinct rights, or instead one and the same right that is enforced or waived through different stages, are sometimes unclear.

ability to make those sorts of choices.[22] Particularly, if there is a conflict (even a hypothetical one) between a right-holder and some other party over a matter falling within the right's ambit, then the former party ought to prevail *because* of the right. This would seem to entail that, even if you were personally unable to trigger a third-party dispute resolution process, you would or should emerge triumphant from one (were the proceedings to be initiated at any rate) because of your right-holder status. Other people (the community, the legal authorities, etc.) will/should side in your favour because of your right. Rights therefore entitle their holders to triumph in a (potential) combat of wills over some matter.[23]

In turn, Arthur Ripstein claims that Immanuel Kant's account of rights differs from WT. For Ripstein, WT treats *legal* rights as mere instruments for making choices regarding their enforcement or waiver, or for some ulterior ends. A given right, on this view, may thus be modified or terminated based on how well it serves those functions. Focusing on the capacity to facilitate freedom in other spheres of life, however, renders legal rights liable to performance evaluations regarding how well they do that job.[24] From Ripstein's Kantian standpoint, that instrumentalism (supposedly) undermines rights' forcefulness. This is because, for Kant, rights and their correlatives form the very structure of legal and political freedom. Legal rights are not apparatuses for effectuating goals outside of the legal system, malleable tools for making choices, or otherwise just means to an end. Instead, they *constitute* a system of equal freedom and each person's independence.[25]

[22] Wellman (1985: 61–80). But see also Wellman (2000: 954–5).

[23] Wellman (1985: 56, 65–73, 80, 89–90, 92–4, 95–102); Wellman (1995: 8, 25, 107, 110–1). Wellman's account implies that it is actually the right-holder's identity or status that gets protected and vindicated. Legal officials (judges, say) are meant to take your side because of your right-holding status, no matter what enforcement choices you make vis-à-vis the right. Seemingly, then, a right-holder's will can or should be vindicated (or be vindicable) without the need for any actual *personal act of will*. Were this the end of the matter, Wellman's would just seem to be a version of IT. In response, he could claim that WT differs because it holds that rights are really about having one's status recognised and vindicated, not (protecting, effectuating, etc.) the interests upon which the right is predicated. E.g., Wellman (1995: 124). (As shall be noted below, Wellman's account, like Kant and Hart's, makes control mechanisms essential too, but perhaps does not place them in the direct centre).

[24] Ripstein (2009: 34). See also ibid 5, 15–7, 33–4.

[25] Ibid 30–1, 34–5. Cf. Ripstein (2017: 194–5); Ripstein (2013b: 162, 180–1); Spector (2009: 362).

Ripstein's charge is odd because Kant is sometimes taken to be among WT's fathers.[26] More importantly, Wellman[27] and Ripstein[28]—equally hold (1) that enforcement power is essential to AN RCTD (and, indeed, for all kinds of rights on Wellman's view); and (2) thus rights perforce afford both a modicum of *control* and some sort of *standing* within the normative system. This is why, despite the stated alternative focuses, their accounts are really just versions of WT.[29] All versions of the theory stand

[26] E.g., Simmonds (1998: 135–6, 176, 179). Kant himself conceives of a right as authorising coercion, power one rightfully has over another within a given system. See Appendix 1.

[27] As discussed in Chapter 2, for Wellman, all rights are dynamic complexes. Despite having some fungible 'associated' components, rights afford 'dominion' status, which is to be understood in terms of providing freedom and control. Further, a right's containing at least one enforcement power plus a liberty to exercise that power seems to be the minimal level of freedom and control (a liberty:freedom::a power:control). See Chapter 2 notes 60–77 and the accompanying text. Hence, despite his emphasis on the will being vindicable in potential disputes, Wellman equally holds that rights necessarily afford some control via normative power. Indeed, control over others via (at least one of) the powers to claim, enforce, and waive (along with the freedom—Hohfeldian liberties—to exercise those powers) is essential to 'dominion' status. This in turn entails that rights perforce afford some kind of special standing. Wellman (1985: 192).

[28] Ripstein claims that (i) Kant identifies a right with a 'title to coerce' and that rights are justifiably employed to counteract unjust interferences with the right-holder's independence. Ripstein (2009: 30, 54–6, 146, 159). Indeed, he notes that Kant deems rights to necessarily be enforceable. Ibid 146. However, Ripstein also construes a right to be (ii) freedom from, or a constraint upon, others' choices (ibid 13–4, 35) and (iii) a power, authorisation, or entitlement to act in certain ways to effectuate the holder's own purposes (ibid 17, 36, 39, 42, 48, 50–1); cf. Ripstein (2017: 194–6). (This inconsistency would lead Hohfeldians to identify these capacities and entitlements with distinct normative positions, i.e., claims, powers, liberties, etc., which may or may not be serving as components within a singular right complex). Moreover, even if Ripstein were correct about their role in structuring independence, again, Kant deems rights to *necessarily* be enforceable and to include the capacity to make choices regarding such coercion. (See Appendix 1 note 9). Hence, the indispensability of control to A RIGHT. Rights also afford their holders standing within a system of equal freedom. See Ripstein (2017: 195–6); Ripstein (2008: 230 n.5, 247); Ripstein (2015: 19). Cf. Ripstein (2013b: 171, 176). One therefore cannot explain Kant's conception using independence (and correlative constraints borne by others) alone. The explanation must also include authorisation to coerce, which can, in turn, be further fleshed out in terms of control, empowerment, and its affording you standing within a system of equal freedom, if not also positive legal rights securing and protecting independence and the choices and choice making freedom that that independence affords.

[29] For a more detailed explanation of Wellman and Ripstein's respective theories and how they both figure under the rubric of WT, see Frydrych (2019).

or fall on these propositions.[30] Indeed, what unites all such accounts under the banner of 'WT' is their holding: (1) enforcement power (or, at least one such power) is essential to A RIGHT; and (2) that rights perforce afford both a modicum of control and some sort of standing within the normative system.

Most versions of the Interest theory (hereinafter '**IT**') lack an equally developed teleology.[31] Still, each tries to delimit the relevant sorts of interests in some way. Certain versions (*seemingly*) present accounts of interests in terms of wellbeing. Joseph Raz's ostensibly counts as one.[32] His IT criteria for A RIGHT are only partly covered by his 'philosophical definition':

[30] Nigel Simmonds' WT is only somewhat exceptional here. He defends Hart's 'earlier' version of WT, according to which a singular Hohfeldian claim, liberty, power, and an immunity can each count as a right. Hart (1983: 35 n.15, originally published in 1954; Simmonds (1998: 211–32). Further, each does so without requiring additional enforcement powers or liberties by which to exercise either those powers or other positions, per Hart's 'later' *Essays on Bentham* WT view of private law RCTDs, powers, and liberty-rights. Hart (1982: 183–92). Simmonds nonetheless believes that all four Hohfeldian (basic) kinds of rights are afforded choices regarding whether to use them or not. The choices, however, are factual matters, not a function of separate normative positions. Simmonds (1998: 218–20); Hart (1983: 35 n.15). Second, and more importantly, Simmonds interprets a Hohfeldian claim to be a kind of enforcement power over the correlative duty. Simmonds (1998: 222–3).

According to his 'early' view, Hart said that a singular Hohfeldian claim, liberty, power, or immunity protects its holder's ability to choose either affirmatively by giving legal effect to the choice (claims and powers) or negatively by not impeding or instructing it (liberties and immunities). Hart (1983: 35 n.15). Hart's 'early' view may be found in his 'Definition and Theory in Jurisprudence' piece, which was originally published in 1954. He changed his mind on the matter by the time of writing *Essays on Bentham*. Hart (1982). See also Simmonds (1998: 215–21).

[31] On older IT of *legal* rights as 'legally protected interests', see, e.g., Jhering (1865: 316–7); Salmond (1902: 219). Cf. Pound (1959: 53).

[32] Raz (1996), particularly the chapter 'Rights and Individual Well-Being'; Raz (1986), particularly the chapter 'The Nature of Rights'. Cf. Kramer (2001: 28). As shall be further discussed in Chapter 6, however, Raz's theory is not actually so delimited, because he posits that legal rights need not really protect considerations of wellbeing: there can be rights predicated upon officials' corruption or mistakes, rights that protect trivial interests, etc. Raz (1986: 186, 262).

Definition: 'X has a right' if and only if X can have rights, and, other things being equal, an aspect of X's well-being (his interest) is a sufficient reason for holding some other person(s) to be under a duty.[33]

Other versions differ from Raz's in several ways. Take Matthew Kramer's IT of legal RCTDs as an example. For one thing, it does not include a grounding story, i.e., of one normative position being the reason for another. Kramer also denies that the relevant sort of interest must be 'the one' which catalysed a particular normative position's generation, e.g., legal officials' justification for positing a given legal RCTD and correlative duty in order to advance the RCTD-holders' interest in personal safety or in wealth accumulation, say. Instead, the pertinent sorts of interests are those actually effected by the normative position: the protection of interests the right (and correlative position) in fact provides.[34] Hence, versions of IT divide over whether a right must have a predicate interest and *justify* the imposition of normative positions (e.g., a duty) on others, or whether a right merely *protects* or fulfils an interest via the right-correlative position relationship.[35] (One could conceivably advance a justification-protection version, though.)

To Kramer's mind, moreover, determining which sorts of interests legal rights ought to protect is a matter for political philosophy, not analytic jurisprudence (and hence not for an *analytic* IT like his). Hence, ascertainment of the kinds of interests which rights serve would just seem to be system- or domain-contingent inquiries.[36] Nevertheless, Kramer (along with Neil MacCormick, another Interest theorist) maintains that the interests in question are delimited to ones that are normally, standardly, or typi-

[33] Raz (1986: 166). Raz's setup to his analytic definition makes it clear that he intends it to be of A RIGHT, not RIGHT HOLDING. Ibid 165–6. (He claims that it 'aims to encapsulate the common core of all rights, and thus to help to explain their special role in practical thought'. Ibid 167.) Still, he immediately thereafter provides this additional definition about right-holding capacity. '*Capacity for possessing rights*: An individual is capable of having rights if and only if either his well-being is of ultimate value or he is an 'artificial person' (e.g. a corporation)'. Ibid 166.

[34] Kramer & Steiner (2007: 289–90). Even so, we can say of such versions that this (effectuation of protection of interests) is a claim about rights' ultimate purpose, even if the underlying justification or purpose for positing a particular right is not pertinent.

[35] Rainbolt (2006: 86–7).

[36] Kramer (1998: 79). Kramer also suggests there can be both 'political-philosophical' and 'jurisprudential' versions of IT and WT and deems Raz's to be of the former variety. Kramer (2013: 245). However, this cannot be squared with what Raz says and does with his IT—especially in his article-cum-book-chapter 'Legal Rights', e.g., which aims to explain how judges use legal rights to generate new rights, duties, and other positions. Raz (1996).

cally beneficial or advantageous for the class of agent to which an individual right-holder belongs.[37] (Kramer also claims that there are 'nominal' legal rights.[38]) Here is Kramer's most recent phrasing of his IT:

> (IT-1) Necessary though insufficient for the holding of a legal right by *X* is that the duty correlative to the right, when actual, normatively protects some aspect of *X*'s situation that on balance is typically beneficial for a being like *X* (namely, a human individual or a collectivity or a non-human animal).
>
> (IT-2) Neither necessary nor sufficient for the holding of some specified legal right by *X* is that *X* is competent and authorised to demand or waive the enforcement of the duty that is correlative to the right.[39]

§ II.2. Criterion 2: Means of Protection/Effectuation

The theories are equally concerned with how rights effectuate their candidate ultimate purposes. Determining the relevant means for doing so, however, is part of a more complicated story; for whilst the debate is about A RIGHT's *intension*, it does not necessarily aim to govern the concept's *extension*. Even so, when it comes to the criterion for means of protecting or effectuating rights, the short version of the story is this: the theories dispute whether enforcement powers are essential to (or essentially associated with) A RIGHT.[40]

If you think that all rights ultimately protect holders' wills or interests, then you must explain *how* they do so. Interest and Will theorists generally

[37] MacCormick (1977: 202); Kramer & Steiner (2007: 289–90, 302–4); Kramer (2017: 49). Kramer's preference is 'typically'. See also Raz (1986: 180).

[38] There nevertheless appears to have been an evolution in Kramer's view on what a right's being 'nominal' means. In his earlier writings, they were unenforceable legal ones. More recently, he seems to mean instead those rights that are liable to be nullified by others against the holder's wishes, i.e., nominal rights are Hohfeldian claims that are unprotected by immunities against their nullification. If so, he has altered things without explanation. He also leaves it unclear why genuine legal rights *must* be so protected by immunities. See Kramer (1998: 8–9, 34, 46, 63–5, 100, 106); Kramer (2000: 476–7, 481–2); Kramer & Steiner (2007: 297); Kramer (2007: 187); Kramer (2008: 417, 418); Kramer (2010: 33); Kramer (2013: 247).

[39] Kramer (2017: 49). But see *infra* note 102 on Kramer's potentially evolving view.

[40] E.g., Simmonds (1998: 141, but just on WT); Steiner (1994: 57, but just on WT); Kramer (2000: 474); Kramer (2013: 246–7); Cruft (2004: 347–8, 369); Eleftheriadis (2008: 8); Wenar (2005: 237–8); Wenar (2013: 226); Stewart (2012: 319); Gorman (2003: 74).

agree that many rights are enforceable via powers.[41] Their disagreement is about whether all rights (or all legal rights, or all legal RCTDs, etc.) *must* be. Will theorists either hold that an RCTD is simply to be identified with enforcement powers, or that such powers are constitutive features of the concept.[42] Interest theorists deny that.[43] Instead, they believe RCTDs are protected or effectuated by the existence of, or imposition of, duties on other parties. (Note, however, that they do not insist upon this always constituting *adequate* protection for the right.) For Interest theorists, rights can of course additionally be protected by enforcement powers. They merely deny that (1) such protection is invariably available and (2) that such protection is a necessary feature of the concept, A RIGHT. This is another reason why the two theories are deemed to be mutually exclusive.

To clarify, the debate does not centre upon any and all sorts of powers. It is primarily concerned with those of enforcement and waiver. Per Chapter 4, a broad understanding of RIGHTS ENFORCEMENT is that it concerns defeasible efforts to try to seek a remedy for (anticipated) breaches of correlative duties, or to try to vindicate a right in other ways. In legal contexts, this often means being able to initiate and prosecute institutional dispute resolution processes, e.g., lawsuits. 'Waiver' means a capacity to forego such processes despite being entitled to them. Moreover, a legal official or authorised agent presumably oversees such proceedings in order to provide determinative, binding resolutions. Whilst moral and social domains need not have analogous third-party dispute resolution mechanisms, they may have other ways to enforce rights.

[41] E.g., Raz (1996: 256–7); Kramer (1998: 9, 64–5, 100); MacCormick (2007: 129).

[42] Examples of Will theorists who identify (at least certain) RCTDs with powers include Hart and Simmonds. Hart (1982: 184); Simmonds (1998: 223). (However, note again Hart's view of the need for bilateral liberties by which to exercise, or not exercise, those private law powers. Hart 1982: 188–9). Will theorists who hold that RCTDs are (parts of) enforceable right complexes, or invariably accompanied by enforcement powers include Wellman and Steiner. Wellman (1985: 59–60, 93–4); Wellman (1995: 8–9); Steiner (1994: 61). As mentioned in Chapter 3 note 32, Pavlos Eleftheriadis, a Will theorist, distinguishes between 'rights' (reasons with some force) and 'relations' (Hohfeldian complexes meant to effectuate rights). Eleftheriadis (2008: 123–8, 168). However, even on his view, the relations must include enforcement and waiver powers.

[43] E.g., Kramer (2013: 246); Kramer (2017: 78); Raz (1996: 255–8). (See ibid for Raz's concern about scholars wrongly presuming the necessary existence of, or overemphasising the importance of, enforcement mechanisms for moral rights).

§ II.3. Criterion 3: Specifying Candidates

The rival theories also specify which (subsets of which) types of basic positions, and which combinations thereof (i.e., complexes), are actually rights—in accordance with the proposed ultimate purpose and identified means of protection or effectuation. Using the *schema of jural relations* to explain, there are at least 11 *theory*-driven interpretations of Hohfeld:[44]

1. The only real type of a right is a claim.
2. Only 'complexes' containing a claim and enforcement and/or waiver power(s) are rights.
3. Rights are any one of Hohfeld's four types of rights.
4. Rights are any one of Hohfeld's four types of rights *and* complexes composed of such types.
5. Rights are any of Hohfeld's four types of rights plus one or more type of ligation (e.g., a duty-right, a liability-right, etc.) and complexes thereof.
6. Rights are only some of Hohfeld's four types of rights.
7. Rights are only some of Hohfeld's four types of rights and complexes containing such types.
8. Rights are suitable tokens of any of Hohfeld's types.[45]
9. Rights are suitable tokens of only certain Hohfeldian types.
10. Rights are only suitable tokens and complexes containing such tokens.
11. Rights are only complexes containing suitable tokens.

For Interest theorists who endorse interpretation 1 above, only a single Hohfeldian claim is a right; for them, Hohfeldian liberties, powers, and

[44] This builds on Eleftheriadis' classification:

(a) Legal rights are claims.
(b) Legal rights are any one of the four concepts: claim, liberty, power, immunity.
(c) Legal rights are any of the four concepts and any combination of such concepts.
(d) Rights are only suitable incidents or combinations of Hohfeldian incidents, and
(e) Rights are only suitable combinations of Hohfeldian incidents.

Eleftheriadis (2008: 7).

[45] Once again, 'token' just means an instance of a class here. The theoretical criteria delimit which subsets of a type, or which types, count as rights and which do not. For example, some liberties may be rights, but perhaps not all. Notice the difference between saying that some but not all Hohfeldian claims are rights, versus saying that liberties and powers are not rights.

immunities are not types of rights.[46] More expansive versions of IT nonetheless treat some or all of those other positions, and/or complexes containing them, as rights too.[47] All versions of IT allow for single positions or complexes to be accompanied by, or include, enforcement and waiver powers; they merely deny that being conjoined or associated with such powers *is necessary to what makes* those positions (and complexes) count as rights.[48]

By contrast, WT usually considers a right to be, at a minimum, a complex composed of a Hohfeldian claim plus at least one enforcement or waiver power (interpretations 2 and 7).[49] ('Usually', because a minority of Will theorists interpret a Hohfeldian claim *to simply be* such a power.) Most versions, though, suggest that multiple enforcement and waiver powers obtain.[50] Still, WT has no set number of required enforcement powers for a given right, save for a floor of at least one such power—but no specification of which one that must be.[51]

Concerning *legal* rights, many versions of WT explain the different stages of institutional dispute resolution processes in terms of multiple powers, i.e., 'secondary' and 'tertiary' rights. However, some Will theorists reject the characterisation of matters in terms of distinct rights, i.e., primary versus secondary versus tertiary—especially if they conceive of rights themselves as admitting of fuller or lesser measures of control.

More capacious versions of WT (would or could) allow for liberty-, power-, and immunity-rights, and for right complexes that do not contain component Hohfeldian claims, so long as one or more enforcement and/ or waiver powers is included in the package.[52] As examples, a right could be composed of: an immunity plus three enforcement powers; a liberty

[46] E.g., Kramer (1998: 13–4).

[47] As dicussed and critiqued in Chapter 2 § IV, some scholars, including certain Interest and Will theorists, believe that Hohfeldian liabilities and other kinds of ligations can serve as the 'core' of a right complex too. (For the Will theorists who do, enforcement powers of some sort must of course be included in any such case). See Wellman (1985: 93–4, 206–7; Wellman (1995: 190); Cruft (2004: 358–9); Rainbolt (2006: 34–9).

[48] E.g., Stepanians (2005: 72).

[49] E.g., Sumner (1987: 43).

[50] Hart (1982: 183–4); Simmonds (1998: 229–30). See *infra* § III for further discussion.

[51] E.g., Hart (1982: 183–4): private law rights admit of 'fuller' or 'lesser' measures of control; Simmonds (1998: 229–30): a given legal right may have a variable set of enforcement powers.

[52] E.g., Wellman (1985: 93–4, 206–7); Wellman (1995: 8–9); Cruft (2004: 367–8); Wenar (2005: 239, 243–6); Wenar (2013: 226).

plus two such powers; etc. Even so, almost all versions of the theory focus on RCTDs plus enforcement powers.

Again, a small minority would deny the need to aggregate different elements into a right complex in the first place. This is because they adjudge an RCTD (e.g., Hohfeld's claim) to be a species of enforcement power.[53] For this minority, analysing rights in terms of complexes creates redundancies. What need is there to explain a right as bearing a separate enforcement power when it already has a Hohfeldian claim—understood as being a self-enforceable normative position?

Notice also the use of the type/token distinction in the classification above. Given what they count as rights, both IT and WT need not track ordinary language[54] or 'theory neutral' rights models such as Hohfeld's *schema* completely.[55] This is because they provide competing qualification tests for candidate tokens of the various types of normative positions, thereby demarcating the set of rights from the total set of all normative positions. A candidate position (or a complex) only counts as a right if it fulfils a theory's specified theoretical ultimate purpose and means of protection or effectuation.[56] Some theorists even deny that any and all tokens of a type of basic position (e.g., a Hohfeldian claim) are actually rights. IT asks whether the candidate token protects or advances the holder's interests, whilst WT asks if it protects or effectuates the ability to vindicate the holder's will. If the candidate does not meet the theory's preferred *raison d'être*, then it is denied rights status.

Consider these examples. If a given Hohfeldian claim does not protect the holder's interests (or does not normally protect the interests of the class of persons that that kind of claim generally benefits, e.g., property

[53] E.g., Hart (1983: 35 n.15); Simmonds (1998: 223 & n.137). Technically, Hart's 'later' view found in his *Essays on Bentham* could be explained as allowing for the 'least' amount of control in terms of a single private law RCTD (a kind of power), e.g., the right to waive a correlative duty. Absent the bilateral liberty by which to exercise that RCTD, however, it is unclear whether Hart would adjudge it to be a proper private law right (although he admits there are other legal rights that do not afford such control).

[54] See, e.g., Cruft (2004: 372–3, 382, 384).

[55] See Chapter 1 note 46 and the accompanying text.

[56] Wenar discusses the possibility of an 'Any Incident' theory, which would treat any token of a Hohfeldian type as a right. (He leaves this ambiguous, though: does he mean all eight positions, the four usually called 'rights', or some other combination?). He rejects any such theory on the grounds that not all Hohfeldian tokens are rights, as some fail to meet his specified criteria. Wenar (2005: 243–6). Cf. Cruft (2004).

holders, citizens, etc.), then that claim is not a right.[57] The token claim is simply something else—exactly what, such theorists leave unclear. Second, in discussing a hypothetical expansive version of his IT that would treat more Hohfeldian positions than just legal claims as rights, Kramer argues that certain legal liberties which get nullified and replaced with 'morally legitimate' paternalistic legal duties to forbear would not really have been classifiable as legal (liberty-)rights (as they were not typically beneficial after all).[58] Third, Hart thinks it mistaken to designate a token immunity as a legal right if it prevents its holder from benefiting from *advantageous* changes to his or her legal positions.[59]

The theoretical criteria not only identify which normative positions count as rights based on whether they protect the holder's will or interest (or justify the imposition of different normative positions on other parties); they also specify the modes of protection, effectuation, justification, etc. For notice that from the mere idea that a right is a normative position protecting an interest or the will, it is impossible to say *why* a given Hohfeldian claim is a bona fide right whilst a given power—of the enforcement variety or otherwise—is not. The criteria are therefore not simply a matter of one preferred candidate ultimate purpose (interests or will) plus some arbitrary list of tokens or types of normative positions. They also *delimit* the ways in which rights must protect or effectuate interests or the will. Only if a candidate meets the specified means does it count as a right.

Here are two examples. First, when certain Interest theorists assert that only Hohfeldian claims are rights, their criteria include the idea that rights *protect* interests *via* duties borne by, or imposed upon, other parties. According to this subset of theorists, then, whilst a liberty may be based on a person's interest, because it fails to protect that interest *in the relevant way* it is not a right. Second, most Will theorists believe that the relevant forms of protection for an RCTD include the power to control the (non-) fulfilment of the correlative duty, rather than just the duty (and its normatively required action or forbearance in furtherance of the right's content).

[57] E.g., Wenar (2005: 244–5).

[58] Kramer (2017: 64). See also ibid 70 for examples of other Hohfeldian liberties and powers which Kramer thinks would not be 'properly classifiable as rights'.

[59] Hart (1982: 191). Whilst Hart's theory mostly concerns private law rights, he also suggests that there are constraints on what *theorists* should call rights. He does not mention advantageousness as a factor in regard to RCTDs, so it is unclear if it really is part of his theoretical criteria for all rights, or if his account is just inconsistent or incomplete on the matter. For the idea of disadvantageous *powers*, see Wellman (1985: 84).

For them, a right quintessentially protects the will *by affording* right-holders, or authorised agents acting on their behalf,[60] capacities by which to enforce or waive it. Hence, for most Will theorists, the bilateral liberty to park your automobile in a parking spot or not, alone, is not a right. For whilst it could be said to either afford its holder the ability to vindicate his or her will, the bilateral liberty does not do so *in the relevant way*, i.e., affording the person the capacity to enforce that choice, his or her normative status, etc.

§ II.4. Why Are Such Criteria Thought Necessary?

Why are such criteria for A RIGHT thought to be necessary? Theorists generally believe their accounts are indispensable for several reasons. First, they provide the concept's essential features and ascertain what it is that all rights (or, at least those falling under their particular version of a theory) have in common. How can we know, let alone agree about, what a right even is, without having criteria—of this sort—for the concept? It is also tempting to ask what, if anything, rights *all* do *as* rights? '*Surely*' there are certain necessary properties they all contain.

Second, the theories provide a standard by which to assess theory-neutral models. How can you otherwise judge which rights model is accurate without using—this sort of—theoretical criteria as the standard? For example, how can you assess the *schema of jural relations*' accuracy, flaws, or utility, without already knowing what A RIGHT is? How, can we judge whether powers and immunities really are types of rights? Thus, theorists who adopt an existing model, like Hohfeld's, superimpose their criteria upon it. Again, these function as a qualification test to determine which of the model's components actually count as rights and which do not. (Hence the 11 different theory-driven interpretations of Hohfeld, listed above.) Third, rights theories provide guidelines for constructing new rights models.[61] Fourth, there are legal, social, institutional, moral, and

[60] See *infra* § III on versions of WT that allow for the divvying up a right's parts, e.g., an RCTD, its enforcement powers, and the liberties by which to exercise those powers, amongst different people.

[61] For example, Raz starts his chapter 'The Nature of Rights' by providing the analytic definition quoted above, distinguishing between duties grounded on rights and those that are not, and by differentiating between rights and other normative positions that can support them (e.g., liberties, powers, immunities, etc.), but which are not themselves rights. Raz (1986: 165–7).

game rights. On what other grounds could it be determined, aside from via a theory of rights of this sort, whether those are modal kinds, functional kinds, or mere homonyms?[62]

Fifth, some proponents seem to contend that their theories help to determine (perhaps in conjunction with other legal theories, facts, etc.) where real-world rights obtain.[63] We need guidance, if not some definitive basis, for determining where they do. Not all instances will be found just by searching for the term 'a right', because other words may signal the existence of rights: 'shares', 'equity', 'property', 'capacity', 'entitled', etc. How, then, can we tell whether instances obtain in such cases without knowing what counts as a right in the first place?

The last point requires further comment, as not all theorists believe it is a rights theory's job to do that sort of work. Their criteria are not meant to be mere stipulative definitions of 'a right'; they are not candidate rules for the usage of the term, especially as multiple words or phrases might fall under the concept (e.g., 'claim', 'liberty', 'power', 'right', 'entitlement', 'equity', etc.). Whilst the theories are concerned with words and terms, they are also not simply philosophical efforts to provide clearer meaning to ordinary usage. For example, versions sometimes exclude what ordinary people or lawyers would call 'rights' from counting as genuine cases.

As will be discussed in greater detail in Chapter 6, the theoretical criteria nonetheless govern potentially divergent matters. Particularly, a debate about rights protecting or effectuating interests or the will *could* be carried on without an excessive focus on duties and enforcement powers. Moreover, the bases for delimiting the relevant modes of protection, advancement, etc., specified in each theory are neither readily discernible from, nor necessarily entailed by, their candidate ultimate purpose in terms of interest or will protection. Although the debate could allow for more expansive considerations, only a handful of theorists have really entertained the idea of larger sets of rights and means of will or interest protection/effectuation.[64]

[62] On the functional/modal distinction, see Chapter 1 note 28.

[63] Cf. Kramer (2012: 129); Wenar (2013: 210). Consider legal rights. They cannot always be identified simply by looking for the term 'a right' in legislation, case law, etc. Sometimes, the law uses other words instead. Other times, legal rights can be gleaned or inferred from, legal sources. How, then, can we tell whether certain laws give rise to rights without knowing what makes something count as a right in the first place?

[64] E.g., Rowan Cruft, Hart, Simmonds, and Leif Wenar.

§ III. Directed Duties

Recently, a few scholars have claimed that the theories of rights debate is, or ought to be recast as being, about how best to explain a 'directed' duty's direction.[65] This, as opposed to seeing that issue as being (at best) just one of several falling out of, or under, the debate, as others seem to have suggested.[66]

The directed duties issue is this. Jurists often distinguish between 'absolute' and 'relative'/'directed' duties. The latter kind is owed to another person, the former is not. How do we determine to whom a directed duty is owed, though? Is it owed to: the 'intended' beneficiary of the obligatory action or forbearance; unintended beneficiaries (too); the party with the power to try to seek a remedy in the face of a (threatened) breach; a party possessing no correlative right? Might it be owed to some other sort of person altogether?

Part of the problem theorists aim to address here is whether there is a difference between (i) the action forming the content of a duty that may affect some party and (ii) the duty being 'directed' to that party. For example, *A* may owe *B* a contractual duty to fix *C*'s roof. *A* therefore must do something for *C*, but the duty might not be directed towards, or owed to, *C*. How, then, can we determine who *A*'s duty is really directed towards: to *B*, *C*, both, some other party too, none of them?

Despite its recent prominence in the literature, it is misguided to think that the directed duties issue shapes the *entire* theoretical debate. Primarily, this is because it is just another way of getting to the 'what is a right' question. Indeed, on these theorists' own reckoning, the question about A RIGHT is a logically prior one:[67] determine what that concept is, and you will know the correlative duty's direction—by definition (or so theorists *appear to assume*, at any rate. For, for better or worse, neither theory

[65] E.g., Sreenivasan (2005: 258 n.5); Stewart 2012: 322; Cruft (2017:169); Wenar (2013: 207–8); Stepanians (2005: 47–8). Gopal Sreenivasan wishes to refocus efforts onto the direction of duties issue. 'But I think we shall see that even the original dispute about rights is better addressed once we have *first* settled the narrower question about directed duties'. Sreenivasan (2010: 482, emphasis added). Cf. Ibid 473, 482–3, 487 n.59.

[66] E.g., Waldron (1984: 8–9); Sumner (1987: 24, 39–47, 100). Cf. Cruft (2004: 366–7); Preda (2015: 409–10); Kramer (2013: 245–6. But see also ibid 246 n.3); Jhering (1865: 313–4 on der Destinatar).

[67] Cf. Kamm (2004: 481). This holds even for Raz's IT, despite his analytic definition of A RIGHT entailing that A DUTY is logically or conceptually prior.

would actually posit that a directed duty is or can be directed to a non-right-holder).[68]

The Interest and Will theories' respective answers are that a duty is directed to a party who is a right-holder *because* the right and its correlative duty (exist in order to) protect or effectuate the right-holder's interest or will. Hence, it seems that no real work is done from the DIRECTED DUTY side of things, i.e., determining an answer to the question independently of each theory's conception of A RIGHT.

Second, the theories need not produce different results on the directionality of directed duties. The reason why certain debaters believe the contrary holds, and hence why they presently try to frame the debate on this issue, is because they assume or insist that WT invariably holds that a directed duty is owed to the person bearing the relevant enforcement and/or waiver power(s).[69]

This is false. As shall be explained in greater detail below, some versions of WT posit that a duty can be owed to one party even though a second party possesses the relevant enforcement power(s).[70] Hence, some Will theorists can agree that legally incompetent agents can be right-holders despite not personally possessing the relevant enforcement powers. Thus, it is erroneous to claim that WT *invariably* posits that an RCTD-holder's *self*-possession of (an) enforcement or waiver power(s) is a necessary condition of A RIGHT.

[68] E.g., Sreenivasan (2010: 468–9). It is for this reason that Sreenivasan can switch from 'directed' to 'correlates with a claim-right' language ('But it remains controversial whether these duties are directed or not, that is, whether they correlate with claim-rights or not'). Ibid 473. (Hence, *pace* ibid 467 n.7: the answer for the identity of a directed duty's direction is the reason why the theory deems the correlative claim-holder to be a right-holder). A possible exception to this would be if you think that self-regarding duties are directed to oneself (i.e., where you do not have a correlative right that you perform a duty owed to yourself). However, employing the term 'directed' in this way cannot be squared with its usage elsewhere, particularly its being used as a synonym for 'relative' (i.e., relative duties).

[69] E.g., Stewart (2012: 322: '[a]ccording to the will theory, the duty corresponding to a claim-right is directed towards the person who is authorised "to waive or to seek enforcement of the duty"'); Sreenivasan (2010: 484: '[b]ut (WT) implies that a duty cannot be owed to someone with no measure of control over it'.); Wenar (2013: 208: '[w]ill theorists say that duties are owed to those who have choices to waive or enforce the duty'); Preda (2015: 410).

[70] See *infra* notes 77–9 and the accompanying text on WT's divvying up of a right's components.

Divvying up a right's components amongst different agents allows WT to identify the same person as IT for a directed duty's direction. Both theories can hold that such duties are directed to RCTD-holders, and not necessarily the party possessing the enforcement powers (if the latter happens to be a separate person). Such Will theorists could deny that the duties are also directed to the enforcement-power-holders—when that person is not identical with the RCTD-holder.

Moreover, for Hohfeldian Will theorists, a duty's being directed towards the correlative claim is seemingly axiomatic.[71] Nevertheless, how it is that a singular right's components can be distributed amongst different agents is an issue WT has yet to (and, I will contend in Chapter 6, cannot) sufficiently explain. As they consider enforcement powers to be essential to A RIGHT, and as they think a right effectuates its holder's will, Will theorists might want to deem cases wherein the right-holder does not personally possess the enforcement and waiver powers to be 'exceptions to the rule'. Whether they should be allowed to do so, without also providing a robust justification for the manoeuvre, is another matter.

Regardless, because versions of WT can hold that, in certain cases, two or more parties may possess a given right's component RCTD and powers (but not exceptions to the rule that rights must include powers, irrespective of who possesses them) the direction-of-duties matter can define neither WT nor the entire theories of rights debate. The rival theories can always identify the same party as the correlative right-holder. WT simply

[71] John Finnis states that the two candidate means for identifying the direction of (relative, as opposed to absolute) duties—the beneficiary, or the remedial power-wielder—need not even be *theories*. Finnis (2011: 202–3, 465 n.32). (Finnis is responding to Kramer (1998: 61 n.23)). In a personal correspondence Finnis clarified his view: one could adopt either candidate by one of two means. The first is by mere stipulation. This resolves a purely technical problem, which is not, and does not involve, a philosophical explanation (a 'theory') of rights. The second is as the result of an analysis seeking an explanatory rationale for rights. Email from John Finnis to the author (24 November 2014).

Another noteworthy case, but not an exception to the idea of a (directed) duty being directed towards a claim-holder, is Simmonds' WT. Again, Simmonds thinks Hohfeldian claims are a species of power. Simmonds (1998: 223). He also explicitly rejects a 'mirror image' notion of correlativity, holding instead that the tethered normative positions need not reflect each other's content entirely. Ibid 222–3. Regardless, he still thinks that a duty correlates with a claim, and not some other kind of power. Moreover, he holds to an 'atomic' view of rights: he rejects the idea that rights are complexes composed of the more basic Hohfeldian positions, and thus rebuffs the idea that secondary and tertiary rights all constitute the 'elements of control' for one legal right, as Hart posits in *Essays on Bentham*. Simmonds (1998: 220–1). Cf. Hart (1982: 183–4).

demands that, if one wants to identify a right, one must locate both an RCTD and the relevant sort of powers—even if they are parcelled out amongst different parties. On its view, a *purported* finding of one component without the others simply marks the absence of a bona fide case.

Even though the theories need not produce divergent sets of right-holders as a result of their respective conceptions of A RIGHT, one might still object that they produce different explanations of why those right-holders have their rights, e.g., in terms of their being grounded in interests, or to effectuate the parties' wills. This is true, but it does not explain what theorists are doing when trying to reframe the debate in terms of competing explanations of directed duties. Again, they are really just asking the 'what is a right' question. Moreover, theorists who (re-)frame matters in this way wrongly assume, and erroneously proceed as though, the theories must identify different parties as being the object of a directed duty as a result.

§ IV. Flawed Charges

Some of the most famous, and supposedly most damning, charges levied by the theories against one another, staples of the debate, are arguments criticising what each's conception of A RIGHT entails. These arguments aim to establish over- and under-inclusivity: that the rival theory's conception leads to certain classes of normative positions being wrongly excluded from, or included in, the set of real rights (and so incorrectly entailing that certain agents are not really right-holders). Disputants present them as constituting fatal flaws. The charges include IT's incompetency and inalienability arguments, plus WT's third-party beneficiaries argument.

This section nonetheless makes two interrelated claims. First, all of these arguments are unsuccessful, at least insofar as they aim to *falsify* a given theory. Second, those arguments do not support the idea that the debate is really about either providing accurate sets of (possible) right-*holders*, or about being able to identify right-holders in any given data set.

§ IV.1. The Incompetency Arguments

Given its views about enforcement powers, WT purportedly cannot account for clear cases of rights (and erroneously entails that certain sorts of agents are not real right-holders). WT's set of possible right-holders is often said to be restricted to mentally competent adult humans capable of *personally* enforcing their rights.[72] The set of wrongly excluded cases, then, includes the rights of: children; the mentally handicapped; the comatose; the dead; non-persons; third-party beneficiaries; substantive criminal law victims; and animals.[73]

Interest theorists offer several grounds to try to substantiate this charge. One is their 'incompetency' argument, which chastises WT for not recognising certain legal rights simply because their holders are not *personally* competent and/or authorised to enforce them, e.g., minors, the mentally handicapped,[74] and victims' rights under substantive (as opposed to procedural) criminal law in common law jurisdictions.[75] Second, in response to Will theorists' 'third-party beneficiary' argument against IT (addressed below), some Interest theorists respond that, instead of marking their inability to explain why third-party beneficiaries lack rights, WT itself cannot explain why such parties *do* in fact have rights.[76] Each of IT's grounds relies on the same point: *pace* WT, real rights can obtain even if their holders cannot personally enforce them.

Debaters nevertheless miss the fact that this under-inclusivity charge cannot falsify WT. This is because, as mentioned above, some—superior—versions of the theory allow for the separation and apportionment of a single right's components—e.g., its RCTD, various enforcement powers (if construed to be distinct from the RCTD), and/or liberties by which to exercise those powers—amongst different people. Namely, between one party and a second legally competent and authorised party, e.g., between a child and a legal guardian; citizen and a legal official; etc.[77] These ver-

[72] E.g., Kramer (2008: 419).

[73] E.g., Jhering (1865: 310 n.438, 312 n.440, although his theory need not afford children or the insane rights either); MacCormick (1982a: 154); MacCormick (1977: 196–9); Cruft (2004: 347, 369, 380); Wenar (2005: 240); Kramer (1998: 4, 69–75); Kramer (2000: 487). By rejecting the (personal) enforceability requirement, IT ostensibly allows for a much more expansive set of right-holders, which can include children, the mentally ill, the dead, the comatose, animals, vegetation, etc.

[74] E.g., MacCormick (1982a); MacCormick (1977); Kramer (1998: 4, 69–75).

[75] Whilst victims may be legally competent, they are generally unauthorised to personally enforce their rights in criminal law proceedings. Hart (1982: 182–3) tries to defend WT from this charge.

[76] E.g., MacCormick (1977: 205–6).

[77] E.g., Hart (1982: 184 n.86); Feinberg (1980: 209); Simmonds (1998: 226 n.138); Wenar (2013: 226). Cf. Wellman (1985: 192: 'the representative does not thereby become the possessor [of the right]'). Some Will theorists nonetheless posit differences between moral and legal rights in this regard. E.g., Wellman (1985: 192); Wellman (1995: 135);

sions of WT acknowledge the existence of rights even where their holders' neither possess nor can exercise enforcement powers and/or the liberties by which to exercise those powers.[78] Hence, it is false to claim that WT must hold that being personally enforceable by the right-holder is a necessary condition of A RIGHT. For on some versions of the theory, a right can obtain so long as *someone* (e.g., a legal guardian, a government prosecutor, a principal's agent, etc.) can have and may use the relevant sort of powers.[79]

§ IV.2. The Inalienability & Unwaivability Arguments

IT's inalienability and unwaivability arguments against WT are also not as devastating as they are presented as being. As certain rights are unwaivable or inalienable, WT is charged with erroneously holding or entailing that: (a) unwaivable and inalienable legal positions do not qualify as rights (and so certain agents do not really qualify as right-holders); or that (b), if they are rights, then they are actually much weaker than they otherwise could be—despite legal officials having intentionally removed the elements of

Simmonds (1998: 226 n.138); Agnafors (2015: 938). Whilst Hart himself understands an RCTD to be a power, it is open to *Hohfeldian* Will theorists to distinguish between the two and apportion the normative positions amongst different people. (See also Vallentyne (2007: 196–7) on a right-holder having the power to authorise someone else to enforce his or her right.)

Not all Will theorists can benefit from this distributive manoeuvre. For example, Steiner believes that rights must be identified with the enforcement-power-holders. Despite being called 'children's rights', the rights of the handicapped, etc., in ordinary and legal discourse, Steiner posits that these are really the rights of state officials or legal guardians, whose powers are employed on behalf of legal incompetents. Steiner (1994: 62); Steiner (1998: 258–62). It seems that many contemporary Interest theorists treat Steiner's WT as being the only possible version. Wellman, another Will theorist, believes that only certain legal incompetents and children (but not infants) can have some rights based on their respective levels of agency, which are enforced by legally competent adults. E.g., Wellman (1995: 135).

[78] For example, Hart deems the powers to belong to the non-*sui juris* parties, even though they are exercised exclusively by the (competent and authorised) representatives. Hart (1982: 184 n.86).

[79] As shall be argued in Chapter 6 § II.1, WT's real problem here is instead that it lacks principled grounds to make or allow for these sorts of divisions. See also Frydrych (2016: 132–5, 155–8); Frydrych (2017b: 199–200); Cruft (2017: 170).

control (waivability, alienability) in order to *better* protect the rights and their holders.[80]

Neil MacCormick's 'inalienability' argument goes further: if enforceability is essential to the concept, why is it that, sometimes, a right's *lacking* certain such powers is more valuable than having them? If all (legal) RCTDs protect their holders' wills via enforcement powers, why is it that our more politically significant legal rights, such as constitutional ones, are inalienable or unwaivable in certain ways? WT, he claims, therefore generates a paradox: the fewer the means of control afforded, the less of a right it is.[81]

Nigel Simmonds, a Will theorist, tries to overcome the inalienability argument. To his mind, there are no discernible standards for determining which enforcement powers are more critical to, or weightier for, a given right.

> Where we are confronted by different facets of control, the strength or efficacy of the protection given to the individual will cannot be judged simply by the number of facets present in any particular entitlement. The different dimensions of autonomy represented by the different forms of control cut across each other; just as the worker's autonomy to alienate his rights may cut across his continuing autonomy to choose whether or not to sue his employer. To provide all the different facets of control will not necessarily offer the most effective or extensive protection to the right-holder's will. Much depends on the circumstances and the nature of the threats to choice in any concrete set of circumstances. Given these complexities, there is no reason to assume that it will be possible to range monotonically upon a single scale of strength or weakness; there is still less reason to expect such

[80] See especially MacCormick (1977: 196–9). MacCormick also chastises Hart's WT for excluding Hohfeldian immunities and certain RCTDs for counting as rights per Hart's own WT for want of an associated power to waive or 'assert' them. Ibid 196.

[81] MacCormick (1977: 195–9). The 'inalienability' label appears to have been affixed to MacCormick's argument by others. He himself discusses both alienability and waivability, and so covers more ground than is generally supposed. *Waiver* can change a correlative person's duty, e.g., to do φ by adding a liberty not to do φ for a certain time. The right may nonetheless persist post-waiver and may be exercisable or enforceable at a later date. A waiver power can also alter a duty-bearer's requirement to fulfil a secondary or tertiary duty altogether without thereby nullifying the primary duty and correlative right. *Alienability* entails forfeiture of a right through transfer or nullification. Consider the difference between waiving your right to collect a debt *on a certain specified date* versus selling the chose in action to a third party.

strength or weakness to be a simple function of the number of different facets of choice associated with the right.[82]

Whilst he accounts for the very possibility of unwaivability and inalienability, Simmonds does not overcome the paradox. This is because his strength/weakness and effective/ineffective distinctions do not adequately cover Hart's fuller/lesser measures of control.[83] For example, why is it untrue, simply by definition, that right *A*, which is both enforceable and waivable, affords more control than does right *B*, which is merely waivable?[84]

Although the 'inalienability' argument is on point (if control mechanisms serve to protect the will, why are certain ones unavailable for some rights?), it cannot falsify WT. For one thing, inalienable rights may nonetheless be enforceable or waivable.[85] For another, Will theorists disagree amongst themselves about which enforcement and/or waiver powers are essential. Hart claims that private law rights admit of 'fuller' and 'lesser' measures of control,[86] whilst Simmonds, again, suggests that any right may have (or be) a variable set of such mechanisms.[87] Hence, the absence of a given power is no proof that other relevant powers fail to obtain.

For the incompetency and 'inalienability' arguments to succeed, one would instead need to establish the possibility of a right with *no* cognate enforcement mechanisms. Specifically, it would have to be shown that: (I) any given *type* of element of control need not obtain in a given case, and then (II) *adduce* that a right could exist lacking any such control in

[82] Simmonds (1998: 229–30).

[83] See Hart (1982: 183–4); Hart's 'elements of control' in Appendix 1.

[84] Simmonds also begs the question about how rights vindicate the will: certain legal rights are rendered unwaivable or inalienable in order to vindicate the holder's will in ways the *legal system* has decided are appropriate, not in ways the right-holder might personally decide such matters. For legal rights, this will always be the case, at least to some extent, given that they are institutional normative positions shaped by officials. Furthermore, the idea of limiting the range of options for waiving, alienating, or enforcing cuts across the will enhancing/protecting aspect of rights, which is integral to WT.

[85] Simmonds (1998: 229–30).; Wellman (1995: 109). For an argument that an immunity (as opposed to inalienability, which is a Hohfeldian disability from being able to alienate) actually protects its holder's choices, see Simmonds (1998: 218–9). Cf. Ibid 153–4, 228.

[86] *Supra* note 16 and the accompanying text.

[87] *Supra* note 82 and the accompanying text.

anyone's hands.[88] The problem, though, is that Will theorists might simply deny that the candidate instance constitutes a bona fide case…

§ IV.3. The Third-Party Beneficiary (3PB) Argument

Will theorists claim that IT can neither explain nor delimit which interests warrant rights? To see why, let us first consider both WT's three general charges and the argument standardly employed to advance (at least) one of them.

> *Purported Flaw 1*: IT is said to systematically register false positives and be incapable of delimiting the set of genuine rights. For example, the theory misattributes particular rights to people (undisputed classes of right-holders, e.g., sane, adult humans) who nevertheless do not actually possess *those specific* rights.
>
> *Purported Flaw 2*: Relatedly, IT cannot explain why particular interest-bearers—those known to have had particular laws created in their favour, which impose duties on other parties—do not possess correlative rights.[89] Critics therefore 'condemn the Interest Theory for its failure to specify why some interests receive legal protection (in the form of rights for the interest-bearer) while others do not'.[90]
>
> *Purported Flaw 3*: The theory cannot but attribute rights to *types of beings and entities* that, despite arguably bearing interests, do not actually possess (specific, real-world) legal rights. Take, for example, individual blades of grass and their 'interests' not to be stepped on.[91]

WT's third-party beneficiary (hereinafter '**3PB**') argument is standardly used to exhibit *Purported Flaw 1*, about misattributing particular rights to people (individuals who otherwise qualify as undisputed types of right-holders). It runs thus.[92] A 3PB of a contract situation is one where

[88] This will be attempted in Chapter 7.

[89] E.g., Steiner (1994: 62–3). Hart uses Rudolph von Jhering's domestic manufacturer challenge to advance this charge. Hart (1982: 180–1 & n.78). See *infra* note 110 and the accompanying text on Jhering's challenge.

[90] Kramer (1998: 79).

[91] E.g., Kramer (2010: 34). Though an Interest theorist, Kramer explains this charge (and provides the example). Even so, it is debatable whether WT actually levies it and whether it is not instead a misreading by certain Interest theorists of the 3PB argument. See, e.g., Hart (1982: 180).

[92] E.g., Hart (1982: 187).

A and *B* enter a contract whereby *B* must either perform a service for, or provide a good to, *C* (to fix *C*'s roof, say). *C* is the 3PB. Legally, it may be irrelevant whether *C* is aware of the contract's existence. The issue is this: does *C* have a legal right under the contract? What about *C*'s neighbours on the same street, who have an interest in *C*'s roof being fixed (e.g., it may affect their own properties' value). How about neighbours on different streets, whose property values may also be affected by *B*'s work? Etc. (All of the parties are *sui juris* persons who are otherwise right-holders of other rights; the question is whether they have additional rights per the contract in question.)

IT, so the 3PB argument goes, lacks sufficient grounds to deny that parties *C*, *D*, *E*, etc., possess legal rights per their criteria for A RIGHT, even though those parties, along with an indeterminate set of people, might be said to have interests in seeing that the roof gets fixed.[93] (It should also be added that the 3BP argument need not be structured so that a third-party, *C*, is intended to benefit, or is even considered, under the *A*-*B* contract.[94])

Again, the 3PB argument aims to serve a dual role. First, to mark a problem with IT's criteria: identifying rights in places where, according to certain legal systems, they do not (and need not). Second, to show that the theory cannot establish which interests warrant rights protection or mark where rights obtain.

Interest theorists generally adopt one or two strategies to respond to these charges (though some apologists adopt both). The first is simply to deny the misattributions claim by insisting that the purportedly problematic candidate parties, or, at least, party *C* (per the roof fixing

[93] To be sure, some legal systems explicitly grant *certain* 3PBs rights. Even within that subset of legal systems, though, the law might only recognise rights for certain sorts of 3PBs and not others. Historically, most 3PBs did not have legal rights in common law systems, and many still do not in some jurisdictions. The BVI, for example, retains unto this day a more traditional view of privity of contract.) There is also no reason why any system *must* recognise such rights or be rendered incapable of rescinding them. Until a recent change in law in 1999 which impacted the privity doctrine, many 3PBs in England did not have rights of action either. Contracts (Rights of Third Parties) Act 1999 c 31. Even with that legislative change, some sorts of 3PBs still lack secondary rights. WT could nevertheless hold that some 3PBs (now) possess rights *because* the law affords them, or others authorised to act on their behalf, enforcement powers. E.g., Hart (1982: 187 n.91). (It should also be noted that 3PB scenarios are not limited to contracts. They can arise from other legal arrangements such as trusts as well.)

[94] E.g., Simmonds (1998: 197).

contract example above), actually do possess legal rights after all.[95] The second is to try to show that IT can credibly delimit the relevant sort of interests and rights.

Both strategies are nevertheless misguided; for what scholars have all failed to notice is that the charges are off the mark. Rights theories aim to explain A RIGHT's structural and purposive features. It is not their job to (i) identify all instances, or (ii) decide who counts as a right-holder, in any given domain or system, and on what bases. The latter is either a task for a different kind of (legal) theory, or is simply a system-contingent query.[96] Some versions of IT nevertheless offer problematic *sufficient* conditions of A RIGHT—a task they need not even undertake. To understand why, though, requires further explanation of the charges.

That 3PBs may have contract-based rights should be of no great concern to IT, as it is conceivable that a legal system could afford all of them (and even some larger set of people) such legal positions. Different systems can have different rules for determining which parties possess rights and on what bases, i.e., which interests warrant rights protection. Thus, WT's charges are not real problems for any Interest theorist who does not offer (the full set of) sufficient conditions for A RIGHT, irrespective of which theory of law that rights theorist also endorses.

The 3BP argument is also impotent if, as is often the case, one's version of IT is tethered to Legal Positivism.[97] For, then, it is not simply that the relevant types of interest warranting legal rights may be a system-contingent matter, it is also the case that determining whether candidate instances constitute bona fide cases of rights is a job for Legal Positivist theses, e.g., about the rule(s) of recognition. Real-world legal systems' sets of rights need not track some normative theory which insists that only certain kinds and sets of rights are morally or politically warranted. Just because the roof-owner, the next-door neighbour, etc., have an interest in the roofing contract being fulfilled, it need not follow that IT must attribute (legal) rights to them. On a Positivist view, a legal system may afford rights to some such parties and not others—for whatever meritorious or unmeritorious reasons. However, this itself undercuts the credibility of, and need for, an IT espousing a robust conception of wellbeing or some other

[95] E.g., Kramer (1998: 67–8); Wenar (2013: 213).

[96] On the latter view, determining which interests warrant legal recognition is simply a matter of a given jurisdiction's laws, not a theory of rights or of law.

[97] On Legal Positivism, see Chapter 1 note 81 and the accompanying text.

delimited subset of interests. (We shall return to the relationship between theories of law and of rights in Chapter 6 § III.2.)

If they are even credible undertakings in the first place (a notion which will be challenged in the next chapter), rights theories need only offer a *pro tanto* basis for identifying rights, or just the necessary conditions for A RIGHT (not the sufficient ones). They must therefore be supplemented by a different kind of legal theory in order to help do any identificatory work in a given real-world legal system. As Kramer says:

> On one point, the Interest Theory and Will Theory concur. That is, each theory accepts that the sheer fact that a certain right would tend to benefit *X* is not a sufficient condition for *X*'s holding of that right. Also needed is the existence of some law—a statute, a judicial ruling, a constitutional provision, an administrative regulation, an incorporated moral principle, a contract, or some other authoritative legal norm—that bestows the specified right on *X*.[98]

[98] Kramer (2010: 33). See also Kramer (1998: 67). On the sufficient conditions for the concept, he has stated:

> [I]n my formulations of my version of the Interest Theory, I have always deliberately forborne from specifying the sufficient conditions for the holding of a legal right. My caution on that point is due to the fact that those conditions include the existence of a correlative legal duty—which means that a full specification of those conditions would include the conditions that are sufficient for the existence of a legal duty. Accordingly, a full specification would have to draw upon a theory of the nature of law and upon an account of legal interpretation. Because no exposition of the nature of right-holding should carry so many jurisprudential commitments, there are solid grounds for my disinclination to recount sufficient conditions for the holding of a legal right.

Kramer (2017: 54). He has furthermore claimed:

> [T]he Interest Theory (the Interest Theory expounded here, at any rate) is not a political theory; like Hohfeld's analytic jurisprudence, it does *not* attempt to prescribe the appropriate distribution of entitlements. Questions concerning who should hold which entitlements are questions not for analytic jurisprudence but for political philosophy and for ordinary political discourse. When the Interest Theory contends that rights are modes of protection for interests that are treated as worthy of such protection, it is setting forward a general thesis about the general nature or structure of rights. It is not advancing any criterion or set of criteria for what should count as the 'worthiness' of an interest. Instead of flowing from the Interest Theory and instead of serving as essential aspects of it, any criteria for worthiness would supplement it.

Even so, some Interest theorists offer delimitation criteria or tests to account for which interests generate rights—including Kramer. Building on a suggestion from Jeremy Bentham, Kramer provides such a criterion, a 'Minimum Sufficiency' test (aka the Bentham test), which claims to be able to distinguish those people who possess valid legal RCTDs from others who, despite bearing seemingly relevant interests, lack legal RCTDs.[99] Kramer thus aims to 'delimi[t] the range of people who count as right-holders under ***any*** particular legal mandate'.[100] The Minimum Sufficiency test is as follows:

> [I]n order to determine whether someone holds a legal right under a contract or under any other legal norm, we need to ask what facts are ***minimally sufficient*** to constitute a **breach** of the contract or norm. If and only if at least one minimally sufficient set of facts includes the undergoing of a detriment by some person *Q* at the hands of some other person *R* who bears a duty under the contract or norm, *Q* holds a right—correlative to that duty—under the contract or norm… [The phrase "undergoing of a detriment" should really be [read as] "undergoing of some development that is typically detrimental for a human being."] … A set of facts is minimally sufficient to constitute a violation of a legal mandate if and only if (1) the set is sufficient to constitute such a violation, and (2) every element of the set is necessary for the set's sufficiency. In other words, a minimally sufficient set contains no redundant elements.[101]

Kramer (1998: 79). However, he also seems to hold that the work of delimiting the potential classes of right-*holders* must preface, rather than supplement, IT.

> Before the Interest Theory can be applied, the class of potential right-holders has to be demarcated; the task of demarcating that class has to be undertaken on the basis of factors outside the Interest Theory itself. Such a task is a moral endeavor, albeit at a high level of abstraction.

Kramer (2010: 35). But see Kramer (2012: 128–9).

[99] '[T]he Interest Theory needs a criterion for deciding when the beneficiary of a duty does indeed have a right to the fulfillment of the duty'. Kramer (1998: 85). 'My philosophical theory of rights, which incorporates Bentham's test for identifying right-holders… Bentham's standard for the identification of right-holders is an integral component of my theory of rights…'. Ibid 88.

[100] Kramer (2010: 31). This revises Kramer's earlier version of the test. Kramer (1998: 81–2).

[101] Kramer (2010: 36–7, bolded emphases added and with Kramer's footnote 9 embedded into the text in brackets). It is unclear why Kramer does not think this constitutes an effort to provide the *sufficient* conditions for A LEGAL RCTD.

Kramer's example differs in structure from the 3BP one above about roof fixing. In this new case, an employer has a contractual obligation to pay his employee named Doris. Doris usually uses part of her salary to buy groceries at the local supermarket. If the employer fails to pay Doris, does the supermarket owner, who relies in part upon Doris' patronage to make a living, have a right that Doris' employer pay her?

Not according to Kramer's Minimal Sufficiency test. **Fact A** is Doris not being paid. **Fact B** is that the supermarket gets no money in sales from Doris. **AB** is a set of facts. By itself, Fact A suffices to constitute a breach. Fact B, by contrast, is relevant if and only if Fact A obtains. Hence, B is rendered redundant. This in turn disqualifies the set AB. Fact A alone suffices to make a complete, non-redundant set. Since the facts that would underpin any additional right are rendered redundant by Fact A's 'self-sufficiency', the supermarket owner is excluded from having a right.[102]

Pace Kramer, as his own example of Doris and the Shopkeeper shows, the test really concerns where *rights* obtain, not who can count as a right-*holder* per se or what it is to be a right-holder. (This is nevertheless a good thing, as WT's 3PB argument is primarily about rights, not right-holders).

[102] Kramer (2010: 36–7). Nevertheless, Kramer's most recent stance (as of 2019) appears to be that: (1) he is offering a conceptual clarification of RIGHT-HOLDING, not A RIGHT; (2) a moral theory must be employed to delimit the set of right-holders before IT can even be applied; and (3) following Visa Kurki, the revised Minimum Sufficiency test, not IT-1 of his earlier formulations (*supra* note 39 and the accompanying text), constitutes the true core of his IT. Personal conversation with Matthew Kramer, *Festschrift for Matthew Kramer*, Churchill College, Cambridge, July 2019. See also Kramer (2017: 49); Kurki (2018).

At the *festschrift*, Kramer also told me that, as it is a conceptual clarification, his IT is insusceptible to empirical refutation. (He has said the same thing about Hohfeld's *schema*. Kramer (1998: 22)). Its virtue, he said, tracks those mentioned in Chapter 2 note 33 and the accompanying text in '(VI)' of providing a precise vocabulary for conducting philosophical disputes about rights.

However, his version of the Bentham test was posited in 1998 and 2010 in order to respond to the 3BP argument. If the test no longer serves that function, and if its metatheoretical goal is simply to posit a perspicuous concept for usage in philosophical debates, but it conflicts with what the law holds and/or with Legal Positivism, then those are reasons not to adopt it as your preferred theory of rights. You may think that its virtue of precision is outweighed by its inaccuracy or divergence from the *explananda*. Whether or not empirical counterexamples suffice to falsify a conception of a concept, they can provide grounds for non-subscription and for preferring alternatives. (Nor does the revised Bentham test make Kramer's conception more precise; for what constitutes breach is outside of its bounds. IT-1 is precise without the cost of inaccuracy, i.e., false positives and negatives, generated by the Bentham test). More will be said about assessing conceptual clarifications in Chapter 6.

The standard versions of the 3PB argument involve *sui juris* persons (e.g., sane, competent adults) who otherwise possess a panoply of other real rights, but who IT—so the argument goes—incorrectly affixes with additional legal rights, under a contract or otherwise, which the law does not in fact recognise.[103] Both Doris and the Shopkeeper already have many other legal rights and their status as right-holders is otherwise not in doubt, given that they are both *sui juris* persons. The question is whether they both have legal rights under Doris' particular employment contract. Even if one were to grant the need for a 'moral' judgment to determine the class of legal right-holders, that does not delimit the set of rights each legal right-holder may have.

Additionally, the Minimum Sufficiency test is not a norm of a given legal system or set of such systems. So, why lend it any credence—especially if the concern here is with legal rights? It is also unclear how this test can be squared with Legal Positivism.[104] The conflict between Positivism and IT here is this. Whether the third party has a valid legal right within the system or not is ultimately a matter for the rule of recognition, not the Minimum Sufficiency test. That test can yield results which do not accord with a given system's rule of recognition the test can either identify rights which the legal officials would or can themselves deny obtain per their master rule(s), or exclude rights which officials would insist do obtain—and which common understanding of doctrines across different systems suggest are valid legal positions too. The (set of) legal rights one does or can have therefore cannot be a matter of 'conceptual' truth, even for Kramer, because a Legal Positivist cannot credibly deny that some legal systems could afford or deny legal rights based on 3PB contracts (or to 3PBs of corrupt tariff laws, e.g., to domestic manufacturers) to *sui juris* people. Further, if indeed a *moral* theory must be applied to delimit the set of right-holders before IT can apply, then *a fortiori* the rights theory cannot be a matter of 'conceptual truth' regarding which (set of) rights right-holders do or can have. (The difficulty of squaring certain rights

[103] Hart (1982: 187); Simmonds (1998: 197).

[104] As an *Inclusive* Legal Positivist, Kramer believes that moral norms can (but need not) form part of a legal system's rule of recognition. Kramer (2003). However, that does not speak to all legal officials in all systems adopting a *moral theory* about the proper set of genuine right-holders.

Further, what counts as a 'breach' or a 'detriment', 'at the hands of' some person, are either just system-contingent matters, or at least dependent upon some other kind of legal theory, e.g., *Exclusive* Legal Positivism's Sources thesis. (See Chapter 1 note 81).

theories with Legal Positivism will be addressed in greater detail in Chapter 6.)

If one's theory aims to provide the sufficient conditions for A LEGAL RIGHT via such a test, then the metatheoretical desideratum seemingly ought to be accuracy of identification, i.e., a candidate's relative superiority in determining where legal rights really do obtain and where they do not. If not, it is unclear why legal theorists or others would adopt the theory or test.

However, it is actually unclear what the Minimum Sufficiency test claims to be able to identify: real-world rights or only those the theory posits that a person *should* have—and if so, which sort? Does the supermarket owner have an RCTD under Kramer's test, just not a *legal* one, or does the owner lack any sort of a right?[105]

At any rate, insofar as it aims to prevent IT from providing an over-inclusive account of rights, the Minimum Sufficiency test disappoints for at least two reasons. First, the very conceivability of a legal system affording supermarket owners (and similarly situated persons) legal rights in Kramer's example (thereby rendering the test under-inclusive) seemingly undermines this test. Second, whilst it might work when there are two or more relevant actions, the test fails to delimit in one-relevant-action scenarios.[106] Kramer's Doris-Shopkeeper example concerns a salary payment and a shopping transaction. However, the test cannot correctly or credibly delimit the set of rights when there is only one relevant action, e.g., where *A* pays *B* to fix *C*'s roof. Do *A* and *C* both have legal rights because the roof was not fixed? The answer is system contingent: some legal systems may afford *C* legal rights here, other systems might not.[107] Further, pointing to the existence of a breach does not necessarily answer where all of the correlative rights obtain; indeed, even a minimally suffi-

[105] Siegfried Van Duffel notes that the Minimum Sufficiency test fails to cover moral rights, or non-RCTD legal rights (e.g., liberties, powers, etc.). Van Duffel (2017: 198–9). (Kramer might respond that that is beyond the purview of both his version of IT and this test, though.) Van Duffel also provides convincing reasons to think that an analysis of A RIGHT is independent from the identification of (possible) right-holders (ibid 190–1), which is undermined to some extent by his own insistence that an adequate theoretical analysis requires the provision of both the necessary and sufficient conditions of the concept. Ibid 196.

[106] Frydrych (2016: 171); Frydrych (2017b: 203). Mark McBride, who was emailed this material in February 2016 and August 2018 respectively (and assessed the former), has subsequently adopted my argument. McBride (2020: 296–7); emails on file with author.

[107] Frydrych (2016: 171); Frydrych (2017b: 203).

cient set of facts about a breach of some duty may not tell you who all of the correlative right-holders are.

Consider also whether additional parties possess rights because the roof was not fixed. Here are two scenarios. (**Example I**:) In the first, *A* owns a house and, through its property management company, *C*, lets it out to *D*. *D*'s bedroom suffers leaks because of an unrepaired roof. *C* enters into a contract with *B* to fix the roof, but *B* does not do the job. (**Example II**:) As an alternative scenario, *C* is the trustee of a house. (Trustees are the legal title holders of trust fund assets. Here, *C* holds legal title to the house on trust for others.) *A* is the life tenant of that house per the trust's terms. *C* the trustee contracts with *B* to fix the roof. *B* breaches the duty by not doing the job.

Let us apply the Minimum Sufficiency test to both scenarios. *A*, *C*, and *D* have a legal right based on the *C*-*B* contract to repair the roof. Why? Because there is one minimally sufficient fact (an unrepaired roof), a breach of duty, and harm affecting *A*, *C*, and *D*'s interests (a party bearing a 'detriment' at the hands of *B*'s failure to fulfil the contractual norm).

I. *C* contracts with *B* to fix *A*'s roof. (That the property either happens to be let out to other parties, or is being occupied by a life tenant, is irrelevant for affixing the minimally sufficient set of facts.)
II. *B* breaches the contractual duty by not undertaking to fix the roof.
III. I and II constitute the minimally sufficient set of facts.
IV. There has been a breach, one which is typically detrimental to property owners, lessees, life tenants, and contracting management companies (if acting as agents). Yet whether *B*'s duty is owed just to *C*, or also to *A* or *D* is a system-contingent matter. Still, mere knowledge of there being a breach does not, alone, answer that question. A lessee's or life tenant's situation is typically affected detrimentally by living in a dwelling without a fixed roof (or paying for one). As such, Kramer's test ascribes a right to the lessee or the life tenant. However, it is untrue that lessees *perforce* have legal rights under a contract between the property owner and a service provider because of that fact about typical detriment. Thus, the test does not delimit appropriately here either. Life tenants, by contrast, *qua* trust beneficiaries, may have (enforceable) rights under the contract, but not in all common law jurisdictions. (More in this below.)

Consider also the following situations involving a trustee. (**Examples IIIa & b**:) The trustee, who, again, is the legal title holder of the trust assets, may enter into a contract with some party, e.g., with an investment manager regarding investment of the trust assets. If that party is given trust assets without proper authority (per the trust instrument's requirements), or if the third party breaches the contract with the trustee, then the trust's beneficiaries may, in some circumstances, be able to initiate legal action to reclaim the assets on behalf of the trust.[108] However, a minimally sufficient set of facts describing the breach of contractual duty here, under either variant, need not include the beneficiaries. Hence, the Minimum Sufficiency test is under-inclusive here.[109]

(**Example IV**:) That test also fails to meet Rudolph von Jhering's challenge. The nineteenth century scholar was not insensitive to the issues of theoretical identificatory power, the potential for false positives, and determining what counts as a legal right. He presents the following case (to which an alternative is appended). To embellish Jhering's example somewhat, through political or financial pressure, or corruption, a domestic manufacturer gains the government's favour. The domestic manufacturer convinces it to pass a law prohibiting importation (*schutzzölle einführt*) of certain foreign manufactured goods that compete with his own. (Consider further, as an alternative to a tariff, an outright ban.) The domestic manufacturer has an interest in the new law being enforced. Indeed, it was grounded in his interests. The law in question also benefits him—and intentionally so, in a sense. Does he therefore have a right under that law? Is it a right correlative to importers' and others' duties to pay the relevant import taxes (and, per the modification to Jhering's example, to avoid importing the good illegally)?[110]

Kramer's Minimum Sufficiency test seems incapable of avoiding attribution of a legal right to the domestic manufacturer. Here, as well, there

[108] This may be per a *Vandepitte* procedure. *Vandepitte v. Preferred Accident. Insurance Corp. of New York* [1933] A.C. 70. (Contracting parties are sometimes unaware that the other party to their bargain is actually acting *qua* trustee of a trust.) In some common law jurisdictions, trust protectors and enforcers may also have standing to enforce the contract.

[109] The trust's settlor *may* be part of the minimally sufficient set of facts, but is not a right-holder unless he or she is also one of the trust beneficiaries. Consider further *in rem* tort law duties. A breach of duty and a description of the minimally sufficient set of facts will not expose who all the correlative legal right-holders are here (Thanks to Mark Reiff for this point). Cf. McBride (2020: 307).

[110] Jhering (1865: 327–8).

is a breach and there are parties who (non-accidentally) typically suffer detriment therefrom.

I. The minimally sufficient set of facts is this: a duty-bearer failed to pay the relevant tax. Either a domestic importing retailer not paying the custom duty, say, or not charging the relevant tax to the customer.
II. The fact of non-payment is typically detrimental for domestic manufacturers to compete with foreign goods that bypass importation bans/tariff-based taxes. (The domestic manufacturer's existence is the raison d'être for the law.) Non-payment is also detrimental to governments. Additionally, it may typically be detrimental to businesses in related fields who benefit from the ban's/tariff's existence.
III. The case therefore meets Kramer's test. However, no domestic manufacturer has such legal rights in any legal system.

Now, someone might bite the bullet and say that the domestic manufacturer does indeed has a legal right here. It would be odd, but of course not impossible, for Kramer to agree.

This is not the end of the story, though, In 2018, Visa Kurki provided a revised version of Kramer's IT. Kurki claims that the Minimum Sufficiency test constitutes the theory's real core (instead of Kramer's earlier formulation)[111] and that it offers both the necessary and sufficient conditions for A LEGAL RCTD.[112] Kurki provides two formulations of his revision.

Formulation 1 (the negative formulation)

X holds a right correlative to currently existing duty D if and only if

(i) X can hold rights and
(ii) a set of facts minimally sufficient to establish the contravention of duty D includes a fact that affects X's situation in a way typically detrimental for beings such as X.[113]

[111] *Supra* note 39.
[112] Kurki (2018).
[113] Ibid 438.

Formulation 2 (the positive formulation)

X holds a right correlative to currently existing duty D if and only if

(i) X can hold rights and
(ii) a set of facts minimally sufficient to establish the fulfilment or non-contravention of duty D includes a fact that affects X's situation in a way typically beneficial for beings such as X.[114]

At a *festschrift* for Matthew Kramer in 2019, Kurki insisted that Kramer's version of the test implicitly includes an 'existence condition', which delimits the relevant sort of actors in the minimally sufficient set of facts: if you do not need to establish anything about a person's existence in order to establish that a duty was infringed, then that person is not a correlative right-holder.[115] (Aside from replacing the IT-1 + IT-2 components of Kramer's theory, Kurki also alters the concern from 'breach' to fulfilment or (non-)contravention of duty, whilst the negative and positive formulations differ on being typically detrimental versus typically beneficial.[116])

At any rate, whilst it would constitute an improvement for the Minimum Sufficiency test insofar as it may help to curb some cases of over-inclusivity, Kurki's existence condition does not resolve the test's

[114] Ibid 439.

[115] See also Kurki (2018: 440 n.36). (However, *pace* Kurki, see *supra* note 98 on Kramer's remarks about the sufficient conditions for A DUTY.) Mark McBride and I nonetheless agreed at the *festschrift* that this existence condition was something Kurki had himself added into the test.

[116] In more recent work, Kurki accuses me of erring in suggesting that the breach of a primary duty entails a primary right. (Instead, he claims, it is the duty's content which specifies which rights the duty entails and how the duty itself can be breached.) Kurki (2021: 14/21), *discussing* Frydrych (2017b: 203). This is bizarre, as it is *Kramer* who advances the 'breach' prong of his test whilst my article offers criticisms of that test. Again, Kramer posits that, to determine whether someone holds a legal right under a legal norm, we need to ask what facts are minimally sufficient to constitute a *breach* (his term) of that norm, and that a party holds a correlative primary right when a detriment is suffered at the hands of some other person who bears a duty under a contract or norm. (See *supra* note 101 and the accompanying text). Kramer's language consciously tracks Hart's explication of Bentham: 'It seems therefore that we may interpret the statement that a law is intended to benefit assign able individuals (and so confers rights upon them) as meaning no more than that to establish its breach an assignable individual must be shown to have suffered an individual detriment' Hart (1982: 179). Best not to shoot the messenger.

under-inclusivity/false negatives problems, and nor does it affect the idea that 3PB (or '4PB') rights are system contingent. Legal systems *can* either afford correlative rights to parties who are unaccounted for under minimally sufficient sets of facts, or deny them such rights—irrespective of what the test suggests they ought to possess.[117] Consider the life tenant in Example II and the beneficiaries in Examples IIIa & b above: their existence is irrelevant for the minimum sufficient set of facts, yet many (but not all) common law systems *do* afford them (enforceable) rights vis-à-vis contracts with outsiders to a trust. So too, a legal system could conceivably afford domestic manufacturers rights relative to other private parties' duties under tariff or importation laws. Hence, Kurki's theory cannot supply all the relevant sufficient conditions for A RIGHT. In

[117] Indeed, Kurki's version may make things worse insofar as, under either formulation, it can erroneously attribute correlative rights even for *absolute* duties (i.e., duties without correlatives). He claims to be 'neutral' regarding whether there are any absolute duties. Kurki (2018: 442 n.43). By contrast, following Hohfeld, Kramer seems to deny that there are any such duties. Kramer (1998: 24–5 & n.11).

Kurki also tries to problematise my criticisms of the Minimum Sufficiency test by claiming that they are ambiguous between a concern over where rights obtain and over what kind of beings can be rendered into right-holders (Kurki 2021). This merely aims to obscure my argument (that which legal rights obtain are system-contingent matters, and that the test generates false negatives and positives), as my examples all concern *sui juris* individuals (per Hart's 3PB argument).

Additionally, Kurki baldly asserts that, in my roof fixing example, *C* has a right ('especially if *C* is specified as a beneficiary of the contract'), while *D* does not Kurki (2021: 14/21). Regarding party *C*, this is empirically false: 3PBs (*qua* 3PBs) do not possess legal rights in all jurisdictions, let alone (secondary) rights of action. Kurki is also silent about why a legal system could not deny any such third party this specific right. Similarly, he leaves it mysterious why a system could not choose to afford *D* (an otherwise *sui juris* person) with a primary right and secondary right regarding the contract. For example, *A* contracts with *B*, the trustee of Blackacre, to fix a roof on the property. If *C*, the life tenant, was entitled to lease out the house on Blackacre (or if *B* the trustee just leased it out himself), why could the legal system be incapable of affording *D*, the lessee, a right under the *A-B* contract?

Strangely, Kurki furthermore states: 'In one sense… it is obviously always up to the lawmaker to make a determination of whose interests warrant legal rights status. This is because rights are the correlatives of duties, and the lawmaker is free – in accordance with the Contingent Norms requirement – to enact whatever duties it likes, and this enactment is likely partly based on a determination of who. Hence, which interests are protected by duties is obviously system-contingent' Kurki (2021: 16/21). He needs to explain why this does not just concede the whole argument.

For different (perhaps unsuccessful) arguments deeming Kramer's test to be over- and under-inclusive, see Sreenivasan (2005); Sreenivasan (2010); Sreenivasan (2017).

the least, as Kramer noted originally, additional legal theories would be required to do so.

Concerning other versions of IT, Gopal Sreenivasan argues that Raz's IT avoids the proliferation charge. '[Raz's] threshold requirement that Y's interest must itself suffice, other things equal, *to justify* X's duty may be regarded as formidable enough to set a suitable limit on the number holding a claim-right correlative to X's duty to φ'.[118] However, not only does this beg the question (e.g., about who else may be afforded correlative rights), it also cannot be squared with Raz's view that officials can: make mistakes when weighing those interests; disagree about the weight of those interests; be disingenuous about the importance of those interests; etc. Concerning the former, Raz's justificatory element, alone, also lacks the ability to explain why certain 3PBs have rights in one jurisdiction but not another; it is rather his Legal Positivism which does so.

One could take Raz's IT as providing a different kind of delimitation test, though: that rights are restricted to protecting certain important values, ones concerning wellbeing, even if other people's interests are sometimes needed to buttress an individual being's interests in order to ground specific rights.[119] However, admitting a legal system's ability to generate 'mistakes', 'trivial' rights, and other rights that do not actually advance wellbeing makes quick work of that candidate; indeed, it shows that wellbeing is not actually integral to Raz's rights theory after all.[120] His version, too, therefore fails to meet Jhering's challenge. Again, though, it is not one Interest theorists need even answer.

As an aside, one ought not to assume from the prominence of these charges and the 3PB argument in the literature that the debate is actually framed by the 'who counts as a right-holder' question. Again, it is not even the case that the rival theories must generate divergent sets of holders. As some versions of WT allow for the separation of a right's parts amongst different agents, allowing the theory to cover (almost) all of the same candidate rights and all of the types of right-holders (children, animals, etc.) as IT. This is not to deny that the theories can create divergent candidate sets. The reason for the divergence, however, will be if IT identifies rights even where *no* relevant enforcement powers are to be found in

[118] Sreenivasan (2005: 265).
[119] Cf. Raz (1986: 247–8); *supra* note 33 ('Capacity for possessing rights').
[120] For further discussion, see Chapter 6 notes 34–7 and the accompanying text.

anyone's possession. Establishing the existence or possibility of such a right is a task IT has nonetheless yet to accomplish. (For its part, WT would deny that such a case would constitute a bona fide finding of a real right anyway.)

One might object that, even if the theories basically agreed upon a set of right-holders, their explanations as to *why* someone counts as a holder will differ. This is true, but only shows that what is really at stake are rival conceptions of A RIGHT, not *who* is a right-holder: the grounds for who counts as such are, for better or worse in the theories of rights debate, predicated upon these conceptions.

§ IV.4. *The Redundancy Argument(s)*

Many people believe that rights are somehow distinct from rules, standards, tests, and ligations (duties, liabilities, etc.). It therefore seems incumbent upon theorists to either explain this distinctiveness, or to demonstrate why it is instead just a common misperception. What do rights do uniquely, if anything? WT famously charges IT with rendering A RIGHT superfluous by 'reducing' it to A DUTY. There are actually different versions of this charge, though, some of which shall now be addressed in order to show why it is off the mark. (Chapter 6 will nevertheless explore whether *alternative* reduction charges—to interests, instead of duties—may be sounder.)

§ IV.4.1. Rights as Duties

Kelsen's Argument

Let us return to Jhering's domestic manufacturer case. Jhering presents the problem of being able to distinguish instances of legal RCTDs from cases where parties are intended to benefit from someone else's duty but without possessing correlative rights. He styles the latter cases, such as the domestic manufacturer from the customs law, as being the mere 'reflex operation' (*reflexwirkung*) of that duty.[121] The issue also reflects a worry about treating a right as nothing more than a passive entitlement to another's duty.[122]

[121] *Supra* note 110.

[122] Ibid, *discussed in* Hart (1982: 180–1); Stepanians (2005: 11, 59–62). Note that the second concern is different, as the domestic manufacturer case could concern the lack of a right altogether.

Hans Kelsen adopts this notion, or a variant of it, in order to argue that legal rights are not merely the reflex operation of duties.[123] One person's duty, he claims, provides other parties with 'reflex-rights'. These are normative states of protection. Reflex-rights, Kelsen nevertheless thinks, are nothing more than those duties. To treat them as distinct normative positions would be to err by double-counting the legally relevant facts.[124] A real right avoids such problems because it is a complex composed of a 'reflex-right' plus enforcement powers.[125]

Hart's Version

Influenced by Jhering and Kelsen on this matter, Hart presents his version of the redundancy argument.

> The principal advocates of benefit or 'interest' theories of rights correlative to obligations have shown themselves sensitive to the criticism that, if to say that an individual has such a right means no more than that he is the intended beneficiary of a duty, then 'a right' in this sense may be an unnecessary, and perhaps confusing, term in the description in the law; since all that can be said in a terminology of such rights can be and indeed is best said in the indispensable terminology of duty. So the benefit theory appears to make nothing more of rights than an alternative formulation of duties:

[123] Kelsen (1911), *cited in* Stepanians (2005: 11, 59–71); Kelsen (1967: 125–30, 132–6). Markus Stepanians argues that Kelsen misconstrues Jhering's conception. Jhering intends for REFLEXWIRKUNG to apply in cases where there are *unintentional* effects on third parties 'beyond [the duty's] proper sphere of effects as posited by the law or by the intention of the agent or the right-holder'. Jhering (1871: 218), *translated by* Stepanians (2005: 60 n.19). Kelsen is said to have modified the conception to concern a duty's 'intended' effects.

Whether or not he has correctly interpreted Jhering, Stepanians' intentional/unintentional normative effects distinction cannot explain the difference between Jhering and Kelsen here. For to say that the government did not intend to create a right for the manufacturer does not answer the question of whether it nevertheless did so. Why should rights obtain only where the lawmaker *intended* rights to be created? What if judges later hold that the law in question generated such rights anyway? The answer depends too much on a particular theory of law, one Stepanians does not present at any rate. The distinction fails, moreover, because the government *does* intend for the duties to benefit the domestic manufacturer. This is why Jhering does not adequately resolve his own challenge.

[124] Kelsen (1967: 127). Compare this with Max Radin on A JURAL RELATION in Chapter 3 notes 8–9.

[125] Kelsen (1967: 134–6).

yet nothing seems to be gained in significance or clarity by translating [statements of duties into statements of rights].[126]

Hart's argument requires some unpacking. First, Markus Stepanians is partially correct to identify it as a semantic version of Kelsen's.[127] It concerns apt terminology, the translation of statements, and meaning. To have a right, per IT, purportedly means no more than being an intended beneficiary of a duty. The argument moves from the idea of *X*'s ***meaning*** *Y* to the ideas that:

(i) All that can be said in a terminology of *X* (1) can be, and (2) is best, said in terms of a terminology of *Y*;
(ii) This renders *X* to be ***nothing more than*** an alternative formulation of *Y*; and
(iii) There is no gain in (1) significance or (2) clarity by translating *Y* into *X*.

Hart has IT in mind here, but these matters equally affect certain rights *models* too, such as Hohfeld's. Understood as a passive position,[128] a claim merely entitles its holder to receive the benefits provided by another party's duty. For Hart, though, this robs 'a right' of a distinct meaning, because it allows all propositions about rights to be 'translated' into propositions about duties. If so, then such matters might even be better understood in terms of propositions about duties. This too renders A RIGHT reducible to A DUTY, which in turn deprives us of a distinct ***conceptual*** resource, one that is ostensibly constitutive of our moral, social, and legal practices. Actually, Hart claims that this view about rights suffers two vices: (1) it makes the language of 'rights' unnecessary (for being redundant) and (2) it can cause confusion too.[129]

[126] Hart (1982: 181–2).

[127] Stepanians (2005: 12, 71–4).

[128] See Chapter 3 § III on the active/passive distinction.

[129] Hart (1982: 181–2). I believe that Hart's rejection of the passive interpretation of a Hohfeldian claim is what motivated him to present his own non-Hohfeldian model of a private law RCTD in *Essays on Bentham* as a (variable) set of powers and liberties and so to abandon his earlier commitment to Hohfeld (as evidenced in his 1954 article 'Definition and Theory in Jurisprudence', reproduced in Hart (1983)).

A Rebuttal

Markus Stepanians, an Interest theorist, offers the most thoughtful responses to WT's redundancy argument(s). For one thing, he tries to show that Kelsen's version is fallacious. Kelsen wrongly moves from the idea that a reflex-right is a state of protection provided by a duty to the idea that the reflex-right simply *is* that duty; for this is to conclude that the cause is the effect. It also leads to the absurdity that, as 'husband' and 'wife' are correlatives, being a wife is being a husband and vice versa.[130]

One problem with Stepanians' argument is that it presumes a particular conception of CORRELATIVITY—despite his being aware that different ones abound.[131] It is thus open for someone to simply deny the aptness of the right:duty::husband:wife analogy. For it could be said that the husband-wife relationship simply involves a different conception or sense of 'correlativity' from that which is most appropriate for right-duty.

Second, Stepanians converts the duty/reflex-right relationship into a causal one, wherein the duty creates a state of protection for another party. This might work for Jhering's conception, but not Kelsen's. For the latter, the duty simply is part of the protection: a normative requirement to (refrain from) undertaking action φ *simply is* the protection for another party. Indeed, for IT generally, the paradigmatic mode of rights protection is the existence or imposition of a correlative duty on another party; the protection is not some intended or unintended by-product, but the very duty itself (i.e., the normative restriction on the duty-bearer's deliberative processes, requiring the person to fulfil his or her requirement to act or forbear from acting). Thus, if Kelsen's argument is fallacious, it is not because of an invalid inference from a normative state of protection produced by a duty to the identification of that state with the duty, because no such inference is necessary: it is already constitutive of the conception.

Stepanians also presents three 'so what' responses to Hart's version of the argument.[132] First, as Hart's is a semantic argument it cannot show that the *concept* is redundant, even if the *term* 'a right' happens to be.[133]

[130] Stepanians (2005: 64, 68–9).

[131] Ibid 11.

[132] Ibid 74–6.

[133] Ibid 71. Technically, Stepanians believes Hart's argument only concerns the predicate 'has a right', because Stepanians thinks the theories only concern what it is to have a right, not what rights are. Ibid 68. However, he also holds that the 'classical' IT is 'based on a certain view of the normative function of rights: they are normative tools at the service of the wellbeing of persons'. Ibid 5.

Second, Hart cannot show that the concept is redundant either. 'For if concept *F* is identical to concept *G*, then neither is redundant since there is only *one* concept to begin with'.[134] Third, Hart's argument can be taken to be a gripe about the substitutability of the *definiendum* ('a right') by the *definiens* ('a duty'). However, Stepanians notes that redundancy is a *requirement* for proving an analysis to be correct; indeed, this is how analytic definitions are supposedly meant to work. If redundancy is objectionable in this context, then it is so for *all* analytic definitions.[135]

Even granting Stepanians' first argument, his second and third ones are unconvincing. Hart's objection is that there is something more to rights than a *duty-qua-definiens* can provide. *If* rights (or RCTDs at least) either are or necessarily include enforcement powers (or other additional enforcement positions, or other features), then that is a basis for deeming the explanation to be inadequate; the IT conception would fail to meet the theoretical desideratum of relative explanatory power (over alternatives that could cover the concept's additional features). If WT's redundancy argument has any force, it is not due to the mere 'fact' of redundancy per se, but rather because of the putative inaccuracy of the reduction here—*if*, that is, a *duty-qua-definiens* alone is in fact explanatorily inadequate. WT's charge is that there are more considerations at play for the *explanans/* analytic definition of A RIGHT. (Hart and other Will theorists may be mistaken about there actually being missing analytic features, thereby warranting a superior *definiens* or *explanans*, though.)

Instead, the charge of redundancy fails because it is probably mistaken. Hart himself acknowledges the existence of cases of unenforceable legal RCTDs. He wishes to account for private law (and certain other) legal rights, believing that this subset is distinct, and that the differences are important. Even so, and whether or not this subset is itself subject to counterexamples, Interest theorists can claim that Hart himself shows the

[134] Ibid 74–5. Other ITs who support the *symmetrical view* of correlativity (Chapter 3 § II) have also offered rebuttals to the redundancy argument along these lines, none of which is compelling. For example, Kramer argues that, given the correlativity of rights and duties, we can say the same thing about duties being rendered redundant. Kramer (1998: 27). Yet those who are unconvinced by Kramer's arguments against the existence of absolute duties (i.e., that all such duties correlate with collective rights, ibid 59), will have the same reasons to doubt this argument too.

[135] Stepanians (2005: 75–6).

need for a larger 'theory' of A RIGHT than his own, one which would explain the relationship of this subset to all other sorts of rights.[136]

§ V. Would-Be Alternative and Hybrid Theories

The last two decades have seen several efforts to move the theories of rights debate forward. Some scholars aim to provide either hybrids of, or alternatives to IT and WT. This section nevertheless argues that they all amount to versions of IT. (It will also point out certain defects in these accounts but takes no stance on whether they constitute superior versions of IT.)

In 2005, Gopal Sreenivasan presented a 'Complex Hybrid' theory of Hohfeldian claims. His (more recent) formulation for it is this:

> (CH) Suppose X is duty bound to φ. X *owes* a duty to φ *to Y* just in case Y's measure (and, if Y has a surrogate Z, Z's measure) of control over a duty of X's to φ matches (by design) the measure of control that advances Y's interests on balance.[137]

In that same year, Leif Wenar put forward a 'Several Functions' theory. Characterising all theories as being concerned with a right's 'functions' (rather than an *ultimate* purpose), Wenar denied that it has a singular, architectonic one. Instead, a right is a Hohfeldian position, or combination of positions, exhibiting one or more of six possible functions. The six identified functions are these:

> The provision of:
>
> 1, an exemption,
> 2, discretion, or
> 3, authorization,

[136] Cf. Hart (1982: 188–93).

[137] Sreenivasan (2010: 488). Cf. Sreenivasan (2005: 271). Sreenivasan cites Hart for the 'measures of control': enforcement or waiver powers over the correlative duty by which to waive the latter, enforce it in the face of its breach, waive enforcement, etc. Sreenivasan (2010: 482), citing Hart (1982: 183–4).

Or the entitlement to:

4, protection,
5, the provision of something, or
6, some performance[138]

In keeping with the idea that not all tokens of the various types of normative positions count as rights, Wenar's Several Functions theory implies that if a Hohfeldian claim does not fulfil at least one of three functions of 'rights that are claims'—protection against harm or paternalism, provision in case of need, or to some specific performance—then it is not a bona fide right.[139]

Kramer and Steiner have already shown that Wenar's 'several functions' account is simply a version of IT.[140] The same, however, ought to be said of Sreenivasan's: positing that a right's 'measures of control' (enforcement powers, etc.) must match the measure of control that advances the right-holder's interests on balance *makes* his an IT.

For one thing, Sreenivasan makes a category mistake, as it were, by treating 'measures of control' as being at the same level as 'interests'. Whether restricted to enforcement or waiver powers, or extended to include other positions like immunities, liabilities, etc., Will theorists hold that the 'measures of control' are means for, exist for the sake of, protecting the will by providing control: affording the right-holder the status of a 'small-scale sovereign' or 'private legislator' and the *locus standi* by which to assert one's personhood or status;[141] effectuating a person's capacity to choose;[142] a 'dominion' status entitling right-holders' wills to prevail over

[138] Wenar (2005: 246).

[139] Ibid 244–5.

[140] Kramer & Steiner (2007). There are also grounds to be sceptical of the theory. Whilst a token right must exhibit at least one of the six stated functions, Wenar posits that it need not possess any specific one. Wenar (2005: 238, 246). He also mentions the possibility of a token Hohfeldian liberty or immunity failing to fulfil any one of the six functions, and thus failing to count as a right. Wenar (2005: 246–7). How could a Hohfeldian liberty fail to exempt, or a power fail to authorise, though? Could a token Hohfeldian claim really fail to fulfil any of those six functions and thus fail to count as a right? Furthermore, the first three putative functions are simply aspects of normative positions that are best explained by rights *models* like Hohfeld's. If a token right need only possess only one (or more) of those three 'functions' (if not also the fifth and sixth), however, then this would be a reason for thinking that the *theory* is superfluous.

[141] E.g., Hart (1982: 183); Hart (1994: 41); Feinberg (1980: 151).

[142] E.g., Hart (1982); Steiner (1994).

others' in any confrontation in which the right is relevant;[143] free and equal status within a legal system;[144] etc. Moreover, for Sreenivasan, there may be times when no measures of control, no enforcement and waiver powers, are warranted. However, something lacking *any* such means of control is no right at all under WT. Hence, his theory is not really a hybrid.[145]

Again, Interest theorists have always believed that rights can be afforded measures of control. It is simply that, on their theory, such measures are neither necessary nor sufficient for A RIGHT (nor for being a right-holder).[146] For IT, a right is a normative construct used to effectuate or protect a predicate interest, and an RCTD, particularly, is primarily protected by, and/or justifies the imposition of, a duty.[147] The theory can even account for modifications to the measures of control. Legal officials, say, can add or subtract a particular enforcement mechanism in order to try to better effectuate the interest. (These additional measures can be said to actually strengthen or weaken the right.[148]) Critically, though, IT explains the grant of such measures and/or their being imposed upon other parties in terms of the right-holder's interests. Even if all rights in a given jurisdiction were, as a matter of historical fact, accompanied by enforcement powers, IT would still account for them as effectuating some interest or other, rather than as protecting the right-holder's will. Hence, they will deny that what is (quint)essential to A RIGHT is what it does for the will.[149]

[143] E.g., Wellman (1985: 96).

[144] E.g., Ripstein (2009). Ripstein would object to this instrumentalist framing, however.

[145] Mark McBride's 'Tracking theory' of rights is, for this same reason, also just a version of IT. McBride (2017). So too, Peter Vallentyne's putative hybrid theory is just a version of WT, because, even with variations in enforcement powers to prevent or compensate rights violation, the power to transfer the right remains essential and inviolable on his account. Vallentyne (2007: 190, 193, 196–7).

[146] E.g., Kramer (2013: 246).

[147] Raz (1986: 166–8); Kramer (2013: 246).

[148] E.g., Raz (1986: 168 & n.1, 171). It would be somewhat odd, though, for an Interest theorist to claim that changing the enforcement mechanisms can weaken or strengthen an RCTD; for a right according to that theory is just the interest or entitlement to a correlative duty, and so its strength or weakness ought to just concern the *force* of its claim and the strength of the correlative duty.

[149] Cf. Raz (1986: 168): '[w]hen the condition which activates the duty is an action of some person, and when the duty is conditional on it because it is in the right-holder's interest to make that person able to activate the duty at will, then the right confers a power on the person on whose behavior the duty depends').

Sreenivasan's is also problematic in ways that other Interest theories are not. Specifically, his 'by design' clause, which qualifies the theory's explanation of the amount of control (i.e., it matches that measure of control which advances the right-holder's interest on balance) cannot be squared with Legal Positivism and the possibility of *legal* rights born of corruption, rights created by mistake, etc.[150] Some legal rights can be afforded measures of control they ought not to have, given their right-holders' interests; other legal rights can have either no measure of control, or at least not the requisite measure, despite the right-holder's predicate interests potentially warranting otherwise.

Three other would-be alternative theories are also just versions of IT. First, Rowan Cruft presents an Interest-theory-with-exceptions. According to Cruft, whilst most rights (of any basic Hohfeldian type) serve their holders' interests by protecting them, justifying the imposition of ligations upon others, etc., there are nonetheless subsidiary or peripheral cases of rights that have nothing to do with the holder's interests.[151] His examples include promissory rights and certain property rights.[152]

Second, influenced by Wayne Sumner and Hillel Steiner, George Rainbolt offers a 'Justified [Normative] Constraint' theory as an alternative to IT and WT. For Sumner and Steiner, imposing normative constraints on others is but one amongst several essential features of any right.[153] Rainbolt, however, combines that notion with the idea of rights being based upon a particular sort of justification as together constituting all rights' *raison d'être*.[154] Rights impose justified normative constraints on other parties.[155] A right obtains when: (i) a second party bears a normatively constraining correlative position, such as a duty or a disability, and (ii) the justification for the existence or imposition of that normative constraint is *some* feature or other of the right-holder.[156] Specifically, Rainbolt believes that claims, immunities, and certain complexes containing tokens of both or either of those two more basic positions count as rights because

[150] Sreenivasan states that his theoretical interests are primarily in morality rather than law, but that his theory applies to law too. Sreenivasan (2010: 468).

[151] For the term 'ligation', see Chapter 1 note 23.

[152] Cruft (2004: 372–3, 384, 387).

[153] Sumner (1987: 35); Steiner (1994: 59).

[154] Rainbolt (2006: xii–xii).

[155] Ibid 27–8.

[156] Ibid xiii, 118. In this way, Rainbolt believes he overcomes the shortcomings of Raz's IT, which (ostensibly) focuses upon wellbeing as the sole basis for justification. Ibid 118–9.

only these impose 'normative constraints' on others.[157] (Hence, singular powers and liberties are not rights.[158])

Third, in 2013 Wenar presented a 'Kind-Desire' theory of an RCTD, although he does not believe that to be the only kind of a right.[159] This theory appears to purport to be able to identify RCTD-holders in any normative system that has such positions.[160] At any rate, the kind-desire builds upon an extensionally inferior 'Role' theory, which attributes desires to members of a given class.[161] As examples, property owners *qua* owners want others not to intrude on their land; promisees *qua* promisees want the agreements to be fulfilled; journalists *qua* journalists want their sources to be protected; etc. Wenar then extends this role-based desire approach to natural and social kinds.

The Kind-Desire theory incorporates three conditions: (1) identify a duty within a normative system; (2) attribute desires to a role-bearer or kind-bearer (who is distinct from the duty-bearer) in virtue of which that sort of agent wants that duty to be fulfilled; (3) a genuine RCTD must be enforceable, whether by the right-holder personally or by another party acting on his or her behalf.[162] Wenar believes 'desire' is at 'the same conceptual space' as 'will' or 'interest' and thus not reducible to either. It is even deemed to be conceptually prior to 'interest' in certain regards.[163]

These three sophisticated accounts are neither alternatives to, nor hybrids of, the Interest and Will theories. They are all just versions of IT. With respect to Cruft's theory, it is doubtful whether his examples of rights-sans-interests actually fail to advance or protect right-holders' interests. Even if they do not, his account leaves it uncertain why, conceptually, rights must otherwise generally advance interests. Further, his divergences

[157] Ibid xi–xii, 25–39.

[158] Ibid 30, 32.

[159] Wenar (2013: 207–8).

[160] '[It] is an analysis of what rights *are*, not of what rights *there are*. The analysis merely says that if there is a system of norms, and if these norms refer to certain roles, and if one norm relates role-bearers in a particular way, then there is a claim-right within that system of norms. The analysis does not endorse or condemn any system of norms. It does not endorse or condemn any roles or duties within any system of norms. That is to say: given any system of norms with roles, *this analysis will show where the rights are*. Describe any role-laden practice you like—real or imagined, sacred or wicked—and this analysis *will find* the claim-rights within it'. Ibid 210. Cf. Kramer (2012: 129).

[161] Wenar (2013: 208–18).

[162] Ibid 218–9, 226.

[163] Ibid 225.

from ordinary usage seem to be based on wholly unsupported moral or political preferences.

Regarding the Justified Constraint theory, Rainbolt never fully justifies why rights must be, or include, normative constraints. This is mostly assumed or posited as being axiomatic.[164] However, following Hart, he also questions whether it makes sense to call a liberty or a power 'a right' if their exercise can be interfered with at any time.[165] Even so, Rainbolt believes that at least one desideratum for comparing accounts of rights is whether it better matches our ordinary language of rights.[166] Yet we talk about 'the right to park' your vehicle in parking lots (a liberty), even when someone beats you to a particular parking spot, thus depriving you of it, and even if there are no available spots in the entire lot (no duty on current spot holders to let you park there; no duty borne by lot owners to ensure that spots are available; etc.).

Indeed, there are many important ordinary legal counterexamples to Rainbolt's view, e.g., rights to solicit for and enter contracts, to sell one's property, and to offer to buy property. None of these involves a correlative normative constraint borne by another party per se, rather than protection afforded by a perimeter of protection relationship by an RCTD, say, which is a distinct right from those just mentioned. (More on this below.[167]) Thus, Rainbolt excludes powers and liberties from counting as rights without warrant.

Rainbolt also begs the question vis-à-vis justification. As intimated above, there is no need for a direct connection between the normative positions in many such cases. For example, (normatively constraining) duties can instead form what Hart called 'perimeters of protection' on behalf of the exercise of liberties (an *indirect* relationship between normative positions).[168] This, rather than being generated directly because of

[164] See especially Rainbolt (2006: 25–7). He appeals to both Hohfeld and Steiner for the idea that it is simply an 'uncontested' feature of rights that they impose normative constraints on others. Rainbolt (2006: 27), citing Steiner (1994: 55, 59).

[165] Rainbolt (2006: 29–31). Again, for Hart, liberties count as rights ('liberty-rights') if directly *or indirectly* protected by duties (i.e., via perimeters of protection). Liberties that are not so protected (at all) do not count as rights. Hart (1982: 171–4); Appendix 1.

[166] Rainbolt (2006: 27).

[167] Furthermore, *pace* Rainbolt, Van Duffel provides historical examples of liberty-rights that lack correlative normative constraints. Van Duffel (2017: 195–6). His examples come from Tierney (1997: 81–5).

[168] On perimeters of protection, see Chapter 1 § II.2.

(being justified by) a right, e.g., a complex containing a claim and a liberty.[169] The protection that duties afford in these situations are thus distinct from the liberty. Such cases do not involve *justified* normative constraint because the constraints obtain for distinct reasons.[170] If the liberty is generally protected, albeit indirectly, then why not call it a type of a right—even on Rainbolt's theory?[171] Without more definitive bases, the proposition that all rights *must* (directly) impose constraints upon others is suspect.

Regardless, Rainbolt's justified constraint view is simply a version of IT. Even if the justification for imposing a normative constraint on another party can be *any* (sort of) reason, it does not follow that that reason fails to be an interest of the right-holder, in the right-holder's interests, or perceived or *claimed to be* in the right-holder's interest.

Turning to Wenar's Kind-Desire theory, critics have already questioned why such desires or wants cannot be explained in terms of the 'interests' inherent in such roles or kinds.[172] All of his '*X qua X*' and '*X* wants *Y*' statements can be rephrased without loss into 'in the interests of the role/kind-bearer *qua* role/kind-bearer'. Second, Wenar does not explain why claim-rights must be enforceable. (Excising that condition appears to do no damage to his theory, though.) Third, it is unclear whether the Role theory or the more expansive Kind-Desire theory can explain secondary and tertiary rights—if, that is, such rights are either RCTDs or complexes

[169] E.g., Rainbolt (2006: 31).

[170] Cruft argues that, if it is a theory, a Pure Normative Constraint account (where Rainbolt's justification prong is discarded) *may* be distinct from IT or WT. This is because it would allow for rights that are neither of value or benefit to the holders, nor protect their wills. Cruft then argues that such a theory would be over-inclusive because it would count many more instances of rights than our ordinary and legal usages allow; and, despite himself, he also shows that a *normative constraint* view is also under-inclusive, because ordinary usage treats liberties and powers as rights, even though they do not impose constraints upon others. Cruft (2004: 355, 359–60, 362–4).

Pace Cruft, though, Interest theorists often say that rights need not be idiosyncratically tailored to the holder's interests but must *normally* or *generally* be in the interests of persons in their situation. Hence, a *normative constraint* view can be seen to promote a right-holder's interest, as it were. E.g., Kramer (1998: 96); MacCormick (1977: 202).

[171] Rainbolt is aware of the general notion of a perimeter of protection and vaguely sees how it might serve as an objection to his theory. Rainbolt (2006: 40–1) However, he fails to adequately address how, given his reliance on Hart's view, it explicitly undermines his own version of the liberty-right/mere liberty distinction (see *supra* note 165 and Chapter 2 note 5) and why it has the same implication for his power-right/mere power distinction.

[172] Ripstein (2013a). Cf. Kramer (2017: 81); Cruft (2017: 175–6).

that include them.[173] For example, Americans and others have rights to be heard in United States Federal courts. Those courts employ standing requirements. One is that, for diversity jurisdiction, plaintiffs must bring claims of more than $75, 000.[174] So, what is the nature of the plaintiff's desire or role as such, rather than the nature of his or her dispute, which reflects this pecuniary quality so as to enable the Kind-Desire theory to identify the holder of such a (secondary) right?[175]

§ VI. Attacks on Analytic Versions

There have also been a couple of critiques levied against *analytic* versions of the theories. These efforts try to characterise the theories of rights debate as being a wholly 'normative' (in the sense of being morally or politically evaluative) affair, entailing that there are no genuine analytic versions.

According to Pavlos Eleftheriadis, the debate is really just about competing moral views about political institutions and about how to interpret legal doctrine.[176] Hence, analytic versions are misguided enterprises. Whilst he recognises the possibility of a philosophical project of 'describing' or interpreting a normative position's (ultimate) purpose, Eleftheriadis finds it dubious that such a project would take the form of theories which just happen to track the ones found in the moral-political debate. Is it a

[173] See, e.g., Hohfeld (1917: 752). Cf. Hohfeld (1913a: 35 n.39; Hohfeld (1909: 293–4).

[174] 28 U.S.C. § 1332(a): Diversity of citizenship, amount in controversy; costs.

[175] Wenar denies that his two accounts are just versions of IT. He claims that the two outline (i) several different 'functions' that rights can serve and (ii) the 'desires' inherent in certain roles or natural kinds, respectively. He suggested to me that his 2013 Kind-Desire theory differs from IT because the latter is (always) ultimately about interests-as-wellbeing. (Conversation with Leif Wenar, Stanford Law School, Palo Alto California, 15 June 2018). Again, in the 2013 article he claims that 'desire' is that 'the same conceptual space' as interests or the will, and not reducible to either. Wenar (2013: 225).

Whatever their merits and improvements upon others', Wenar's theories are nonetheless just versions of IT. Not only are early versions of IT not necessarily tied to conceptions of wellbeing, but, as shall be explained in greater detail in Chapter 6, Legal Positivist Interest theories (e.g., Raz and Kramer's versions) cannot really be about wellbeing either. Positivists admit that there can be rights predicated upon mistakes, corruption, trivial rights, etc. Cruft's 2004 Interest-theory-with-exceptions is yet a further example divorcing interests from wellbeing, as, *pace* Cruft himself, his examples (e.g., property rights) *do* point to right-holders' interests after all, even if he denies that they advance their wellbeing. Cruft (2004: 372–3, 384, 387).

[176] Eleftheriadis (2008: 10–15).

mere coincidence? Not likely. Analytic versions are therefore crypto-normative: scholars are really just presenting moral arguments disguised as analytic theories.[177] They 'ignor[e] their own methodological constraints by pursuing normative projects under the guise of analysis'.[178] This, he thinks, is evidenced by the fact that their theories do not track the facts of legal practice well. Further, each theory even admits it is inconsistent with at least some of the data, 'the facts of legal practice'.[179] Hence, analytic rights theories 'are distortions rather than accurate explanations'.[180]

Hamish Stewart also basically considers 'definitional' (i.e., analytic) rights theories to be fruitless enterprises. On his view, these versions simply lay down stipulative definitions of 'a right' and present counterexamples to their rival's definition.[181] Analytic rights theorists want their definitions to both (i) reflect ordinary and legal linguistic usage (at least to some extent) and (ii) be able to provide a precise, technical vocabulary, which can later be used in normative debates about what rights people ought to have and what sort of beings ought to count as right-holders.[182] However, these dual aims are said to be in 'irreconcilable conflict': the more precise one's definition, the less it will track or reflect ordinary usage; the more it tracks ordinary usage, the less precise it will be.[183]

Further, Stewart believes analytic rights theories are not really doing what they claim to do. As discussed above, WT purportedly cannot account for cases of inalienable and unwaivable rights, or the rights of certain people (e.g., children). In turn, IT is said to be unable to either explain or exclude the rights of 3PBs. Stewart thinks that, if the analytic

[177] Ibid 14–5.

[178] Ibid 15.

[179] Ibid.

[180] Ibid.

[181] As mentioned in § II.4, however, theorists *claim to* present complex criteria for what count as A RIGHT, not (just) definitions (if at all) of the term 'a right'. They do not believe themselves to be simply concerned with rules for the usage of words, but with capturing the essential features of a concept.

[182] These metatheoretical desiderata come from Kramer & Steiner (2007: 296). See also Chapter 2 § III on Kramer and Steiner.

[183] Stewart (2012: 320). He suggests that the best way to understand a basic concept is not to begin with a definition and then defend it against every possible counterexample. Instead, one should 'grasp the main features of the concept as they present themselves in the relevant body of material and then try to understand the role the concept plays in the material'. Ibid 338. If this is a feasible approach, then it still seemingly leaves the door open to analytic rights theories. They need only modify their modus operandi.

versions really are correctives to ordinary usage, then such counterexamples should not prove bothersome. Yet analytic rights theorists *do* treat them as being important. That attempts to address counterexamples are even undertaken belies the fact that analytic theorists' own conceptions of rights are not really delimited by their proffered definitions, and nor are their definitions what really motivates them to concoct counterexamples and responses. Like Eleftheriadis, Stewart believes that the means by which analytic theorists attempt to accommodate the counterexamples are really crypto-normative arguments. Their analyses and counterarguments incorporate evaluative components that undermine their theories' efforts to be morally neutral.[184]

According to Stewart, then, what motivates such theorists to craft counterarguments is a belief that certain classes of agents (e.g., children, 3PBs, etc.) *should* (not) have (certain) rights. They manipulate their definitions and their applications to accord with these beliefs. Doing so, however, undermines the very reason for constructing such definitions in the first place: they are no longer morally neutral tools fit for philosophical discussion. Again, this practice belies the fact that the definitions do not actually represent analytic theorists' own proffered conceptions.

Whilst space does not allow for a full discussion of the debate's genealogy, calls to preclude analytic versions are misguided. For one thing, Eleftheriadis ignores the possibility that such versions are either simply inadequate, or just the relatively best analytical jobs that can be done. Even if a theory has many explanatory gaps or failings (e.g., it does not track the facts well, covers only so much of them before counterexamples run rampant, etc.) it does not follow that its proponents are really

[184]Stewart's particular arguments are as follows. First, both Interest and Will theorists really believe it is morally or politically unpalatable for WT to exclude certain classes of people from being right-holders. Some Will theorists stretch their accounts to include such agents or provide outlandish justifications for their exclusion from the set of right-holders. Either way, their motivation is moral or political, not analytic. Second, when Interest theorists like Kramer try to distinguish amongst different kinds of interests in order to determine whether a 3PB possesses rights or not, their analyses are really based on substantive grounds about why such people should (not) have rights, and not their definitions. (Kramer would be the first to admit this, though, and would not deem it to be problematic for his theory. See Kramer (1998: 79); Kramer (2010: 35)). Third some Interest theorists distinguish between what is 'generally beneficial' from what is 'generally detrimental' to people or a class of persons in order to deny that a parent would have a right to be informed upon (one correlative to a duty borne by his or her child to inform on the former for seditious sentiments under a hypothetical law). Stewart (2012: 325–6, 332–3).

motivated by moral or political impulses, or that their accounts are actually moral or political ones.

For example, one of Hart's reasons for favouring WT over IT is 'the' redundancy argument(s), addressed above in Section IV.4. [185] This serves as a counterexample to Eleftheriadis' view because, sound or not, Hart's argument, which charges IT with creating inaccurate and unnecessary (conceptual and) semantic redundancy, need neither be construed as a moral or political one, nor as necessarily being predicated upon (crypto-) moral or political impulses.

One might think that Hart only advances this argument because he really believes that rights *ought to be* enforceable and exercisable, that rights *ought to* afford one control, etc. I have nonetheless argued elsewhere that many people—Will theorists generally, but others too—harbour a 'conceptual archetype' of rights as perforce being exercisable and utilisable tools.[186] The idea is that you invariably *do* things with your rights. This notion is centuries old, at least.[187] Regardless of whether the archetype is accurate or not, it would be a mistake to believe it to *necessarily* be a moral or political one, or that its endorsement and utilisation *must be* predicated upon such normative impulses.

Although they tend to focus on the debate's standard charges of a given theory's putative under- and over-inclusivity, would Eleftheriadis and Stewart deem as crypto-normative the analytic debate over whether A DUTY is or includes: (i) an exclusionary reason; (ii) just a weighty reason; or (iii) simply an act or forbearance that can be exacted from another party?[188] It is hard to see why preferring one option here over the others must necessarily be morally or politically motivated either.

Now, Stewart certainly demonstrates that particular rights theorists go awry, methodologically speaking. The simple solution for such theorists,

[185] Again, see Hart (1982: 181–2).

[186] Frydrych (2019: 466–9). As examples, see Hart (1982: 184): '…it is hard to think of rights except as capable of *exercise*…'; Steiner (1994: 57): '[t]he idea that rights are things which are exercisable deeply permeates both ordinary language and standard legal usage. Next to our minds and our muscles, rights are what we exercise most'; Simmonds (1998: 216): '…reflects our sense that rights are involved with the choices of the right-holder: rights are things that may be exercised, and right-holders have a choice about how they shall be exercised'. See also Wellman (1995: 109).

[187] See Tierney (1997).

[188] See e.g., Hart (1982: 157–60, 266–8); Raz (1977: 233); Raz (1986: 195); Raz (1984: 131).

which he himself provides, is to simply avoid those sorts of arguments. Stewart might reply that these normative matters form the 'central moves in the debate' between the theories[189] and are therefore unavoidable. Whilst Section IV argued that those 'central' moves miss their mark anyway, Stewart's take is still worth challenging because there are alternative, non-normative (again, in the sense of being morally or politically evaluative) explanations for analytic theorists' providing responses to the putative counterexamples. For example, they may very well think it 'ghastly' to deny children the status of right-holder for normative reasons, but may additionally believe it reflects a *mistake* whereby the analytic theory entails the exclusion of salient data from ordinary parlance, from law, etc. Its exclusion or inclusion from (the implications of) a definition (in the name of a precise vocabulary, or some other metatheoretical/epistemic desideratum) need not be based on the moral or political idea that children ought to have rights. Second, ascribing rights to 3PBs need not be based on moral or political preferences. It may simply be an attempt to handle the data. Third, analytic theorists need not (and perhaps ought not) try to deny that real and hypothetical laws can and would generate morally abominable legal rights.

Stewart is nevertheless correct to notice something troublesome with the analytic theories, even if his diagnoses are off the mark. Instead, he ought to have gone further because there is something awry with the *entire* theories of rights debate. Indeed, as the next chapter will argue, it is doubtful whether *any* theories—of this sort, at any rate—are necessary or helpful.

§ VII. Conclusion

The theories of rights debate about how best to explain A RIGHT. Rival theories present competing criteria for the concept, which include the following. 1: an ultimate purpose that all rights serve, which in turn gets expressed as a requirement that a right protect something, justify something, promote something, or effectuate something. 2: specification of the means of protection, justification, etc. e.g., *by* imposing a duty on another party; *via* enforcement powers over that duty. 3: declaring which (subset of which) basic types of normative positions (e.g., Hohfeldian claims, immunities, etc.) warrant rights-status.

[189] Stewart (2012: 320).

Some Interest theorists hold that only RCTDs are rights. Others posit that liberties, powers, etc., and 'complexes' can be rights too. All Interest theorists agree, however, that normative positions which fail to serve the ultimate purpose of generally protecting/promoting the interests of a class of agent, either by imposing duties on other parties, or through other specified means, are not really rights.

By contrast, many Will theorists think that only a complex composed of an RCTD plus (at least) one enforcement or waiver power (at a minimum)—if they construe RCTDs to differ from powers, that is—used to protect or effectuate the holder's will, count as a right. A minority, though, hold that rights can be combinations of various positions (e.g., Hohfeldian immunities, liberties, etc.) on the condition that such complexes also involve the relevant sorts of enforcement power(s). All Will theorists nevertheless agree that rights protect their holders' wills via enforcement powers over other parties' correlative normative positions. For WT, rights afford you a modicum of control in addition to a sort of normative status, recognition, and standing within a normative domain.

Despite the debate's provenance, debaters must nevertheless address some fundamental methodological concerns. Particularly, the theories' respective criteria warrant greater scrutiny. *How* did theorists come up with them? On what grounds were certain features added whilst other candidates were rejected? *Why* must rights protect interests or the will? Why must rights protect or effectuate anything? Why are there not a greater variety of means of will and interest effectuation or protection? Why do certain normative positions, which seem fully capable of effectuating or protecting their holders' interests or wills, not count as rights under particular versions' criteria? Demanding greater accountability along these lines leads to even more searching questions about the debate's utility and worth. The next chapter addresses these concerns, along with other serious—fatal, it shall be argued—problems suffered by the theories and their very debate.

CHAPTER 6

The Case Against the Theories

§ I. Introduction

The theories of rights provide competing criteria for A RIGHT.[1] As mentioned in Chapter 1, philosophers, jurists, and others may be attracted to such theories in part out of a wariness of the mass proliferation of rights language over the last few decades, replete with ubiquitous disputes over what counts as genuine cases, and a fear that this will devalue the concept(s).[2] It would help to be able to appeal to a definitive standard or test by which to resolve all disputes about: (i) what rights are and (ii) where genuine instances obtain (let alone credible criteria of fundamentality for what ought to constitute constitutional and human rights).[3]

This chapter nevertheless argues that (1) the theories are irredeemably flawed and (2) the debate itself ought to be abandoned. It proceeds as follows. Section II argues that each theory contains serious idiosyncratic

[1] Certain versions of the Interest and Will theories qualify their accounts. Particularly, proponents may specify that their version only concerns (1) a particular normative domain or system (e.g., legal rights, but not moral ones) and/or (2) a certain kind of a right (e.g., Hohfeldian claims, but not liberties, powers, or immunities). See Chapter 5 § II.1. These delimitations do not affect these versions of the theories' susceptibility to the criticisms presented herein.

[2] See Chapter 1 note 3.

[3] Some scholars nonetheless claim that the debate having reached a stalemate; despite their (purported) flaws, neither theory seems capable of definitively besting its rival. E.g., Sumner (1987: 51); Wenar (2008: 269); Van Duffel (2017: 187).

D. Frydrych, *The Architecture of Rights*,
https://doi.org/10.1007/978-3-030-76039-7_6

defects—ones that mostly differ from the canonical charges levied in the debate literature (addressed in Chapter 5 § IV). Section III then shows that the theories also bear common problems that have hitherto gone undetected, and why any theory *of this sort* is unnecessary for understanding rights.

§ II. Each Theory's Idiosyncratic Failings

§ II.1. Will Theory's Particular Problems

A. Divvying Up a Right's Components

This section addresses each theory's unique flaws, i.e., ones its rival does not bear. Let us commence with WT's. One of its unique defects is that it lacks a principled explanation of how a given right's components, e.g., a right-correlative-to-a-duty ('an RCTD') and enforcement powers, can be held (and exercised) by different people.[4]

To see why, though, recall IT's under-inclusivity charge. WT purportedly fails to account for clear cases of legal rights (and erroneously entails that certain sorts of agents are not right-holders), including those of: children; the mentally handicapped; the comatose; the dead; non-persons; third-party beneficiaries of contracts; criminal law victims; animals; and others.[5] As mentioned in the last chapter, this charge actually misses the mark. This is because some versions of WT allow for the separation and apportionment of a single right's components—e.g., an RCTD, various enforcement powers (if construed to be distinct from the RCTD), and/or liberties by which to exercise those powers—amongst different people.[6] For these versions of WT, a right can obtain so long as *someone* (e.g., a legal guardian, a government prosecutor, a principal's agent, etc.) possesses and/or may exercise the relevant sort of powers.

WT's real problem is rather the lack of a principled, cogent basis for these distributive manoeuvres. How can you believe that a right's components can be divvied up amongst different people if you also insist that it perforce affords *its holder* some 'control' over others? Whose will actually gets protected or effectuated here? Given WT's criteria, what makes the parcelled out normative positions count as components of 'a' right? Why treat it as a unified construct, rather than as distinct (kinds of) rights held

[4] Frydrych (2016: 132–5, 155–8); Frydrych (2017b: 199–200); Cruft (2017: 170).

[5] See Chapter 5 § IV.

[6] Chapter 5 notes 77–8 and the accompanying text.

by different people? Additionally, versions of WT allowing for this apportionment cannot explain why, given their conception of A RIGHT, the powerless party (or power-holder) is nonetheless deemed to be a right-holder,[7] nor why the power-holder/wielder is not the true right-holder—as certain other versions of WT insist.[8] If, moreover, RCTDs necessarily protect their holders' wills via enforcement powers, then how could such cases count as 'mere exceptions to the rule' of one person holding all of a right's components, including those necessary for enforcement?[9]

Nigel Simmonds, a Will theorist who rejects the rights-as-complexes approach, nevertheless presents an argument that could be repurposed to try to defend WT's distributive manoeuvre. Imagine a legal order wherein only legal officials possess the relevant enforcement powers. In such a system, Simmonds thinks, private citizens would not actually have any rights.[10] This, on the grounds that right-holders would always be at the whim of officials to see whether their 'rights' will be enforced. Hence, the 'rights' afford no real control.

Matthew Kramer tries to rebut Simmonds' argument by showing that, adjuding such a condition to be morally abominable, dystopian, etc., is no basis for denying or affirming whether rights actually obtain.[11] Most Will theorists will be unpersuaded by Kramer's claim. For them, a right's ultimate purpose is to protect/effectuate the right-holder's will. If people

[7] These versions therefore do not (and perhaps cannot) offer the sufficient conditions for A RIGHT.

[8] E.g., Steiner (1998: 248–62). What if no one possesses the relevant enforcement powers? WT will simply deny that there are actually particular rights in those cases. (That does not necessarily amount to a denial of the possibility of right-holder status for an entire *class* of agent, though). Interest theorists will of course reject that assessment, which reflects the theories' clashing fundamentals.

[9] Imagine WT abandoned its essentialism and adopted a central case method instead, whereby the theory advanced the proposition that the central case of a right is held by a rational, competent agent, and is self-enforceable. Even then, the grounds for identifying such instances as *the* central case would remain suspect: why is it any more or less of 'a right' because of its holder's qualities and whether he or she is competent to self-enforce it?

[10] Simmonds (1998: 225). Given his interpretation of a Hohfeldian claim as a kind of normative power (ibid 223), Simmonds' own view prohibits the separation of a right's components amongst different agents (save, perhaps, the separation of the claim-power and the liberty to exercise it. Simmonds (2013: 299-300)). His argument need not stand or fall with his (active) interpretation of A CLAIM, however. It could be reconstructed to say that, if citizens only bore passive claims, whilst officials held all of the relevant enforcement powers and liberties by which to exercise them, that would be problematic.

[11] Kramer (2000: 476–81).

never had the means by which to do so (via WT's specified modes, at any rate), then it would be senseless to style them as right-holders.

Now, imagine a second legal system with the same comprehensive division of RCTDs, enforcement powers (and liberties by which to exercise those powers) amongst private citizens and legal officials respectively, but where the officials (the power- and liberty-holders) systematically refuse to ever enforce any citizen's RCTDs. Would the citizens actually have legal rights?[12] One reason for thinking that they do concerns duty fulfilment, rather than enforcement. Private citizens may have reasons to conform to, or comply with, their legal duties-correlative-to-rights, independently of the possibility of enforceability—even in a loathsome legal regime.[13] Of course, this is far from determinative. Regardless, WT still cannot properly account for certain rights (where there is a division of their components) that do not meet its first two criteria (the ultimate purpose of vindicating the holder's will by affording control via enforcement mechanisms).

B. *Explaining Control*

Another of WT's idiosyncratic defects is that it does not adequately explain why only certain modes of control are germane to will vindication. Chapter 5 § IV noted that the 'inalienability' argument, the (narrower) charge of WT being unable to account for certain rights' inalienability or unwaivability, cannot falsify the theory. For the theory, which may only require a floor of just one enforcement power (without specifying *which one* it must be), can also allow for a right's set of enforcement mechanisms to vary over time. Further, an inalienable or unwaivable right may nevertheless be enforceable. Even so, WT provides no clear reason for excluding alienation power from the pertinent set of modes of control. More generally, the theory lacks a principled explanation about why only certain sorts of powers (and other normative positions) are germane to will vindication.

C. *A Mere Version of the Interest Theory*

WT's third major idiosyncratic defect is that it is wholly subsumable under its rival. Even if all rights were enforceable, IT could still deny that

[12] Suffice it to note that some Interest and certain Will theorists (i.e., that subset which identifies rights exclusively with enforcement powers) will disagree—and not necessarily on party lines—about whether these citizens have rights.

[13] This will nonetheless prove unsatisfactory to those who think such cases are better explained in terms of 'absolute' legal duties.

enforceability is essential to A RIGHT. Imagine there was universal agreement that all rights are enforceable and thus afford some form of control. That would still leave open the question of whether all rights (exist in order to) facilitate or protect interests or the will. IT might also claim to have a better explanation of why enforcement mechanisms obtain, i.e., as tools to help protect the interests behind, or effectuated by, the right. (Early versions of IT may even have maintained that all legal rights are enforceable.[14])

Moreover, WT lacks an adequate account of why the locus of concern for rights is or ought to be the will in the first place. Now, some versions claim to emphasise will vindication via right-holder-status recognition, rather than via the ability to make choices regarding enforcement.[15] Even so, all versions are subsumable under IT. For, in response to the possible objection that IT and WT's ultimate purposes still clash, it must still be asked: is right-holding status vindicated for its own sake, i.e., for the sake of one's will, personhood, soul, etc., or in order to advance one's interests? What might the differences between personhood vindication and those interests be?[16]

D. *The Threat of Redundancy*

Another of WT's idiosyncratic problems is somewhat ironic: it erroneously reduces rights to powers.[17] Through its 'redundancy' argument(s), WT charges IT with erroneously reducing, analytically, AN RCTD to A DUTY and/or making the term 'a right' superfluous. The theory purportedly entails that all propositions about RCTDs can be (better) restated in terms of duties.[18] IT could nevertheless levy a 'redundancy' argument of its own,

[14] See Pound (1915: 111); Pound (1959: 62–3, 67). For example, according to Jhering, A LEGAL RIGHT (or A PRIVATE LAW RIGHT, at least) has two aspects, one substantial the other formal. The substantial aspect is the benefit/advantage/gain to be had, which serves as the right's core. The formal aspect, *die klage* (entitlement to sue), serves as the core's shell, providing legal protection. Jhering (1865: 316–7 in § 60). See also ibid 328 on *die klage* (a 'criterion' for private law rights) being exercised by the right-holders themselves or a guardian on their behalf. See further Stepanians (2005: 72 n.28, 144–50); Hart (1982: 181 n.76). Apparently, certain medieval scholars such as Marsilius of Padua and William of Ockham believed that rights (*ius*) were both (i) necessarily enforceable in courts and (ii) protected interests. See Tierney (1997: 117–21, 189).

[15] E.g., Carl Wellman. See Chapter 5 notes 22–3 and the accompanying text.

[16] For a different reason to think WT is wholly subsumable under IT, see Edmundson (2012: 102).

[17] Frydrych (2016: 191–2).

[18] See Chapter 5 § IV.4 on the redundancy arguments.

charging WT with erroneously reducing AN RCTD to A POWER.[19] However, we already have the concept, A POWER, which concerns the capacity to change (create, modify, or terminate) parties' normative positions and statuses. Further, even if normative powers are a subset of rights, not all rights are powers.

Some Will theorists would deem this to be a misplaced charge, as their versions hold that rights are complexes composed of an RCTD (*not* construed as a power on their conception, but rather as a passive position) plus enforcement powers, and that these components can be distributed amongst different agents. This understanding of A RIGHT therefore requires including the feature of being entitled to someone else's duty-bound action or forbearance, which is not covered by A POWER per se. Hence, they will insist that their version of WT does not make this reduction.

The charge nonetheless remains apt because enforcement powers are equally integral to the 'distributional' versions of WT's conception of A RIGHT. Take away all of the enforcement power(s) and there is no real right left according to WT—even if it contains a distinct (passive) 'RCTD'.

Other Will theorists might nevertheless insist that this reduction charge misses the point of their distinct versions: to recognise or vindicate a party's right-holder status (his or her 'dominion') in the face of real or hypothetical disputes. However, their versions of WT suffer the same difficulty: the inability to explain the passive 'RCTD' component.[20] Hence, the charge of reducing rights to powers applies to their versions too.

§ II.2. IT's Particular Problems

A. Fails to Delimit

IT also contains serious idiosyncratic defects. One is failing to credibly delimit the set of relevant interests—the only way to render the theory

[19] Frydrych (2016: 191–2). For example, HLA Hart, a Will theorist, even says that rights are powers—at least concerning private law rights. 'These legal powers (for such they are) over a correlative obligation…'. Hart (1982: 184). Cf. Simmonds (1998: 223). Hart distinguishes between powers and liberties by which to exercise those powers. Hart (1982: 184 n.86, 188). Whilst, for example, legal minors have some minimal capacity to create valid contracts, it is nevertheless unclear how a legal incompetent can even possess such enforcement powers (sans exercise liberties) on his view.

[20] For example, Wellman denies that singular Hohfeldian claims count as rights and defines 'claim-rights' as including a power to enforce. Wellman (1985: 28, 39, 59–60); Wellman (1995: 123, 186–7).

potentially worthwhile and illuminating. (As shall be discussed below, an '*Interests-Simpliciter*' version of IT is basically useless.) For example, legal rights need not be predicated upon beneficial, weighty, or important interests, let alone ones based on their holders' individual interests either—as certain versions of the theory insist. Leif Wenar suggests this is typical of IT, because rights 'outrun' interests of any sort.[21]

All versions of IT nevertheless (seemingly) deny this. They claim to delimit the relevant sorts of interests in some way or other. Their reason for doing is at least in part because they consider the charges of their theory's (i) suffering from proliferation problems and (ii) being incapable of explaining why certain rule-governed situations do not include rights to be on point. However, all such delimitation efforts, e.g., to interests that concern wellbeing,[22] or ones which are normally, typically, or standardly beneficial for a class of beings or entities,[23] are unsuccessful.

However, many Interest theorists are also Legal Positivists. By virtue of their positivistic commitments, and because of the acquiescences made to that theory of law by its Normativist rivals, all Interest theorists are, or ought to be—in the name of consistency—committed to the idea that *legal* (and other institutional) rights can reflect any sorts of interests, including ones that cut against wellbeing, being typically beneficial, etc.[24] Their theory therefore cannot, and need not be, delimited to those sorts of normative concerns. Understood thus, IT becomes rather trivial as a *theory*.[25]

[21] Wenar (2008: 256). Cf. Jeremy Bentham on useless legal duties (without correlative rights) that benefit no one, discussed in Hart (1982: 168).

[22] E.g., Raz (1996: particularly in Chapter 3).

[23] E.g., MacCormick (1977: 202); Kramer & Steiner (2007: 289–90). Kramer also hints at further specifications to his version by distinguishing between 'vicarious' and 'altruistic' interests. Kramer & Steiner (2007: 302–4).

[24] Frydrych (2016: 162–73, 182–3); Frydrych (2017b: 205). Note that this is an argument about legal rights and not about legal right-*holders* per se. For more specific arguments against Raz's and MacCormick's respective versions of IT's compatibility with Legal Positivism, see Rainbolt (2006: 89–93); Simmonds (1995: 316 n.23). See also Martin (1993: 70): *pace* Raz, authoritative legal recognition is sufficient to make something a legal right regardless of whether it is an 'important' interest or an aspect of wellbeing. So too is an authoritative denial that a candidate right and correlative duty are actual legal positions within the system.

[25] Additionally, with no specific subset of interests being endorsed, there is no reason why certain versions of WT could not embrace the notions of rights being grounded in, or protecting, interests (whilst still denying that that is the most important feature).

Consider Joseph Raz's IT first.[26] His is not what it appears to be at first glance because its 'wellbeing' prong is not actually integral to it.[27] Following John Salmond, Joel Feinberg, H.J. McCloskey, and others, Raz believes that rights are sufficient (i.e., non-exclusive) *grounds* for correlative duties.[28] Rights are not merely correlatives, but also grounds. More precisely, they are 'intermediate conclusions' between certain sorts of interests and duties.[29] Raz therefore treats A RIGHT as being logically dependent upon A DUTY: being a reason for imposing a duty, the former is *logically* posterior to the latter. Still, in being able to ground some duties, rights are *justificationally* prior to them—even if both positions are created at the same time, i.e., they are existentially correlative;[30] *A*'s right is the reason for *B*'s bearing a correlative duty.[31] Although they primarily serve as the non-exclusive grounds for correlative duties, rights can additionally ground, and be protected by, other positions: liberties, powers, further rights, liabilities, etc.[32]

To provide further context, Raz's account of LAW includes the ideas that (i) the law can be identified simply by its sources (not its moral or other merits, if any) and (ii) law necessarily claims to possess legitimate authority (whether it has it or not).[33] In accordance with his (Exclusive) Legal Positivism, and despite his IT criteria, he also notes that authorities can create legal rights for any reason they see fit. 'One has a legal right because the authority declared that one has an interest which justifies holding others to be subject to duties. One has that legal right even if the authorities' declaration is mistaken'.[34] There are also trivial legal rights.[35]

[26] For Raz's analytic definition of A RIGHT, see Chapter 5 note 33.

[27] Frydrych (2016: 117, 162–3, 173, 182–3); Frydrych (2017b: 201 n.24); Frydrych (2018b: 571).

[28] Salmond (1902: 223, 231); McCloskey (1965: 116, 121); Feinberg (1980: 148–9). Cf. Hudson & Husak (1980); Raz (1986: 170, 181, 183–4, 16, 188, 192–3, 202, 210). In other words, for Raz, some duties are grounded in rights, but others are not.

[29] Raz (1986: 181). Rights therefore do not merely reflect an interest, but also add an additional, independent reason. Raz (1996: 46).

[30] See Chapter 3 § II.2 on existential correlativity. Raz also treats CORRELATIVITY as possibly obtaining between two—or more, *contra* Hohfeld—distinct normative positions. See Raz (1986: 170–1).

[31] Ibid 169–71, 181, 183–4, 188, 192–3, 202, 210.

[32] Ibid 167–8.

[33] Raz (2009b: 29–30); Raz (1996: 215).

[34] Raz (1986: 262).

[35] Ibid 186.

Further, legal officials can create rights that fail to work as hoped or designed.[36] For example, legislators may address some concern with an individual or class of persons' wellbeing (which ostensibly catalysed the officials to act in the first place) by codifying a right that either unwittingly protects different interests instead, or which is actually incapable of advancing or protecting the intended interest. One may add that officials can even intentionally misrepresent a legal right as promoting people's wellbeing, knowing full well that it does not and will not. They might therefore simply ignore considerations of wellbeing altogether when constructing the right.[37] In light of these considerations, Raz cannot really be taken to hold that rights perforce protect wellbeing; and when taken together with his overall account of LAW, his rights theory turns out to be neutral about which (sorts of) interests legal rights can actually protect or advance.

The same can be said of Kramer's IT, even though it does not include 'justificatory' considerations. At least until just recently, Kramer has insisted that his version does not, and that rights theories generally need not, provide A LEGAL RCTD's sufficient conditions.[38] The question of which interests to recognise is, he has convincingly suggested, a jurisdictionally contingent matter.[39] *Qua* Legal Positivist, though, Kramer ought to believe that officials may deem that a putative (class of) right(s) is legally valid if it meets the jurisdiction's rule(s) of recognition—irrespective of whether it is 'typically beneficial' for a class of beings or entities.[40]

[36] Ibid 170. Cf. Raz (1996: 45–9, 269–74).

[37] *Contra* Raz's thesis that law necessarily claims legitimate authority (Raz (1996: 215)), Kramer argues that wicked legal systems need not even feign belief in the morality of their laws, or of a given law. Kramer (2003: Chapter 4). Cf. Kramer (2007: 186); Finnis (2011: 432 n.13). Kramer's argument ought also to be considered adequate to undermine Raz's Modal view of rights and other normative positions. (See Chapter 1 note 28 on the functional/modal distinction). For if legal rights need not be weighty interests, *or even be (mis-)represented* as being weighty interests, then they need not be said to be, or be presented as, the codification of (purported) moral rights. In other words, lawmakers need not present legal rights as being morally legitimate, as being anything other than expressions of their power, and thus need not claim to protect or promote the holders' wellbeing. Alone, this may not suffice to demonstrate a structural difference between moral and legal rights, save insofar as the latter need not be (predicated upon) weighty reasons. Cf. Kramer (2018: 408).

[38] Kramer (2017: 54). See Chapter 5 § IV.

[39] Kramer (1998: 79).

[40] Now, at one point, Kramer suggests that, even for IT, not all instances of legal rights must invariably protect such interests. Indeed, in 'extremely rare' circumstances a particular right may even prove detrimental to its holder. Kramer & Steiner (2007: 292). Nevertheless, the question here is about whether the 'generally/typically beneficial interests' proposition

Furthermore, whilst he (correctly) denies the need to do so, Kramer nonetheless tries to provide the sufficient conditions via a revised version of Jeremy Bentham's test. As shown in Chapter 5, however, Kramer's version, the 'Minimum Sufficiency' test, can neither delimit the relevant sorts of interests accurately nor be squared with Legal Positivism.[41] Stripped of the test, his version of IT is therefore best understood, like Raz's, as concerning any sort of interest. Authorities may very well *claim* to either be advancing right-holders' wellbeing or to have in its legal repertoire rights that protect interests which are typically beneficial for some class of beings. For Positivists, however, the officials' claims need not be true or accurate, and nor are they even relevant to determinations of a right's legal validity.

The same can also be said of non-Positivist versions of IT, such as John Finnis'.[42] For theirs too can admit the existence of legal rights born of corruption or mistakes, trivial instances, ones with design flaws, etc. This, even if such theorists would want to deem these to be 'peripheral' or 'degenerate' cases, per the central case method. However, after admitting that such rights do exist, or that the relevant sorts of interests are jurisdictionally contingent (even if there is some central set of interests with which you think officials ought to concern themselves), you are shorn of the pertinent delimitation of the relevant sort of interests serving as a necessary condition for A RIGHT per your rights theory's criteria.[43]

Additionally, if one insists that IT must delimit the relevant sorts of interests to those concerning right-holders' wellbeing, then it is difficult to see how a contemporary normative version of IT can account for status-based, inegalitarian rights, e.g., those that help structure aristocratic or priestly classes. For example, had *primum noctum* been a real medieval right, how would we determine if it was really a matter of the lord's wellbeing? (Since it is in the right-holder's interest to increase his chances

actually constitutes part of the 'essential features of rights'. Ibid 281. Legal Positivism suggests it need not be.

Kramer (but not Raz) could also argue that trivial legal rights, ones borne of corruption, etc., may still be typically beneficial for the type of person who holds those positions. Still, it does not follow that rights perforce are typically beneficial for their holders, or that a legal system cannot generate a legion of rights for otherwise run-of-the-mill right-holders which typically are not beneficial for them. Kramer may deny that those should be counted as genuine instances, but at the cost of his own theory's credibility.

[41] Frydrych (2017b).

[42] Finnis (2011: Chapter 8).

[43] You are also left with a theory that is basically unobjectionable to WT, save in terms of the latter's insistence about rights perforce offering some modicum of control.

of having offspring?) *A fortiori* if the theory needed to hold that this right's existence was buttressed by the community's interests. What about the rights to select wager of battle and to designate a champion to do the actual fighting?[44] (Is it in a combative community's strategic interests to allow the more skilled fighters, or their employers, to escape/establish justice in this fashion?) It is also worth mentioning possible legal rights to hunt minority groups or to murder the bourgeoisie and other enemies of the revolution under communist and fascist legal systems. Additionally, in his *Politics*, Aristotle mentions the law of a society wherein a man was forbidden to wear a real belt, rather than a halter, until he had killed an enemy.[45] Today, we might say that you only earned the right to wear a belt by committing murder or homicide in combat.

This is not to say that such rights fail to protect or advance any interests. A theory could even insist that such rights *do* advance their holders' wellbeing. However, it would be incongruous with the dominant values of this epoch, with most (if not all) contemporary Western normative theories of law, and with those (stated) values of any Interest theorist of the last two centuries.

Stripped of any credible delimitations of (i) interests and (ii) a particular form of interest-right connection (i.e., grounding, advancing, protecting, etc.), we are left with a version of IT that is no real rival to WT:[46] *qua* theory, it provides no reason to believe that rights serve some unique ultimate purpose.[47] An *Interests-Simpliciter* version of IT holds the following:

I-S IT: A right is invariably related to an interest. Any right is either grounded in an interest, protects it, effectuates it, and/or advances it. Additionally, a right is connected to that interest either by design or by accident. The interest may be important, trivial, or even counter-productive to its holder's (or a class of persons or beings to which the holder belongs) aims and ends.

[44] As mentioned in Chapter 2 notes 44–5 and the accompanying text, whilst Kramer (a Hohfeldian) deems 'rights of action' to be powers, Hohfeld himself posits that they are, or include, claims.

[45] Aristotle (*Politics*: 1324b: 15–17). On 'hunting minorities' rights, see *infra* note 63.

[46] Cf. Simmonds (1998: 201–2, 222–3). This is also why Wenar's 2013 Kind-Desire theory is not on par with IT, but a mere version of it. 'Desire' would only be at 'the same conceptual space' as interests, as he claims (Wenar (2013: 225)), if IT's interests were actually delimited in some fashion, e.g., to wellbeing.

[47] This is not to insist that rights in fact have one. It is simply to note that almost all theorists (save Wenar) insist that they do.

Furthermore, Interest theorists present purported cases of rights lacking (one or more) enforcement mechanisms in order to falsify WT. However, we do not need a *theory* of this sort to do that. In other words, rights theories are not needed to advance or resolve the (older) debate about whether rights are perforce enforceable.

B. Cannot Adequately Distinguish Rights

IT's second major defect is that its putative necessary conditions for the concept do not help distinguish rights from other normative positions or certain other usual suspects of the normative world, e.g., rules, standards, principles, liabilities, etc.; for these others may be predicated upon, advance, protect, or fulfil interests too. IT may not even be able to help to sufficiently distinguish rights from 'absolute' duties: ones not grounded in, or correlated to, rights.

C. Interests Versus Normative Positions

Certain versions of IT, particularly justificatory ones, bear a third idiosyncratic defect: insufficiently accounting for (i) again, the relationship between interests and rights[48] and (ii) rights *qua* normative positions. As suggested above, legal rights need not be predicated upon genuine or weighty interests. Moreover, although aware that officials may misrepresent the real reasons for codifying a right or err in constructing it, some Interest theorists tend to ignore a distinction raised by Roscoe Pound generations ago: there is a difference between the legally codified right and the interest it is (purportedly) predicated upon.[49] Furthermore, in response to Wesley Hohfeld's deeming 'a claim' to be the '*stricto sensu*' case of a right, Pound asserts that '[i]f we define [a right] in terms of claim, we put in the foreground the idea of interest, whereas we are defining something conferred by law to make the interest effective'.[50]

Again, even though a given interest might catalyse the construction process for a legal right, it might not be the same interest the position actually protects. Additionally, legal officials could *claim* to create a right

[48] For different arguments to this effect, see Rainbolt (2006: 88–99).

[49] See Pound (1959: 67–8) for differences between predicate interests and the 'legally delimited and secured' ones that form part of legal rights as normative constructs. (Pound nonetheless deems it to be a virtue of Jhering's account to be able to distinguish the two interests. Ibid 62, 67). See also Hohfeld (1917: 726 n.34) on interests versus a legal relation that protects them.

[50] Pound (1959: 70).

that protects interest *X* but instead intentionally posit one either that does not do the work, or is entirely useless. (Here, one could resort to *Interest-Simpliciter* IT and go fishing for some interest or other that the right might accidentally advance.)

For another thing, whilst Pound's assertion about 'a claim' may be disputed, a (purported) predicate interest does differ from understanding the features of a right *qua* normative position, entitlement, normative advantage, etc. By construing rights to be interests (or interests-reasons), some versions of IT, but not all, cannot adequately account for this aspect of A RIGHT.

Although WT's redundancy arguments (discussed in Chapter 5) incorrectly charge IT with reducing rights to duties, certain versions of IT may nonetheless be said to wrongly reduce rights to interests and/or reasons. Here is why. Some Interest theorists might simply deny that rights have a unique job to do despite bearing an ultimate purpose. Raz seems to advance this view. Whilst he thinks WT's redundancy charge (of rights to duties) is a genuine problem,[51] by ascribing to rights a justificatory role (vis-à-vis other normative positions) he seems to do a better job than most other Interest theorists in trying to overcome it.

Recall that Raz believes rights to be the grounds of some duties, and thus be justificationally prior to them. Margaret Holmgren nevertheless demonstrates why rights are not actually prior in this way within Raz's own account.[52] On Raz's view, in order for a candidate interest to be deemed sufficiently weighty to generate a legal right, potential duty-bearers must also be determinable within the first step of the (legal officials') deliberative process.[53] As such, his IT is really about the justificational priority of *interests* to both rights and duties.[54] Hence, my strong interest

[51] Raz (1996: 269).

[52] Holmgren (1985).

[53] Raz (1996: 35); Raz (1986: 169, 183–4). Raz posits a two-stage analysis. Stage 1: Determine whether certain interests ground a right. A duty analysis figures in here too, though, in determining whether there *could even be* someone on whom a duty might be imposed. Without that possibility, no right can obtain. In other words, if there cannot even be a *potential* duty-bearer, then there cannot be a right either. Stage 2: Analyse whether the right grounds duties. When assessing whether an interest grounds a right, examine both the interests of the potential right-holder (and perhaps other parties), and those of potential duty-bearers to see if the would-be holder's concerns *outweigh* the potential burden that would be imposed on others. Raz (1996: 35–); Raz (1986: 171–2, 181–4).

[54] Cf. Simmonds (1998: 196): Raz's and other versions of IT conflate interests and rights. But see Kramer (1998: 44).

(perhaps buttressed by others') is a reason both for me to have a right *and* for you to have a correlative duty.[55] What is the difference between a right and an interest, then? What distinct work does A RIGHT do? Raz says we start with the original interest, which then justifies a right—a distinct, additional interest—that in turn justifies imposing a duty on someone.

Raz's IT may therefore be said to be vulnerable to the charge of reducing A RIGHT to AN INTEREST. He would nonetheless insist that rights are something more than the predicate interests: they are additional, independent *reasons*.[56] However, he fails to demonstrate a real difference in kind. Are rights *weighty* interests? Not necessarily.[57] Might rights involve morally or politically significant interests? Sometimes. Interests that are also reasons? Sure. But interests all the same.[58]

However, explaining rights wholly in terms of interests and/or reasons is problematic. Each is an inadequate *explanans*, because interests and reasons miss the fact that rights are (also) *entitlements* and *normative positions*, and not simply the grounds for other normative positions such as duties, liberties, powers, etc., or motivations for others to fulfil their duties.

[55] Neil MacCormick agrees that the redundancy argument is a problem for versions of IT that utilise existential correlativity. He tries to overcome it by holding that rights are logically and sometimes *temporally* prior to duties, thereby rejecting both the *symmetrical view* of correlativity *and* the necessity of existential correlativity. For him, rights ground duties and can obtain without any correlatives. His examples, and criticisms of the *symmetrical view*, are addressed in Chapter 3 § II.2.

[56] Raz (1996: 46).

[57] Raz (1986: 186). The same legal positivistic stripping of delimitations (of IT qualifications regarding which interests may ground rights) applies when interests are discussed in terms of reasons too.

[58] Further distinguishing between interests and reasons will not help here because a-right-as-a-reason could equally be said to be 'reducible' to a-duty-as-a-reason. One might object that the former does not include an exclusionary quality, per Raz's conception of A DUTY. (See Raz (1999)). The right-holder, in other words, need not exclude anything from his or her own deliberations. However, a right is not actually a reason *for* the right-holder on Raz's account: it too is a reason for another person to act or forbear. See also McBride (2018).

Space does not allow for a full-blown discussion of Raz's conception of A DUTY. Many scholars have questioned the idea of exclusionary reasons as such. I wish only to add that, if one simply cannot practically determine the true scope of the exclusion, i.e., what must be (and what need not be) excluded from consideration, then this undermines the idea of the duty in question even being an exclusionary one. If ascertaining the proper scope of exclusion is a problem for all duties, then this also calls into question Raz's very conception.

§ III. Shared Problems

Chapter 5 § IV and this chapter's Section II argued that most of the standard debate charges are inaccurate and that each theory's serious idiosyncratic faults lie elsewhere. This section will now argue that (1) the theories suffer from common defects and (2) the very theoretical enterprise is not worthwhile. For one thing, any such right theory's criteria are suspect. Undertaking repair work, or constructing alternatives, is unmotivated because the very construction process for criteria of this sort is somewhat arbitrary. For another, other kinds of accounts of rights, and legal theories, render such theories of rights unnecessary anyway.

§ III.1. Questionable Criteria

Rights theorists generally fail to establish, let alone justify, (i) the *selection criteria* for their theoretical criteria for A RIGHT and (ii) how they fix the content for each criterion. Subjecting the theories to greater scrutiny is long overdue. How were the criteria devised? On what grounds were certain features added whilst other candidates were rejected? Why *must* rights protect or effectuate just one thing?[59] Why do particular normative positions, which seem fully capable of effectuating or protecting their holders' interests or wills, not count as rights under certain versions of each theory's respective criteria? For WT, why must an RCTD be protected by (some variable number of) enforcement powers? Why must a right typically protect the will via personal control mechanisms, why are there exceptions to this rule, and why should such cases count as mere 'exceptions' to that rule?

In the last couple of decades, certain scholars have presented more expansive versions of both theories (or, 'hypothetical' versions thereof) that account for more kinds of rights than just RCTDs.[60] Still, most

[59] Wenar's Several Functions theory was a step in the right direction against this feature of rights theories. However, it did not go far enough, and its own candidate features (or, at least the latter three) can all be explained in terms of interest protection/effectuation. See Chapter 5 § V.

[60] Here are some examples. At least in 1994 Hillel Steiner considered rights to be Hohfeldian claims *or* immunities protected by enforcement and waiver powers. Steiner (1994: 61). (He also believed the theories of rights debate to just be about whether rights are perforce enforceable. Ibid 57–8.) Again, whilst Wellman allows for different kinds of right complexes (with various Hohfeldian positions serving at their fixed cores), he nonetheless believes that every complex contains an enforcement power and liberty. Chapter 2 notes

versions of WT delimit will vindication to enforcement mechanisms: means by which to try to remedy or vindicate a right. Enforcement *powers*, especially.[61] However, those sorts of powers do not exhaust the ways by which rights can be exercised or enforced, let alone constitute the full set of means by which rights can vindicate the will. Why, then, restrict consideration to just them? As examples, the powers used to create, modify, and terminate rights (e.g., to buy property, or for entering and ending contracts) seem no less utile than those concerning enforcement for the purposes of will effectuation. All versions of WT lack adequate accounts of will vindication to justify limiting their concern to rights enforcement as opposed to considering rights exercise more generally.[62]

60–77 and the accompanying text. George Rainbolt's Justified [Normative] Constraint theory considers rights to be claims, immunities, and complexes. To count as a right, though, a complex must contain either a claim or an immunity (or both). However, singular powers or liberties do not count as rights on their own. Rainbolt (2006: xi–xii, 30–9).

Rowan Cruft and Wenar also suggest the possibility of more expansive versions of IT and WT, in addition to other hypothetical theories that no one actually endorses, i.e., 'Normative-constraint[-sans-justification]' and 'Any Incident' theories. Cruft (2004); Wenar (2005). (On the last, see Chapter 5 note 56). Wenar's Kind-Desire theory of RCTDs holds that they are necessarily enforceable. (Wenar (2013: 218–9). He also suggests that such powers need not be held by the right-holder personally, but leaves it unclear whether the RCTD plus powers nevertheless form a complex, with its various components being held by different agents. Ibid 226. (Cf. Wenar (2005: 239–40), which suggests that they do not.) Cruft's expansive WT, which he does not personally endorse, treats normative positions other than RCTDs as kinds of rights, but maintains that each must be accompanied by enforcement powers. Cruft (2004: 367–8). Further, Cruft's Interest-theory-with-exceptions can cover instances of all four basic Hohfeldian kinds of rights. (Hence, only this version of IT could cover the idea of rights exercise beyond rights enforcement.) Strangely, though, Cruft's version of IT also seems to posit that rights perforce come with a claim for an apology or recompense upon violation in some form or other. Cruft (2004: 381, 387–8); (Cf. ibid 360 n.25). Kramer entertains the idea of a more expansive version of his IT but still rejects it. Kramer (2017: 49).

[61] Hart and Simmonds are important exceptions. Again, see Hart (1982: 188) on legal liberty-rights and power-rights, but ibid 183–4, 188 on private law (and certain other legal) RCTDs *being* enforcement powers plus liberties to exercise them. Simmonds allows for singular Hohfeldian liberties, claims, powers, and immunities to count as rights, but interprets a claim *to be* an enforcement power. Simmonds (1998: 218–25).

[62] WT's various ways of fleshing out of a right's putative ultimate purpose in terms of protecting the will and affording control, e.g., of a private law right-holder being rendered a 'small-scale sovereign' or 'private legislator', of having 'dominion' status, etc., are also woefully underdeveloped. E.g., Hart (1982: 183); Hart (1994: 41); Wellman (1985: 95–6). (This may be especially problematic for those versions which advance liberty-rights/liberties *qua* kind of rights.)

In turn, IT's ideas that rights *must* protect or advance some notion of wellbeing, interests that are typically beneficial for a class of beings, or some other subset of interests has already been put into doubt. What, therefore, would justify its proponents deeming it to be a *conceptual* impossibility for legal systems to contain sets of evil rights, entitling their holders to (do) horrible things?[63] Even in the face of trivial and corrupt legal rights, how can such an assertion be maintained? Why cannot there also be certain sets of rights designed to run contrary to their holders' (or the class of beings to which the holders belong) best interests? (Utilising the—albeit questionable—critical/positive morality distinction,[64] why believe this to be impossible for any given society's positive moral rights, or for a given institution's rights, etc.) Why, moreover, do unenforceable rights not simply count as defective cases? Aside from those who explicitly argue in favour of restricting the term 'a right' to RCTDs, why do some Interest theorists exclude normative powers and immunities, which could be said to 'justify' others bearing Hohfeldian liabilities and disabilities?

Now, Interest theorists may complain here that the debate's enforcement-centricity is not their fault and insist that they are simply responding to WT's claims about enforcement mechanisms being essential to A RIGHT. This defence is unsatisfactory because many versions of IT present or adopt monistic rights models. These versions have equally helped to cabin both (i) the debate and (ii) potential explanations of the relationship between rights and interests, e.g., by excluding liberties, powers, and immunities from counting as types of rights and appreciating how those positions, *qua* rights, can advance or protect interests.[65] Hence, IT

[63] Normative Will theorists Judith Thomson and Pavlos Eleftheriadis claim that immoral legal rights in wicked legal systems (a right to hunt certain minority groups, say) are not 'real' rights in some sense. Thomson (1990: 74–5); Eleftheriadis (2008: viii). Officials, they believe, cannot change the meaning, or the conceptual features, of a legal right simply by fiat, by creating immoral rights. This, Eleftheriadis further insists, cannot be done because it betrays the 'ordinary' sense of the term '[a] right'. Eleftheriadis (2008: viii). *Pace* both theorists, it simply begs the question that the concept(s) cannot already accommodate these sorts of cases. Being morally disgusted by such examples and stipulating that 'real' rights necessarily contain moral content, moreover, is insufficient reason to believe that all rights do and must.

[64] On the critical/positive morality distinction, see Chapter 1 note 20.

[65] See Chapter 2 § III against monistic modelling. Rainbolt, Cruft, and Wenar present certain theories that treat positions other than just RCTDs as rights. Their own theories, which Chapter 5 showed to be mere versions of IT, fail to exculpate it here because: Wenar's *kind-desire* RCTDs are held to be perforce enforceable (*supra* note 60); Cruft seems to think

equally neglects alternative means for vindicating rights other than via enforcement powers.

Again, theorists generally fail to establish, let alone justify, (i) their *selection criteria* for what ought to form part of the criteria for A RIGHT (i.e., what makes them the necessary, and, if offered, sufficient conditions in the first place) or (ii) how they fix the content for each criterion. One tends to just get expressions of theorists' intuitions.[66] Without credible methods (and accounts of those methods), however, the theories' respective criteria for the concept are unjustified and unmotivated. This is so even for normative versions. (There are nonetheless reasons to doubt that the theories' rivalrous criteria are significantly marred by political prejudices.[67])

Furthermore, both theories also fail to address plausible additional criteria for A RIGHT. For example, rights are also sometimes said to possess the qualities of weight, (peremptory) force, or trumping power. The absence of any of these latter—purported—features of rights from the theoretical criteria, or at least reasons for their exclusion, is somewhat surprising, given certain theorists' discussions of them.[68]

that rights also necessarily include claims for apology or recompense (*supra* note 60); and Rainbolt needlessly excludes the possibility of rights which do not constrain others (see Chapter 5 notes 165–8 and the accompanying text).

[66] See, e.g., Chapter 5 note 186 and the accompanying text on WT being predicated upon a conceptual archetype of rights (one that is not held by Will theorists exclusively) as utilisable tools, which is or need not be morally or politically evaluative in origin or nature either.

[67] Wenar claims that many scholars put forward their theories, not as efforts in conceptual analysis, but as a 'prelude to advancing a substantive theory of what rights there really are'. Wenar (2008: 270–1). By this he means a (crypto-) moral or political account. Ibid; Wenar (2005: 224). In 2005 he explicitly framed the division as being between Kantianism and Welfarism. Wenar (2005: 250–1). Per his 2008 examples, though, Wenar also seems to suggest that perfectionist liberals and the political left support IT, whilst other liberals and libertarians support WT. Wenar (2008: 270–1).

There are good reasons to doubt this. For example, if the libertarian Robert Nozick's conception of A RIGHT is really just a side constraint on other people, then enforcement mechanisms are not integral to it. Nozick (1974: 29); Flikschuh (2007: 69). But see Mack (2018). Cf. Hart on public welfare rights, which, although enforceable, extend beyond the scope of his (mostly private law) WT. Hart (1982: 185). Consider further John Finnis' IT. (Finnis 2011). For additional reasons to be sceptical that subscription and promotion of one theory or the other must be due to moral or political reasons/impulses, see Chapter 5 § VI.

[68] Raz and Simmonds, an Interest and Will theorist respectively, insist that rights do possess peremptory force, but neither sufficiently accounts for it in their (rivalrous) criteria for A RIGHT. See Raz (1986: 192, 249–50); Simmonds (1998: 114, 176, 200–5, 214–6, 225); Simmonds (2013). Simmonds also argues that Raz cannot actually account for this (putative)

Another often ignored, or at least under-analysed, candidate criterion is this: rights as entitlements. Rights scholars (not just rights theorists) do not really analyse or explain AN ENTITLEMENT. Even so, some baldly insist that it is the key to understanding A RIGHT. For example, HJ McCloskey suggests that rights are best explained, positively, as entitlements to do, have, enjoy, or have done, rather than negatively as something against others, or as something one ought to have.[69] Others, by contrast, think the notion is too 'thin' or 'imprecise' to serve as a/the criterion for A RIGHT,[70] or that it provides no deeper explanation of the concept *qua explanans*.[71] They also disagree about what counts as types of entitlements and about the relationship of rights to entitlements. (Are all entitlements rights, or only some, and on what bases is this to be established?[72]) Until a better account of AN ENTITLEMENT is worked out, its potential *qua* candidate part of the criteria for A RIGHT therefore cannot be assumed. On the other hand, the inclusion or exclusion of weight, force, trumping power, or being an entitlement would have to be in accordance with credible, forthright selection criteria for the theoretical criteria, which do not exist.

Whilst one might deem these to be surmountable difficulties, repairing the theories or constructing alternatives remains unmotivated because there is no reason to even believe that all (specified) rights *must* meet this sort of criteria. Rather than simply questioning the very idea of credibly identifying a normative concept's essential features,[73] it suffices here just to note that both analytic and normative versions' criteria are methodologically suspect. First, the idea that all rights, or even just some designated subset of a kind-of-a-right and/or a right within one normative domain, necessarily bear some singular, non-trivial, ultimate purpose is under-motivated. Theorists offer no good reason to believe that rights

feature. I would add that, at best, Razian *duties* could account for it, but these do not mirror Razian *rights* in structure.

[69] E.g., McCloskey (1976: 99).

[70] E.g., Lindahl (2001: 162–3).

[71] E.g., Bayles (1992: 141–2).

[72] E.g., Chapter 2 § III on Kenneth Campbell's entitlements/capacities distinction.

[73] As mentioned in Chapter 1 § V, scholars lack a shared paradigm within and by which to weigh their rights theories' respective faults and virtues. For example, many theorists remain stalwart in the face of putative counterexamples—which they nonetheless believe count as genuine cases of rights. Moreover, legal philosophers tend to appeal in vain to metatheoretical desiderata (consilience, extensional adequacy, etc.) as tools for assessing and comparing legal theories, as they lack common grounds and metrics by which to quantify and weigh such factors.

must have one, and there probably is not just one.[74] So too, a criterion specifying a mode of protecting, justifying, etc.: there is no reason to believe that all (designated) rights perforce *must* do only one of these sorts of things.[75] As such, there is little reason to put faith in theoretical criteria of this sort.

§ III.2. Superfluous Theories

Here are two more bases for thinking that rights theories are unnecessary and that their debate ought to be abandoned. First, there are both *Hohfeldian* Interest and Will theorists. (Indeed, there are both normative and analytic Hohfeldian rights theorists.) They all agree that Hohfeld's *schema* identifies what lawyers, judges, and others call (and what legal sources style as) 'rights'. Still, they insist that their theoretical criteria are indispensable for determining which (tokens of which) types of normative positions within the *schema of jural relations* really count as rights.

On the contrary, rights theories are superfluous supplements to, and restrictions upon, the *schema*. Their criteria are complicated stipulations about which of the model's normative positions count as rights, on grounds that depart from why these rights theorists came to adhere to it in the first place. How, though, was Hohfeld able to construct a model, one many (but not all) rights theorists believe to be basically sound, *without* relying on any rights theory's criteria? Is it a mere coincidence? Did he stumble upon the appropriate conceptions?[76]

[74] Or three, or six, depending on how one interprets Wenar's Several Functions theory, other than all of the functions ultimately just being explainable in terms of interest protection and advancement.

[75] As an example of a right that does not *justify* the imposition of any normative positions upon other parties, consider once again the right-of-way when two vehicles arrive at a traffic intersection at the same time (discussed in Chapter 3 § II.3). The first driver's right is not a reason for the other driver's duty to wait. That right adds no further justification for the imposition of legal positions; it is not an 'intermediate conclusion' between the interest in having a functioning, safe coordination system and drivers bearing such duties in the appropriate circumstances.

[76] Actually, the *schema* is largely unoriginal. Even so, Hohfeld's jurisprudential predecessors did not rely on a rights theory's criteria in order to construct their models either. See Chapter 2; Pound (1915); Frydrych (2018a).

No. Rights modellers can look at legal and moral sources and discourses to decide whether the term 'a right' is used equivocally (e.g., compare '*A*'s right to do φ' with '*A*'s right that *B* must φ for *C*') and if the different meanings concern different concepts. Modellers can then make practical judgments and stipulations about those concepts (e.g., distinguishing between an RCTD, a liberty, a power, etc.) and about how they connect to one another (if at all) and to other sorts of normative positions, e.g., in terms of correlativity, logical contradictoriness, etc.

As the process involves making practical judgments, modellers need not try to justify their accounts via comprehensive inquiries into all possible data sets—even if they must be receptive to empirically driven critiques. Additionally, they need neither posit some *ultimate* purpose that all rights must serve, nor provide other candidate necessary conditions for their conceptions (which are then to be tested against actual and hypothetical cases—a method that both analytic and normative rights theorists employ). Hohfeld never did so.[77]

Of course, Hohfeld's popularity with many rights theorists is no proof of the *schema*'s soundness. For example, you might believe that A CLAIM cannot accommodate the idea of rights being reasons (of varying weight) that can ground duties and other normative positions.[78] Even if it could not,[79] you still do not need a *theory* of rights to advance that view. Take Raz's overall account of A RIGHT. It ostensibly holds that rights perforce justify others' bearing duties that advance right-holders' (beings of ultimate value or corporations) wellbeing.[80] The 'theory' portion of his account could be excised, leaving a model according to which a right is often or generally a reason (good, bad, weighty, trivial) that has been

[77] Hohfeld also showed that rights modelling need not be normative—again, in the sense of being morally or politically evaluative. For example, endorsing or rejecting the distinction between A CLAIM and AN IMMUNITY need not be based on moral or political judgments. Consider also the following once more: no one seems to believe that the debate over whether A DUTY (simply) involves weighty reasons or (also) exclusionary ones is *necessarily* a moral or political dispute.

[78] See MS Green (2007).

[79] Kramer (1998: 45–9) nevertheless shows that Hohfeld's and Raz's conceptions could be rendered compatible. One could also tack on to Hohfeld's *schema* the idea of rights generally being predicated upon interests of any sort without thereby creating a cognate Hohfeldian rights *theory*. Cf. Hohfeld (1917: 725–6 n.34).

[80] Raz (1986: 166).

deemed (by officials, by a community, etc.), or presented as being, sufficiently weighty to justify imposing normative positions on others and/or creating new derivative rights. This need not constitute a necessary condition, let alone one characterised as fulfilling a singular ultimate purpose. Further, even if you reject all existing rights models, you could create a new one without relying on 'theoretical' criteria to do so. There are more credible alternative methods.[81] Hence, rights theories are, at best, superfluous additions to rights models, for understanding A RIGHT.[82]

Second, as shown in Section II, Legal Positivists (should) find it difficult sticking to a rights theory's criteria. Indeed, for Positivist rights theorists, it is both problematic and unwarranted for them to make claims about A RIGHT's necessary features (not just the sufficient ones) that can run contrary to their positivistic commitments.[83]

Consider first Positivist Interest theorists. How can they claim to delimit the relevant interests to those concerning wellbeing, or those which are 'typically' or 'standardly' beneficial for a certain class of being or entity, and deem these to be essential to A LEGAL RIGHT?[84] If a legal system's rule of recognition identifies as valid certain rights that do not meet such criteria (especially ones attributed to *sui juris* persons), Positivists

[81] Cf. Halpin (2017: 21–3). Halpin's sound critique nonetheless misses the fact that some rights theorists deny that all tokens of each Hohfeldian type, let alone certain types, count as rights, and believe their theories to be the indispensable bases by which to make such determinations.

[82] Some theorists insist that Hohfeld alone cannot explain the direction of duties that correlate with rights. A rights theory, they believe, must do that job. E.g., Finnis (2011: 202–5); Simmonds (1998: 222); Sreenivasan (2005: 322). It doubtful, however, whether Hohfeld would have considered this to be a genuine problem. For one thing, his 'passive' conception of an RCTD correlates with a duty by design. He also insists that there are no necessary or logical connections between any of the *non-correlating* normative positions (e.g., claims to powers, duties to powers, duties to liabilities, etc.). Hohfeld (1913a); Hohfeld (1917); Frydrych (2021). Why, then, should rights theorists problematise this, unless they either just disagree (in part) with Hohfeld or wish to modify the *schema* to suit their own ends?

[83] See Frydrych (2016: 182–3); Frydrych (2017b: 204–5).

[84] An Inclusive Legal Positivist, Kramer suggests that a moral judgment about demarcating the set of proper kinds of right-holders must be made before IT can be applied. Kramer (2010: 35). Even if a Legal Positivist believes that an account of right-*holders* should be so constrained, why believe that this has any effect on which legal *rights* may be granted by a legal system—especially vis-a-vis certain rights granted or denied to *sui juris* humans? How does, or could, this affect which legal rights a right-holder may possess? (Why, additionally, must a 'genuine' RCTD be protected by immunities from nullification?). See Kramer (2013: 247); Kramer & Steiner (2007: 297).

should consider them to be genuine cases *and* counterexamples to IT (rather than as constituting pseudo-rights for failing to meet the rights theory's criteria). Once again, Kramer's argument against Raz's view that law necessarily claims legitimate authority[85] applies equally to legal rights: a wicked legal system's officials need not even pretend that all of the system's rights are typically beneficial, advance wellbeing, etc., and nor must the rights be so in order to count as genuine, valid cases.[86]

For Positivist Will theorists, would even hypothetical cases of wholly unenforceable rights fail to establish that A LEGAL RIGHT does not perforce afford control, dominion, or private legislator status? For example, if officials can recognise unenforceable legal rights (albeit not via dispute resolution processes triggered by a right-holder or guardian's enforcement powers) as being valid per their rule of recognition, why would they fail to count as bona fide instances within the legal system?[87]

Rights theorists might object that officials' merely positing of certain laws creating (aberrantly, putatively) what they *claim* to be bona fide rights cannot thereby change the very concept, A LEGAL RIGHT. They could also insist that their theories merely offer 'conceptual clarifications': although beholden to empirical evidence to some extent, these are 'correctives' to the messiness of rights discourse and practices and are therefore not subject to empirical falsification.

These objections miss the point. A conceptual clarification is beholden to the real world. You cannot insulate the *explanans* from the *explananda*.

[85] *Supra* note 37. Raz would need to abandon his Modalism in order to distinguish legal and moral rights, e.g., whereby moral rights are grounded in aspects of their holders' wellbeing, whilst legal rights need only be treated by officials as if they are. (Doing so would also lead to an *Interests-Simpliciter* IT for legal rights, if not also positive morality). Raz nonetheless reaffirmed (what I style) his Modalist stance to your author. Personal conversation with Joseph Raz, NYU School of Law, November 1, 2018).

[86] The same could be said for all of the moral rights of a given society's positive morality, even if its members do not believe or recognise this.

[87] Whilst rights theories need not provide A RIGHT's sufficient conditions, some Will theorists might claim to be able to bypass a charge of providing inaccurate ones or others that are incongruous with Legal Positivism. For once you have identified an enforcement and/or waiver power, then you have also found a bona fide right. In response, even on certain versions of WT, not all such power-holders or wielders are actually right-holders: some hold such powers on behalf of RCTD-holders. If Will theorists respond that one need only take the further step of discerning who the power-holders are acting on behalf of in order to find the relevant right, then they need only be reminded that certain powers can be exercised without any cognate RCTDs.

Even if they are in part correctives (and there are credible bases to doubt they are 'correcting' using reliable techniques), it is simply untrue that rights theories are immune from empirical falsification. On the contrary, actual and hypothetical cases *qua* counterexamples provide grounds for deeming a theory's criteria to be erroneous.[88] Indeed, an abundance of counterexamples affords one (1) grounds to deem an account of the concept suspect and (2) a basis for seeking a superior alternative available on the jurisprudential marketplace. If rights theories were otherwise immune from this sort of scrutiny, then there would probably be no reason for anyone to lend credence to them.[89]

Furthermore, a demand for methodological consistency across one's theories of LAW and A RIGHT should lead to scepticism about all such rights theories. This has already been shown for Legal Positivist rights theorists. The same may also be said for 'Normativist' theorists of LAW.[90] For Natural lawyers who profess to rely upon the central case method,[91] why utilise the central/peripheral distinction when it comes to LAW, but then present or assume necessary conditions, particularly of the demanding sort provided by these rights theories, when it comes to A RIGHT? (Even if one believes that *some* features of a central case can also be characterised as necessary ones, it does not follow that all are. Moreover, credible bases would be needed for determining which rights really constitute the paradigmatic ones, so that their features (ones which might not be exhibited in rival candidate paradigms) are reflective of the entire concept.)

[88] See Chapter 5 note 102. Now, you may very well harbour doubts about the activity of presenting singular counterexamples to serve as first-order logic counterexamples deemed sufficient to falsify a claim of something's constituting a putative necessary feature of a concept. Even if you do, those doubts should be channelled appropriately; namely, scepticism about such methods should lead one to be dubious of the very enterprise of constructing rights theories of this sort—including normative versions.

[89] Hamish Stewart believes that, whilst normative rights theories are fine, analytic versions are flawed, crypto-normative accounts. (He also thinks the latter are incapable of meeting two putatively conflicting metatheoretical desiderata. However, only a handful of rights theorists actually appeal to both, let alone deem them to be indispensable standards). Hence, analytic scholars should just 'retreat' to Hohfeld's claim. Stewart (2012: 320). Chapter 5 § VI showed that his reasons for thinking thus about analytic versions are nevertheless erroneous. More importantly, he does not see that *both* analytic and normative versions offer unnecessary criteria and that the entire debate ought to be abandoned.

[90] See Chapter 1 § IV on 'Normativist' theories of law, i.e., Natural Law and Interpretivism.

[91] See Chapter 1 § IV on the central case method. The selection criteria for what counts as a 'central' case is insufficiently discussed in legal philosophy, if not also elsewhere.

Take John Finnis' IT as an example. A Hohfeldian Interest theorist and Natural Lawyer, he advances a teleological view of law. Sound legal theorisation, he furthermore believes, utilises the perspective of the *central* case of the internal point of view: that of the *spoudaios*.[92] Moreover, a rights theory is needed to explain what it is to have a right and what all the Hohfeldian types of a right have in common.[93]

Even so, as mentioned in Chapter 1 § IV, Finnis neither employs the stated methodological approach, nor the central case method generally, when either endorsing and utilising Hohfeld's *schema* wholesale, or when presenting his IT.[94] It is also difficult to square his claim about the need for a rights theory with his avowed methodological stances. Laying down such criteria for A RIGHT does not seem to be integral to the latter methodology, e.g., for both putative central and peripheral cases of rights, if it is not simply outright inconsistent with it.

Imagine, then, that both analytic and normative rights theories were radically transformed by abandoning their theoretical criteria and switching to the central case method sans necessary conditions. Even then, the

[92] Finnis (2011: 14–9). What is often missed in discussion of Finnis' work is that, not only is this standard meant to affect which data is collected and a theory's overall shape, but also the very concept *formation* process. Ibid 12, 16, 17–8.

[93] Finnis (2011: 202–3, 465 n.35).

[94] Ibid 198–205. Finnis seems to equate the basic needs underpinning certain constitutional and human rights with 'basic aspects of human flourishing'. Ibid 205. He nonetheless believes it is unnecessary to settle the theories of rights debate 'as regards strictly legal rights', seemingly just because Hart's WT does not claim comprehensive coverage over the set of all legal rights. Ibid. He therefore states:

> It suffices that, for the less restricted purposes of this chapter, we may safely speak of rights wherever a basic principle or requirement of practical reasonableness, or a rule derived therefrom, gives to A, and to each and every other member of a class to which A belongs, the benefit of (i) a positive or negative requirement (obligation) imposed upon B (including, inter alia, any requirement not to interfere with A's activity or with A's enjoyment of some other form of good), or (ii) the ability to bring it about that B is subject to such a requirement, or (iii) the immunity from being subjected by B to any such requirement.

Ibid. See also ibid 227.

As noted in Chapter 5 note 71, as concerns determining the direction of directed duties, Finnis believes that only an additional mere stipulation is required (choosing between one of two options, ones which happen to track the stances of the Interest and Will theories of rights), but without suggesting that one is superior to the other per se and noting that neither will 'always correspond with legal usage'. Ibid 203. See also ibid 227.

theories would likely still suffer comparable difficulties and be subject to doubts about their worth. For example, for pluralist WTs (i.e., those who believe there are more kinds of rights than just RCTDs), why would the rights to buy property and to solicit for contracts (which involve powers) be more or less paradigmatic than the right of a judgment creditor (which is, or includes, an RCTD)? In turn, for IT, why would an unenforceable RCTD count as the paradigm case, rather than just as a peripheral or 'degenerate' one?[95] For *protection* versions of IT, at any rate, surely having both enforcement mechanisms and a correlative duty affixed affords rights more security than does a mere correlative duty alone. Relying on the proposition that the paradigm selection method is wholly normative, moreover, would not render such versions of the theories any less suspect.

§ IV. Conclusion

The theories of rights provide seemingly rivalrous criteria for A RIGHT, or for some subset of rights. This chapter nevertheless argued that the existing theories are irredeemably flawed and that theories of this sort are unnecessary for understanding rights anyway. The dominant existing ones, the Interest and Will theories, contain both significant idiosyncratic and common defects. (Most of the idiosyncratic ones, moreover, differ somewhat from the standard charges levied in the debate literature.)

WT's idiosyncratic defects are these. First, its thesis that rights perforce afford some form of control is untenable. In the least, this is because it cannot adequately explain or justify the distribution of a single right's components amongst different people (e.g., a child's possessing an RCTD, but a legal guardian having the enforcement powers), let alone why such divvying up should constitute an exception to the rule. Secondly, WT cannot explain why some rights have more enforcement powers available to them than others. Thirdly, the theory is subsumable under IT. Fourthly, WT erroneously reduces AN RCTD, if not also A RIGHT, to A POWER.

IT's idiosyncratic failings are in turn these. First, as no version of IT credibly delimits the set of interests, we are left with a (vacuous) *Interests-Simpliciter* version. However, an *Interests-Simpliciter* version is unilluminating—especially in terms of an ultimate purpose all rights serve and as a necessary condition for the concept. An explanation of all rights' ultimate

[95] Raz, for example, suggests that the paradigm cases of legal rights *are* enforceable, and that unenforceable ones are in a sense 'parasitic' upon enforceable ones. Raz (1996: 256).

purpose in terms of interests *of any sort*, where rights either—intentionally or accidentally—protect or advance an interest, or purport to justify others bearing normative positions, is, at best, trivially true. Further, not all legal rights are predicated upon individuals' actual interests or those of some class to which they belong. Even when catalysed by a genuine interest, a posited right might not actually protect or reflect that interest.

Secondly, IT offers unhelpful necessary conditions for A RIGHT, as other sorts of normative concepts may also advance and/or protect interests (and even be the basis for imposing duties on people), e.g., rules, principles, absolute duties, etc. Thirdly, certain versions of IT fail to adequately address: (i) the difference between rights and the interests upon which they are (purportedly) predicated; and (ii) the notions of rights *qua* entitlements and *qua* normative positions. Fourthly, one does not need an entire *theory* to counter the proposition that rights are perforce controllable.

Whilst there are grounds for deeming each theory's respective idiosyncratic flaws to be fatal, this chapter also provided reasons for adjudging *any* rights theory of this sort and so the very debate, to be unnecessary. For one thing, the very bases for constructing such theoretical criteria for A RIGHT are suspect. (The existing criteria are also under-inclusive in terms of: (i) which normative positions count as rights; and (ii) the ways in which a right can protect, vindicate, effectuate, etc., interests or the will.) Lest one be tempted to alleviate these problems by undertaking repair work or constructing new theories, the chapter suggests that, the selection process for theoretical criteria of this sort is both somewhat arbitrary and unmotivated, because there is little reason to believe that all rights do, or must, meet these sort of criteria, e.g., an ultimate purpose with a singular mode of effectuation.[96]

For another thing, rights theorists *themselves* point to (i) non-arbitrary alternatives for understanding rights and (ii) grounds for believing that their own rights theories are incongruous with their overall views about

[96] Further, not all rights 'protect' or 'justify' something. Additionally, IT's and WT's respective specified modes of protecting or justifying rights are posited without sufficient argument, and nor are they necessarily dependent upon their respective candidate ultimate purposes (the will or interests). Moreover, the one (version of the Interest) theory that aimed to provide multiple 'functions' instead of a singular ultimate purpose really just provides candidates that are already covered by rights *models*, rendering the theory superfluous.

law, let alone views about philosophising. In fact, their commitments to other kinds of (1) theories of law and (2) rights models (which can rely on different methodologies for their construction) render these sorts of rights theories superfluous. Although the chapter mostly developed the case in terms of analytic theories about legal rights, the same can be more fully done for normative versions—and for non-legal rights too.[97] It is therefore time to abandon the theories of rights debate. Scholars can look to both ordinary and legal discourses and practices to harvest the relevant data to shape their explanations of rights, without concocting these sorts of 'theoretical' criteria.[98]

One last point. Rights theorists who present domain or kind-of-a-right qualifications might complain of unfair treatment here. Their versions have a more limited aim: not to explain the ultimate purpose of all rights, but rather just that of certain kinds of rights and/or those in certain normative domains. The gripe is unwarranted, as this chapter's criticisms apply equally to those versions. Theirs are equally problematic in terms of whether all such instances really concern interests or the will. Their criteria, moreover, still assert global scope over the specified domains or particular kinds of positions, determining or entailing which instances count as real rights. Some even purport to explain what makes these sorts of normative positions count as rights, despite acknowledging that other kinds of rights obtain. Hence, their theories are under-motivated: why adopt them if we already know that there are other kinds, ones that do not rely on their specified criteria?

[97] For example, White (1984: 11, 13-4) suggests that, as concerning rights about what one is entitled to do or to receive, the theories of rights are inadequate because they cannot cover (putative) rights to be in a certain state, to feel certain things, or to take certain attitudes.

[98] Alternatively, scholars (normative or analytic, Legal Positivist or Normativist) might instead just try using the central case method to compare candidate instances of rights (and avoid levying theoretical criteria of the sort discussed in Chapters 5 and 6). That is, if they can somehow credibly establish which ones count as the paradigm cases. If so, they might, for example, take their paradigms from what ordinary and technical discourse users call 'a right' and then compare the conceptual structures of different instances of rights to those paradigms.

CHAPTER 7

Legal Rights Enforcement

§ I. Introduction

This chapter and its successors demonstrate how the philosophy of rights can proceed perfectly well without relying upon the 'theories' of rights. It addresses the relationship of legal rights-correlative-to-duties ('RCTDs') to legal enforcement powers. There is almost universal agreement that legal rights are typically enforceable.[1] The chapter, however, offers an analytic reconstruction of a stronger view, one which is popular amongst quite a few legal philosophers, lawyers, and laypeople: that legal rights are either perforce, or invariably, enforceable in some way or other. For adherents, the notion of 'a wholly unenforceable, passive legal right' is no real right at all. The reconstruction of this stance shall be called the Control View [hereinafter 'CV'].[2]

[1] Interest theorists agree. They just believe that not all rights need be so, and that enforceability is not a necessary feature of A RIGHT. E.g., Raz (1996: 256–8).

[2] Scholars should find this label congenial, especially as the various enforcement mechanisms are often discussed in the literature in terms of measures of control. (It is, however, under-inclusive: for there are more ways to control rights than just by enforcing or waiving them). Markus Stepanians, however, uses 'Control View' to simply re-label the Will theory of rights. Stepanians (2005: 8). There is merit in this, especially as most contemporary Will theorists no longer hold robust metaphysical views about 'the will'. Again, the most famous twentieth century Will theorist, HLA Hart, was keen to use the word 'control' to explain his view. Indeed, the idea of enforcement powers being 'elements of control' is adopted here from him. Hart (1982: 183–4). Even so, there is greater value in using the label for this

D. Frydrych, *The Architecture of Rights*,
https://doi.org/10.1007/978-3-030-76039-7_7

CV is nonetheless contested—and has been since at least the middle ages.[3] However, whilst largely subsumed under the theories of rights debate for the last hundred years or more, this 'necessarily-enforceable-or-not' dispute need not stand or fall with that 'theoretical' one. (The reconstruction nevertheless includes some Will theorists' views, albeit stripped of their 'theoretical criteria'; for all Will theory ('WT') proponents—would, if aware of it—endorse CV, which is conceptually more basic than their theory.)

This chapter focuses on *legal* RCTDs because legal systems present the clearest examples of enforcement mechanisms: power-based 'elements of control'. Moreover, CV concerns *legal* enforcement mechanisms for legal rights, rather than merely *lawful* and unlawful means of enforcement. Section II explicates the pertinent mechanisms: legal enforcement and waiver powers. (Other modes of 'controlling' legal rights obtain, but they do not concern enforcement per se.)

CV nevertheless admits of variations, some of which will be explained below. The most important differences concern the relationship of RCTDs to powers. Does a legal RCTD necessarily *contain* one or more enforcement powers (Version A), or should it be *identified* with such powers instead (Version B)? Version C posits a different relationship: the invariability of legal rights' enforceability is rather due to (a conceptually necessary feature of) A LEGAL SYSTEM; accordingly, the elements of control can, but need not be, constitutive features of a legal RCTD itself.

Section III then argues that, howsoever construed, CV is erroneous. A legal RCTD could exist without any of these elements of control also obtaining. Whilst many scholars have attempted to show this before, their efforts were either inadequate or question begging. Their arguments, put forward to advance the idea that the relationship between a legal RCTD and enforcement powers is conceptually contingent, all use examples that concern only one or two elements of control. However, showing that a given power is not necessary to A LEGAL RCTD, or is not necessarily available when such a right exists, does not and cannot demonstrate that *other* elements of control fail to obtain as well.

Successfully demonstrating the conceptually contingent nature of the relationship between legal RCTDs and legal enforcement powers is challenging. For legal rights can have 'fuller' or 'lesser' measures of

rational reconstruction, which covers a wider group of scholars and ordinary persons than the Will theory does, and which avoids certain 'theoretical' difficulties in ways that shall be discussed below.

[3] E.g., Tierney (1997: 117–8, 189).

control.[4] A given case may have one, some, or all of the various elements. Moreover, legal rights may have variable sets of such powers.[5] Given their dynamic nature, legal rights may lose or gain some elements of control over time—but never all of them at once (according to CV, at least). Positing that there is no magic number of how many enforcement powers a given legal RCTD must have (other than a floor of one), and that the number of such elements can fluctuate over time and with changing circumstances, renders CV something of a moving target. For adherents need only defend the proposition that a given legal right must bear at least one element of control at any given time, without stipulating which element it must be.

Section III therefore takes a more comprehensive approach. By analysing the power-based elements of control in terms of primary, secondary, and tertiary rights, the aim is to establish the conceptual contingency of any and all legal RCTD and legal enforcement power relationships.[6] An abductive inference can then be made: if all the elements of control are only contingently related to legal RCTDs, then it should be possible to construct legal RCTDs that lack, or are not associated with, any of them.[7]

Nevertheless, even this tack cannot falsify CV completely. For it can undermine Versions A and C, but not Version B, which identifies an RCTD itself as a kind of power. Version C adherents could therefore retreat to a minimalist stance of an RCTD being just one controlling power, absent which, they would insist, there is simply no legal right at all.

In response, we must ask: what is the 'powerless' RCTD, then, if not a right? Even if it is 'defective', why is it not a genuine, valid instance? Further, what term should we use for the impotent entitlement instead of 'a right'? The theories of rights' criteria will not help here. A fuller response to this approach will have to wait till the next chapter. For a CV sceptic can equally ask: what is the point of a right if it cannot be enforced? An answer is that it marks its bearer as being legally entitled to something from

[4] See *infra* § III 'Argument 1' and Appendix 3.

[5] Cf. Simmonds (1998: 229–30).

[6] This chapter is unconcerned with the relative strength or weakness of any given element of control, or combinations thereof. In advancing his WT (which includes a rights model that constitutes an instance of CV), Nigel Simmonds argues that the quantum of control over a right is not strictly determinable by the number of (constitutive) elements alone. Simmonds (1998: 229–30), *quoted in* Chapter 5 note 82 and the accompanying text.

[7] There are several modes of *secondary* rights enforcement (e.g., self-help efforts, commencing litigation, arbitration, or mediation), but perhaps an indefinite number of *quaternary* rights enforcement techniques (e.g., ways to enforce a court order).

someone else. Often being so entitled is advantageous; sometimes it is not. This may be unsatisfying, but nonetheless true.

A question also arises about how valuable abductive inference generatable by the work in Section III might be. Conceptual analysts' claims of being able to present concepts' 'necessary' features has been under considerable attack for some time. The weight one should therefore lend to an analysis predicated upon the existence of first-order logical counterexamples used to cleave off what is 'contingent' from what is 'necessary' to a concept is debatable.

That methodological issue is not as pressing here, though, because the worry about essentialism runs the other way around. Instead of trying to show what is conceptually necessary to either A LEGAL RCTD, or to A LEGAL SYSTEM, the analysis here aims to undermine CV's claims about a necessary relationship between A LEGAL RCTD and legal enforcement powers. Furthermore, the chapter does not rely exclusively on counterexamples; it also requires critiquing certain views about law and the effectiveness of rules and legal positions.

§ II. The Control View

§ II.1. The Elements of Control

CV holds that some or all of the following are either necessarily features of, or essentially tied to, A LEGAL RCTD: powers by which to try to seek a correlative duty's fulfilment, for alleviating that duty, and by which to seek (or forego seeking) the right's vindication in light of the correlative duty's non-fulfilment. Various versions of CV can nevertheless differ over:

1. The total number of elements that must form part of, or be available to, a right;
2. Whether:
   (2a) Passive RCTDs must be included in the tally of total elements; or
   (2b) RCTDs should instead be identified with certain enforcement and waiver powers;
3. If (2a), whether enforcement powers are:
   (3a) constitutive of rights *qua* components of a right complex, or
   (3b) not parts of rights—albeit invariably co-obtaining;
4. Whether it is helpful and important to distinguish between primary, secondary, and tertiary rights; and
5. Whether rights are functional or modal kinds.[8]

[8] On the functional/modal distinction, see Chapter 1 note 28 and the accompanying text.

CV considers the most relevant and typical sorts of control to be capacities by which to enforce and waive rights. (Certain other capacities, such as ones by which to *nullify* a right and its correlative duty, also fall within the set. These are often ignored but are important for flagging a control/enforcement distinction whereby enforcement is but a subset of means of control.) Such capacities are generally understood in terms of legal powers. However, auxiliary liberties and immunities also fall within the set.

Whilst all CV proponents would agree that rights must include, or be associated with, at least one power,[9] they can disagree about how many powers are actually necessary. Here is a brief list of the legal 'elements of control':

I. Powers by which to waive, extinguish, or demand a second party's duty.
II. Powers to initiate institutional dispute resolution processes (litigation, an administrative proceeding, etc.) or to undertake self-help measures.
III. Powers to waive undertaking such processes and to cease prosecuting them once commenced.
IV. Powers to either enforce a prescribed remedy (e.g., a court order) or to waive it;
V. Auxiliary liberties by which to exercise or forego exercising each of the above-listed powers (as opposed to bearing duties proscribing or mandating those powers' usage).
VI. Supporting immunities that protect the above-listed powers from nullification by others.[10]

[9]For examples of minimalist accounts, see, e.g., Simmonds (1998: 115): '[t]he modest version of the Will Theory treats rights as powers of waiver *or* enforcement over legal duties' (emphasis added); Sumner (1987: 43): the 'one indispensable measure of control' is a primary power to self-extinguish both the right and correlative duty, which 'requires no institutional mechanism'.

[10]As mentioned above, versions of CV can posit that the number of elements of control in any given right can vary. Further, the CV list of elements presented here is not necessarily exhaustive. For example, one might believe that there must be immunities protecting the liberties that are required to exercise the powers. Yet those liberties and immunities do not seem to be *invariably* available legal positions—even on a CV account. For example, what if someone contracts with the right-holder so that the latter cannot use such powers? (On the other hand, right-holders may still use those powers with effect, e.g., if the other parties do not raise the matter in court). See Appendix 3 for a more comprehensive list of elements of control.

CV proponents can also disagree about whether the elements of control must form part of the legal right itself, e.g., as part of a complex. This is partly because they can also divide over whether legal rights are, or include, a passive conception of AN RCTD. Again, Version B proponents deny the need for any such passive component because they hold that legal RCTDs are actually powers. Others may instead hold that legal rights are complexes composed of: (component type a) a legal position marking an entitlement to receive a duty from other parties and (component type b) enforcement powers, with supporting liberties and immunities.

§ II.2. CV and the Primary/Secondary/Tertiary Rights Distinction

Chapter 1 § II.1 noted that scholars divide over whether the primary/secondary/tertiary rights distinction (PST distinction): (View 1) correctly notes the existence of distinct normative positions, but mistakenly presents them as being different rights, as they ought to instead be construed as mere components of a singular right complex; or (View 2) incorrectly presents secondary and tertiary enforcement mechanisms as types of rights when they are instead something else, i.e., powers that do not count as rights.

Most CV advocates endorse View 1, but some are amenable to View 2. (View 2 is not bothersome to CV minimalists because, as will be shown below, they believe there is at least one power available for a primary right.) For a full picture of CV's conception of A LEGAL RCTD with all of the attendant elements of control (i.e., the relevant powers, liberties, and immunities), see Appendix 3. Appendix 4 presents CV's variances, e.g., passive RCTDs versus RCTDs-as-powers models, and PST distinction advocates versus the unified-right (complex) alternative.

§ II.3. CV Versus Theories of Rights

Despite reflecting philosophical and jurisprudential stances of great provenance, the need to present an analytic reconstruction of the belief that legal rights are invariably enforceable here is as follows. First, to the extent that people even reflect on such matters, they differ over the relevant number of elements of control. Second, they harbour rivalrous conceptions of some of those elements. For example, is an RCTD a passive position requiring separate ancillary powers to enforce it, or is it instead self-enforcing? Third, the reasons why adherents believe rights to be invariably enforceable requires clarification. For some it is based on their conception of A LEGAL RIGHT; for others it is the very functioning of a legal system, rather than the rights themselves, which explains why rights can invariably be controlled. Fourth, CV is not a 'theory' of rights, in the sense outlined in Chapters 1 and 5. It does not offer that sort of criteria for a concept. CV neither posits nor relies upon an *ultimate* purpose for all rights, e.g., the furtherance or protection of wills or interests. Still, people might be attracted to CV because they believe there is no real 'point' to the idea of an unenforceable right. (One can attribute a 'point' or purpose to rights without it constituting a raison d'être or explanation for all (legal) rights and/or without A RIGHT having a *singular*, *ultimate* explanation.)

CV is nevertheless compatible with the theories of rights. For example, it would be perfectly consistent for Interest theorists to suggest that legal rights are always enforceable, so long as they are understood in terms of the protection or justification of a party's interests or wellbeing, rather than affording control. Indeed, early Interest theorists appear to have held that rights are always enforceable in these ways.[11]

CV can also avoid some of those theories' biggest problems. Particularly important is WT's difficulty in providing a principled explanation for the potential separation and distribution of a right's components (i.e., a passive RCTD from the relevant enforcement and waiver powers) amongst different people, e.g., a legal guardian holding the enforcement powers for a child's right.[12] Being devoid of 'theoretical' commitments about advancing or protecting the will, CV adherents can, by contrast, deem it immaterial whether right-holders or other authorised parties possess the relevant powers. What is important to CV is just that rights be enforceable; it does not matter who does the job so long as *someone* could do so.

Of course, proponents of CV Version B would find the separation of rights possession and the enforcement mechanisms problematic. They identify an RCTD as a kind of power, rather than a complex composed either of (i) a passive position plus powers and liberties by which to exercise the powers, or (ii) powers plus exercising-liberties.[13] For them,[14] if a given right *simply is* a single power (to waive another's duty, say, which does not require an exercising-liberty), then it makes no sense to say that

[11] See, e.g., Chapter 6 note 14 on Jhering's conception.
[12] See Chapter 6 § II.1.
[13] It might here be said that *A* can *wield B*'s right, rather than *possess* it.
[14] E.g., Simmonds (1998: 223).

A can enforce *B*'s right. Generally, though, being free of 'theoretical' commitments to the idea that rights protect or effectuate the holder's will, most CV proponents may have no qualms with the elements of control being distributed amongst different agents—regardless of their independent moral or political assessment of that sort of state of affairs.

Again, the idea that RCTDs are always enforceable need not depend on the idea that they are either in themselves elements of control or necessarily contain the latter as components; enforcement mechanisms can instead be understood as separate but invariably co-obtaining normative positions. For the CV majority, unlike WT, distinguishing between an RCTD and its enforcement mechanisms is unproblematic, regardless of whether the latter are construed as: (a) components of a complex, parts of which can be held by different parties; or (b) simply different normative positions held by different people, which for reasons having to do with the nature of legal systems, invariably co-obtain.[15]

Is CV wholly normative, in the sense of reflecting a moral or political belief or prejudice? Is the idea, moreover, that rights *ought* to be enforceable, or that it is invariably the state's (or some other body's) responsibility to enforce all rights? No. The idea, or 'intuition', is that an unenforceable right is no right at all, and not simply a 'defective' case.[16] Further, despite deeming all legal RCTDs to be enforceable, CV proponents are also free to believe there are good reasons why certain rights ought not to be enforced, e.g., because they are the product of legal corruption, lead to bad social results, etc.

One opposes CV by insisting that there are valid legal rights which are wholly unenforceable. This contrasting view, of course, need not include a judgment that a right's unenforceability is a good or bad thing, or that some or all rights ought (not) be enforced. The dispute is over whether legal rights are all perforce or invariably enforceable in some way or other. Although some philosophers may dislike the very idea of rights, no rights scholar, to the best of my knowledge, takes the stance that rights generally *ought not* to be enforceable, that it would be morally wrong to enforce rights in most or all cases.

[15] See Chapter 1 § II.2 and Chapter 9 § II on perimeters of protection and support respectively.

[16] Cf. Chapter 5 § VI for arguments against analytic versions of WT all simply being crypto-normative accounts. See also Chapter 5 note 186 on a conceptual archetype of rights as invariably utilisable tools.

§ II.4. CV, Rights Enforcement, and Control

Chapter 4 provided a working conception of RIGHTS ENFORCEMENT, whereby it concerns attempts to vindicate a right and/or right-holding status in the face of (threatened) challenge, infringement, or violation, or the capacity to waive such efforts. Some CV advocates would add that there must be liberties by which to exercise or forego exercising enforcement and waiver powers. The liberties *exercise* those powers, whilst the powers *enforce* the RCTD.

I believe this points to a distinction between control and enforcement, whereby the latter merely constitutes a subset of the former. For there are ways to control rights beyond merely enforcing them. Examples are by modifying the right-duty relationship, and by creating additional or supplementary rights and duties.[17] Furthermore, *alienation* (say, of property, through sale, gifting, transfer, etc.) and *nullification* both seem to be ways of controlling rights, but not means to enforce them per se. Scholarly CV proponents nonetheless tend to count these latter two amongst the relevant 'elements of control' without considering this divergence and/or whether they ought to instead be concerned with (a more expansive understanding of) control.

At any rate, CV's (internally disputed) set of elements of control might also be said to constitute the 'central case' of legal rights enforcement. Whilst the view posits that rights are necessarily enforceable, it does not claim that they are either invariably *vindicable* or *remediable*.[18] Just like WT, CV neither endorses the phrase '*ubi jus, ibi remedium*', nor construes rights as guarantees that holders will get what they want—especially as a minimalist proponents posit that there need only be one enforcement or waiver power. Even on the most robust version of CV, aside from waiver powers, the RCTD-holder (or other party acting on the former's behalf) possesses a set of normative positions that merely enable *attempts* to undertake self-help, to seek successful procurement of third-party-granted remedies, or to gain other modes of rights vindication.

[17] For example, Joseph Raz's Dynamic rights model—a non-CV one—includes the idea of a right sufficing to ground new supplementary rights, duties, and other legal positions. Raz (1986: 168–9, 171, 185–6); (Raz (1996: 259–61).

[18] Even Dworkin's idea of constitutional rights as trumps need not be construed as going so far as to entail that rights are invariably remedy-securing. Perhaps only certain American Legal Realists, who believe rights to be determinable only after a judge or other legal official has levied a legal decision, might take such an extreme stance. See Frydrych (2018a: 315–22).

§ III. The Relationship of Enforcement Powers to Legal RCTDs

CV is falsifiable. There are legal rights lacking (associated) primary, secondary, or tertiary enforcement powers (Arguments 1, 2 and 5 below). Further, the view relies on erroneous ideas about the nature of law (Argument 4) and what makes legal norms 'valid', 'effective', and 'genuine' (Argument 5). Even when elements of control obtain, RCTDs may nevertheless be unenforceable because they can conflict with, and be hindered by, legal, social, or moral rules (Argument 6).

Prominent legal philosophers originally put forward Arguments 1, 3, and 5. Whilst presenting them I will flag if and where the arguments go awry both to improve them and to demonstrate how they connect to larger issues in legal philosophy. Even so, it is critical to once again note that CV adherents know that certain mechanisms may not be available for a given right; for them, there are 'fuller' and 'lesser' measures. Thus, CV cannot be falsified just by showing that a particular power fails to obtain; for any singular absence, it is open to proponents to claim that other pertinent elements of control may be available.

Further, CV does not offer thorough criteria for A LEGAL RCTD or an analytic definition, which may then be tested using first-order logic counterexamples to try to establish under- or over-inclusivity. Indeed, on Version C, the elements of control need not even be components of the rights themselves. Moreover, it is doubtful that one will be able to find a single real-world legal RCTD that lacks *all* of the elements of control. Even if examples were found, CV's problems are not restricted to A LEGAL RCTD; they require addressing certain views about legal systems.

Section III overall argument therefore takes a different tack. It is instead inferential or abductive: if every enforcement mechanism within the CV set is only contingently available (i.e., a given element might not obtain in a given case of a legal RCTD), then there can, or could, be unenforceable legal rights, i.e., ones without any (associated) elements of control.

Argument 1: Primary Waiver Powers

HLA Hart's (mostly) private law rights model (i.e., his account stripped of its 'theoretical' commitments) represents a version of CV.[19] For Hart, RCTDs entitle their holders, or others acting on their behalf, to various

[19] Hart (1982).

levels of control over another party's duty.[20] Within his main depiction of the elements of control, though, he does not explicitly distinguish between primary, secondary, or tertiary rights. Instead, the elements all seem to form part of one unified construct—although he notes that, as some afford greater or lesser degrees of control, not every right contains them all.[21]

Let us style Hart's 'first' element (or, more accurately, the first component within his Roman numeral (i)), a *primary waiver power*. Importantly, this power appears to obtain even absent (the perceived threat of) a primary duty's violation and without the need to commence legal proceedings. (It is numeral (ii), his 'second' element, which discusses what may be done in the face of a breach or *threatened* breach.)

In criticising Hart's view, Neil MacCormick provides counterexamples to the idea that all rights include a primary waiver power. His cases include the inability to waive duties of non-interference or assault for flagellation by (or of) a prostitute and statutory rights to workplace safety conditions.[22] However, given Hart's express belief that legal RCTDs may afford fuller and lesser measures of control, MacCormick's arguments and examples cannot falsify CV. Hart knows that there are unwaivable legal rights, mentioning statutory duties (implying statutory rights, or a subset thereof) as examples that might fall under this category.[23] (Again, he also prefaces his account by stating that there can be fuller and lesser measures of control.) Regardless, for our purposes, all we need are the bona fide examples of unwaivable primary legal RCTDs to add to our overall collection of instances of valid legal RCTDs lacking a certain kind of enforcement power.

[20] See Chapter 5 note 16 and the accompanying text on Hart (1982: 183–4).

[21] Hart (1982: 183 & n.85). Cf. Simmonds (1998: 230). On the other hand, Hart refers to some of the correlative duties in element (ii) as 'secondary' ones. Hart (1982: 186).

[22] MacCormick (1977: 196–8). He also discusses an immunity from being enslaved.

[23] Hart (1982: 183 n.85). Another problem with some of MacCormick's counterexamples, at least insofar as they concern Hart, rather than CV or WT, is that they ignore Hart's stipulated domain limitations. Hart admits that legal immunity-rights, such as one against being enslaved, fall outside of the scope of his private law rights *theory*. Ibid 189–92. The question then becomes one about the scope of Hart's CV commitments. Particularly, whether, on his view, *statutory* rights admit of the same fuller or lesser measures of control.

Argument 2: Primary Enforcement Powers
Hillel Steiner provides a Hohfeldian interpretation of Hart's model of a private law RCTD. He partitions Hart's elements into six Hohfeldian powers:

1. To waive compliance with the duty (i.e., extinguish it);
2. To leave the duty in existence (i.e., demand compliance with it);
3. To waive proceeding for the enforcement of the duty (i.e., for the restraint of, or compensation by, the duty-bearer in the face of threatened or actual breach);
4. To demand proceeding for the enforcement of the duty;
5. To waive enforcement;
6. To demand enforcement.[24]

Steiner's explanation does not track Hart's elements precisely. First, Steiner either conflates waiver and extinguishment, or simply excludes the latter. Thus, 'leav[ing] the duty in existence' should be counted as the third element (corresponding with the third component within Hart's Roman numeral (i)). Hence, the tally of total Hartian enforcement mechanisms should be at least seven. Steiner also conflates the idea of leaving a primary duty in place with a demand for compliance. Although he is correct to list both as features of Hart's view, these are nonetheless distinct—if 'leaving in place' is even a genuine normative capacity, that is. Matthew Kramer criticises Steiner for 'treat[ing] "leave the duty in existence" and "demand compliance with it" as interchangeable predicates'.[25] Demanding is an affirmative act or capacity over and above one of simply maintaining the status quo. Nevertheless, Hart *does* actually suggest something like what Steiner says:

> In most cases where *public* duties are thought of as having correlative rights, the duty to supply the benefits are conditional upon being demanded and the beneficiary of the duty is free to demand it or not. Hence, though he has no power to waive or extinguish the duty he has a power by presenting a demand to substitute for a conditional duty not requiring present performance an unconditional duty which does, and so has a choice.[26]

[24] Steiner (1998: 240). Steiner rightly adds a 'sixth' enforcement power to Hart's list 'for the sake of logical completeness' (ibid 240 n.14), though there is in fact more than power at play here.

[25] Kramer (2013: 256).

[26] Hart (1982: 186, emphasis added). Although not necessarily a CV proponent, MacCormick also suggests that normal, adult right-holders are usually free to demand or

Hart has in mind here public welfare rights: public assistance, unemployment relief, farming subsidies, etc.[27] I will call these *primary enforcement powers*. Now, as Hart notes, rights can sometimes be enforced even when there is just the threat of breach. Still, he correctly assigns such enforcement capacities to the second stage (his Roman numeral (ii))[28] because they are used to try to remedy matters, by triggering institutional involvement in order to try to prevent or stop the breach. Whether characterised as secondary or 'remedial' rights, secondary powers, or the element(s) of a unified right complex, there are many clear examples of this. Private law ones include injunctions for anticipatory breach of contract and a trust beneficiary's efforts to prevent another party (e.g., a trustee, a life tenant, etc.) from causing waste.

However, is the use of legal powers *pre-duty-violation* (or even the threat thereof) to enforce legal RCTDs a bona fide legal capacity, let alone a commonly recognisable phenomenon? Trying to prevent a breach does not seem to be the same thing as either demanding compliance in the absence of some perceived threat of breach or going to court after a breach.

Chapter 9 posits that there are actually different ways by which to claim or invoke rights, and that some of these involve using *liberties* to make claims of right, because they remind the duty-bearers of their already-existing responsibilities, rather than changing their normative position or requirements. One is therefore tempted to suggest that what is really happening in cases of (what I have styled) 'primary enforcement powers' is instead one of three things: (A) people are demanding their rights but in ways that do not involve enforcement *powers*; (B) the relevant enforcement actually concerns secondary rights, not primary ones, i.e., that 'procedural'/'remedial' rights are being used to try to vindicate the primary ones; (C) people are merely *exercising* their rights using legal powers, rather than *enforcing* them. (Option C seems to explain Hart's brief discussion of public duties—especially insofar as it concerns converting conditional duties into unconditional ones, which is not the same thing as demanding compliance with an existing duty.)

forego demanding observance of an RCTD even before (threatened) breaches of the correlative duty. MacCormick (2007: 129).

[27] Hart (1982: 185).

[28] Ibid 183–4. Again, see Chapter 5 note 16 and the accompanying text.

Consider further Joel Feinberg's example of handing in a chit,[29] say, to claim your coat at a restaurant's coat check. *Pace* Feinberg, *exercising* your right by handing in your chit does not involve the use of a legal power.[30] The duty-bearer is merely complying with the pre-existing duty. Nor is it necessarily a *demand* for compliance: the right-holder may be making a claim, but not a demand. Alternatively, if a legal power is involved, then it still concerns exercising your right to collect the coat, rather than enforcing your rights over it.

William Buckland nevertheless provides more credible candidate examples of primary enforcement powers.

> Most definitions of right make... a definite reference to enforcement. It is possible to argue that primary rights are not within this definition, for enforcement implies, in general, a wrong done... This proposition, however, is in fact far from true. The Roman *praeiudicia*, the German *Feststellungsklagen* and our own [common law] 'originating summonses' bring primary rights into court—no right need have yet been infringed.[31]

Whilst Buckland's examples are not *compliance demands* made to either a duty-bearer or a legal official per se, they can be used to *vindicate* a legal RCTD's bona fides. These Roman, German, and common law actions concern clarificatory procedures about what the parties' respective rights and duties even are, leading to a declaration of status. From this, enforcement procedures aiming to procure remedies for duty violations may, but need not, be subsequently initiated.[32]

Would such actions ever be initiated but for the threat of a breach of duty? Would you need to vindicate your rights using those three procedures otherwise? The answer may be 'yes' for at least one of the three.[33] Even so, it suffices for our purposes (of collecting examples of legal RCTDs without such power) to note two things. First, that they all seem to involve

[29] Feinberg (1980: 150).

[30] Ibid.

[31] Buckland (1945: 97). Cf. Salmond (1902: 95) on declaration of right proceedings.

[32] On *praejudicia*, see, e.g., Lee (1946: 363, 423).

[33] A *praejudicium* may concern just getting a duty-bearer to declare his or her status as such. For example, if a creditor lends money to a debtor, but the former has in turn received funds from a third-party suretor, the suretor can get the creditor to make a public declaration of his or her own liability and number of sureties. Lee (1946: 363).

'procedural'/secondary rights over and above the 'substantive'/primary ones—thus putting back into question the very idea of 'primary enforcement powers'. Second, even if these procedures really do just concern primary powers, they are not always available for all legal RCTDs. One can also imagine primary enforcement powers being excluded via contract.

Argument 3: 'Inalienable' Rights

The following legal power relationship to CV is, or should be, controversial.[34] Aside from Hart and Wayne Sumner, few CV proponents might consider the capacity to alienate to be integral to their accounts; for, again, despite the label, the view's real emphasis is on rights enforcement and not the larger notion of control. It is also worth distinguishing alienation, nullification, and waiver. Alienation does not enforce rights, but waiver does. All three might nonetheless be said to constitute ways of controlling rights. *Waiver* can alter a correlative duty, e.g., to do φ, by adding a liberty not to do φ for a certain time. The right may nonetheless persist post-waiver and may be exercisable or enforceable at a later date. A waiver power can also alter a duty bearer's requirement to fulfil a secondary or tertiary duty altogether without thereby nullifying the primary duty and correlative right. *Alienability* means forfeiture of a right through either transfer or nullification. Consider the difference between waiving your right to collect a debt on a specific date versus selling your property and thereby making someone else the new owner.

Certain legal RCTDs are inalienable. You cannot sell your constitutional rights to other parties or permanently contract around them in many jurisdictions. Now, citizens of many states can forfeit their citizenship and thereby lose constitutional rights afforded by their former jurisdictions. Not all regimes allow you to abandon your citizenship, though.

[34] It is sometimes discussed in the theories of rights literature because of Hart's remarks about 'extinguishing' a private law right and MacCormick's 'inalienability' argument against Hart's theory. On Hart, see Chapter 5 note 16 and the accompanying text; on MacCormick's argument, see Chapter 5 note 81 and the accompanying text. CV is less vulnerable to MacCormick's argument than is WT. For it is open to most proponents to not only suggest that inalienable rights may nonetheless be enforceable or waivable, but also that CV is uncommitted to the idea that the more modes of control there are, the more of a right something is.

Argument 4: Secondary Rights as Contingent Distributions
For hundreds of years, people have debated whether rights are necessarily enforceable in legal proceedings. Let us consider more recent arguments that they are not. John Gardner believes that many if not all legal rights are 'institutionalised' moral or customary ones. Unlike purely moral or customary ones, conferring or imposing primary and secondary legal rights and duties is done as a matter of distributive justice or injustice.[35] In part, this is because legal rights, unlike their moral or social analogues, are entitlements subject to distribution. For example, some rights require the use of state assets: courts of law, legal officers, their time and efforts, public funds to cover the costs of such institutions' operations, etc.[36] These relatively scarce and expensive resources are subject to allocation considerations. Gardner also posits that secondary legal rights and duties are not logically entailed from primary ones.

> If one locates the primary duties in the law of torts, as we saw, one inevitably includes a secondary duty of corrective justice as part of the 'tort law' package. But one need not use the law of torts, and more generally, one need not grant a secondary duty of corrective justice. One may choose a different (non-corrective) legal response to some legal wrongs, or indeed, no legal response at all. So, there are always two questions for the court or legislature: which 'initial entitlements' to include in the law, and how to respond—correctively or otherwise—to their violation.
>
> It follows that the corrective duties are not mere automatic implications of the initial entitlements… They are distinct entitlements that also need to be distributed by the law.[37]

[35] Gardner (2014: 339–40).

[36] Ibid 340–1. By 'secondary', though, Gardner is sometimes referring to what (the literature often calls) *tertiary* positions. For example, compare ibid 338–9 with ibid 344–5. Gardner's stance can furthermore be contrasted with that of Henry Terry. Terry considers rights of action as correlating with legal officials' (e.g., clerks of court) duties to perform their tasks when required, and which, he submits, exist irrespective of whether the right-holders have valid, sustainable causes of action. Terry (1884: 120). (It is for this reason that Terry actually classifies rights of actions as primary rights.) Regardless, this is not what CV means by controllability; it is not about being able to initiate groundless legal processes with no chance of surviving a motion to dismiss, let alone of securing victory. CV instead concerns, amongst other things, the capacity to initiate proceedings wherein the right-holder has a real shot at vindication.

[37] Ibid 345.

Gardner is adopting and modifying Guido Calabresi and Douglas Melamed's account of legal rights here.[38] Those two scholars picture the legal construction of rights and their enforcement mechanisms in two (conceptually, if not temporally, distinct) 'stages'. In the first, legal officials generate entitlements, understood as titles to resources. In the second, the officials determine which modes of protection the right-holders are to enjoy.[39]

> The state not only has to decide whom to entitle, but it must also simultaneously make a series of equally difficult second order decisions. These decisions go to the manner in which entitlements are protected and to whether an individual is allowed to sell or trade the entitlement. In any given dispute, for example, the state must decide not only which side wins but also the kind of protection to grant.[40]

'Wins' here is ambiguous between victory in: (a) a competition over who should be initially entitled or (b) dispute resolution proceedings (litigation, arbitration, etc.). Calabresi and Melamed seem to mean the former here. Further, Gardner parts company with them if they imply that mere possession of the primary right (invariably) determines that there will be state intervention or mode of protection of any sort, let alone the outcome of such legal proceedings. Indeed, his articulation of this view helps to emphasise the contingency of *secondary* rights: not only their very generation, but also in constituting just one possible mode of protecting rights, or basis for helping to resolve disputes generally.[41]

[38] Calabresi and Melamed's view can in turn be traced back to nineteenth century German jurisprudence.

[39] Calabresi and Melamed (1972: 1090–2, 1105–15). Protection and enforcement need not always require state force. Ibid 1090 n.4.

[40] Ibid 1092.

[41] Cf. John Finnis on the specification of rights. 'Employing a useful contemporary jargon, we can say that people (or legal systems) who share substantially the same *concept* (e.g. of the human right to life, or to a fair trial) may none the less have different *conceptions* of that right, in that their specifications [the features and contents of specific legal positions] differ, partly because the circumstances they have in mind differ and partly because specification normally involves choices, *by some authoritative process*, from among alternatives that are more or less equally reasonable'. Finnis (2011: 219, emphasis added). See also Raz (1996: 266–7) on secondary rights not being based upon primary ones, but rather a second, distinct *moral* judgment.

Not everyone accepts this two-stage analysis. For example, Pavlos Eleftheriadis argues that segregating entitlement and protection into two 'questions' or 'stages' renders the first devoid of content. If the modes of protection are not specified at the same time as the initial assignment, then the entitlement will be indeterminate.

> The problem with the idea of entitlement is that it specifies the winners but not the losers. It gives [an entitlement, e.g., to property] without specifying who is excluded and how… The problem lies with the apparent distinction between the two stages: the stages of recognising the entitlement and specifying its protection. The distinction is false. And if it is false, the simplicity of entitlement is also false. Winners and losers must be defined at the same time. If exclusion is left to the stage of remedial enforcement, then the first stage has not resolved anything at all. If so, the allocation of entitlements at that stage is an empty and useless process. So if legal rights are to be standards whose general rationale is to resolve conflicts of interests they must guide the action of all sides.[42]

Pace Eleftheriadis, exclusion is not left to the second stage. It is constitutive of the first. Winning or losing can be understood in terms of entitlement to, or exclusion from, resource usage itself—regardless of how winners enforce their entitlements. *A* may have a legal duty to stay off of *B*'s land without anyone knowing how *B* or anyone else could remedy *A*'s potential transgressions, if at all.[43]

Holding that entitlements are indeterminate absent specific means of remedying breaches also constitutes a form of Sanction theory of law. Sanction theories posit that all (unexcused) breaches of legal duties will be met with system-imposed liabilities (e.g., to provide court-ordered remedies) or punishments. Over time, the theories have expanded the relevant

[42] Eleftheriadis (2008: 71).

[43] Consider this jurisprudential debate about PROPERTY: is it composed of multiple, fungible normative positions, or is a right to exclude the keystone of the concept? James Penner, Thomas Merrill, and Henry Smith take various approaches to 'the' right to exclude stance. They nevertheless disagree about what this means: is it a claim that others self-exclude, or also powers by which to enforce others' exclusion in the face of threatened breach? Whether or not they are correct about the overall debate, Penner was correct in 1997 that the RCTD is a right of exclusion, whilst the right to exclude concerns powers and liberties by which to remedy transgressions of that RCTD. See Penner (1997); Merrill (1998); H.E. Smith (2002). Cf. Terry (1884: 100).

sort of 'liabilities' to include mere susceptibility to litigation and comparable legal processes.[44]

Sanction theories present at least three ways by which to understand A RIGHT and A DUTY. Option A: some versions analytically reduce AN RCTD to A POWER, because they treat RCTDs as powers by which to enforce duty compliance or to pursue remedies for breaches. A DUTY, in turn, is reduced to A LIABILITY: susceptibility to such enforcement efforts. Adherents therefore tend to identify legal rights with secondary or tertiary ones. Option B: other versions present enforcement capacities and correlative liabilities as being necessary, but non-exclusive, features of AN RCTD and A DUTY respectively. Option C: *primary* rights and duties are only rendered real via an official's say-so in a decision or decree.[45]

Some CV proponents may nevertheless rebuff the Sanction theory label. First, holding that rights and duties are invariably or perforce enforceable does not necessarily entail the imposition of a sanction. To hold that RCTDs are necessarily enforceable does not entail that rightholders must always emerge victorious; not only may they lose a proceeding, but, given the fluctuating measures of control, a given position may not even involve the power to commence a remedy-seeking process. For a CV minimalist, moreover, the 'sanction' in question is not even necessarily the duty-bearer's liability to participation in such legal processes, let alone a requirement to provide a remedy, compelled performance, or subjection to punishment. It might instead just be the duty-bearer's liability to primary enforcement or waiver power.

Second, whilst some CV proponents might deem the analytic reductions to be accurate, for others, RCTDs can correlate with both duties and Hohfeldian liabilities concurrently.[46] On their approach, the liability to a duty's potentially being waived (to the duty-bearer's own advantage, perhaps) is best understood as one position (the liability) being required for

[44] E.g., Kocourek (1928: 345). See also Raz (1984: 131) on the supposed 'Kelsenian twist' in Hart's account of private law RCTDs and duties.

[45] See, e.g., Frydrych (2018a). Sanction theories are criticised for ignoring or rejecting a distinct role of legal duties as requirements to act or forbear. They also tend to (but need not) reduce or replace the normative sense of duty—a belief in a requirement to comply—with motivations to conform out of fear of punishment or other undesirable repercussions. See Hart (1994); Woozley (1968); Hacker (1973); Raz (1999: 156–61); S.A. Smith (2012: 227–38).

[46] E.g., Simmonds (1998: 223); Wellman (1985: 28–9, 39).

the modification of another (the duty). A DUTY is thus logically prior to A LIABILITY (to enforcement), and thus indispensable.

Third, as there are no established, shared criteria for A RIGHT, why hold that the Calabresi-Melamed stance counts as an argument rather than a rival view or mere stipulation?[47] For example, why hold that *B*'s entitlement to *A*'s exclusion from some resource, absent specific means for modifying the parties' relationship in terms of the entitlement's enforceability, counts as a right? People can benefit from legal rules without necessarily having a right.[48] Is their stance thereby put under pressure?

Keeping in mind the rejection of 'theoretical' criteria for A RIGHT in Chapter 6, consider the following hypothetical case. *B* is legally entitled to enter some land, to use it, and to live there. No one else may move there, live there, use the land, or sell it, etc. However, the law in this jurisdiction is such that *B* cannot: sue *A* for entering the land; waive *A*'s duty from refraining to traverse the land; etc. Nor can anyone else do so on *B*'s behalf. Are we then to say that *B*'s entitlements fail to count as a set of property rights? Further, that unless the capacities to (at least) commence institutional dispute resolution processes obtain, if not ones to procure particular remedies, people in *B*'s situation are inaptly styled as 'right-holders'? Is it a mistake to claim that *B* has the right to live there? If it ought not to count as a right, what alternative label would be appropriate? For Legal Positivists, if the system's officials can officially recognise the entitlement as a legal right per their rule(s) of recognition, does that suffice for it to count as a right of that system—even the position alone cannot catalyse litigation or other official proceedings in which it might garner recognition?

Pulling ourselves out of this rabbit hole, it suffices for this chapter's purposes just to collect examples of legal RCTDs without secondary enforcement powers. Such cases do exist. For example, recent US Supreme Court cases hold that American states have the right to tax Native Americans under US *federal* Indian law and state law, but no right to enforce those rights to tax against certain Indian tribes, e.g., to force remittance of the tax revenue.[49] Another standard example are valid con-

[47] They themselves insist that theirs is just one amongst many ways of conceiving matters here. Calabresi and Melamed (1972: 1089 & n.2).

[48] See, e.g., Chapter 4 note 3 on adverse possession and dishonest transferring, and Chapter 5 note 110 on Jhering's domestic manufacturer case.

[49] E.g., Fletcher (2017: 236–7, 239 & n.11, 255), *discussing*: *Michigan v. Bay Mills Indian Community* 572 U.S. 782 (2014) and *Oklahoma Tax Commission v. Citizen Band,*

tract rights which are unenforceable for not being in writing (e.g., per England's *Statute of Frauds* 1677 Section 4).[50] Still another might be Section 53(1)b of Victoria Australia's *Property Law Act*, whereby an oral declaration of trust over land is legally valid without written evidence, but is unenforceable without one.[51]

Argument 5: Genuine Rights and Law's Effectiveness

How should scholars explain legal rights that lack modes of enforcement in terms of being able to initiate lawsuits or comparable dispute resolution proceedings? How can such rights be squared with the notion of legal validity? The following discussion places rights enforcement in the context of a greater debate about law: what makes something count as a legal system? Must laws be 'effective' in order to count as rules of a system? What makes something a 'valid' norm of a system?

According to many legal philosophers, in order for a legal system to continue as 'a going concern', then its rules must 'have force' and be 'effective'. In turn, laws must be effective to maintain their status as norms of the system. Without offering an in-depth explication of effectiveness, many scholars take it to roughly entail a state of affairs of general conformity with some critical mass of a system's norms by those subject to them. Effectiveness is often established through sanctions, punishments, liabilities, and other forms of rule enforcement and conformity measures. Despite the lessons learned about Sanction theories' failings, certain legal philosophers remain stalwart that some form of liability must accompany many, if not all, of a human (as opposed to hypothetical alien or angelic) legal system's duties.[52] It seems to follow, then, that, if legal rights and duties must be enforceable to ensure both (i) duty fulfilment and (ii) the rules grounding the duties continuing to be viable parts of a legal system, then institutional mechanisms must exist for their enforcement and valida-

Potawatomi Indian Tribe of Oklahoma 498 U.S. 505 (1991). See also White (1984: 25) for further examples of primary rights and duties without secondary positions. (Some of his examples, however, are erroneous. For example, regarding statutes of limitation, a time-barred right-holder may nonetheless commence an action but is subject to the statute being raised as a knock-down defence).

[50] See, e.g., S.A. Smith (2012: 235 n.33).

[51] Property Law Act 1958 (Vic) Section 53(1)b; *Secretary, Department of Social Security v James* [1990] FCA 213.

[52] E.g., Schauer (2010); Kramer (2003). See also Chapter 1 note 59.

tion. In other words, legal duty-bearers must (generally? for the most part? usually?) be liable to compelled participation in effective institutional dispute resolution procedures.

To clarify, these legal philosophers believe there must be an integral association or relationship (*not* an identity) between some critical mass of legal duties and legal liabilities (the latter in the sense of punishments, fines, etc., and not merely subjection to institutional processes). Let us call this the Effectiveness thesis. Its proponents can agree that duties and liabilities serve distinct conceptual and normative roles, and so would therefore rebuff any Sanction theory charges levied against them as inapt.

Moreover, endorsing the Effectiveness thesis does not necessarily entail subscription to CV. The latter view merely holds that legal *rights* must be, in some way, enforceable. It takes no stance on whether the rest of a legal system's rules, standards, etc., must be as well. By contrast, those scholars who only endorse the Effectiveness thesis are free to say that many, *but not all*, legal rights are enforceable.

With this in mind, Kramer (a non-CV proponent) divides legal rights and their correlatives into genuine and nominal varieties (although he may no longer believe that the difference turns on enforceability).[53] As shall be discussed in Chapter 9, other scholars nonetheless maintain a genuine/nominal distinction based on rights enforceability. However, as Kramer's is the most sophisticated treatment of the distinction, his—older—account will be employed here simply for elucidatory purposes.

Kramer also believes that a legal right may be either 'operative' or 'inoperative'. An 'operative' legal right is one that is (or would be) regularly enforced. For every operative right there are enforcement powers by which to respond to (anticipated) breaches of duties. Rectification must take place 'regularly' if an operative right is to exist. An 'inoperative' legal right is either (Class A) *unenforceable* for a want of any such associated powers, or (Class B) regularly *unenforced*—or, would be unenforced were duty violations to occur—by the relevant power-holders. Class B inoperative legal rights are nevertheless 'genuine': whilst it may go unenforced and thus be inoperative, such a right may still be genuine because it is potentially enforceable (i.e., the relevant powers obtain). This generates three classes: (I) operative-genuine legal rights; (II) inoperative-yet-genuine

[53] Kramer (1998: 8–9, 34, 46, 63–5, 100, 106); Kramer (2000: 476–7, 481–2). On Kramer having perhaps changed his mind about what makes a legal RCTD 'genuine' or 'nominal', see Chapter 5 note 38.

legal rights; and (III) inoperative-nominal legal rights.[54] Kramer's view therefore stands in opposition to CV by positing that some legal rights are simply unenforceable, i.e., inoperative-nominal ones.

This stance is nevertheless problematic, as it entails more than just the idea that some 'critical mass' of a system's norms must be enforceable: it additionally suggests that legal right is 'genuine' only because of such powers. In other words, it is immaterial to appeal to an integral relationship between *some* critical mass of rights and certain sorts of powers in order to explain law's effectiveness because, on this view, *no genuine* right lacks associated powers.

Whilst Kramer does not explicitly identify legal validity with enforceability, this version of the genuine/nominal distinction seems to get us there, nonetheless. To what extent is this merely stipulative? Why must legal RCTDs be enforceable (or be protected by associated immunities against divestiture, say) in order to count as 'genuine'?[55] On the one hand, if they are valid norms of the system, then it is inapt to construe unenforceable rights as 'nominal'.[56] On the other hand, if inoperative-nominal rights are not valid norms of the system after all, then Kramer's distinctions have not accounted for unenforceable *legal* rights; if they are rights at all, inoperative-nominal cases are instead moral or social ones.

A rejoinder to those charges might turn on what makes something a valid norm of a legal system. A Legal Positivist such as Kramer could say that the criteria of validity per a system's rule of recognition held by officials settle the matter. Being deemed 'valid' presumes the existence of an institutional context wherein legal officials *qua* officials apply the law. Legal rules may regularly go unenforced for considerable periods of time. Even so, applying Kramer's account to all legal norms, those are inoperative-yet-genuine (applications of) norms of the system. However, per Positivist strictures, legal rights, like other elements of law, must be stamped with that official imprimatur. (This recognition, moreover, must seemingly occur in or via an official proceeding of some sort.)

Even if both (i) officials' potential employment or recognition of legal positions and (ii) correlative duty-bearers' regular conformity with

[54] Kramer (2000: 482–4).

[55] Kramer & Steiner (2007: 297).

[56] It is equally groundless to say that legal RCTDs unprotected by immunities against nullification are also merely 'nominal' ones, rather than genuine ones—if that is indeed now Kramer's view—since being protected thus has nothing to do with whether the RCTDs are valid components of the system.

their duties are indispensable for RCTDs to count as valid positions of a given legal system, why is the use of enforcement powers the exclusive means by which to render them effective? It might be begging the question about rights' unenforceability to narrowly construe enforceability to a limited set of legal powers used in very specific ways. Are there no other means by which legal officials can validate rights, save via litigation or comparable remedial dispute resolution processes (or declarations)? Like most in the philosophy of rights, this sort of view ignores the possibility that there might be other ways to use rights to make them and laws 'effective'. For example, would it suffice if judges or other legal officials simply *referenced* them periodically, without claimants needing to specifically mention or imply their rights in pleadings in litigation or in other dispute resolution processes?[57]

One might insist that, even though the existence or implementation of sanctions is not conceptually necessary for a legal system to obtain, they are nonetheless integral in order for legal rights to do so. There is no compelling reason to believe that proposition, however. Instead, it is better to salvage Kramer's classification by noting that: (1) certain legal rights are or can be (Type I) enforceable via powers, or (Type II) unenforceable for a want of associated powers, and (2) that Type I legal rights divide into (Ia) the typically enforced variety and (Ib) those which are typically unenforced despite being enforceable. Type I legal rights are compatible with CV, but the very possibility of Type II rights is a problem for the view.

Even so, Kramer does not establish that any Type II legal rights actually obtain. (The end of Argument 4 presented candidate cases thereof, though.) Instead, he provides the grounds for a further argument that legal rights can meet a legal system's validity conditions despite being unenforceable. We can imagine a legal system wherein the state will never enforce a party's rights, but where the officials acting *qua* officials make mention of them, laud them, or broadcast their status as valid legal positions all the time—even if merely as showpieces. Again, that alone ought to constitute the relevant sort of official imprimatur, at least per Legal Positivism's rule of recognition.

Recall further Nigel Simmonds' Dystopia argument from Chapter 6 § II.1. Let us now add a new element to it. Imagine a legal system replete

[57] This invites larger questions about theories of law, which are beyond this chapter's purview. However, we will re-tread upon this theme of alternative modes of rights usage in the next chapter.

with corrupt officials who perennially deny proceedings to hear legal disputes for reasons that are unique to each case. Yet each time they do so they nevertheless officially affirm the legal validity of one party's right. Whether the subjects of that regime actually have legal rights thus depends on a theory of law and one's conception of LEGAL VALIDITY. For Positivists, at least, an affirmative answer seems possible. It is also unclear why a Natural lawyer or Interpretivist must disagree, even if they find the rights in question (let alone the legal system as a whole) to be morally problematic or adjudge them to constitute mere 'peripheral cases' of the central cases of rights and law.

Argument 6: Tertiary Rights
Tertiary rights are not logically entailed from secondary ones. As CV proponents themselves are happy to admit, being able to start a lawsuit does not mean you will win it—even if you deserve to do so. (Even if you do succeed, you may not get what you want from the process either). (Further, just because a legal official orders a remedy for the rights violation, it does not follow that the right-holder will necessarily be able to secure that remedy).[58]

There are a number of reasons why even in legitimate, just, and efficient legal systems a given right will not always entail victory in institutional dispute resolution processes. Two are that officials can make mistakes or can be corrupt. A third is that a right-holder's claim, although valid, may be outweighed by other considerations; legal rights may conflict directly with certain laws, other legal rights, or even government policies. One consideration may be outweighed by another in certain circumstances, or deemed limited in its application vis-à-vis some other party's concerns (contrary to the first right-holder's wishes or expectations).[59] Of course, someone must weigh the competing norms and considerations (a law versus a right, one right versus a second) in order to adjudge their respective extensions, relative weaknesses, capacities for being trumped, or inapplicability in a given case.

[58] On what I call 'quaternary rights', see Appendix 3.

[59] Far too much ink has been spilled debating whether rights conflicts are even possible, or whether rights are instead 'compossible' (i.e., supposed conflicts between competing rights claims are merely ephemeral and serve only to demonstrate each right's true scope). Subscribers to the Compossibility view, however, are few and far between today. See, e.g., Steiner (1998).

§ IV. Conclusion

Whilst legal RCTDs are typically enforceable by legal powers, they are not invariably so. The chapter presented an analytic reconstruction of a popular belief amongst lawyers, ordinary people, and many legal philosophers, that they nevertheless are perforce enforceable in one way or another. Although many adherents treat them as such, this 'Control View' is not actually committed to the idea that all of the 'elements of control' must serve as conceptual components of A LEGAL RCTD. On some versions of CV, enforcement can be the function of distinct rights, i.e., 'secondary' and 'tertiary' ones, which can be possessed and used by various parties.

The chapter then showed why each listed mode of control may or may not obtain in particular cases. First, some primary legal rights are unwaivable. Second, if there really are 'primary enforcement powers', they are not always (or even regularly?) available. Third, some rights are inalienable (i.e., non-transferable and non-nullifiable). Fourth, 'remedial' rights are not logically entailed from the mere existence of primary ones, and cases of primary legal RCTDs that do not give rise to secondary rights obtain. Fifth, right-holders do not always win lawsuits, let alone get awarded remedies. It is also erroneous to identify a norm's *genuineness* or *validity* with its enforceability; for rights recognition and validation need not be accomplished exclusively via the use of (associated) enforcement powers.

With all of these counterexamples *plus* the arguments exposing CV's misconceptions about law, genuineness, and legal validity at hand, an abductive inference can then be made that legal rights could be created, or might already exist, which lack, or are not associated with, *any* of the listed elements of control. Even so, alternative means may exist for the right's recognition as a valid normative position within a legal system.

What is the payoff of this analysis? Does it prove that enforceability is either (a) not a constitutive feature of A LEGAL RCTD or (b) not an otherwise invariably obtaining option? In terms of a legal RCTD not being either invariably *remediable* or *vindicable* (whether by the holder personally or by someone acting on his or her behalf), then the answer is 'yes'—though CV advocates themselves already agree with that proposition. If what is meant instead is that mechanisms by which to waive the correlative duty, to engage in self-help, or to initiate and participate in official (or other third-party) determinations of the content of legal rights and correlative duties need not obtain for a given legal RCTD, the answer is also 'yes'.

Nevertheless, wholly unenforceable legal rights—at least in terms of the legal power-based modes of control specified in this chapter—are not completely impotent. They can successfully accomplish specified tasks, such as coordinate property relations, without such powers. (This is not to claim that they would do a particularly good job of things, though.)

At best, enforcement powers are essential to secondary and tertiary rights—understood as distinct rights, and probably best in terms of complexes composed of RCTDs, powers, and liberties. Still, not all legal RCTDs must come equipped with the means to commence, let alone triumph, in legal processes. Neither do such rights necessarily constitute 'trumps' over social policies or the will of others, and nor must they start off as trumps that shed (associated) powers over time, e.g., in the face of statutes of limitation. Instead, they are better conceived as *generally* having, or being associated with, potent-but-defeasible capacities.

Even so, there is something to the idea of wholly unenforceable legal rights being 'defective' in some sense. The next three chapters will therefore explore how legal rights can be employed in more ways than CV addresses, by claiming and invoking rights using liberties rather than powers for example, and what is in fact wrong with wholly unusable (let alone unenforceable) cases.

CHAPTER 8

Imperfect Legal Rights

§ I. Existing Explanations

There is something to the idea of legally unenforceable rights being 'imperfect' or 'defective'. People often dispute what their rights and duties are and require. Only legal officials can provide authoritative, binding determinations of what people's positions entail. So, if there are no means by which to trigger authoritative determination processes (regardless of who holds such powers: private parties, legal guardians, government agents, etc.), then rights and duties might fail to provide determinate guidance to the parties.

Whatever one thinks about the very possibility of wholly unenforceable legal rights, the possibility of which was adduced in Chapter 7, the following consideration is also worth bearing in mind. For various—often unarticulated or underdeveloped—reasons, even some Control View opponents agree that there is something wrong with the idea of legally unenforceable rights. Such instances are deemed to be 'imperfect',[1] 'degenerate' or 'vitiated',[2] 'nominal',[3] or to be conceptually parasitic upon enforceable

[1] E.g., Terry (1884: 116–9); Salmond (1902: 223); Vinogradoff (1924: 61–2); Feinberg (1980: 150); MacCormick (2007: 122–3, 129).

[2] E.g., Martin (1993: 60, 83–4).

[3] See Matthew Kramer, Chapter 5 note 38; Chapter 7 note 53.

D. Frydrych, *The Architecture of Rights*,
https://doi.org/10.1007/978-3-030-76039-7_8

ones.[4] Why think so, though?[5] This 'defect' view appears to reflect a conception of rights reflected in the following concern: 'what is the *point* of rights if they cannot be claimed or enforced'? Hence, adherence to an unenforceable-legal-rights-are-problematic stance does not cut neatly across pro- or anti- Control View lines.[6]

Legal rights may still have a point even in the absence of any enforcement capacities. For example, one might believe that a right need only ground a legal duty in others and mark its holder as the intended beneficiary of that duty's required conduct. These (distinct) purposes are not necessarily rendered useless or defective simply for want of invariably associated enforcement features. That legal rights-correlative-to-duties ('RCTDs') may therefore be less potent normative or legal tools than if they always married to elements of control is no argument against the idea that such rights nevertheless serve some sort of function.

Still, that response does not really capture *why* people think unenforceable legal rights are imperfect or defective. Joseph Raz provides the beginnings of one possible explanation of why such cases ought to be deemed so. For him, the very notion of an unenforceable legal right is parasitic upon an enforceable one because the law is primarily concerned with enforceable norms.[7] Further, Rex Martin believes that nominal rights 'fail to function as rights' because they '[give] no effective normative direction to the conduct of other persons'; other people do not take the right as a basis for acting as it directs.[8] Martin's claim nonetheless exaggerates the extent to which enforcement mechanisms, rather than the predicate (primary) RCTD, must provide the normative guidance function for duty-bearers.[9]

[4] Raz (1996: 256–7). For discussions of hypothetical systems with legally unenforceable rights, see Reiff (2005: 47–9).

[5] There are different senses of 'imperfect rights' and 'imperfect duties' in the philosophy of rights literature beyond that of rights being imperfect for being unenforceable in some way or other. For example, a duty is sometimes deemed to be imperfect: for lacking a correlative right (e.g., Etinson (2013: 465)); because the holder lacks a liberty or claim by which to fulfil it (cf. White (1984: 58)); or because it is unenforceable (e.g., Varden (2011: 280)). Sometimes, a right is also deemed imperfect for altogether lacking a correlative duty. E.g., MacCormick (2007: 123); cf. White (1984: 71). See also Terry (1884: 116, 119).

[6] This candidate 'point' of rights need not be reducible to will vindication or protection per se and need not be framed in terms of a 'theory' of rights either.

[7] Raz (1996: 256).

[8] Martin (1993: 83).

[9] To my mind, no jurisprudential account (and not simply in the philosophy of rights literature) has, to date, provided an adequate account of the extent to which a right, rather than just the correlative duty, provides duty-bearers with information to guide them—especially if

§ II. A Functionalist Answer: Rights as Action-Guiding

Here is a superior, albeit partial, explanation of why wholly unenforceable legal RCTDs constitute imperfect cases of rights: they lack the means for securing officials' binding determinations of their existence, content, and/or scope. Hence, legal right-holders (and correlative duty-bearers) might lack sufficient information and guidance about what their respective normative positions mean and entail.[10] Imperfect rights also lack means for catalysing authoritative proceedings wherein officials can *fix/decide* what the rights and duties in question, or just certain features thereof, ought to be.

There is sometimes a need for the content and contours of legal rights and duties to be determined and shaped by legal officials' binding opinions. Reasons for officials to provide them will often arise when right-holders and duty-bearers are either unclear about, or dispute, their legal positions. Both Raz's and Martin's answers point in the same direction about RCTDs and duties functioning as action-guiding and/or reason-providing normative positions. Nevertheless, deeper reasons for construing typical legal RCTDs to be enforceable are to be found in the idea of law's effectiveness.

Let us first turn to one of Raz's arguments, which can be used to show that enforcement mechanisms are not necessary features of A LEGAL RCTD or A LEGAL DUTY. As mentioned in Chapter 1, Raz presents the case of a legal system for a community of angels. Given the nature and disposition of its community members, angelic legal duty-bearers will not require (the fear of) punishments to motivate conformity (if not compliance) with their duties.[11]

If a community of angels actually needs law, it would be because it needs to resolve (at least) certain coordination problems, if not also distribution issues. Even so, the conceptual possibility of legal subjects with

and when the correlative positions are not deemed to be identical in content. See also Chapter 2 note 87 for some worries about how rights, rather than duties, contrain others.

[10] It is not a complete explanation because it does not explain what would be 'defective' about lacking waiver powers for primary rights or enforcement powers for tertiary rights. For an argument that could be characterised as showing what would be defective about a legal system lacking tertiary rights (and, I would add, *their* enforcement), see Hughes (2013: 196).

[11] More specifically, Raz's argument aims to show that sanctions are 'inessential' to 'our' concept, LAW. See Raz (1999: 157–61); Chapter 1 note 59.

purer-than-human motivations and dispositions does not resolve the question about the relationship between primary, secondary, and tertiary legal rights and duties. For even sincerely motivated, morally superior, non-omniscient agents might still generate conflicts about what their legal positions really entail. If not (amicable) dispute resolution processes akin to the variety found in human legal systems, such beings will at least require authoritative binding decisions and answers to their queries about what their rights entitle, and their duties require, specifically. Angel *A* may believe its legal duty requires it to take action φ. Correlative right-holder Angel *B* may think that *A*'s duty instead requires both φ and ψ. *A* wants to fulfil its duty, but politely disagrees with *B* about what the legal position entails.

Alternatively, imagine that both the legal right-holder and correlative duty-bearer are simply uncertain about some critical aspect of their legal positions (ones they themselves did not generate. In other words, the parties do not dispute the matter, as in the previous case, as neither harbours firm views about what the right and duty entail precisely. So, together, they seek out authoritative guidance.[12] Some legal official must decide (providing an authoritative, binding decision about) what the right and duty really are and entail.[13]

This is not to say that a legal official in any system must hear the parties' issue, let alone resolve it. Thus, wholly unenforceable rights' imperfection follows from the occasional need to clarify legal positions' contents and extensions; if it is impossible for a legal RCTD and its correlative duty's existence or content to be *officially* determined and/or clarified, then both are somewhat defective.

§ III. Objections

Consider the following objections. First, does a functionalist account of RCTDs not take us back to *theories* of rights? Second, assume arguendo that lacking the means to provide binding determinations of what some rights and duties actually entail constitutes a defect in a legal system. Even then, it does not follow that those rights and duties are *themselves* defective for failing to contain, or be associated with, the means for triggering such

[12] Co-trustees who (have the right to) seek direction from a court about the content or scope of their duties or powers, via an original summons, need not use their imaginations here.

[13] See Raz (2009b: 108); Chapter 4 note 112. Alternatively, the parties may just seek counsel from lawyers about what their legal rights and duties entail. They might do this for both a substantive answer and as a ground to try to avoid future liability.

official determinations. Third, certain scholars distinguish between general 'abstract' rights and 'concrete' determinate rights derived from the former.[14] A concrete position's being somewhat under-determinate does not render the *general* right 'defective'. Fourth, one might believe that morally upright people simply follow their legal duties; they do not need to be compelled via enforcement mechanisms.

§ IV. Rejoinders

Functionalist accounts of legal rights need not depend upon the 'theories' of rights. An account of rights as action-guiding or reason-giving need not be explained in terms of an ultimate purpose protecting or fulfilling right-holders' wills or interests, to protect their role-bearing status (e.g., as property owners, as citizens, etc.), or any other components of the 'theoretical criteria' addressed in Chapters 5 and 6. The problem is instead when and where functionalist explanations are taken to be the starting point for a *theory* of rights—or worse still, the all-encompassing, predominant aim for the philosophy of rights.[15]

The objection also aims to distinguish a legal system's failings vis-à-vis a legal RCTD from the idea of the right's own imperfection. However, if certain legal RCTDs and duties cannot *even in principle* be clarified, which may be necessary to provide guidance about what exactly is owed to whom and when, what actions must be taken, etc., then those normative positions are themselves defective, not just the system.

Third, as far as your author is aware, discussions of defective cases in the philosophy of rights literature concern the 'concrete', particular ones. If, however, the abstract general legal rights provided no guidance to legal officials whatsoever, rather than wholly vague or conflicting directions, about which concrete rights were entailed or about their specific contents, then they too would be somewhat defective. Further, the idea of making general abstract rights determinate through binding decisions does not make sense, given the very abstract/concrete distinction: only concrete ones would be made determinate via an official's say-so.

[14] For example, see Pavlos Eleftheriadis' view discussed in Chapter 3 note 32 and the accompanying text. Eleftheriadis (2008: 123–8, 168).

[15] Furthermore, even if social practices or concepts ought to be interpreted in light of their purpose or function, that does not take us all the way to the Normativists' (e.g., Ronald Dworkin and John Finnis') claim that one must engage in *moral or political* evaluation and justification in order to explain that function. See Dickson (2004: 142–3).

Fourth, even if a legal right in question is, pro tanto, a morally acceptable one, duty-bearers still might not comply for failure to comprehend their positions' full scope or implications. They might disagree with right-holders and others about their duties' applications/entailments (albeit honestly disputing them), or simply not know what their positions actually entail. The law therefore needs a way to determine the content in order to guide the parties.[16]

This view neither explains who should possess the capacity to trigger legally binding official guidance or clarification of legal positions, nor entails that the right-holder must be the exclusive party authorised and competent to do so. Still, a legal system lacking *any* means for determining the existence, content, and scope of its rights and duties would be defective too. *Some* such official determinations are seemingly indispensable to any legal system—or at least those replete with legal rights—howsoever initiated.

Legal systems need not rely on a 'case or controversy' method for raising rights matters in institutional proceedings. It is imaginable that a system could authorise its officials to unilaterally raise such issues. However, that approach would rely on them being able to discover and learn about such concerns in order to initiate the requisite procedures by which to determine the legal positions' contents. Barring omniscient legal authorities, much of the time the right-holders and duty-bearers will often be better placed to determine the need for an official determination.

Regardless of who wields these powers, rights enforcement helps to catalyse determinations of a legal RCTD and its correlative duty's content and contours. Without such means, both positions would be defective. Hence, the conceptual chasm between duties and Hohfeldian liabilities is not as large as one might suppose from Raz's Community of Angels argument. Of course, this does not establish a necessary conceptual connection between rights and enforcement mechanisms; and nor does it presume that litigation or some analogous official dispute resolution process is the exclusive means by which to bring legal rights and duties before legal officials in order to have them deemed valid and clarified.

[16] What if the legal right in question is not a moral one? A person who finds a given legal RCTD morally repugnant might not comply with its requirements. Irrespective of whether legal duties are exclusionary reasons or merely weighty ones, there may be overriding moral or prudential reasons militating against conformity. This may also be the case even when the duty is a moral(ly acceptable) one.

CHAPTER 9

Claims & Invocations of Right

§ I. Introduction

Having a legal right does not perforce entail (also having) a power to commence legal proceedings or to undertake self-help remedies—let alone success in such endeavours. There is nevertheless a life of legal rights outside of institutional settings, one that need not rely exclusively upon legal powers for their enforcement. This chapter explains two ways by which to utilise rights in private and social settings: making claims and invocations of right.

In doing so, the chapter advances three unique, albeit narrow, theses. First, rights claiming can be made using liberties, not just powers. Second, it is worthwhile to distinguish between two kinds of liberty-based ones: (i) *claims* of right and (ii) *invocations* of right. Both concern the use of liberties in support of rights-correlative-to-duties ('RCTDs'), but differ in content.[1] Third, legal liberty-based claims and invocations of right constitute (weak) forms of lawful rights enforcement.

Rights can be claimed directly of duty-bearers or invoked to other people. Such communications can renew duty-bearers' sense of legal obligation and remind them of what is due; they can stimulate duty-bearers' deliberations about how and when to act. Invocations of right can also

[1] The distinction is not between so called 'second-personal' and 'second-person-plural' addresses. See Darwall (2006: 9); Thomas (2015: 153–4).

D. Frydrych, *The Architecture of Rights*,
https://doi.org/10.1007/978-3-030-76039-7_9

influence other parties' beliefs about: what is due to a right-holder; a duty-bearer's (inappropriate) conduct; and whether they ought to assist the right-holder.

The literature on claims of right on behalf of legal RCTDs typically focuses on institutional proceedings: courts of law, arbitration, administrative hearings, etc. Further, scholars who do look beyond those contexts nonetheless tend to focus almost exclusively upon *powers* (be they understood in terms of Hohfeldian powers or 'active' Hohfeldian claims) by which to: waive duties; make 'demands'; or undertake self-help measures.[2] This focus stems at least in part from the fact that philosophers and jurists have long debated whether to define or conceive of rights as containing, or being constituted by, enforcement powers. However, legal, moral, and political philosophers concerned with analysing *private and social* claims of right generally identify claimability with normative powers.

Focussing just on powers, whether in institutional contexts or otherwise, is myopic. It underrepresents the ways in which rights can afford their holders options by which to shape their lives. This chapter therefore aims to begin to broaden scholarly horizons. Legal claims and invocations of right made outside of institutional proceedings can be authorised by (and rely on) legal *liberties*, not just powers, because the claimant or invoker must legally be permitted to both (i) communicate to other parties via a particular means and (ii) convey the kind of content that comprises the communication. Whilst not particularly potent tools for getting right-holders what they want, liberty-based claims and invocations nevertheless bear legal significance.

§ II. Perimeters of Support

This section outlines the inverse of a perimeter of protection relationship: instead of RCTDs protecting or facilitating the exercise of liberties, liberties can be used to protect or facilitate RCTDs.[3] I will style such relationships 'perimeters of support'. Whereas perimeters of protection concern one normative position protecting actions that are themselves permitted by a different position, perimeters of support concern permitted actions undertaken on behalf of a different normative position. Any accurate

[2] See the discussion in Chapter 4 § V.

[3] See Chapter 1 § II.2 on perimeters of protection.

rights model must be able to account for these sorts of capacities and relationships.

My notion of perimeters of support and forthcoming argument about liberties being used in support of RCTDs (which is not the only form a perimeter of support relationship can take) of course builds on earlier work. Particularly important is that of Stephen Darwall, Joel Feinberg, Mark Reiff, and Jean Thomas. Their respective works point the way towards the existence of two sorts of claims of right, ones *which differ from* those directed towards (and via) legal bodies and officials. These two sorts of claiming are addressed to either duty-bearers or to other community members, be they made by right-holders themselves or by others on their behalf.[4] (Thomas notes that both forms of address, one to the duty-bearer, the other to the normative community at large, help to enforce a right; the latter form of address, too, ultimately concerns 'effectuation or support' of the duty-bearer's duty.[5]) Rights are frequently brought to people's attention in these ways.

However, those scholars either: (i) err in deeming claims of right to be a function of 'active' Hohfeldian claims or Hohfeldian powers (and hence fail to recognise the need for A PERIMETER OF SUPPORT) or (ii) fail to identify the relevant type of normative position under which the claiming is authorised.[6] This is important because it affects how weak or strong, potent or impotent, this subset of claims of right are and can be.

With perimeters of support in mind, I will argue that a subset of claims of rights are better explained in terms of Hohfeldian liberties. There are furthermore at least two kinds of legal *liberty*-based claims of right, ones which help to try to enforce and support RCTDs outside of institutional settings. Legal liberties can be used to: (i) *invoke* one's RCTD publicly and/or (ii) *claim* one's rights directly from duty-bearers (or from others). Further, these liberties neither rely on legal officials (judges, administrative tribunals, tribal leaders, etc.) nor the threat of their involvement or participation for their employment, and nor do they change anyone's legal positions.

Here is an example of *claiming* rights directly from a duty-bearer. Sally agrees to lend her next-door neighbour Peter her lawnmower for two

[4] See Reiff (2005: 25–34); Darwall (2006: 9); Thomas (2015: 152–5). Thomas seems to suggest that the second form perforce addresses the entire normative community, not just a subset thereof. Ibid 154.

[5] Thomas (2015: 155).

[6] Darwall (2006: 18); Darwall (2013: 41); Eleftheriadis (2008: 117); Feinberg (1980: 148, 150, 157); MacCormick (1982b: 350–62); Reiff (2005: 25–34); Thomas (2015: 152–4).

weeks. Having failed to return it after three months, Sally calls a forgetful Peter on the telephone and says: 'In case you have forgotten, the mower is mine. I bought it and lent it to you some time ago. Return it'. This remark is neither a mere request nor a command. It reminds Peter of what he already owes Sally, and it might provide him with an incentive to fulfil his duty (i.e., to return the item) sooner than he might otherwise have done.

Here is an example of *invoking* rights. Peter has not returned Sally's lawnmower for several more months. Sally would like it returned but has been unsuccessful in getting it back from him. Frustrated, she sends an email to their whole neighbourhood stating: 'Peter from Logic Lane will not return the mower I lent him months ago. I can prove to y'all that it's mine. Can you tell him to return it to me if you see him? Be wary of lending him anything of yours!'.

Why are claiming and invoking rights different here? Are there actually two distinct concepts represented? When is something a case of invocation rather than claiming, and vice versa? Moreover, what can these accomplish?[7] The two modes are communicated with different goals in mind and their contents are distinct too. This kind of *claim* of right directly asserts that something is due to the claimant (or to another party). Its content concerns that which is already due. By contrast, an *invocation* of right asserts that, because something is already due, some further thing ought to be done, believed, or understood. Whilst both may try to enforce the duty's fulfilment, the latter may also concern efforts to have social sanctions imposed upon the duty violator.

Invoking and claiming rights in these ways bear the potential to influence other people's attitudes, views, and actions. They enable someone to *try* to demonstrate an entitlement to receive something that is already due. Claiming a right in this fashion may instil in the duty-bearer a renewed sense of obligation. Invoking a right may engender a sense of correctness, appropriateness, or validity (e.g., that the duty-bearer should do φ for the right-holder) in those who hear or learn about the claim. In turn,

[7] This section only aims to provide a rough outline of the two modes. Even so, the following questions are important for further investigation. Question 1: Are there not rather *four* kinds of rights usage being discussed here: two ways to invoke and two to claim, each with one directed to the duty-bearer and another to some other group of people? Question 2: When you communicate your rights to a legal official, must you claim it, or is it possible to just invoke it? Does the answer differ if the communication is posed to a judge/arbitrator/mediator in a legal case, rather than posed to sorts of officials, such as a police officer?

duty-bearers can be persuaded to act simply by bringing rights to their attention in these ways.[8]

Claims of right can influence duty-bearers' legal reasons to act. They can trigger a 're-cognition' of their legal requirements. For example, duty-bearers may believe that, whilst the claims are morally dubious and the legal system is itself abominable, there are nevertheless good legal reasons for responding and conforming. *Invoking* legal rights—your own or another person's—can also help to shape other people's views, e.g., a given community's. It can influence recipients' judgments about: what the right-holder is entitled to receive or do; how other parties ought to act; and whether certain people should be praised or blamed for their behaviour.[9]

§ III. Characterising the Two Modes

With which normative positions ought these sorts of claims and invocations of right be identified? Second, how can we be certain that they are indeed *legal* positions? Good starting points for this inquiry appear to be trying to ascertain whether such they can modify normative positions and whether they possess or entail any compulsory force vis-à-vis duty-bearers or third parties. For, as will be explained below, in lieu of modificatory capacities or compulsory qualities, it would be a mistake to identify them with RCTDs, powers, or combinations thereof.[10]

Modifying the lawnmower example, imagine that Sally and Peter live in a common law jurisdiction with civil and criminal law statutes of limitations governing actions concerning personal chattels (for theft, conversion, actions for replevin, detinue, trover, etc.) of six years, but no adverse possession rule for chattels. Peter has the item at his house, but Sally

[8] Duty-bearers may act out of a sense of obligation, out of self-interest, social, political, or legal pressure, or from a combination of these factors. This is akin to what is sometimes styled the Any Reasons thesis: allegiance to a legal system (and conformity with its norms) can be for any reason, e.g., calculations of long-term interest, concern for others, tradition, a desire to conform, etc. See Hart (1994: 203, discussing legal officials' reasons for showing allegiance to the system's norms).

[9] Of course, these need not be the only aims behind claiming or invoking rights. For example, a claimant might also be seeking public recognition or other sorts of validation.

[10] The analysis understands a duty's compulsory quality in *normative* terms, i.e., not in terms of physical power. The matter under consideration here is whether issuing a communication—an invocation or claim—to fulfil a duty contains a compulsory quality.

retains superior title. Six long, cruel years of mowerlessness pass for Sally. Even so, she can no longer successfully sue Peter to get her property back, and nor can the state convict him of theft if he raises the relevant statutes of limitations as defences. Undeterred, Sally calls Peter on the phone and claims the chattel. She reminds him that the mower is her property and that it was only loaned to him. Does Sally's communication have any *legally* compulsory quality? If so, how should it be explained and characterised?

Here are some candidate explanations. Option I: Sally uses a legal power to create a new duty for Peter, one differing from his original duty to simply return the mower. In Hohfeldian terms, Sally used a power to create for herself a new claim—albeit one that *might* be unenforceable in the courts given the statutes of limitation—and a new correlative duty in Peter. Under this option, though, the power does not nullify the pre-existing claim and correlative duty. Option II: Sally uses a legal power to modify Peter's original duty and her own correlative Hohfeldian claim. Option III: Sally uses a Hohfeldian claim to *make* a claim of right, reaffirming Peter's duty. Option IV: Sally uses legal liberties to assert or reaffirm Peter's duty.

Options I–II The first two candidates are legal powers. Does Sally's phone call alter the parties' legal relations, either by adding new legal positions, or by modifying the parties' original ones? How exactly would either an additional duty, or a modified one, differ from the original? On the one hand, it might be thought that the communication alters the timeframe for the chattel's return. Perhaps Peter's duty is modified from being required to return the item in, say, a reasonable period of time (even given his tardiness till now) to instead returning the item forthwith. Alternatively, as Carl Wellman argues, maybe a power-based claim of right alters the correlative duty's stringency and adds force to other people's reasons to act negatively to what has happened.[11] As Sally's ownership status has not been completely altered (again, there is no adverse possession rule regarding personal chattels in this hypothetical jurisdiction), there seems to be no reason why she could not unilaterally alter Peter's relationship to her vis-à-vis the mower.[12]

[11] See Chapter 4 note 118 and the accompanying text.

[12] This, if we assume her property rights track something like Anthony Honoré's eleven incidents of ownership. Honoré (1961). See Chapter 1 note 71.

These power-based explanations of such claims of right are nevertheless inapt because there is no reason to think that Sally's communication changes the parties' legal positions in these ways. Peter's duty to return the item is already well past due. As he already ought to return the mower forthwith as a matter of the original duty, there is no need to understand Sally's communication as altering the content, nature, or stringency of his legal duty. It just seems to be a matter of calling attention to existing reasons, rather than adding to them or their force. Any increased gravity of the duty-bearer's wrongdoing is based upon what he himself has done (e.g., holding on to the mower for so long), *not* based on the claimant's mere communication calling attention to that fact. (Moreover, giving others reasons to react negatively to the duty-bearer need not change their normative positions either. It merely alerts them to how they might have been warranted to treat him had they already known the details.) Of course, this does not prove the absence of legal powers. If Peter already must so act, however, then even if such powers do obtain, they are explanatorily superfluous here.

Pace Margaret Gilbert, moreover, there is no need for a concept, A POWER, which maintains the status quo, i.e., one that does not alter normative positions. Aware of the problems of trying to attribute claimability to a 'passive' Hohfeldian claim, Gilbert tries to explain it instead in terms of a non-altering power for her demand-rights.[13] However, there is either some correlative liability built in to a duty-bearer's position (complex or 'basic' position) such that he or she is susceptible to these demands in ways that change the duty or how to fulfil it (along the lines Wellman suggests), in which case Gilbert ought to adopt the regular concept (a power which alters positions), or she ought to instead adopt a liberty-based account of claimability.[14]

Options III–IV Alternative explanations are that Sally's attempt to catalyse Peter's compliance reflects something already inherent in Peter's existing duty: he already owes her the mower. So, Sally uses either (III) her existing Hohfeldian claim, or (IV) liberties to press for the item's return. In turn, Peter is either bound to accede to Sally's communication as a

[13] See Chapter 4 notes 129–34 and the accompanying text.

[14] The same may be said for HLA Hart and Hillel Steiner's notion, which was styled a 'primary enforcement power' in Chapter 7 § III 'Argument 2'. That too is better understood in terms of a legal liberty.

function of his existing duty to return the mower, or he additionally bears some normative incapacity or is simply not entitled (e.g., Hohfeldian 'no-rights') to prevent her from making such communications to him.

Assessing these two options depends in part upon how one understands a *Hohfeldian* claim. Again, it is a contested concept. As mentioned in Chapter 3 § III, the view of Hohfeldian claims being themselves capable of engendering the making of claims of right depends upon an 'active' interpretation of a Hohfeldian claim. Reasons were provided for preferring the 'passive' interpretation instead; namely, the 'active' interpretation adds the capacity to claim as a feature of the concept, which renders it subject to decomposition. It would then be a composite of: (i) the entitlement to another's required action or forbearance and (ii) the capacity to claim. Not only does this mean that it fails to be 'conceptually basic' (a metatheoretical desideratum Hohfeld thought his conceptions should meet), but the capacity to claim is also *better* explained in terms of other normative positions, i.e., liberties and powers. To discard the 'active' interpretation entails eliminating Option III.

Concerning Option IV, *Hohfeldian* liberties lack modificatory or compulsory qualities. A liberty alone cannot bind another party. So, a liberty to claim could neither modify parties' normative positions, nor compel another party to act or forbear from acting. There are of course alternatives to Hohfeld's conception, including ones positing a direct correlation between *A*'s liberty and *B*'s duty (e.g., against interference).[15] Even so, it is unclear that, on these alternative conceptions, a liberty entails any modificatory capacity vis-à-vis the correlative duty either.

The key to accurately characterising the two modes of claiming and invoking rights outlined here, and identifying which normative domain (law, morality, etc.) they belong, lies in the fact that the very entitlement to communicate with others requires explanation. The very act of communicating requires permission to be undertaken. Furthermore, the relevant permission must be legal. This serves as the strongest basis for identifying the types of rights usage in question with liberties.

Here is the reasoning fleshed out. Many rules place limits on communications or allow for such limitations to be generated. Some laws ban certain kinds of communication based on content (hate speech, libel laws, gag orders, etc.). Others impose time, place, or manner restrictions (e.g., prohibiting telemarketers from telephoning private residences during

[15] E.g., Hart (1982: 172); Robinson et al. (1983: 269).

certain times of the day). Different laws make it is illegal and/or tortious to contact people at all, e.g., restraining orders. Still other laws authorise parties to make contracts which contain duties requiring one or both parties' silence (duties to forbear from making certain sorts of communications) on specific matters.

To make a claim or invocation of right, therefore, one must be entitled both to communicate with given parties and to convey the relevant kind of speech. Thus, at least two liberties are required to explain Sally's communication to Peter about the lawnmower: one enabling her to undertake some means of communication, and a second allowing her to convey certain content. In turn, Peter's position reflects Sally's lack of duties to avoid: (I) attempting to contact him via the specific medium utilised and (II) communicating that kind of speech to him. If this characterisation is apt, then there are ways to claim rights that only involve liberties.

Moreover, such claims and invocations of right are *lawful* actions, using legal positions, because they are dependent upon legal authorisation for their actualisation in terms of the modes of communication and their content. This is important for two reasons. First, it helps to undercut a popular conception of law as simply being a sanction/remedy-driven institution enforced by those with a monopoly of political force. Second, it helps to show how private agents can use legal norms to help to defend their legal positions outside of institutional frameworks.

Now, one might deem this to be a 'thin' sense of 'legal', one that is on par with any trivial activity that is not legally prohibited, such as combing your own hair. This would be a mistake, as it would ignore the difference in normative force and in social implications that such communications can trigger in terms of private responses for compliance and for social responses on large scales in furtherance of legal norms and the law generally..[16] (It would additionally be an error because, outside of the

[16] Gilbert would probably oppose this account in favour of her (Hohfeldian claim-power) 'demand-right' on the basis that her alternative better explains the grounds of the claimant's *standing* to make a claim of right. She notes that 'naked' liberties do not afford such standing, whilst her demand-right both does so and explains its very grounding. Gilbert (2018: 77). However, her account has merely infused claimability into AN RCTD without warrant. Instead, all that is needed is a relationship between an RCTD and a liberty, so that an exercise of the latter in furtherance of the former can come replete with the relevant sort of standing (to make a claim of right, rather than a bald assertion or meritless claim). Indeed, her own account suggests as much: she notes that, for liberty-holders, this standing is the function of the 'protective claim' (here, meaning the passive component of an 'active' Hohfeldian claim,

contexts of these two particular modes of rights claiming, people's legal positions can also be changed through what is said, e.g., by soliciting someone to enter a contract the parties can become offeror and offeree.) *Liberty*-based claims and invocations of right must therefore also be included in general accounts of practical reasoning.

Two more points may be added in favour of counting these sorts of claims and invocations as legal ones are as follows. Officials generally prefer that people peacefully resolve their disputes by themselves, if possible, without having to resort to institutional dispute resolution processes. Liberty-based claims and invocations of right assist in furthering that goal. Moreover, any legal action taken by a communicatee against a valid claimer or invoker (because the recipient believes the right-holder had no right to communicate) will fail because the liberty exculpates the communicator.[17]

Additionally, if one accepts the working conception of RIGHTS ENFORCEMENT offered in Chapter 4, then liberty-based claims and invocations of right count as types of rights enforcement because they either aim to see a duty fulfilled, its breach remedied, or the securement of some form of vindication for the right and/or right-holding status. To be sure, claims and invocations of right do not determine outcomes. Claiming is simply a means by which to *try* to get a right recognised, remedied, or otherwise vindicated. Legal enforcement mechanisms, generally, are only defeasible tools. Just like powers to enforce or waive an RCTD, legal liberties to claim or invoke do not guarantee success or a remedy. They are mere means by which to lawfully try to vindicate rights.

if not simply the passive interpretation of a claim itself) which allows for them to make assertions of right rather than mere assertions (ibid). This in turn suggests the superfluity of either (a) incorporating the capacity or entitlement to claim into the RCTD itself, or (b) a 'protective claim', as the assertion is ostensibly done via a 'non-altering' power, not a liberty (on her view), and so would be function of a direct relationship between a demand-right and a duty. As discussed in Chapter 2 § III, moreover, the RCTD and correlative duty may assist a liberty-holder in reminding others why and how not to interfere, but his or her *being entitled to so act* is a function of the liberty itself. A liberty-holder permitted to do *X* thus has 'standing' to claim (via a different liberty) that she be free to do *X because* she possesses the (former) liberty. Whether absent a perimeter of protection the claim would be respected is another matter.

[17] See Hohfeld (1913b: 554); Goble (1922: 104–5); Radin (1938: 1151); Reiff (2005: 193). Indeed, *A's* liberty may be a ground for *B* to be rendered liable to cover *A*'s costs.

§ IV. Objection and Response

Objection There seem to be cases of rights invocation that would be inappropriate to identify as forms of rights exercise or enforcement. For example, imagine that Lord Bob walks into a bar. Eager to impress, Lord Bob invokes the fact that he owns Downton Abbey (which is true). He proves his ownership by showing patrons the deed, photos of him in the house, etc., which he always carries around on his person for just such purposes. Whilst Lord Bob has, in a sense, 'invoked' his property rights to the others, it seems odd to say that he thereby 'exercised' his property rights, let alone 'enforced' them. If this involves a different sense of 'invoking' rights than that outlined above, what is the distinguishing basis? If it is the same sense, what makes it an instance of exercise or enforcement?

Response The particular senses of liberty-based claims and invocations of right outlined above differ from each other based on the intended addressees and the reasons why each communication is made. A liberty-based *claim* of right is made in order to motivate a duty-bearer to fulfil his or her duty. An *invocation* of right aims to influence other parties, perhaps in order to gain their support or assistance, and perhaps as an indirect way to motivate the duty-bearer. Claiming and invoking rights in these ways are undertaken on behalf of some predicate RCTD.

Further, distinguishing Lord Bob's case from the sense of invocation outlined in this chapter is not difficult. Lord Bob has 'invoked' his property rights, but not in the particular sense discussed herein, because he did so for the sake of something else (i.e., to impress others), and not on behalf of his rights or right-holding status, e.g., the use of his property, to vindicate his legal title, etc.

Must rights be used solely to furthering their contents? No. Again, people can use their rights to extort or punish others, to seek publicity or recognition, etc., and not because they are primarily concerned with either their content or vindicating their right-holder status. Must all forms of claiming or invoking always be done for such purposes, then? No. Even so, there are distinct senses of claiming and invoking rights which do serve such ends. The basic idea is that such communications *can* be the normative—including legal—basis for motivating an action or belief in the public at large, or in some smaller group of recipients of the information, including duty-bearers personally. Perhaps some duty-bearers fear a group's judgment and act on that basis (i.e., modify their course of actions in order to fulfil their duties). Even if they did, that is no reason to deny alternative or additional motivations, such as a desire to comply with the law.

Invocations and claims of right cover a large variety of communications. They are also not necessarily restricted to the right-holder's personal actions: other parties can claim and invoke on a right-holder's behalf. Just as trustees, legal guardians, and state officials can sometimes commence legal proceedings in the name of another party's rights, so too can one sometimes invoke or make claims on behalf of another's. (Of course, not all communications referencing another's rights are instances of the two modes being discussed here.)

Legal liberty-based claims and invocations of rights provide alternative means for trying to vindicate rights in private and social contexts. Although less potent tools than enforcement powers, such liberties need not be devoid of normative force or potential in terms of influencing a duty-bearer's or a third party's thinking. (It also seems possible to invoke or claim immunities, powers, and even other liberties, not just RCTDs.)

CHAPTER 10

The Conceptual Contingency of Perimeters of Support

§ I. Introduction

Either akin to, or extending, the Control View outlined in Chapter 7, it might be thought that liberties by which to claim or invoke rights are either constitutive features of a right-correlative-to-a-duty ('an RCTD') or are invariably associated with them (the latter option perhaps due to a belief about how normative domains must operate). Alternatively, it might be thought that this is the case only for legal (as opposed to moral, social, other institutional, etc.) rights. This would be the last refuge for those who believe that RCTDs perforce engender or entail their own enforceability in some sense, or who wish to conceive of RCTDs as entitling one to make claims of right.[1]

Just like power-based elements of control for an RCTD, however, liberties by which to make claims or invocations of right need not obtain just because an RCTD does. To establish that proposition, this chapter will focus predominantly upon *legal* liberties and RCTDs. Further, as in Chapter 7, this chapter does not, and need not, offer a conceptual analysis of A RIGHT or AN RCTD, wherein perimeters of support are adjudged to (not) be putative essential features of one or the other. Again, any such analysis would fail to be comprehensive, and some proponents of this extended Control View might believe the invariability of claimability to be

[1] E.g., Feinberg (1973: 65).

D. Frydrych, *The Architecture of Rights*,
https://doi.org/10.1007/978-3-030-76039-7_10

due to the nature of normative domains themselves, rather than because of some essential feature of RCTDs, anyway.[2]

Section II addresses Hohfeldian arguments which aim to show that any relationships between claims and liberties are conceptually or logically contingent. In fact, many Hohfeldians argue for 'global' conceptual contingency: there are no necessary logical/conceptual connections or entailments between any (tokens) of the eight fundamental types of rights and ligations within the *schema of jural relations.* (Let us style this the 'Global Contingency proposition'.) If correct, their arguments entail that all perimeters of protection and support relationships are merely contingent.

The Hohfeldians' arguments nonetheless suffer from two kinds of flaws, which make it impossible for them to justify the Global Contingency proposition. Section III therefore presents novel arguments to establish the conceptually contingent nature of any relationship between liberties used to claim and invoke an RCTD, i.e., to form 'perimeters of support' for the latter. These arguments overcome the Hohfeldians' difficulties by concerning rules proscribing all potential liberties of support, not just token liberties.

The chapter then presents some ways to respond to the new arguments. One is simply to express dubiousness about the plausibility of the new arguments' hypothetical cases. A second, speculative response is to suggest that connections between RCTDs and liberties invariably obtain because positions can have normative effects across normative domains or systems, e.g., moral liberties on behalf of legal RCTDs.

§ II. *Pace* Invariable Support Perimeters Part I: Hohfeldian Arguments

Many Hohfeldians argue that any connection between claims and liberties is entirely for contingent, rather than logically/conceptually necessary, reasons. Hohfeld himself suggests there are no such necessary connections amongst any of the *schema*'s eight positions, save for that of being

[2] Embedded within his larger argument that there is no logical connection between rights and claims/claiming, Alan White believes he has shown that 'having a subjunctive claim' to something, i.e., a call or demand that something should be the case (White 1984: 117–20), and hence being able to make a claim of right, is not implied from simply having a right to that thing. Ibid 130–2. However, he does not actually establish this.

correlatives and 'opposites'.[3] Even so, neither he nor his adherents demonstrate this general proposition for *all possible* relationships amongst normative positions (e.g., between a liberty and an immunity, between a claim and an immunity, etc.).[4] Of course, if all such relations are conceptually

[3]Hohfeld (1913a: 35–7); Hohfeld (1917: 745–7). Hohfeldians' arguments to this effect actually aim to accomplish several goals concurrently. Goal I: to show that possessing a right against one ligation-bearer does not necessarily entail possession of (cognate) rights against additional persons—in part, because a given right does not necessarily hold against everyone. Possessing multiple rights in a given state of affairs does not entail that a given position will obtain against anyone other than a specific ligation-bearer. (This reflects Hohfeld's Interpersonal and Strict Bilaterality theses, discussed in Chapter 3 note 18. For Hohfeld, *A*'s right that *B* stay off *A*'s land differs from *A*'s right that *C* stay off. Although the rights are similar in content, they are distinct). Hence, having a right does not guarantee a particular (social) outcome; just because one has a right does not mean one's aims cannot be thwarted.

Goal II: to show that no Hohfeldian position is logically entailed from the possession of any other kind of Hohfeldian position, be it a right or a ligation. Goal III: to resolve certain paradoxes about the usage of the term 'a right' in certain cases: (*Paradox Type A*) where it might be said that one has a right and does not have a right at the same time (e.g., making legally valid exercises of a power despite having been duty-bound not to do so); and (*Paradox Type B*) where it might be said that one has a right to do wrong. E.g., Kramer (1998: 4–5, 17 n.6, 19, 62–5, 68–72, 82–3, 99–100, 106); Simmonds (1998: 152–5, 220, 223 & n.137); Steiner (1998: 242 n.16, 245 n.20).

According to Nigel Simmonds, these sorts of Hohfeldian arguments are (additionally) meant to show that rights are neither inviolable, nor composed of logically necessary parts. The components are simply the product of—historically contingent and sometimes also erroneous—judgments of policy and justice. Arguing that a right can contain distinct, basic normative positions (e.g., claims and liberties) as components was meant to be an argument against Kantians and others who either denied that rights bore such complexity, or thought that the components invariably co-obtained. Simmonds (1998: 172, 180, 194). Cf. Hohfeld (1913a: 27 n.21, 36). (Simmonds himself, though, rejects the idea of rights as complexes. Simmonds (1998: 220)). Even so, Hohfeld's predecessors never denied that one person might have distinct (legal) relationships with different parties; and it is doubtful that anyone ever really disagreed with the proposition that *A* could have a right against *B* but not against *C* (and indeed have a different sort of legal relationship with *C*).

[4]Hohfeld's own examples concern either relationships between claims and liberties, or between powers and liberties by which to exercise them. E.g., Hohfeld (1913a: 52); Hohfeld (1917: 756–7). It remains an open question, however, what Hohfeld thought about the relationship between primary, secondary, and tertiary rights, and whether a breach of the first *necessarily* gave rise to a secondary one, and so forth. See Hohfeld (1909: 293–4); Hohfeld (1913a: 34–6); Hohfeld (1913b: especially at 569–70 nn. 32–4); Hohfeld (1917: 745, 747, 753–5). See also Frydrych (2018a: 300–3).

Hohfeldians also discuss other sorts of connections that do not necessarily rise to the level of conceptual necessity, but which seem to come close. On the connection between duties to act and liberties to undertake the actions necessary to carry out the duty, see, e.g., Steiner

contingent, then all perimeter of support relationships are too. Let us now address the Hohfeldian arguments. The first three are Hohfeld's own.

§ II.1. Case A: Hohfeld's Salad

Liberties can exist without associated Hohfeldian claims. You may be free to undertake an action (or to forbear from acting) without being entitled to be free from interference by others whilst doing so. Building on an example from John Chipman Gray, Hohfeld notes the difference between having a claim to a salad and the liberty to consume it. One may be at liberty to eat the salad without also having a claim 'to do' so. *A* offers *B* some salad. *A* makes the offer on the condition that, whilst *B* can eat what he can of the food, *A* does not promise to refrain from interfering with *B*'s consumption thereof.[5] It being *A*'s property, *A* can rightfully grab the salad bowl from under *B*'s nose, i.e., legally interfere with *B*'s eating. *B* thus has a liberty to consume the salad but no claim to do so without interference.

§ II.2. Cases B & C: Blackacre and Whiteacre

Hohfeldian claims can also obtain without corresponding liberties. Hohfeld provides two cases. The first concerns having a claim but not a liberty. The second is about having a liberty to φ and a 'no-right' to φ concurrently.

> *A*'s privileges… are strikingly independent of his rights or claims against any given person, and *either might exist without the other*. Thus *A* might, for $100 paid to him by *B*, agree in writing to keep off [his own land,] ***Blackacre***. *A* would still have his rights or claims against *B*, that the latter should keep off, etc.; yet, as against *B*, *A*'s own privileges of entering on Blackacre would be gone. On the other hand, with regard to *X*'s land, ***Whiteacre***, *A* has, against *B*, the privilege of entering thereon; but, not having possession, he has no right or claim, that *B* shall not enter on Whiteacre.[6]

(1994: 74–85); Kramer (1998: 17–8); Simmonds (1998: 162, 183–6). On immunities against divestiture purportedly being necessary for claims to count as 'genuine' ones, see Kramer & Steiner (2007: 297–8). For the notion of duties delimiting power usage ('directed powers') by an anti-Hohfeldian, see Raz (1996: 241–4).

[5] Hohfeld (1913a: 34–5). Cf. Gray (1909: 20).

[6] Hohfeld (1917: 747, emphases and bolding added). Cf. Hohfeld (1913a: 32–3, 52).

Case B concerns *A*'s land, Blackacre. *A* has a claim against *B*'s entrance, but not a liberty vis-à-vis *B* to personally enter his own estate. **Case C** concerns a third party's land, Whiteacre. There, *A* has a liberty vis-à-vis *B* to enter the third party's land, but no claim against *B*'s entering Whiteacre. Why does *A* actually have a liberty in the latter case? For Hohfeld, it is because *A* does not owe *B* a duty to forbear from entering Whiteacre, even though *A* owes such a duty to *X*, the landowner. For Hohfeld, the absence of a duty perforce entails the existence of a liberty. Further, the *A*-*B* relationship does not define the *A*-*X* relationship, or vice versa.

§ II.3. Cases D & E: Kramer & Singer's Remaindermen

The following Hohfeldian arguments involve a remainderman and trespassers.[7] Joseph Singer provides the first, **Case D**. Having a right to keep trespassers off some land (a claim that they stay off) does not entail that you also have a liberty to use the land yourself. For example, a remainderman may have no liberty to enter the land personally whilst nonetheless having a claim to keep trespassers off.[8]

Matthew Kramer thinks Singer's point is glib because the rights in question have different contents: keeping others off the land versus entering it yourself. (This criticism applies equally to Hohfeld's Blackacre case.) Singer, he believes, ought to have gone further by demonstrating that a claim to be free from interference with *one's own* entry onto some land does not entail one's also having a liberty to enter the land.[9] Whilst Kramer does not offer examples, Case C (mostly) seems to fit the bill: *A* has a liberty vis-à-vis *B* to enter Whiteacre, but no liberty to do so vis-à-vis *X*, Whiteacre's owner. (It must be added that, even so, *A* may also have RCTDs that *B* not interfere with *A*'s entering *X*'s land in certain ways,

[7] A remainderman is someone designated in a trust or will to inherit property after another person, the life tenant, who is also identified in the legal instrument, ceases to have a right to it. For example, a husband may stipulate in his will that, after he dies, his wife may live in his house until she herself dies, after which their son is to get the property. The son here is the remainderman.

[8] Singer (1982: 988). If the remainderman really does have a claim here, she does not have the power to enforce it against the trespasser. It is the job of a trustee, as the legal title holder to the property (who does have a claim against trespassers), to initiate and prosecute any civil actions against trespassers. The trustee has such a claim, but no liberty to enter the property itself so long as the life tenant (who holds a beneficial interest in the property) dwells there. (That is, unless the trustee is granted such liberty by the life tenant).

[9] Kramer (1998: 16–7).

e.g., by assaulting him. Still, *A's* claim does not entail a liberty vis-à-vis *X* to enter the land.)

§ II.4. Case F: Rainbolt's Lake

George Rainbolt aims to show that: (I) a Hohfeldian claim can exist independently of any other normative positions; (II) that singular claims constitute genuine rights; and (III), that rights are neither necessarily enforceable nor exercisable.[10] His main argument is this. *A* plans to visit Squam Lake, New Hampshire, USA. That lake is of sentimental value to *B*. *A* promises *B* that, when he gets to the lake, he will dip his feet in the water. Thus, *A* has a duty to *B* to do so whilst *B* has a correlative claim that the dipping be done. This is all that is required for *B* to have a genuine right. *B* need not additionally possess a power to sue *A* for failing to perform, since *B* may waive that power. Nor must *B* possess an immunity from *A*'s unilaterally extinguishing the duty by some means.[11]

Why does *B* have a bona fide right, despite lacking additional positions? Why does a singular (passive) Hohfeldian claim count as a right? At first, Rainbolt seems to punt to Hohfeld for the idea that it is a right *because* it correlates with a duty. *A* has a duty to act (to dip his feet in the lake), and duties are the 'invariable correlative' of rights.[12] Why is *that* relevant or required for something to count as a right, though? Hohfeld gives no

[10] Rainbolt (2006: 42–4).

[11] Ibid 43. Aside from questions about whether it is a legally binding agreement, Rainbolt's argument is superficially flawed. Whilst it aims to show that a singular Hohfeldian claim can be a right without relying on associated normative positions (liberties, powers, etc.), it presumes, without need or warrant, the existence of a waiver power. That only helps buttress the *opposite* view, though: the idea that rights are always enforceable, and thus are to be understood in terms of complexes. His argument can therefore be improved by assuming that *B* has neither enforcement nor waiver powers.

[12] Rainbolt (2006: 43), *quoting* Hohfeld (1913a: 31). Rainbolt seems to contradict himself on the matter, however. Despite the lake example being an argument in favour of single claims constituting rights, he nevertheless holds that '[n]o actual rule system gives people a single claim all by itself'. Rainbolt (2006: 43). These propositions seem irreconcilable, e.g., by trying to frame one or the other as being a conceptual claim and the other as an unsubstantiated empirical assertion; for he considers the lake example to concern a bona fide (albeit hypothetical) *legal* position. Ibid. It is at least conceivable that a legal system could recognise *A* and *B*'s agreement as a legal contract, even if the parties could not enforce it, and even if other legal considerations, such as the common law doctrine consideration, are neither required nor met, e.g., *B* giving *A* something in return for the toe-dipping. (Further, a rights functionalist might object that this can only concern *moral* RCTDs and liberties, not *legal*

answer, but Rainbolt does. As discussed in Chapters 5 and 6, Rainbolt's *theory* of rights is that, by their nature, rights impose justified, normative constraints on other parties; all that is required for one party to have a right is for a second person to (justifiably) bear a normatively constraining position that correlates with the first party's position, and where that normative constraint is justified by being predicated upon *some* feature or other of that first person. A duty is one kind of normative constraint. Whilst not all duties bear correlatives, for those that do, the counterpart positions count as rights.[13]

§ II.4.I. Pace *the Hohfeldian Arguments*

Insofar as they aim to demonstrate the conceptually/logically contingent nature of the relationships between normative positions, the arguments addressed above all suffer from at least one of two flaws. Flaw 1: fallaciously assume that showing a token of one type of normative position does not obtain *establishes* that no other tokens of the same type obtain. Just because a right-holder lacks, abandons, or forfeits a given liberty, it does not follow that he or she lacks others.[14] This is like trying to demonstrate that no birds live in Europe by showing that there are no American bald eagles there. Flaw 2: you cannot demonstrate the conceptual contingency of such relationships by showing that party *A* may have one kind of a right against party *B*, but not against party *C*. (Instead, you must try to show that *A*'s various normative positions vis-à-vis *B* are all contingently related.)

The Hohfeldian arguments therefore all suffer from the same structural difficulty: being unable to prove a negative. They aim to show that, because one token of a type of Hohfeldian position (e.g., a claim) does not obtain whilst a token of some other type of position does (e.g., a liberty), that different tokens of the first type of position, or tokens of any other basic types, do not obtain. By design, however, their arguments cannot demonstrate the non-existence of any additional normative positions (liberties, powers, etc.), let alone whether such positions are either logically entailed or merely contingently connected to the one identified token normative position. For any revised arguments of this sort to even have a

ones. Much work would have to be done to actually distinguish the cognate positions, though).

[13] Ibid xiii, 118. See also Chapter 5 § V on Rainbolt's theory.

[14] For a similar view, see Halpin (1997: 38).

hope of success, Hohfeldians would need to undertake a comprehensive process of elimination, establishing the non-existence of any other token positions. Let us nonetheless address the specific examples.

The Salad Situation. Hohfeld says *B* can have a liberty to eat a salad without also possessing a claim to do so without interference. However, his argument wrongly implies that, because some means of interfering are available to *A* by which to reclaim the salad from *B*, all possible means obtain. This is false.[15] Whilst the salad owner, *A*, who gives *B* the liberty to eat, may try to take the salad back, *A* cannot assault *B* in order to do that. For example, *A* cannot punch *B* and then grab the food. *B* has claims against *A*'s doing so. Hence, in addition to the liberty to consume, *B* might also be said to have *some* right to do so without interference—although not, of course, against all possible means of interference.

One could object that this argument trades on an ambiguity in the notion of 'a right against interference' and that there is no real 'claim to consume without interference' here. Instead, there is just a right against being assaulted, which has nothing to do with the liberty in question. *A* owes *B* no duty to forbear from interfering with the salad eating per se, and *A*'s duty not to assault *B* has nothing to do with the activity of salad consumption. Thus, it is mistaken to characterise *that* duty—or a further specified version of it, if construed as being a general one—as correlating with a right to non-interference with salad consumption. The objection is unconvincing. The claim against being assaulted indirectly protects *B*'s liberty to eat the salad. The claim to consumption-sans-meddling, at least, concerns assault (but not *A*'s snatching the salad without touching *B*). In other words, the claim creates a perimeter of protection for the liberty, howsoever mediate.[16]

Case B: Blackacre. Although vis-à-vis *B*, *A* cannot go on to his own land, Blackacre, *A* has not necessarily lost any of the other liberties usually associated with ownership. As examples, the right to alienate property normally includes liberties to exercise that right. Barring the creation of duties

[15] Hart (1982: 171); Halpin (1997: 37–41); Kramer (1998: 12 & n.3); Kramer (1999: 316).

[16] Cf. Kramer (1998: 16–7 n.6) on the issue of characterising rights and duties against interference. He notes that, for such arguments, one need only to show that one's characterisation of the parties' positions is accurate, not that it is *uniquely* accurate.

otherwise, *A* can and may alienate. *A* may also have the liberty (and power) to hire repairmen for the property, to purchase and add new chattels for the land, etc. Whilst these do not prove that other liberties, including the ones just mentioned, exist for logically/conceptually necessary, rather than contingent, reasons, such a demonstration is not required to establish the Hohfeldian argument's inadequacy, at least insofar as it aims to advance the Global Contingency proposition.

Cases C & D: Whiteacre & the Remaindermen. These cases reflect the second kind of flaw outlined above. Singer's remainderman argument is unhelpful because it concerns one's person's normative positions vis-à-vis two distinct persons. The same holds for Hohfeld's Whiteacre case, wherein two trespassers wish to enter a third party's land. In Hohfeld's view, *A* has a claim to non-interference whilst interloping against one party, but no liberty to actually do so vis-à-vis the landowner. As these concern different legal relationships, what is the significance for establishing the global contingency proposition, or even just between claims and liberties?

At best, the Whiteacre example establishes that it is possible for you to possess a liberty vis-à-vis one person but not vis-à-vis a second. *A* has a liberty to go on to Whiteacre vis-à-vis *B*, but not vis-à-vis *X* (because *A* instead owes a duty to *X* not to enter). Still, this says nothing about the general relationship between claims and liberties.[17] *A* also has a claim against *B* not to interfere with the former's entering Whiteacre, not simply a liberty, because, again, *A* has a right against being assaulted. This is just a perimeter of protection relationship, though.

The remainderman argument also suffers from the first flaw (no birds because no bald eagles). It just shows that the claim-holder fails to possess all the elements of a 'full' property right. One might assume that a property owner usually possesses both a claim against entrance to the land and

[17] Notice, furthermore, the ambiguity in Kramer's 'right to be free from interference' with one's entry onto some land: is it one Hohfeldian position or multiple? Kramer thinks it is only a Hohfeldian claim against interference. Kramer (1998: 14–7). The liberty to enter—if there is one—may shape the content of that claim: a claim against one's interfering (physically, etc.) with the claim-holder's entering the land. That content (against physical assault) shapes the claim's extension, for there may be other legally permissible ways by which to interfere with the attempted ingress, e.g., by calling the police, warning the landowner, etc. Correctly or otherwise, some scholars nonetheless object that a claim alone cannot suffice to explain such '*freedom* from interference'; freedom from interference whilst doing activity φ without *being entitled to do* φ is, for them, a conceptual error. E.g., R.E. Robinson et al. (1983: 269).

the liberty to enter it oneself vis-à-vis the whole world (*in rem*). However, if remaindermen (or trustees, more likely) can try to vindicate their claims against trespassers, which the argument presumes, then they have both the liberty and the power to commence proceedings, even if they lack a 'full' property right. Remaindermen may additionally have liberties to style themselves as 'remaindermen', to contact the trustee regarding the trust (e.g., in order to invoke their rights to inspect trust documents), etc.

Squam Lake. Rainbolt's argument about the promise to go to the lake fails to prove a negative: that no other legal positions obtain, rendering the Hohfeldian claim (that *A* dip a toe into a lake) an independent, 'atomic' position. Again, exposing this inadequacy does not *ipso facto* demonstrate that any other positions do, let alone must, obtain.[18]

Hohfeldians generally also fail to explain why one party's bearing a duty suffices to establish that another party must have a correlative right.[19] Even if *A* owes *B* a duty to touch a lake, and even if it is 'directed' toward *B* (and even if it is in *B*'s interests that *A* do so), why does that suffice to establish *B as a right-holder*—especially a legal one, in cases like the lake example? This is simply assumed or stipulated without warrant or adequate justification—especially for those who are open to the possibility of absolute duties.

§ III. *Pace* Invariable Support Perimeters Part II

§ III.1. A Simpler Approach

There is a simpler way to demonstrate the conceptual contingency of all liberty-based claims of right: establishing that any given means of communication, which is required for providing the relevant 'perimeter of

[18] Rainbolt offers a second example wherein *C* is owed money from *D*, but also bears a duty not to accept it from *D*. For Rainbolt, it does not follow that the creditor lacks a right. *C* has a claim to the money, despite not having a liberty to receive it. Rainbolt (2006: 44). For the same sort of reason, this argument also fails to prove that the right-holder possesses only a claim; the creditor might be at liberty to contact the debtor, to communicate with him or her about the debt, to direct the debtor to give the funds to other parties, etc.

[19] See Chapter 3 § II.1 on absolute duties. But see Kramer (1998: 58–9). Cf. Salmond (1902: 224).

support', might be unavailable.[20] You *may* have 'the' liberty to contact a duty-bearer (via telephone, email, etc.) or to otherwise communicate with him or her, or with other parties, in order to inform them about your rights, or to try to persuade any of them to act. Still, these require entitlements or authorisations to use particularised means of communication. However, there is no reason why a given right-holder *must invariably* be privileged to undertake any or all such actions.

Liberties to make claims or invocations of right are conceptually independent from RCTDs because nullifying the latter would not necessarily thereby eradicate those liberties. Being legally authorised to communicate with duty-bearers or other parties—both in terms of (1) being permitted to contact them and (2) being free to express the relevant content within those communications—is not necessarily predicated upon possession of a legally valid RCTD held against such persons. To return to our example from Chapter 9 § III, Sally may be entitled call Peter on the telephone and tell him to return her mower even if he does not actually have it (e.g., she was mistaken about whom she lent it to, he had already returned it to her, etc.).

Moreover, a perimeter of support relationship between any such liberty and RCTD in part concerns the *content* of the communication. However, *X*'s liberty to communicate to *Y* need not be based upon *X*'s RCTD, and it probably permits discussion about a great many things otherwise.

Now, one could model an RCTD as containing such liberties as components, but the liberties by which to make such communications are not *perforce* reliant upon those claims. Further, given their content-dependence for being identified as the bases by which to claim or invoke rights, the relationships of such liberties with an RCTD could not be systematically formalised in a rights model in the way one can do for RCTDs and powers

[20] Another method would be to try to show the lack of particular means of communication in given cases and then making an abductive argument about the total set of means of communications being unavailable. This technique was employed in Chapter 7 to show the potential unavailability of enforcement and waiver powers for a given RCTD. That approach would not work here, though. For whilst the number of modes of legal enforcement and waiver *powers* is relatively determinate and limited, the set of modes of support for RCTDs via *liberties* is indeterminate, if not also unlimited. The approach would then suffer the same fate as Hohfeldians' tack of only showing the non-existence of some, not all, means. The reason why the method undertaken below differs is because it discusses (i) a distinct *rule* that authorises communications from those granting rights and (ii) different rules prohibiting all forms of communication.

(i.e., in terms of determining and enumerating the features of primary, secondary, and tertiary rights).[21] For example, *X*'s liberty can concern being free to talk to *Υ*, who in turn is simply not entitled to *X*'s forbearance from communicating (or, if you prefer, bears a Hohfeldian 'no-right' that *X* not try to communicate). Yet one cannot add to '*X* has a Hohfeldian claim that *Υ* do φ' that '*X* also has the liberty to claim that *Υ* do φ' *without specifying the particular ways* by which *X* may claim: to call, to write, to visit *Υ*'s home, etc.

§ *III.2.* *Some Hypothetical Cases*

§ *III.2.1.* *Case 1: Secret Contracts with Blackout Clauses*

The following cases suggest the possibility of wholly unclaimable and 'uninvocable' RCTDs. As a methodological caveat, they are not being presented in order to establish the necessary and sufficient conditions of a concept, or to otherwise establish some analytic definition's over- or under-inclusivity. Instead, they simply present hypothetical cases wherein a liberty-based perimeter of support relationship does not obtain.

The first case is this. As part of a contract between them, *A* and *B* agree to the following clause:

> *A* gives *B* the right to φ, but only if *B* never claims it of *A* or anyone else, and never broadcasts its existence to anyone—including to *B* himself—through any form of communication, even just to say that *B* possesses such a right. This includes communications to legal officials, including courts, for the sake of trying to vindicate the right, let alone initiating legal proceedings. *B*'s duty to forbear from making any communications holds so long as *A* has not clearly and conspicuously breached the duty regarding φ, as opposed to either merely having seemed have done so or appearing to threaten breach.

Assume that the contract is for a legally valid purpose. Would *B* have a valid legal right to φ despite lacking accompanying liberties by which to claim or invoke it, at least so long as both parties fulfil their respective ends of the bargain? In other words, would *B* not have an RCTD to receive φ, plus duties to neither invoke nor claim it, let alone to sue, to or from *A*, the legal system, or anyone else? *A*'s conspicuous breach would itself change the parties' legal relations: it would replace *B*'s duties to refrain

[21] See Appendix 3.

from communicating with liberties to claim and invoke and a power to initiate legal proceedings. Still, what happens in the scenario where *A* does not conspicuously breach? Is there any liberty-based claim or invocation of right perimeter of support here?

§ III.2.II. Cases 2 and 3: Statutory Prohibitions

A statute provides a jurisdiction's poor with a right to potable water from their municipal government. Nevertheless, the statute specifically proscribes judicial review, other forms of appeal, or any other way of trying to seek legal remedy for breaches of this particular government duty. (The prohibition does not apply to any other legal rights within the system.) The statute explicitly states that courts shall not take judicial cognisance of such claims, and that the right-holders are themselves duty-bound to avoid trying to remedy breaches. The statute furthermore holds that the right-holders are duty-bound not to invoke, claim, or even make reference to their rights to the municipal government or to anyone else. The jurisdiction's highest court has upheld all of the statute's provisions, deeming it consistent with the country's constitutional rights (freedom of speech, due process, etc.).

Consider also Case 3: *A* owes a contractual duty to *B*. However, a statute, which has been upheld by the courts, states that parties to contracts have a duty not to invoke or claim their rights of duty-bearers, the government, or anyone else.

§ III.2.III. Case 4: Games

Although this chapter is predominantly concerned with legal RCTDs and liberties, this case deals with game-based positions. At the beginning of a fictional board game, players are assigned different roles. The roles are allocated by picking cards out of an opaque bag. Each card contains information assigning a player a specific role. Each player is then obligated to identify his or her role to the others. However, by design, one of the cards assigns two roles to a single player. (Assume that the game can only be played by a minimum number of people, and that one, and only one, player is able to pick a card of this sort every time the game is played.) The second role is both secret and integral to game play. By design, then, the secret role-bearer's identity is kept hidden from the other players, although everyone is aware that someone amongst them fulfils the role. Hence, the dual-role-assigned player may only disclose information about his or her other, non-secret role. Further, if the other players suspect the secret role-bearer's identity, they are duty-bound not to reveal it.

Qua secret role-bearer, the dual-role player is entitled to undertake certain discreet actions throughout the game without interference from the other players, but such actions must be undertaken in ways that do not betray his or her being the secret agent. This involves, for example, reorganising game pieces in ways that are detrimental to others when, during set intervals, all the players are sent to different rooms or areas where they are out of vision or hearing distance of one another, they must close their eyes, etc.

The secret role therefore comes with exercisable rights to act in certain ways (e.g., to reorder the game pieces). It involves liberties to act and RCTDs against interference when doing so, and an RCTD against being outed as the dual-role player. However, these game-based rights are incommunicable to the other players without violating the rules of the game. The secret role-bearer, personally, must not invoke or claim the right: to fulfil the part; to demand non-interference with his or her other actions in furtherance of the role; etc.[22]

§ III.3. Responses

The first two cases (along with the second's variant) seem implausible. Even though Case 1 concerns a contract for legally valid purposes, it seems unlikely that courts would actually uphold a 'total blackout of communications' clause. Most modern legal systems would not want to enable or encourage parties to be able to shirk their legal duties by making the other party contract away every capacity to communicate about the bargain, let alone commence legal proceedings, even when the duty is perceived to be on its way to being fulfilled. On the other hand, the contract in question explicitly allows for communications upon conspicuous breach. Hence, it is not a total blackout: if party *A* does not fulfil the duty, then both communications and legal proceedings are contractually permissible.[23]

[22] One might be tempted to analogise Case 4 to secret courts or proceedings. This would be inapt because legal situations involve government agents, who may communicate such positions amongst themselves, whether done *in camera* or otherwise.

[23] Although he does not develop the idea, Hohfeld mentions 'potential' rights and ligations. E.g., Hohfeld (1917: 718 n.19). Still, this does not answer the question of whether it is a matter of conceptual necessity that such potential rights become actual in the face of the violation of some predicate (actual) rights and ligations.

Even so, what if there is a disagreement between the parties about what a contractual duty actually entails? What if party *B* merely requires clarification? Would legal systems really allow, let alone want, people to exclude the very possibility of seeking private clarifications of what their positions entail, save in the face of conspicuous breach—where elucidations must be procured in courts or other official proceedings (even if not provided by the legal officials but by the parties themselves)?

Cases 2 and 3 are equally dubious. Again, could the parties (the government and private agents) fulfil their duties in silence adequately? The statutory requirements add an additional problem to those found in Case 1: unlike contractual duties, these forms of communication would have to be carved out of the system's constitutional and statutory rights on a case-by-case basis. Moreover, and without presuming a Sanction theory of law, what happens if the contractual or statutory silence duty is systematically transgressed, ignored, or violated?

Despite their implausibility, the rules and states of affairs in Cases 1–3 are not impossible ones. Their violation of certain norms and policy concerns of contemporary modern courts and legal systems does not mean they are conceptually incoherent or that no jurisdiction could adopt them. Whilst they might show that perimeters of support relationships between legal RCTDs and liberties are conceptually contingent, it is nevertheless tempting to say that, where such relationships fail to obtain, not only is something valuable missing, but also that something is defective with those rights. Chapter 8 argued that wholly unenforceable legal rights (whether it be in terms of either constitutive or associated legal powers) constitute 'imperfect' cases because (aspects of) the correlative positions' contents cannot be determined or fixed by officials' authoritative binding decisions. Here too, wholly unclaimable or uninvocable legal rights seem to be defective because their meaning or content cannot be determined or clarified via interlocutory means, i.e., the parties communicating with one another to settle or confirm such matters.

Case 4, the game with the secret role-bearer, is a little different. The players all bear game-based duties not to inquire into the secret role-bearer's identity. These duties are not simply owed to the secret role-bearer, but to all the players. Still, it is easy to imagine a player going on a fishing expedition, asking indirect questions in order to try to bypass the rule and sniff out the secret role-bearer. If this happens, both the dual-role-bearer (presumably in a manner that does not necessarily betray his or her secret role) and everyone else may demand that the inquirer still his or her tongue in order to protect the integrity of the game. That would not be the—social or moral—right[24] of the secret role-bearer *qua* secret role-bearer, but rather of all players.[25]

§ *III.4. Trans-Systematic Norms*

Another way to try to advance the idea of *some* invariable perimeter of support of liberties over claims is this: insist that rights and ligations have effects and applications across different normative systems or domains, e.g., legal positions affecting moral and social normative domains, moral positions impacting games, etc.[26]

For example, in the name of freedom of speech, legal liberties can be used to advocate for moral or social change. They can help to promote conformity with moral or social duties, to advocate for the legal codification of such duties, and to help change a society's ideas about what are morally best, acceptable, etc., ways of going about things. One may exercise the legal right to free speech—including by making mention of the right's very legality—to try to convince people to listen to speech they might otherwise find offensive; to try to convince people to abide by certain manners; etc.

Perhaps more controversial is the notion of using moral liberties to claim legal rights. (Moral liberties can be understood as normative

[24] If there is an RCTD being defended here, it is probably a social or moral one, not a game-based one, because you either play by the rules of the game or you do not. Recreational games generally do not contain a rule holding that you must abide by their rules. Non-abidance simply means that you are either cheating or not actually playing the game. Enforcement of these social norms nonetheless also enforces adherence to the game's rules.

[25] It could be identified as an *invocation* of (a social or moral) right on behalf of that player, even if done by the secret role-bearer personally on his or her own behalf, or if by others despite their not knowing the secret role-bearer's identity.

[26] Albeit within the bounds of one system, Hohfeld argues as much regarding legal and equitable positions. Hohfeld (1913b: 553). Some positions are recognised by both law and equity: 'concurrent' jural relations. Others are only recognised in equity: 'exclusive' jural relations. Ibid 555. Hohfeld believes that, in cases of conflict between law and equitable positions, the equitable ones are paramount and pro tanto 'annul' their rivalrous 'legal' ones, e.g., in a conflict between *A*'s legal duty and *A*'s equitable 'no-right'. Ibid 543–4, 571 n.36. Back when there were separate courts of law and equity, in certain circumstances a common law court could take cognisance of a jural relation created by a court of equity. For example, a chancery decree (creating an equitable tertiary right) based on an *exclusive* (equitable) jural primary right and duty could sometimes provide the basis for a common law action of debt (a 'concurrent' secondary jural relation). Ibid 568. See also Reiff (2005: 22–34) on the moral, social, and 'strategic' enforcement of legal rights.

positions falling under either 'critical' morality, or a given society's positive/conventional morality.[27]) Here, in response to moral claims of right, recipients of such communications may be moved to recalibrate their thinking and to fulfil their legal duties.

Recall once more Chapter 9's example of Sally calling her neighbour Peter on the telephone to tell him to return her lawnmower. Being legally permitted to do so was a basis for identifying her entitlement to communicate as a legal liberty. Modifying the example slightly, what if Sally is legally prohibited from making that call (e.g., Peter has a restraining order out against her), but nonetheless believes she had the moral right to call Peter, as that is the only way she is going to be able to get her property back. Such a phone call may influence Peter's behaviour (e.g., convince him to return the mower), even though making the call would be illegal.

Even if no pertinent *legal* liberties are available by which to claim legal rights in a given system, or at a given juncture—such as in the implausible scenarios provided in **Cases 1–3**, or that by imagining the most oppressive sorts of legal regimes (which might also be too implausible in these regards)—there might still be certain *moral* liberties by which to do so.[28] *If* legal or moral liberties can invariably be used to claim legal rights, then, although RCTDs are not always enforceable via powers (*pace* the Will theory and Chapter 7's Control View) they are still never wholly 'naked' passive positions either.[29] Instead, there would be a more sophisticated relationship between RCTDs and other normative positions, and indeed amongst positions from various domains (perhaps requiring a more nuanced way to model them).[30] Of course, it is difficult to establish causation or a necessary conceptual connection here, and will depend upon one's views of critical/positive morality (if the notion of critical morality is even sensible, that is).

[27] See Chapter 1 note 20.

[28] Daniel Lyons argues there are always opportunities to demand moral rights. Lyons (1966: 119). Kramer takes the stronger view that moral rights are always enforceable. Kramer (2007: 187).

[29] On the vested/naked distinction, see Chapter 1 § II.2.

[30] The notion of using moral liberties to claim legal rights leads to problems accounting for conflicts between normative positions belonging to different domains, e.g., having a moral liberty to do what is legally prohibited.

§ IV. Conclusion

Just because an RCTD obtains, it does not follow that liberties by which to claim or invoke them must as well. The relationship between them is not conceptually/logically necessary. This chapter nonetheless showed why Hohfeldian arguments to this end are ineffective. They wrongly assume that a demonstration of one token of a type of position (e.g., a particular liberty) failing to obtain entails that no other tokens of that type also obtain. Second, those arguments show that *A*'s right against *B* does not also hold against *C*, when what Hohfeldians need to instead establish is that *A*'s various positions vis-à-vis *B* are merely contingently related. Section II thus presents a superior way to make the case: presenting hypotheticals that involve *rules* proscribing all such liberties, and not just tokens of the type.

However, the chapter then suggests that 'perimeters of support' need not exclusively be formed by token positions from the same domain or system. As examples, legal positions may be used to exert moral influence, whilst moral liberties can be used to try to catalyse legal change. Trans-systematicity (or trans-domain interplay) of normative positions is the last hope for those who believe that exercisability and/or enforceability are necessary features of A RIGHT.

Of course, the mere possibility of trans-systemic applicability does not show whether any such associations invariably obtain. For why *must* any given position be exercisable by another from a different normative domain? There seems to be no good reason for thinking thus. It is true that, in responding to the arguments against an invariability-of-rights-claimability (in *some* way or other) view, completely stifling or nullifying any such liberties requires concocting implausible rules and cases such as those presented in Section III. Still, this does not mean they are inconceivable, or that completely stifling the ability to make a claim cannot arise by accident.

The question then becomes how much weight one ought to assign to this sort of analysis. On the one hand, whilst there is good reason for deeming legal rights that are unenforceable via *powers* to be defective (as argued in Chapter 8), the case of enforcement-*liberties* does not present quite as obvious a functionalist analogue job. On the other hand, it does seem reasonable to believe that rights would also be 'imperfect' if there were absolutely no liberties by which to seek *clarification* (which is not the same thing as rights claiming or invoking, but which might result therefrom) of correlative RCTDs' and duties' meaning, content, or entailments from duty-bearers or other parties. Still, the need to devise implausible cases in order to establish the contingency of perimeter of support relationships suggests that, generally, liberty-based perimeters of support are normatively significant and important to account for when modelling and philosophising about rights.

Whether liberty-based means by which to claim or invoke are 'essential' to A LEGAL RIGHT is questionable. Even so, it is for you to decide what to make this chapter's analyses. Hence, you might: find it sound but insignificant for the purposes of understanding *human* (as opposed to angelic or alien[31]) legal systems; deem the very methods of analysis to be suspect; or simply find the examples insufficient to establish that these are just conceptually contingent (as opposed to being conceptually/'logically' necessary) relationships. Assessing the bases and justification for such judgments, and the modes of analysis in question, however, requires further work in philosophy more generally.

[31] See, e.g., Chapter 1 note 59.

Appendix 1 Sample Rights Models

These are only partial presentations of the models, focusing mostly on their constitutive normative positions (rather than their interrelations, etc.*).*

Jeremy Bentham (1782)[1]

A Right: when the law imposes on one party an *extra-regarding* duty to provide a service to a second party[2] where the law intends for that latter party to benefit (where the act has been calculated, by the lawmaker who designs the duty, to benefit the right-holder).[3]

[1] Bentham (2010). This preliminary presentation mostly follows Hart (1982: particularly the chapters 'Legal Duty and Obligation', 'Legal Rights', and 'Legal Powers'), but see also Lindahl (1977: 198–203). Even so, more work must be done to elaborate Bentham's model.

[2] Bentham (2010: 79–80). Take away the notion of punishment and you deprive the words duty, right, power, etc., of all meaning. Ibid 145.

[3] Ibid 300. 'The notion of command leads to that of duty: that of duty to that of right: and that of right to that of power'. Ibid 317. 'If it be any other party [who will benefit from the compelled action], then is it a duty owing to some other party: and then that other party has at any rate a right: a right to have this duty performed: perhaps also a *power*: a power to compel the performance of such duty'. Ibid 317. 'Right is either naked or armed with power'. Ibid 317 n.1. 'Wherein consists the exercise of such a right? In the demanding of the services only, or in the demanding and receiving them accordingly?' Ibid 300 n.2.

D. Frydrych, *The Architecture of Rights*,
https://doi.org/10.1007/978-3-030-76039-7

Type I: *Negative* services
Type II: *Positive* services.[4]

Liberty: the mere absence of duty. A right of exemption from dominion.[5]
Power[6]:

Type I: Power of ***Contrectation***: a normative capacity to physically handle objects (including humans *qua* bodies). 'The right of performing acts of an intransitive nature, the work of law'.[7]
Type II: Power of ***Imperation***: a normative capacity to control a rational being's active faculties.[8]

Immanuel Kant (1797)

Rechtanspruch: coercive powers vis-à-vis another person's duty.[9]

[4] Ibid 80, 301. Both are '*enforced* services'. Hart (1982: 168).

[5] Bentham (2010: 150 in the footnote commencing on 148, 75–6).

[6] Every power is a right, but not every right is a power. Ibid. Powers can be 'corroborated' (i.e., protected by some other normative position, e.g., by a correlative duty), or 'uncorroborated' (i.e., not so protected). Ibid 314.

[7] Ibid 79 n.'a', 149 in the footnote. Aka 'autocheiristic' power. Ibid 103 n.1.

[8] Ibid 42 n.'b'. Hart on Bentham's imperation power: 'a power to procure persons to act in conformity with a command or prohibition by providing motives influencing their will, and it does so in either of two main ways: by threatening punishment if the act is not done or by offering reward if it is done'. Hart (1982: 200–1). Hart is probably correct to identify Bentham's contrectation and imperation powers as being what usually are called 'liberties' or 'permissions'. Hart (1982: 197, 200).

[9] '[I]f a certain use of freedom is itself a hindrance to freedom in accordance with universal laws (i.e., wrong), coercion that is opposed to this (as a hindering of a hindrance to freedom) is consistent with freedom in accordance with universal laws, that is, it is right. Hence there is connected with right by the principle of contradiction an authorization to coerce someone who infringes upon it.' Kant (1996: AK 6:231, pg 25). 'Right and authorization to use coercion therefore mean one and the same thing'. Ibid 6:232, pg 26. Technically, Kant (1996: AK 6:222, pg 15) seems to associate 'authorization' with freedom from obligation, or permission. Even so, the 'authorization' to coerce involves control over another. As Arthur Ripstein (a Kantian) says, '[a]n act is coercive if it subjects one person to the choice of another'. Ripstein (2009: 54). This applies to both legitimate, authorised acts and illegitimate ones. (The contexts, moreover, especially in Kant's (1996: AK 6:233–4, pgs 26–7) discussion of a right in 'the narrow sense', make it somewhat clear that he is referring to 'a right' in these contexts, and not just 'Right'). Furthermore, Kant calls this the 'strict' or 'narrow' sense of a right, but notes that people also think of a right in a 'wider' sense, of which there are two true or 'alleged' kinds: *equity* (right without coercion) and *right of necessity* (coercion without a right). Ibid 25–8 (6:232–35).

ALOIS VON BRINZ (1857)[10]

Rechte: a legal permission, a legal ability, or a combination thereof.[11]

Dürfen (*licere*): legal permission. (***Befugniss*** is also identified with *licere*).[12]

Können (*posse, potestas*): legal ability/capacity.[13]

Brinz also mentions ***Anspruch*** (a claim) as *rechte*, and as a basis for a *klagrecht* (right/cause of action).[14]

WILLIAM MARKBY (1871)[15]

Three senses of 'a right' (of which the first is intimated to be the most appropriate):

Right: the correlative of a duty, which is invariably enforceable.[16]

Faculty/Power: [undefined]. Two types: 'of doing' and 'of not doing'.[17]

Liberty: freedom from all kinds of duty.[18]

Immunity and Privilege: [both undefined].[19]

Duty: the necessity that persons (to whom a legal command is addressed) are under to obey (that law).[20]

Type I: *Relative*: correlates with a right.

Type II: *Absolute*: does not correlate with a right.[21]

[10] Brinz (1857).

[11] Ibid 49–50 (§ 23).

[12] Ibid.

[13] Ibid.

[14] Ibid 52 (§ 24). Compare John Stuart Mill: '[w]hen we call anything a person's right, we mean that he has a *valid claim* on society to protect him in the possession of it, either by the force of law, or by that of education and opinion'. Mill (1863: 78, emphasis added).

German jurists in the second half of the nineteenth century debated the relationships amongst: (i) *recht*, *anspruch*, and a right/cause of action (sometimes distinguished by the terms *klag* or *klagrecht*) and (ii) 'the' German conception of a cause of action to the Roman *actio*. See, e.g., Windscheid (1862: 81 n.1, 89–93, (§§ 37, 43–4)).

[15] Markby (1871: 49–57).

[16] Ibid 50.

[17] Ibid.

[18] Ibid 51.

[19] Ibid 57.

[20] Ibid 49.

[21] Ibid 50.

Ernst Bierling (1877)[22]

Rechtsanspruch (legal claim): In its narrower meaning, it is an imperatival address to a correlative duty-bearer. However, the concept of a liberty to demand [*Forderndürfen*] is insufficient to explain the concept of *anspruch*; for one may possess the latter without having to make such a demand, and without even being aware that one is a right-holder. The *anspruch*-holder is rather in the special 'constant condition of (a) tacit demand(ing)' [*constanten zustande stillschweigenden Forderns*] of the duty-bearer. That condition in turn enables the holder to (performatively) make a demand.[23]

Befugniss:

Type I: ***Rechtliche Dürfen***: (unrestrained legal liberty): 'simple legal permission... the content of which is, in essence, purely negative [i.e.,] not being legally forbidden'.[24]

Type II: ***Rechtliche Können***: (legal power): 'legal ability, i.e., the ability, following some provision of positive law, to produce certain legal effects by "acts-in-the-law"'.[25]

Henry Terry (1884)[26]

Jural Correspondents	Correspondent right	Permissive right	Protected right	Facultative right
	Duty	None	Duty	None

[22] Bierling (1877: 32–73).

[23] Ibid 39–40, 40 in the footnote (§ 141). Of the three concepts expressed in ordinary language by the term 'a right' — *Rechtanspruch*, *Dürfen*, and *Können* — only the first warrants the 'scientific title' of a 'subjective right'. Ibid 74 (§ 160).

[24] Ibid 50 (§ 147), as translated in Lindahl (1977: 196).

[25] Ibid (and ibid). Roscoe Pound translates Bierling here as: 'capacity in pursuance of certain provisions of the positive law, to produce determinate legal consequences through legal transactions'. Pound (1915: 111).

Cf. August Thon, who notes four distinct senses of '*subjektiven rechts*' — ***Normenschutz*** (normative protection), ***Anspruch***, ***Befugniss***, and ***Genuss***. Thon (1878: chapters 5–7). Thon also holds that, of these four concepts, only *ANSPRUCH* truly deserves the title of 'a subjective right'. Ibid v–vi. Cf. Schuppe (1887).

[26] Terry (1884: the chapter 'Duties and Rights in General').

Correspondent rights: the condition of being owed a duty to act or forbear.[27]
Protected rights: the condition of being owed a duty to create a state of affairs, or to preserve the status quo. The duty is enforceable at the right-holder's option.[28]
Permissive: the condition of not being under a duty.[29]
Facultative: powers or capabilities to dispose of rights of other kinds.[30]
Two types:
Type I: Powers: privately exercisable without the aid of a court.
Type II: Charges: only executable/enforceable via judicial proceedings.[31]
Duty: three types: Peremptory Duties, Duties of choice, and Duties of intent.[32]

John Salmond (1902)[33]

Jural Correlatives	Right	Liberty	Power	Immunity
	Duty	Liability (type I)	Liability (type II)	Disability

Jural Absences	Right	Liberty	Power	Immunity
	Liability (type I)	Duty	Disability	Liability (type II)

A Right (*stricto* sensu case)[34]: an interest recognised and protected by a rule of right/legal justice (for *legal* rights, or by the rule of natural justice for *moral* rights) for which a corresponding duty is imposed on one or more other parties.[35]

[27] Ibid 87. '[T]he violation of a mere correspondent right does not give a cause of action; for that a violation of a *protected* right is necessary'. Ibid 99 (emphasis added).
[28] Ibid 97.
[29] Ibid 90. Permissive right versus legal power: one may be under a duty not to do an act without being made legally incapable of doing it. Ibid.
[30] Ibid 100.
[31] Ibid 101.
[32] Ibid 85–7.
[33] Salmond (1902: Chapters X-XI: 'Legal Rights' and 'The Kinds of Legal Rights'). See also Dickey (1971).
[34] Salmond (1902: 231, 234).
[35] Ibid 219, 220–1, 223. The power to enforce via instituting legal proceedings is not essential to A LEGAL RIGHT. (Unenforceable legal rights are 'imperfect' cases, though).

A Liberty: the benefits one derives from the absence of legal duties imposed on oneself.[36] The law allows to one's will a sphere of unrestrained activity.[37]
A Power: when the law actively assists me in making my will effective as against others.[38] A power is usually, but not necessarily, combined with a liberty to exercise it. Hence its exercise may be effectual and yet wrongful.[39]
An Immunity: the benefit derived from the absence of power in other persons.[40]
A Duty: an obligatory act.[41] A duty is the absence of a liberty.[42]
A Disability: the absence of a power.[43]
A Liability: either the absence of a right or an immunity. It is the correlative either of a liberty or a power vested in someone else.[44]

William Galbraith Miller (1903)

Various senses of 'a right':

> It is a claim [with a correlative duty?]; a power; a faculty; a liberty [with a correlative duty?]; an authority; a privilege; a prerogative; a capacity to act or to possess dominion, empire, power, authority, immunity, status, or some interest put forward actively if necessary in the form of a case or action at law, and recognised by the state in accordance with right, law, and justice.[45]

Ibid 223. Nevertheless, 'there can be no right unless there is someone from whom it is claimed…'. Ibid 224. 'I enjoy my rights through the control exercised by it over the acts of others on my behalf'. Ibid 235.

[36] Ibid 231.

[37] Ibid 236.

[38] Ibid.

[39] Ibid 234 n.1.

[40] Ibid 235. 1. Rights (*stricto* sensu) — what others *must* do for me. 2. Liberties — what I *may* do for myself. 3. Powers — what I *can* do as against others. 4. Immunities—what others *can not* do as against me. Ibid 238.

[41] Ibid 218.

[42] Ibid 236.

[43] Ibid.

[44] Ibid.

[45] Miller (1903) 131. Cf. ibid. 138, citing *Quinn v Leathem* (1901) A.C. 495.

Hohfeld's Schema of Jural Relations (1913)[46]

Table of Jural Correlatives	Claim	Privilege*	Power	Immunity
	Duty	No-right	Liability	Disability

Table of Jural Opposites	Claim	Privilege	Power	Immunity
	No-right	Duty	Disability	Liability

Five Types of Rights: claims, liberties, powers, immunities, and complexes.

A Claim/right (*stricto* sensu): one's affirmative claim against another.

A Privilege [liberty]: one's freedom from the right or claim of another.

A Power: one's affirmative 'control' over a given legal relation as against another.

An Immunity: one's freedom from the legal power or 'control' of another as regards some legal relation.[47]

A Right Complex:

E.g.1. a power + a liberty

E.g.2. a claim + a claim + a power + a power + a liberty

E.g.3. a claim + a liberty + a power + an immunity

Types of Ligations: duties, no-rights, liabilities, disabilities (and complexes?)

Some Hohfeldians' Suggested Modifications:

- *Hohfeld preferred the term 'privilege', but this is standardly replaced with 'liberty' in the literature. The differences between a liberty and privilege, say critics, are the mere absence of a duty versus an express permission to act. Hohfeld believes that these amount to the same thing.[48]

[46] See Hohfeld (1913a: 30).

[47] Ibid 55. Despite his definitions, the reader is advised to note Hohfeld's inconsistent usage of his conceptions. For example, are liberties and immunities *freedoms from* others' claims or powers, or do they instead mark the other parties' *lack of* claims or powers? So too with a claim: do we claim with a claim, or is it a passive position? See the discussion of this problem in Chapter 3.

[48] Hohfeld (1913a: 42 n.59).

- Not all of the four basic types count as rights: only one (e.g., a claim) or some are.
- Not all tokens of a type count as rights, e.g., not all powers are rights.
- Some or all ligations (duties, liabilities, etc.) can also be rights. [See Chapter II § IV against this notion].
- It is disputed whether claims and/or immunities are active or passive positions.

Roscoe Pound (1915, 1959)[49]

Juristic Conceptions	Right	Liberty	Power	Privilege	No correlative
	Duty	No correlative	No correlative	No correlative	Liability

- A legal right (in the 'narrow or strict sense') is a capacity to assert a legally recognised and delimited interest before legal officials (courts, etc.).[50]
- *Liberty versus Privilege*: liberty is any action that is not prohibited, whilst privilege is a special exemption from an ordinary legal rule.[51]
- 'A right' also refers to a complex conception, or rather a bundle of (the more basic) conceptions.[52]
- All of these juristic conceptions of 'a right' contain a capacity for asserting them before courts and administrative agencies.[53]
- Hohfeld's no-rights, liabilities, immunities, and disabilities are not genuine legal positions and lack jural significance.[54]

[49] See Pound (1915); Pound (1959: especially 70–1, 75).

[50] Pound (1915: 93); Pound (1959: 70). Why not define the *stricto* sensu case as 'a claim'? 'If we define [it] in terms of claim, we put in the foreground the idea of interest, whereas we are defining something conferred by law to make the interest effective'. Pound (1959: 70). Cf. Hohfeld (1917: 726 n.34) on interests versus a legal relation that protects the interest.

[51] Pound (1959: 81).

[52] Pound (1915: 101); Pound (1959: 58).

[53] Pound (1959: 71).

[54] Pound (1915: 97–8, 100); Pound (1959: 78–81).

HLA Hart (1982)[55]

Legal Liberty-right: norms to act protected indirectly by obligations of non-interference.

Two varieties: unilateral and bilateral

Liberty-rights versus liberties: former are 'vested' (protected directly or indirectly by someone else's duty) or 'naked' (unprotected directly or indirectly by a duty).[56]

Bilateral liberties: entitled to act AND not to act.

To be a liberty-*right* the bilateral liberties must be protected, directly or indirectly, by duties not to interfere.

Unilateral liberties: entitled either to act OR not to act (not both).

To be a liberty-*right* it must be protected, directly or indirectly, by duties not to interfere.[57]

'Naked' (unprotected) unilateral and bilateral liberties do not count as 'rights'.[58]

A Legal Right-Correlative-To-An-Obligation:[59]
Most *private law* tokens of the type: a special case of legal power(s) (plus liberties to exercise the powers) whereby the holder may waive, extinguish, enforce, or leave unenforced another's obligation.[60]

There are nonetheless other legal and moral rights-correlative-to-duties ('RCTDs') that are not liberty-powers. These are instead simply entitlements to a correlative duty-bearer's action or forbearance.[61]

Legal Power: 'the act which there is a bilateral liberty to do is an act-in-the-law, just in the sense that it is specifically recognized by the law as having legal effects in *varying* the legal position of various parties and as

[55] Hart (1982).

[56] Ibid 171–4.

[57] Ibid 173–4. But see Ibid 188 n.93. Whether Hart's designation of certain unilateral liberties as 'rights' can be squared with his *theory* advanced in the same work is a discussion best left for another occasion.

[58] Ibid 172–3.

[59] See Chapter 5 note 16 and the accompanying text.

[60] Ibid 183–4, 188.

[61] Ibid 189, 192–3.

an appropriate means for varying it'.[62] Powers can also be used to 'preserve' parties' positions.[63]
Legal Immunity: legal positions that prevent *adverse* changes to its holder's other legal positions. However, immunities that prevent *advantageous* changes do not count as rights.[64]
Legal Duty: 'Far better adapted to the legal case is a different, non-cognitive theory of duty according to which committed statements asserting that others have a duty do not refer to actions which they have a categorical reason to do but, as the etymology of "duty" and indeed "ought" suggests, such statements refer to actions which are due from or owed by the subjects having the duty, in the sense that they may be properly demanded or *exacted* from them. On this footing, to say that an individual has a legal obligation to act in a certain way is to say that such action may be properly demanded or extracted from him according to legal rules or principles regulating such demands for action'.[65]

Neil MacCormick (1977, 2008)[66]

- Rights are 'logically', and sometimes also temporally, prior to duties.[67]
- Whilst liberties, powers, and immunities by which to protect passive rights (to another's duty) are not always available[68]; passive rights without associated enforcement powers are for that reason 'imperfect'.[69]

[62] Ibid 188. But see again ibid 188 n.93.

[63] Ibid 184.

[64] Ibid 191.

[65] Ibid 159–60 (emphasis added). Cf. Ibid 266. See also John Austin: '[r]ight; — the capacity or power of exacting from another or others acts or forbearances; — is nearest to a true definition'. Austin (1869: 410). Compare also John Stuart Mill: 'It is part of the notion of duty in every one of its forms that a person may rightfully be compelled to fulfil it. Duty is a thing which may be *exacted* from a person, as one exacts a debt. Unless we think it can be exacted from him, we do not call it his duty'. Mill (1863: 71).

[66] See MacCormick (1977); MacCormick (2007).

[67] MacCormick (1977: 200–1).

[68] Ibid 205; MacCormick (2007: 129).

[69] MacCormick (2007: 129).

Conjunction of Active and Passive Rights:

1. A right-holder with 'full active capacity' [e.g., a rational adult] has the choice to demand or forego demanding observance by another or others of one's passive rights.
2. When rights have been infringed, it is normally a matter of free choice whether to demand a remedy from the infringer or to let the matter pass.
3. If the demand is made and rejected, or ignored, one has the right and power to take legal action before a court, calling for it to impose a suitable legal remedy.[70]

Joseph Raz

A Right: reasons that are the sufficient but not necessary grounds of (justify imposing) duties, other positions, and even other rights. Rights are: *justificationally* prior to duties; *existentially* correlative with duties; and *logically* posterior to duties.[71] They are typically but not necessarily exercisable (or enforceable) via liberties and powers and protected by immunities, none of which is a right.[72]

Liberty:

Exclusionary permission: an entitlement to perform an act even though there are conclusive reasons for one not to perform it, provided one is entitled not to act for those reasons, to exclude them from one's considerations.[73]

Weak permission: no norms regulating certain behaviour.[74]

'*Liberty-right*': a spurious category, Raz suggests.[75]

[70] Ibid.

[71] Raz (1986: 180–1, 196); Raz (1996: 33, 35–6).

[72] On rights as reasons, see, e.g., Raz (1986: 169, 181); Raz (1996: 46). On rights as sufficient but not necessary grounds, see, e.g., Raz (1986: 181, 183–4, 188, 192, 193, 202); Raz (1996: 31). On rights grounding other normative positions (duties, liberties, etc.), see, e.g., Raz (1986: 167–8, 170–1); Raz (1996: 31, 46, 268). On the existential, justification, and logical relations between rights and duties, see Raz (1986: 170–1, 180–1, 196); Raz (1996: 33, 35–6). On rights being contingently protected by other positions, see Raz (1986: 181); Raz (1996: 256–8, 266–7). On there being but one basic kind of right, see, e.g., Raz (1980: 179–81); Raz (1986: 176 (rights are nothing but the grounds of duties), 180, 188).

[73] Raz, (1999: 89–91); Raz (2009b: 117 n.4).

[74] Raz (2009b: 117 n.4).

[75] Raz (1996: 275).

Power:

Directed power: a power restricted by duties. The duties specify conditions for the power's use.[76]

Immunity: a reason for not being subject to another's power.[77]

Duty: a first-order reason to act or forbear coupled with a second-order, exclusionary reason (i.e., to preclude from taking into consideration certain reasons for not conforming with the first-order reason to act/forbear).[78]

Duties correlating with rights[79]

Absolute (*Non-correlating*) *duties*, e.g., self-regarding ones[80]

Liability: (undefined?)

Raz's Purported *Order of Justification for Legal Rights and Other Legal Positions:*

Interest → Right → Duty

1. Weighty interest + 2. a weighty moral right grounds a (legal) duty
   - Interest → Duty
     (i.e., rights are not the exclusive grounds of duties).
   - Interest → Right → Liberty
   - Interest → Right → Power (e.g., enforcement powers to protect the right)
   - Interest → Right → Immunity (e.g., to protect the right from nullification)
   - Interest → Right → Another Right

The Actual *Order:*

An interest + a (putative) *moral* right + a conceivable class of duty-bearers *and* a discernible agent who can actually bear the duty. If all four co-obtain, then a *legal* right and a legal duty can be generated concurrently.

[76] Ibid 241.
[77] Raz (1986: 168 n.1).
[78] Raz (1996: 40).
[79] Raz (1986: 170–1, 196).
[80] Ibid 210–3; Raz (1996: 32–40).

Appendix 2 The Theories of Rights

D. Frydrych, *The Architecture of Rights*,
https://doi.org/10.1007/978-3-030-76039-7

	The Will theory			*The Interest theory*	
	'Choice' theories	*Will theories*	*Kantians*	*Interest theories*	*'Wellbeing' theories*
All rights' ultimate purpose	To protect or effectuate domains of freedom and the ability to choose	To vindicate holder's wills	To structure independence in a system of equal freedom	To protect or effectuate interests of any sort	To effectuate holders' wellbeing (not well defined)
Normative positions that count as rights	**A.** A Hohfeldian claim + at least one enforcement power **B.** Any complex that includes such powers	**A.** A claim + at least one enforcement power **B.** Any complex that includes such powers	Only one kind	**A.** A claim **B.** Any Hohfeldian incident **C.** Any complex, whether or not it includes enforcement and waiver powers	A claim of sufficient weight that can ground a duty in others
ID test for a duty's direction	**A.** The power-holder **B.** The claim-holder, where *someone* has the relevant power(s)	**A.** the power-holder **B.** The claim-Holder, where *someone* has The power(s)	The right-holder	The *intended* beneficiary of a duty—Not just any claim-holder	Was the duty generated based on a particular person's interests-cum-right?
Application to rights models	**A.** Not all Hohfeldian *types* (or their analogues in other models) count as rights **B.** All Hohfeldian types (and their analogues) are rights—if they are enforceable **C.** Not all tokens of all types count as rights	**A.** Not all Hohfeldian *types* (or their analogues) count as rights **B.** All Hohfeldian types protect the will *if* claims and immunities are kinds of power **C.** Not all tokens of all types count as rights	Monistic conception of a right	**A.** Not all *tokens* of all Hohfeldian types (or their analogues) are rights. If the position does not generally serve the holder's interests, then it is not 'a right'	Monistic conception of a right

Appendix 3 Legal Elements of Control, Both Real and Purported

(The elements are framed in Hohfeldian terms)

Primary Right
1. A Hohfeldian **claim** to a second party's correlative duty to act or forbear
2+. **Immunities** from that claim being nullified by the duty-bearer or a third party?
3. A **power** to enforce the duty through private means even before (threatened) breach[a]
4–5. Liberties to exercise or not to use the enforcement power
6. An immunity from nullification of the enforcement power by another
7. A **power** to waive the duty
8–9. Liberties to use or not to use the waiver power
10. An immunity from someone other than the right-holder nullifying the waiver power
11. A **power** to nullify the duty
12–3. Liberties to exercise that power or to refrain from doing so
14+. Immunities from having that power being divested by others

Secondary Right
15. A **claim** correlating with a duty-bearer's duty to acquiesce to self-help measures
16+. **Liberties** + **Powers** by which to undertake the relevant self-help actions (**Immunity** from liability for validly undertaking self-help measures)
17. A **claim** to a remedy for breach of the primary duty. The content is either devised by the duty-bearer personally, or specifically 'demanded' by the right-holder[a]
18. A **power** to waive the other party's duty to provide the right-holder-specified remedy
19–20. Liberties by which to exercise or not use the waiver power
21+. Immunities from someone other than the right-holder nullifying the power
22. A **claim** to an official dispute resolution process[b]

(*continued*)

D. Frydrych, *The Architecture of Rights*,
https://doi.org/10.1007/978-3-030-76039-7

(continued)

23. A **power** to trigger an institutional dispute resolution process in light of a (threatened) breach, e.g., commencing a lawsuit, an administrative hearing, etc.
24. A **power** to waive commencement of the dispute resolution process[c]
25–6. Liberties to exercise or not to use the enforcement power
27+. Immunities from someone other than the right-holder nullifying the power
28. A **power** to terminate the institutional dispute resolution process before an official decision is issued
29–30. Liberties to use that power or not
31+. Immunities from having that power divested by others
32+. **Powers** to authorise third parties to enforce your claims
33–4. **Liberties** to *claim* a remedy from the duty-bearer, or to forbear from doing so[c]
35–6. **Liberties** to *invoke* one's right to third party to solicit support for rights violations[c]

Tertiary (and Quaternary) Right(s)
37. A **claim** correlating with a second party's duty to comply with a remedial order
38+. **Immunities** from that claim being nullified by others
39+. A set of **powers** by which to enforce the results of the remedial process[d]
40+. Liberties to exercise or not to use those enforcement powers
41+. Immunities from others nullifying those powers
42. A **power** to waive the duty to comply with the remedy
43–4. Liberties to use the waiver power or not
45+. Immunities from others nullifying the power
46. A **power** to nullify the duty to comply with a remedial order
47–8. Liberties to use or not use that power
49. An immunity from having that power divested by others

[a] Although presented by certain scholars, these two (distinct) candidate types of normative positions may (sometimes) be spurious. For example, concerning element 4, see Hart (1982: 186). For element 17, see Hohfeld (1909); Hohfeld (1917: 752). However, a specific sum (as damages) *can* sometimes be determined by the parties themselves. E.g., Hohfeld (1913b: 554, 'Example 23').
[b] The duty-bearer's duty to participate in an institutional dispute resolution process may be owed to the state, not the claim-holder. Further, one can imagine a legal system wherein duty violations automatically give rise to dispute resolution processes, whether the right-holder desires the process or not.
[c] These liberties are explained in Chapter 9.
[d] There is good reason to consider elements 39 to 49 to be *quaternary* rights, which enforce, but differ from, elements 37–38. The former are means by which to enforce the (tertiary) rights of judgment creditors. Enforcing a court judgment, say, may involve getting the police to procure goods and place liens, compelling banks to comply with money transfers, etc.

Appendix 4 Varieties of Control View

	Primary/Secondary/Tertiary Distinction Adherents	*Unified Conception of a Right*
AN RCTD = a power, or a set of powers	View 1: A right is the power to waive a primary duty View 2: A right is the power to enforce a primary duty View 3: A right is a complex of both primary powers [**'Cp'**] View 4: Cp + alienation and nullification powers [**'Cpan'**] View 5: A right is **Cpan** + the power to enforce a secondary duty View 6: A right is **Cpan** + the power to waive a secondary duty View 7: A right is **Cpan** + the powers to enforce and waive the secondary duty [**Cpan** + the two powers = **'Cpans'**] View 8: A right is **Cpans** + a power to enforce a tertiary duty	Different powers are used to enforce the same right at different stages. (Not all of the powers must be held by a single party, however)

(*continued*)

D. Frydrych, *The Architecture of Rights*,
https://doi.org/10.1007/978-3-030-76039-7

(continued)

	Primary/Secondary/Tertiary Distinction Adherents	*Unified Conception of a Right*
	View 9: A right is **Cpans** + a power to waive a tertiary duty View 10: A right is **Cpans** + the power to enforce and waive a tertiary duty. [**Cpans** + the two power = **'Cpanst'**] View 11: A right is the power to enforce a primary duty + an immunity for that power View 12: A right is the power to waive a primary duty + an immunity for that power View 13: A right is **Cp** + an immunity from nullification for one of the powers View 14: A right is **Cp** + an immunity for both powers View 15+: Etc.	
AN RCTD = a complex composed of (Hohfedian) claims, powers, immunities, and/ or liberties	The same iterations as above, but with claims added to each view	Different powers are used to enforce the same right at different stages

Bibliography

Agnafors M., 'Mixing Interest and Control Assessing Peter Vallentyne's Hybrid Theory of Rights' (2015) 43 Philosophia 933.
Anderson A.R., 'Logic, Norms, and Roles' (1962) 4 Ratio 36.
Aristotle, *The Politics*, tr Carnes Lord (2nd edn, University of Chicago Press 2013).
Austin J., 'Lecture XVI', in Robert Campbell (ed), *Lectures on Jurisprudence, or the Philosophy of Positive Law* (3rd edn, J. Murray 1869).
Baker G., & P.M.S. Hacker, *Wittgenstein: Understanding and Meaning: Volume 1 of an Analytical Commentary on the* Philosophical Investigations. *Part I: Essays* (2nd extensively revised edn by P.M.S. Hacker, Wiley-Blackwell 2005).
———, *Wittgenstein: Rules, Grammar, and Necessity: Essays and Exegesis of §§185–242: Volume 2 of an Analytical Commentary on the* Philosophical Investigations (2nd extensively revised edn by P.M.S. Hacker, Wiley-Blackwell 2014).
Bayles M., *Hart's Legal Philosophy: An Examination* (Kluwer Academic Publishers 1992).
Bentham J., *Of the Limits of the Penal Branch of Jurisprudence*, Philip Schofield (ed) (Clarendon Press 2010).
Beran H., 'Ought, Obligation and Duty' (1972) 50(3) Australasian J. of Philosophy 207.
Bierling E., *Zur Kritik der Juristischen Grundbegriffe* (Friedrich Andreas Berthes 1877) Vol II.
Bix B., 'Raz on Necessity' (2003) 22 Law and Philosophy 537.
Brandt R.B., 'The Concepts of Obligation and Duty' (1964) 73 Mind 374.
Brett A., *Liberty, Right, and Nature: Individual Rights in Later Scholastic Thought* (CUP 1997).

D. Frydrych, *The Architecture of Rights*,
https://doi.org/10.1007/978-3-030-76039-7

Brinz A., *Lehrbuch der Pandekten* (1st edn, Deichert 1857).

Brown V., 'Rights, Liberties, and Duties: Reformulating Hohfeld's Scheme of Jural Relations?' (2005) 58 Current Legal Problems 343.

Buckland W., *Some Reflections on Jurisprudence* (CUP 1945).

Burke E., *Reflections on the Revolution in France* (Hackett 1987).

Calabresi G. & Douglas Melamed, 'Property Rules, Liability Rules, and Inalienability: One View of the Cathedral' (1972) 85 Harvard L. Rev. 1089.

Campbell, A.H., 'Some Footnotes to Salmond's Jurisprudence' (1940) 7 Cambridge L. J. 206.

Campbell K., 'Book Review of Carl Wellman's Real Rights and The Proliferation of Rights' (2001) 110 (439) Mind 881.

———, 'The Variety of Rights', in Rex Martin and Gerhard Sprenger (eds), *Challenges to Law at the End of the 20th Century: Rights: Proceedings of the 17th World Congress of the International Association for Philosophy of Law and Social Philosophy* (IVR), Bologna, June 16–21 (F Steiner Verlag 1997).

Carnap R., *Meaning and Necessity: A Study in Semantics and Modal Logic* (University of Chicago Press 1956).

Cohen M. (ed), *Ronald Dworkin and Contemporary Jurisprudence* (Rowman and Allenheld 1983).

Cook W.W., 'Hohfeld's Contributions to the Science of Law' (1919) 28 Yale L.J. 72.

———, 'Preface' in W.W. Cook (ed), *Fundamental Legal Conceptions as Applied in Judicial Reasoning and Other Essays* (Yale University Press 1923).

Corbin A., 'Legal Analysis and Terminology' (1919) 29 Yale L.J. 163.

Cruft R., 'Rights: Beyond Interest and Will Theory?' (2004) 23 Law and Philosophy 347.

———, 'The Circularity of the Interest and Will Theories of Rights', in Mark McBride (ed), *New Essays on the Nature of Rights* (Hart 2017).

Daly C., *An Introduction to Philosophical Methods* (Broadview Press 2010).

Darwall S., *The Second-Person Perspective: Morality, Respect and Accountability* (Harvard University Press 2006).

———, *Morality, Authority, and Law: Essays in Second-Personal Ethics Vol I* (OUP 2013).

DePaul M. & W. Ramsey (eds), *Rethinking Intuition: The Psychology of Intuition and Its role in Philosophical Inquiry* (Rowman & Littlefield 1998).

Dicey A.V., *A Digest of the Law of England with Reference to the Conflict of Laws* (Stevens & Sons 1896).

Dickey A., 'Hohfeld's Debt to Salmond' (1971–1972) 10 U.W. Austl. L. Rev. 59.

Dickson J., *Evaluation and Legal Theory* (Hart Publishing 2001).

———, 'Methodology in Jurisprudence: A Critical Survey' (2004) 10 Legal Theory 117.

———, 'Law and Its Theory', in John Keown & Robert George (eds), *Reason, Morality, and Law: The Philosophy of John Finnis* (OUP 2013).
Donnelly J., 'How Are Rights and Duties Correlative?' (1982) 16 J. of Value Inquiry 287.
Dworkin R., *Taking Rights Seriously* (Harvard University Press 1977).
———, 'A Reply By Ronald Dworkin', in M Cohen (ed), *Ronald Dworkin and Contemporary Jurisprudence* (Rowman & Littlefield 1983).
———, *Law's Empire* (HUP 1986).
Edelman J., 'Vindicatory Damages', in Kit Barker, Ross Grantham, & Karen Fairweather (eds), *Private Law in the Twenty-First Century* (Bloomsbury 2017).
Edmundson W., *An Introduction to Rights* (2nd edn, CUP 2012).
Eleftheriadis P., 'The Analysis of Property Rights' (1996) 16 OJLS 31.
———, *Legal Rights* (OUP 2008).
Etinson A., 'Human Rights, Claimability and the Uses of Abstraction' (2013) 25(4) Utilitas 463.
Feinberg J., *Social Philosophy* (Prentice Hall 1973).
———, 'The Nature and Value of Rights', in *Rights, Justice, and the Bounds of Liberty: Essays in Social Philosophy* (Princeton University Press 1980).
Finnis J., 'Some Professorial Fallacies about Rights' (1972) 4 Adel. L. Rev. 377.
———, 'Law and What I Truly Should Decide' (2003) 48 American J. Jurisprudence 107.
———, *Natural Law and Natural Rights* (2nd edn, OUP 2011).
Fitch F., 'A Revision of Hohfeld's Theory of Legal Concepts' (1967) 10 (39/40) Logique et Analyse 269.
Fletcher M., 'Rights Without Remedies' (2017) 11 NYU J. L. & Liberty 236.
Flikschuh K., *Freedom: Contemporary Liberal Perspectives* (Wiley 2007).
Fouto A., 'Revisiting "Subjectivity" in Rights Theories: The (Re)Creation of the "Legal Subject in Second Scholatics Juridical Discourse' (2019) 75(2) Revista Portuguesa de Filosofia 1103.
Frydrych D., *The Architecture of Rights* (DPhil Thesis, University of Oxford 2016).
———, 'Down the Methodological Rabbit Hole' (2017) 49(147) Crítica, Revista Hispanoamericana de Filosofía 41 ['Frydrych (2017a)'] (special issue on legal philosophical methodology).
———, 'Kramer's Delimiting Test for Legal Rights' (2017) 62(2) The American Journal of Jurisprudence 197 ['Frydrych (2017b)'].
———, 'Rights Modelling' (2017) 30(1) Canadian Journal of Law & Jurisprudence 125.
———, 'Hohfeld vs. the Legal Realists' (2018) 24(4) Legal Theory 291 ['Frydrych (2018a)'].
———, 'The Theories of Rights Debate' (2018) 9(3) Jurisprudence: An International Journal of Legal and Political Thought 566 ['Frydrych (2018b)'].
———, 'What is the Will Theory of Rights?' (2019) 32(4) Ratio Juris 455.

———, 'The Case Against the Theories of Rights' (2020) 40(2) Oxford Journal of Legal Studies 320.
———, 'Rights Correlativity', in Shyam Balganesh, Ted Sichelman & Henry Smith (eds), *Wesley Hohfeld A Century Later: Edited Work, Select Personal Papers & Original Commentaries* (CUP 2021).
Gardner J., 'Legal Positivism: 5½ Myths', in *Law as a Leap of Faith: Essays on Law in General* (OUP 2012).
———, 'What is Tort Law For? Part 2. The Place of Distributive Justice', in John Oberdiek (ed), *Philosophical Foundations of the Law of Torts* (OUP 2014).
Gilbert M., 'Giving Claim-Rights Their Due', in Brian Bix (ed), *Rights: Concepts and Contexts* (Ashgate Pub. Co. 2012).
———, *Rights and Demands: A Foundational Inquiry* (OUP 2018).
Giudice M., 'Analytic Jurisprudence and Contingency' in M Del Mar (ed), *New Waves in Philosophy of Law* (Palgrave 2011).
———, *Understanding the Nature of Law: A Case for Constructive Conceptual Explanation* (Elgar Publishing 2015).
Glanville, *A Treatise on the Laws and Customs of the Kingdom of England Composed in the Time of King Henry the Second*, tr J Beames (John Byrne & Co 1900).
Goble G., 'Affirmative and Negative Legal Relations' (1922) 4 Illinois L. Q. 94.
Gorman J., *Rights and Reason: An Introduction the Philosophy of Rights* (Acumen 2003).
Goudmit J., *The Pandects: A Treatise on The Roman Law and Its Connection with Modern Legislation*, tr R. de Tracy Gould (Longmans, Green & Co 1873).
Graham G. & T. Hogan, 'Southern Fundamentalism and the End of Philosophy', in M DePaul and W Ramsey (eds) *Rethinking Intuition: The Psychology of Intuition and Its role in Philosophical Inquiry* (Rowman & Littlefield 1998).
Gray J., *The Nature and Sources of the Law* (Columbia University Press 1909).
Green L., 'The Concept of Law Revisited' (1995–6) 94 Michigan L. Rev. 1687.
———, 'Legal Obligation and Authority', (*Stanford Encyclopedia of Philosophy* 23 December 2003) http://plato.stanford.edu/entries/legal-obligation/ Accessed 26 September 2020.
——— & Thomas Adams, 'Legal Positivism' (*Stanford Encyclopedia of Philosophy* December 17, 2019 https://plato.stanford.edu/entries/legal-positivism/ Accessed 5 March 2021.
Green M.S. & commentators, 'Why No Deontic Logic?' (Prawfsblawg 12 October 2007) http://prawfsblawg.blogs.com/prawfsblawg/2007/10/why-no-deontic-.html/ Accessed 26 September 2020.
Grey T., *Holmes and Legal Pragmatism* 41 Stanford Law Review 787 (1989).
Grotius H., I *De Jure Belli ac Pacis* (1625).
Gupta A., 'Definitions' (*Stanford Encyclopedia of Philosophy* 20 April 2015) https://plato.stanford.edu/entries/definitions/ Accessed 26 September 2020.
Hacker P.M.S., 'Sanction Theories of Duty', in A.W.B. Simpson (ed), *Oxford Essays in Jurisprudence* (Second Series) (OUP 1973).

Halpin A., 'More Comments on Rights and Claims' (1991) 10 Law and Philosophy 271.

———, *Rights and Law: Analysis and Theory* (Hart Pub. 1997).

———, 'Methodology', in Dennis Patterson (ed), *A Companion to Philosophy of Law and Legal Theory* (2nd edn, Wiley-Blackwell 2010).

———, 'The Value of Hohfeldian Neutrality when Theorising about Legal Rights', in Mark McBride (ed), *New Essays on the Nature of Rights* (Hart 2017).

———, 'Correlativity and its Logic: Asymmetry not Equality in the Law' 2019 XXXII(1) Canadian Journal of Law and Jurisprudence 82 ['Halpin (2019a)'].

———, 'Choosing Axioms of Correlativity' (2019) 64(2) American Journal of Jurisprudence 225 ['Halpin (2019b)'].

Harel A., 'Theories of Rights', in Martin P Golding and William Edmundson (eds), *The Blackwell Guide to the Philosophy of Law and Legal Theory* (Blackwell Publishing Ltd 2007).

Hart H.L.A., *Law Liberty, and Morality* (OUP 1963).

———, 'Definition and Theory in Jurisprudence', in *Essays in Jurisprudence and Philosophy* (Clarendon Press 1983) (article originally published in 1954).

———, *Essays on Bentham: Jurisprudence and Political Theory* (Clarendon Press 1982).

———, *The Concept of Law* (2nd edn, Clarendon Press 1994).

Hathaway O. & Scott Shapiro, 'Outcasting: Enforcement in Domestic and International Law' (2011) 121 Yale L.J. 252.

Hegel, G.W.F., *Elements of the Philosophy of Right*, Allen Wood (ed), tr HB Nisbet (CUP 2008).

Himma K., 'Laws Claim of Legitimate Authority', in J Coleman (ed) *Hart's Postscript: Essays on the Postscript to the* Concept of Law (OUP 2001).

Hohfeld W. N., 'Nature of Stockholders' Individual Liability for Corporation Debts' (1909) 9 Columbia L. Rev. 285.

———, 'Some Fundamental Legal Conceptions as Applied in Judicial Reasoning' (1913) 23 Yale L.J. 16 ['Hohfeld (1913a)'].

———, 'The Relations Between Equity and Law' (1913) 11 Michigan L. Rev. 537 ['Hohfeld (1913b)'].

———, 'Fundamental Legal Conceptions as Applied in Judicial Reasoning' (1917) 26 Yale L.J. 710.

———, *Fundamental Legal Conceptions as Applied in Judicial Reasoning and Other Essays*, W.W. Cook (ed) (Yale University Press 1919).

———, *Fundamental Legal Conceptions as Applied in Judicial Reasoning and Other Essays*, W.W. Cook (ed) (Yale University Press 1923).

———, *Fundamental Legal Conceptions as Applied in Judicial Reasoning and Other Essays*, W.W. Cook (ed) (Yale University Press 1964).

———, *Fundamental Legal Conceptions as Applied in Judicial Reasoning*, David Campbell & Philip Thomas (eds) (Ashgate 2001).

Holmgren M., 'Raz on Rights' (1985) 94 Mind 591.
Honoré A., 'Rights of Exclusion and Immunities against Divesting' (1960) 34 Tulane L. Rev. 453.
———, 'Ownership', in A.G. Guest (ed), *Oxford Essays in Jurisprudence* (OUP 1961).
———, *UlpianPioneer of Human Rights* (2nd edn, OUP 2002).
———, 'Property and Ownership: Marginal Comments', in Timothy Endicott, Joshua Getzler & Edwin Peel (eds), *Properties of Law: Essays in Honour of Jim Harris* (OUP 2006).
Hudson S. & Douglas Husak, 'Legal Rights: How Useful is Hohfeldian Analysis?' (1980) 37 Philosophical Studies 45.
Huemer M., 'The Failure of Analysis and the Nature of Concepts', in C Daly (ed) *The Palgrave Handbook of Philosophical Methods* (Palgrave Macmillan 2015).
Hughes R., 'Law and the Entitlement to Coerce', in Wil Waluchow & Stefan Sciaraffa (eds), *Philosophical Foundations of the Nature of Law* (OUP 2013).
Jackson F., *From Metaphysics to Ethics: A Defence of Conceptual Analysis* (Clarendon Press 2000).
James S., 'Rights as Enforceable Claims' (2003) 103 Proceedings of the Aristotelian Society, New Series 133.
Jenkins C., 'Intuition, "Intuition", Concepts and the A Priori', in A Booth and D Rowbottom (eds) *Intuitions* (OUP 2014).
Jhering R., *Der Geist des Römischen Rechts auf den verschidenn Stufen seiner Entwicklung*, Vol III (1st edn, Leipzig Breitkopf und Härtel 1865).
——— 'Die Reflexwirkungen oder die Rückwirkung rechtlicher Thatsachen auf dritte Personen' (1871) 10 Jahrbücher für die Dogmatik des heutigen römischen und deutschen Privatrechts 245.
Kamm F., 'Rights', in J. Coleman, K. Himma & S. Shapiro (eds), *The Oxford Handbook of Jurisprudence and Philosophy of Law* (OUP 2004).
Kant I., *Metaphysics of Morals*, tr Mary Gregor (CUP 1996).
Kelsen H., *Hauptproblem der Menschenrechte: Hobbes – Locke – Kant* (1911).
———, *Pure Theory of Law*, tr Max Knight (2nd edn, University of California Press 1967).
Kleinfeld J., 'Enforcement and the Concept of Law' (2011) 121 Yale L.J. Online 293.
Kocourek A., 'Plurality of Advantage and Disadvantage in Jural Relations' (1920) 19(1) Michigan L. Rev. 47 ['Kocourek (1920a)'].
———, 'The Hohfeld System of Fundamental Legal Concepts' (1920) 15 Illinois L. Rev. 24 ['Kocourek (1920b)'].
———, 'Reply to Paper of Professor Corbin', Terminology and Classification in Fundamental Jural Relations Terminology and Classification in Fundamental Jural Relations—A Symposium (1921) 4 American L. School Rev. 614.
———, 'Wanted: Phrase for Legal Capabilities and Restraints' (1923) 9 ABA J 25.
———, *Jural Relations* (2nd edn, Bobbs-Merrill Co Publishers 1928).

Kramer M., 'Rights Without Trimmings', in Matthew H Kramer, Nigel Simmonds & Hillel Steiner, *A Debate Over Rights: Philosophical Enquiries* (OUP 1998).

———, 'Review of Rights and Law: Analysis and Theory by Andrew Halpin' (1999) 62 Modern L. Rev 314.

———, 'On the Nature of Legal Rights' (2000) 59 Cambridge L. J. 473.

———, 'Getting Rights Right', in Matthew Kramer (ed) *Rights, Wrongs and Responsibilities* (2001).

———, *In Defense of Legal Positivism: Law Without Trimmings* (OUP 2003).

———, 'Legal and Moral Obligation', in Martin P Golding and William Edmundson (eds), *The Blackwell Guide to the Philosophy of Law and Legal Theory* (2007).

———, 'Rights in Legal and Political Philosophy', in Gregory A. Caldeira et al (eds), *The Oxford Handbook of Law and Politics* (OUP 2008).

———, 'Refining the Interest Theory of Rights' (2010) 55 American J. of Jurisprudence 31.

———, 'What is Legal Philosophy?' (2012) 43 Metaphilosophy 125.

———, 'Some Doubts About Alternatives to the Interest Theory of Rights—Symposium on Rights and the Direction of Duties' (2013) 103(2) Ethics 245.

———, 'In Defence of the Interest Theory of Right Holding: Rejoinders to Leif Wenar on Rights', in Mark McBride (ed), *New Essays on the Nature of Rights* (Hart 2017).

———, 'Hart and the Metaphysics and Semantics of Legal Normativity' (2018) 31(4) Ratio Juris 396.

Kramer M., & Hillel Steiner, 'Theories of Rights: Is There a Third Way?' (2007) 27 OJLS 281.

Kurki V., 'Rights, Harming, and Wronging: A Restatement of the Interest Theory' (2018) 28(3) OJLS 430.

———, 'Critical Notices: Rights and Demands' (2019) 79(3) Analysis 530.

———, 'Are Legal Positivism and the Interest Theory of Rights Compatible?', in M McBride and V Kurki (eds.), *Without Trimmings: The Legal, Moral and Political Philosophy of Matthew Kramer* (forthcoming, OUP). Draft available on SSRN: Last checked May 1, 2021.

Langlinais A. & B. Leiter, 'The Methodology of Legal Philosophy', in H Cappelen, T Gendler, and J Hawthorne (eds) *The Oxford Handbook of Philosophical Methodology* (OUP 2016).

Laurence S. & E. Margolis, 'Concepts' (*Stanford Encyclopedia of Philosophy* 17 June 2019) https://plato.stanford.edu/entries/concepts/ Accessed September 26, 2020.

Lee R., *The Elements of Roman Law with a translation of the Institutes of Justinian* (Sweet & Maxwell Ltd 1946).

Leiter B., *Naturalizing Jurisprudence: Essays on American Legal Realism and Naturalism in Legal Philosophy* (OUP 2007).

———, 'Explaining Theoretical Disagreement' (2009) 76 U. Chicago L. Rev. 1215.
———, 'Naturalized Jurisprudence and American Legal Realism Revisited' (2011) 30 Law and Philosophy 499.
———, 'Naturalism in Legal Philosophy' (*Stanford Encyclopedia of Philosophy* 27 March 2017). https://plato.stanford.edu/entries/lawphil-naturalism/ Accessed September 26 2020.
Lindahl L., *Position and Change: A Study in Law and Logic* (D Reidel 1977).
———, 'Stig Kanger's Theory of Rights', in Ghita Holmström-Hintikka et al (eds.), II *Collected Papers of Stig Kanger with Essays on His Life and Work* (Kluwer Academic Publishers 2001).
Llewellyn K., *The Bramble Bush: On Our Law and its Study* (Oceana Pub. 1951).
Lyons Daniel, 'Entitled to Complain' (1966) 26 Analysis 119.
Lyons David, 'The Correlativity of Rights and Duties' (1970) 4 Nous 45.
MacCormick N., 'Rights in Legislation', in P.M.S. Hacker & J. Raz (eds), *Law, Morality and Society: Essays in Honour of H.L.A. Hart* (Clarendon Press 1977).
———, 'Children's Rights: A Test Case for Theories of Rights', in *Legal Right and Social Democracy: Essays in Legal and Political Philosophy* (Clarendon Press 1982) originally published as (1976) 62 Archiv Für Rechts– und Sozialphilosophie 305 ['MacCormick (1982a)'].
———, 'Rights, Claims, and Remedies' (1982) 1 L. and Philosophy 337 ['MacCormick (1982b)'].
———, 'Discretion and Rights' (1989) 8 Law and Philosophy 23.
———, *Institutions of Law: An Essay in Legal Theory* (OUP 2007).
———, *H.L.A. Hart [Jurists: Profiles in Legal Theory]* (2nd edn, Stanford University Press 2008).
Mack E., 'Robert Nozick's Political Philosophy' (*Stanford Encyclopedia of Philosophy* 15 June 2018). https://plato.stanford.edu/entries/nozick-political/ Accessed 26 Sept 2020.
Markby W., *Elements of Law: Considered with Reference to Principles of General Jurisprudence* (Clarendon Press 1871).
Marsh T., 'The Legal Continuum' (1969) 64 Nw. U. L. Rev. 459.
Martin R., *A System of Rights* (OUP 1993).
——— & James Nickel, 'Recent Work on the Concept of Rights' (1980) 17 Am. Phil Q. 165.
McBride M., 'The Tracking Theory of Rights', in Mark McBride (ed), *New Essays on the Nature of Rights* (Hart 2017).
———, 'Raz's Definition of a Right' (2018) 31(4) Ratio Juris 460.
———, 'The Unavoidability of Evaluation for Interest Theories of Rights (2020) 33(2) Canadian Journal of Law & Jurisprudence 293.
McCloskey H.J., 'Rights' (1965) The Philosophical Q. 115.
———, 'Rights—Some Conceptual Issues' (1976) 54 Australasian J of Philosophy 99.

Merrill T., 'Property and the Right to Exclude' (1998) 77 Nebraska L. Rev. 730.
Mill J.S., *Utilitarianism* (Parker, Son, and Bourn 1863).
Miller W., *The Data of Jurisprudence* (W. Green & Sons 1903).
Moore A., S. Grattan, & L. Griggs, *Australian Real Property Law* (7th edn, Thomson Reuters 2020).
Mullock P., 'The Hohfeldian No-Right: A Logical Analysis' (1970) 56 Archiv Für Rechts–und Sozialphilosophie 265.
———, 'The Hohfeldian Jural Opposite' (1971) 13 Ratio 158.
Nozick R., *Anarchy, State, and Utopia* (Basil Blackwell 1974).
O'Neill O., *Towards Justice and Virtue: A Constructive Account of Practical Reasoning* (CUP 1996).
Page W., 'Terminology and Classification in Fundamental Jural Relations Terminology and Classification in Fundamental Jural Relations—A Symposium' (1921) 4 Am. L. School Rev. 616.
Patterson D., 'Alexy on Necessity in Law and Morals' (2012) 25 Ratio Juris 47.
Paulson S., 'Review: Rejoinders to Hart on Rules and Rights' (1979) 77 Michigan L. Rev. 484.
Penner J., 'The Right to Property: The Exclusion Thesis', in *The Idea of Property in Law* (OUP 1997).
———, 'On the Very Idea of Transmissible Rights', in James Penner & Henry E Smith (eds), *Philosophical Foundations of Property Law* (OUP 2013).
Pound R., 'Legal Rights' (1915) 26 Int J of Ethics 92.
———, Chapter 21: 'Rights', in *Jurisprudence*, Vol IV (West Publishing Co. 1959).
Preda A., 'Rights: Concept and Justification' (2015) 28 Ratio Juris 408.
Putnam H., 'The Analytic and the Synthetic', in *Mind, Language, and Reality: Philosophical Papers Volume 2* (CUP 1979).
Quine W.V.O., 'Main Trends in Recent Philosophy: Two Dogmas of Empiricism' (1951) 60 The Philosophical Review 20.
Radin M., 'Correlation' (1929) 29 Columbia L. Rev. 901.
———, 'A Restatement of Hohfeld' (1938) 51 Harvard L. Rev. 1141.
Rainbolt G., 'Two Interpretations of Feinberg's Theory of Rights' (2005) 11 Legal Theory 227.
———, *The Concept of Rights* (Springer 2006).
Ramsey W., 'Prototypes and Conceptual Analysis', in DePaul M and W Ramsey (eds) *Rethinking Intuition: The Psychology of Intuition and Its role in Philosophical Inquiry* (Rowman & Littlefield 1998).
Raz J., 'Promises and Obligations', in Peter Hacker & Joseph Raz (eds), *Law, Morality*, and *Society: Essays in Honour of H.L.A. Hart* (OUP 1977).
———, *The Conceptof a Legal System: An Introduction to the Theory of Legal System* (2nd edn, Clarendon Press 1980).
———, 'Hart on Moral Rights and Legal Duties' (1984) 4 OJLS 123.
———, *The Morality of Freedom* (OUP 1986).

———, *Ethics in the Public Domain: Essays in the Morality of Law and Politics* (revised edn, OUP 1996).

———, *Practical Reason and Norms* (2nd edn, OUP 1999).

———, *Between Authority and Interpretation: On the Theory of Law and Practical Reason* (OUP 2009) ['Raz (2009a)'].

———, *The Authority of Law: Essays on Law and Morality* (2nd edn, OUP 2009) ['Raz (2009b)'].

Reiff M., *Punishment, Compensation, and Law: A Theory of Enforceability* (CUP 2005).

Ripstein A., 'Hindering a Hindrance to Freedom' (2008) 16 Jahrbuch für Recht und Ethik 227.

———, *Force and Freedom* (HUP 2009).

———, 'Ethics Discussions at PEA Soup: Leif Wenar's 'The Nature of Claim-Rights' with Critical Precis by Arthur Ripstein' (*PEA Soup* 10 April 2013). http://peasoup.typepad.com/peasoup/2013/04/ethics-discussions-at-pea-soup-leif-wenars-the-nature-of-claim-rights-with-critical-precis-by-arthur.html Accessed 26 Sept 2020 ['Ripstein (2013a)'].

———, 'Possession and Use', in J Penner & H Smith (eds), *Philosophical Foundations of Property Law* (OUP 2013) ['Ripstein (2013b)'].

———, 'Standing, Value, and the Theory of Rights: Discussion of Why Law Matters' (2015) 12 Jerusalem Review of Books 10.

———, 'Reply', in S Kisilevsky & M Stone (eds), *Freedom and Force: Essays on Kant's Legal Philosophy* (Hart Publishing Ltd 2017).

Robinson R.E. et al., 'The Logic of Rights' (1983) 33 U. Toronto L.J. 267.

Rosen G., 'Real Definition' (2015) 56(3) Analytic Philosophy 189.

Salmond J., *Jurisprudence, or The Theory of the Law* (1st edn, Stevens & Haynes 1902).

———, '*Jurisprudence, or The Theory of the Law* (2nd edn, Stevens & Haynes 1907).

Savigny F., *System of the Modern Roman Law*, tr William Holloway (J. Higgenbotham Publisher 1867).

Schauer F, 'Was Austin Right After All? On the Role of Sanctions in a Theory of Law' (2010) 23(1) Ratio Juris 1.

———, 'On the Nature of the Nature of Law' (2012) 98 Archiv für Rechts- und Sozialphilosophie 457.

Schlag P., 'How to Do Things with Hohfeld' (2015) 78 Law & Contemporary Problems 185.

Schuppe W., *Der Begriff des subjectiven Rechts* (Wilhelm Koebner 1887).

Shapiro S., *Legality* (Harvard University Press 2011).

Simmonds N., 'Analytic Foundations of Justice' (1995) 54(2) Cambridge L. J. 306.

———, 'Rights at the Cutting Edge', in Matthew H Kramer, Nigel Simmonds & Hillel Steiner, *A Debate Over Rights: Philosophical Enquiries* (OUP 1998).

———, *Central Issues in Jurisprudence* (4th edn, Sweet & Maxwell 2013).

Singer J.W., 'The Legal Rights Debate in Analytic Jurisprudence from Bentham to Hohfeld' (1982) 1982 Wis. L. Rev. 975.
Skorupski J., *The Domain of Reasons* (OUP 2010).
Smith H.E., 'Exclusion versus Governance: Two Strategies for Delineating Property Rights' (2002) 31 J. Legal Studies S453 [Sic].
Smith S.A., 'Rule-Based Rights and Court-Ordered Rights', in Donal Nolan & Andrew Robertson (eds), *Rights and Private Law* (Hart Publishing 2012).
Spector, H., 'Value Pluralism and the Two Concepts of Rights' (2009) 0 RMM 355.
Sreenivasan G., 'A Hybrid Theory of Claim-Rights' (2005) 25 OJLS 257.
———, 'Duties and Their Direction' (2010) 120(3) Ethics 465.
———, 'Public Goods, Individual Rights, and Third-Party Benefits', in Mark McBride (ed), *New Essays on the Nature of Rights* (Hart 2017).
Stavropolous N., 'Legal Interpretivism' (*Stanford Encyclopedia of Philosophy* 8 Feb 2021) https://plato.stanford.edu/entries/law-interpretivist/ Accessed 5 April 2021.
Steiner H., *An Essay on Rights* (OUP 1994).
———, 'Working Rights', in Matthew H Kramer, Nigel Simmonds & Hillel Steiner, *A Debate Over Rights: Philosophical Enquiries* (OUP 1998).
———, 'Moral Rights', in David Copp (ed), *The Oxford Handbook of Ethical Theory* (OUP 2006).
Stepanians M., *Rights as Relational Properties—In Defense of Right/Duty-Correlativity* Habilitation Thesis, University of Saarland 2005) (on file with author).
Stewart H., 'The Definition of a Right' (2012) 3 Jurisprudence 319.
Stich S., 'Reflective Equilibrium, Analytic Epistemology and the Problem of Cognitive Diversity', in DePaul M and W Ramsey (eds) *Rethinking Intuition: The Psychology of Intuition and Its role in Philosophical Inquiry* (Rowman & Littlefield 1998).
Stoljar N., 'What Do We Want Law to Be? Philosophical Analysis and the Concept of Law', in Wil Waluchow and Stefan Sciaraffa (eds) *Philosophical Foundations of the Nature of Law* (OUP 2013).
Strauss G., 'The Positive Right to Marry' (2016) 102 Virginia L. Rev. 1691.
Sumner L.W., *The Moral Foundations of Rights* (Clarendon Press 1987).
Tamanaha B., *A General Jurisprudence of Law and Society* (OUP 2001).
Tapper C., 'Powers and Secondary Rules of Change', in A.W.B. Simpson (ed), *Oxford Essays in Jurisprudence* (Second Series) (OUP 1973).
Terry H., *Some Leading Principles of Anglo-American Law Expounded with a View To its Arrangement and Codification* (T & J W Johnson & Co 1884).
———, 'Legal Duties and Rights' (1903) 12 Yale. L. J. 185.
Tierney B., *The Idea of Natural Rights: Studies on Natural Rights, Natural Law and Church Law 1150–1625* (Scholars Press 1997).
Thomson J., *The Realm of Rights* (Harvard University Press 1990).

Thomas J., *Public Rights, Private Relations* (OUP 2015)
Thon A., *Rechtsnorm un Subjecktive Rechts: Untersuchungen zur Allgemeinen Rechtslehre* (1878).
Tuck R., *Natural Rights Theories: Their Origin and Development* (CUP 1979).
Vallentyne P., 'Libertarianism and the State' (2007) 24 Social Philosophy 187.
Van Duffel S., 'The Nature of Rights Debate Rests on a Mistake' (2012) 93 Pacific Philosophical Q 104.
———, 'Adequacy Constraints for a Theory of Rights', in Mark McBride (ed), *New Essays on the Nature of Rights* (Hart 2017).
Varden H., 'Duties, Perfect and Imperfect', in Deen K. Chatterjee (ed), *Encyclopedia of Global Justice* (Springer 2011).
Vinogradoff P., 'The Foundations of a Theory of Rights' (1924) 34(1) Yale L. J. 60.
Waldron J., 'A Right to Do Wrong' (1981) 92 Ethics 21.
———, 'Introduction', *Theories of Rights* (OUP 1984).
Weinrib E., *The Idea of Private Law* (OUP 1995).
Weatherson B., 'What Good Are Counterexamples?' (2003) 115 Philosophical Studies 1.
Wellman C., *A Theory of Rights: Persons Under Laws, Institutions, and Morals* (Rowman & Littlefield 1985).
———, *Real Rights* (OUP 1995).
———, *The Proliferationof Rights: Moral Progress or Empty Rhetoric?* (Westview Press 1999).
———, 'Review of *A Debate Over Rights*, (2000) 109 Mind 954.
Wenar L., 'The Nature of Rights' (2005) 33 Philosophy and Public Affairs 223.
———, 'The Analysis of Rights', in Matthew Kramer et al (eds), *The Legacy of H.L.A. Hart: Legal, Political, and Moral Philosophy* (OUP 2008).
———, 'The Nature of Claim-Rights—Symposium on Rights and the Direction of Duties' (2013) 103(2) Ethics 202.
———, 'Rights' (*Stanford Encyclopedia of Philosophy* 24 Feb 2020) http://plato.stanford.edu/entries/rights/ Accessed 26 Sept 2020.
White A., 'Conceptual Analysis', in C Bontempo & SJ Odell (eds) *The Owl of Minerva: Philosophers on Philosophy* (McGraw-Hill 1975).
———, 'Rights and Claims' (1982) 1 L. and Philosophy 315 ['White (1982a)'].
———, 'Reply to Professor MacCormick' (1982) 1 L. and Philosophy 359 ['White (1982b)'].
———, *Rights* (Clarendon Press 1984).
Williams G., 'The Concept of Legal Liberty' (1956) 56 Columbia L. Rev. 1129.
Windscheid B., *Lehrbuch des Pandektenrechts* (1862).
Wittgenstein L., *Philosophical Investigations*, tr GEM Anscombe, PMS Hacker, and J Schulte (4th edn, Wiley-Blackwell 2009).
Woozley A., 'Legal Duties, Offences, and Sanctions' (1968) 77 Mind 461.
Zakrzewski R., *Remedies Reclassified* (OUP 2005).

Index[1]

[1] Note: Page numbers followed by 'n' refer to notes.

D. Frydrych, *The Architecture of Rights*, https://doi.org/10.1007/978-3-030-76039-7